In Memory of

Medora Field Perkerson

WHITE
COLUMNS
in
GEORGIA

White columns and Southern charm. Miss Carolyn Whitehead on the porch of the President's House, University of Georgia, Athens.

WHITE COLUMNS
in
GEORGIA

Medora Field Perkerson

BONANZA BOOKS   •   NEW YORK

LIBRARY OF CONGRESS CATALOG CARD NUMBER:—52—5572

*This edition published by Bonanza Books,
a division of Crown Publishers, Inc.,
by arrangement with Holt, Rinehart and Winston, Inc.*

(G)

To my dear friend

Ella May Thornton,
STATE LIBRARIAN OF GEORGIA

whose inspired assistance in research was invaluable

in the collection of material for this book

CONTENTS

LIST OF ILLUSTRATIONS

Acknowledgments

PRIMARILY to three people who suggested that I write a book about interesting old Georgia houses.

Mimosa Hall at Roswell had already furnished me the setting for a mystery novel, *Who Killed Aunt Maggie?* published in 1939. Heron Point on St. Simons Island, the scene of a second—*Blood on Her Shoe*, 1942—was an imaginary reconstruction of Hampton Point, described in Fanny Kemble's famous *Georgia Journal*.

Historic old houses, said my husband, deserved better treatment than to be used as a dumping place for dead bodies. Yet I found real murder, mystery and tragedy, as well as romance and heroism and statesmanship, when I started out on the trail of that authentic history for which Georgia's ante-bellum houses furnished the background.

And so then, to three people who suggested this third book——

First of all to my husband, Angus Perkerson, editor of *The Atlanta Journal* and *Constitution Magazine*, who made the suggestion over and over for about seven years, and who—when work was finally begun—kept after me like a bloodhound until the book was completed. This means that for nearly three years he was "best friend and severest critic" of a manuscript in process.

Next, to Georgia Leckie, book buyer for Rich's, in Atlanta, who was second in line with the suggestion. Third, to Luise Sims, former book buyer for Davison's, who not only suggested that I write the book but also suggested to John Selby. Editor-in-Chief of Rinehart, that he publish it. Certainly my thanks are also due Mr. Selby for giving me the green light on what turned out to be a happy pilgrimage over Georgia.

My indebtedness to the Librarians of the State reaches out to nearly every town mentioned in the book. Their responses to requests for information or the checking of information were unfailingly prompt and gracious. I wish especially to thank the Library of Congress in Washington, the Georgia State Library, the State Department of Archives and History, the Atlanta Public Library, the Architectural Library at Georgia Institute of Technology, the Emory University Library, the University of Georgia Library, the Atlanta Historical Society and the Georgia Historical Society. The bound files of *The Atlanta Journal* magazine from 1920 to the present time were also a source of much rich material relating to the Georgia scene.

My thanks are due Mrs. L. D. Bolton of Burge Plantation for permission to quote from her grandmother's diary. For permission to quote from *In and Out of the Lines* I am grateful to Mrs. Roger Noble Burnham, of Los Angeles, niece of the author. Also to Dr. E. Merton Coulter, Dr. John D. Wade, Dr. Ralph B. Flanders and Sylvia Porter for permission to quote from their respective works. To Mrs. Rosser Smith, of Macon, for permission to use material from the work of her grandfather, Harry Stillwell Edwards. To Margaret Davis Cate, of Sea Island, for access to source material relating to Georgia coastal history and for many kindnesses. My indebtedness to Ella May Thornton is acknowledged in the dedication of this book.

For assistance in obtaining special photographs I am indebted to Kenneth Rogers, Carolyn Carter and *The Atlanta Journal* and *Constitution Mazagine;* to William Columbus Davis for selections from his collection assembled for *The Columns of Athens; to* Frances Benjamin Johnston, to Wilbur Kurtz, Winship Nunnally, Edward Vason Jones, Mrs. C. Perot Whiting, John A. Sibley, Mills B. Lane, Jr., Colonel Thomas Spencer, Louise Ferguson and others. Also to the Chambers of Commerce in Albany, Augusta, Columbus, Macon, Rome, Thomasville and Savannah. For advice on architecture I am grateful to Francis M. Daves.

For many things I am indebted to many people who had a part in building this book about old Georgia houses. To my friends and their friends, to newspaper editors and writers, to county historians, to garden-club presidents and chairmen, to telephone operators, traffic officers, filling-station attendants—to all those who so eloquently demonstrated that Southern hospitality and good manners are not merely a part of our tradition but a part of life as it is lived in Georgia today.

Especially I wish to thank Mrs. Frank Faulk, of Albany; Mrs. Madison Nicholson, Mr. and Mrs. Wymberly W. DeRenne, Mrs. Dan Magill, Dean John E. Drewry and Dr. Hubert Owens of Athens; Mrs. Frederick A. Ware, Mrs. Rodney Cohen (Senior and Junior), Judge Henry C. Hammond, Mrs. Owen Cheatham, Mrs. Mary Carter Winter, Mr. and Mrs. Edison Marshall and Jacob H. Lowrey of Augusta; Mrs. E. E. Callaway, Mrs. R. H. Patterson, Mrs. R. R. Fowler of Covington; Mr. and Mrs. E. S. Rheberg, Flournoy Branham, Mrs. M. C. Wiley and Dean and Mrs. Virgil Y. C. Eady of near-by Oxford.

Mrs. Donald Hancock of Cartersville; Miss Alice Wardwell, Mrs. J. R. Tweedy, Mrs. J. Frank Walker of Eatonton; Mrs. Howell Newton of Forsyth; Mrs. Kyle Smith and Mrs. Marian Merritt of Greensboro; Mrs. Ethel Dallis Hill, Miss Eleanor Orr, Miss Lucille Bryant Johnson of LaGrange; Mrs. P. M. Marchman and Mrs. R. F. Brooks, Sr., of Lexington.

Acknowledgments

Miss Susan Myrick, Mrs. Frank F. Jones, Mrs. A. C. Morgan, Mrs. Everett Flournoy, Mrs. Walter D. Lamar, Mrs. George S. McCowen, Jordan Massey, Jr. and Ralph Jones of Macon; Miss Kittie Newton, Miss Therese Newton and Mrs. A. S. Ware of Madison; Mrs. Nelle Womack Hines of Milledgeville; Hamilton Hall and Miss Lutie Burkhart of Newnan.

Mr. and Mrs. E. P. Grant, Miss Ann Hamilton, Mrs. Claire J. Wyatt, Miss Inez Henry, Mrs. Ligon Henderson, Lawrence Yancey Lipscomb, Mrs. William N. Randle and Mrs. Lee Ella Dean Temple of Rome; the Misses Evelyn and Katharine Simpson, Mrs. Granger Hansell and Mrs. Nap Rucker of Roswell.

Miss Caroline Meldrim, Mrs. Shelby Myrick, Mrs. Noble Jones, Mrs. Craig Barrow, Mrs. Norman M. Hawes, Miss Edith Duncan Johnston, Miss Emily G. Ravenel and Raiford Wood of Savannah; Alfred W. Jones and Richard A. Everett of Sea Island; Mr. and Mrs. Clarence Moeckel, Mrs. Arthur Ready, Isaac F. Arnow and Tom Sterling of St. Marys; Miss Louise Irwin of Sandersville; Mr. and Mrs. Ed Jerger, Miss Emily Jerger, Miss Nell Pringle and James Gribben, III, of Thomasville; Mrs. Harold Lamb of Union Point; Mr. and Mrs. Rochford Johnson of Washington; Mr. and Mrs. Porter W. Carswell, Jr., of Waynesboro. And among others, Mrs. Jane K. Arnold, Mrs. Colquitt Carter, Jr., Mrs. Paul C. Crowell, Frank Daniel, Mrs. Jesse Draper, Mrs. Lucille Field Dowdle, Mrs. Robert Field, Mr. and Mrs. R. E. Lee Field, Richard B. Harwell, Miss Camille Hilsman, John R. Marsh, Mrs. Alva Maxwell, Mrs. Calhoun McDougall, Mrs. Violet Moore, Mrs. Calvin Prescott, Mr. and Mrs. K. G. Schaid, Mrs. H. O. Barth, Mrs. George C. Biggers, Mrs. Horace Powell, Mrs. Green D. Warren, Mrs. J. H. Crosland, Mrs. Howard Harmon, Mrs. Hines Roberts, Miss Lula Kingsbery, Miss Mary Kingsbery, Mrs. Norman Sharp, Mrs. Harold McKenzie, Mrs. Stephen Barnwell, Mrs. Frank Ridenour, Mrs. Wylly Folk St. John, Andrew Sparks, Dr. Harold Bush-Brown, Mrs. K. M. Drewry, Mrs. Wilmer Moore, Rebecca Franklin, Ward Morehouse and Mrs. Willard Patterson.

CHAPTER 1

Gone with the Wind Country

*T*HE gentleman from the North bowed low and stood aside on the graceful stairway landing to allow a lovely lady in hoop skirts to pass. She inclined her head and gave him a faint smile as she swept by. He was much taken with her Southern charm.

Later the gentleman was shocked to learn he had met the family ghost. He vowed he had even caught a whiff of fragrance from the damask rose in her hair.

It all happened in a fine old white-columned Georgia house, and not so long ago.

Old houses never quite give up the people who have lived within their walls. They hold on hardest to those—however long gone—who lived most vividly, who figured in the most fervid romance, the bravest act of gallantry, the greatest tragedy, the most spectacular scandal or the finest service to posterity. No matter who lives in these houses today, you are likely to meet earlier tenants too, at least in fancy. Atmosphere, no less than architecture, seems to determine the final character of a house.

In Atlanta, visitors constantly make us conscious of our lack of really old houses. For Atlanta is no longer merely the capital of Georgia. Since the publication in 1936 of a book that has outsold everything but the Bible, Atlanta has become the capital—the heart—of Gone With the Wind country. Atlanta's Peachtree has become one of the famous streets of the world.

And it is Gone With the Wind country that the majority of Atlanta's first-time visitors wish to see—a land of legend, of cotton and camellias, mint juleps and magnolias and all the rest of it. To most of these visitors, "the South, in its romantic splendor, is summed up forever in the stately plantation house, with tall white columns and sweeping galleries, set in the midst of rolling green fields."

1

Peachtree Street is a long, long street, leading back into the past for more than a hundred years and far beyond the city limits of the future. But there are no plantations along Peachtree. There aren't even any peach trees. Peachtree Street got its name from the former Indian village of "Standing Peachtree."

It is true that you find a satisfactory number of handsome houses with tall white columns in Atlanta's North Side residential section, a beautiful parklike area now mostly removed from Peachtree Street. But these were all built long after one General Sherman burned the city in 1864. The new Atlanta, which grew up with the New South, is much like any American city of around 700,000 inhabitants. It has little of the old-time Southern flavor of Savannah or Charleston or some other cities below the Mason-Dixon line.

An "over-seer's city" Jonathan Daniels called Atlanta some years ago because a part of its cosmopolitan population is made up of citizens sent South by national concerns as directing heads of branch houses or Southeastern divisions.

More recently James Street likened Atlanta to a lady wearing a Yankee mink coat with a Confederate slip showing.

Though both descriptions are witty, neither is quite accurate, of course. Most of Atlanta's old families made their money by holding on to the local real estate or by investing in Coca-Cola stock, also a Simon-pure local concoction. The "over-seer" citizens who, after all, are selected by their home offices for certain meritorious qualities, soon settle agreeably into the general pattern which they help to create.

And Atlanta, because of its geographical situation, is controlled by forces larger than any of these. As a communications and distribution center, it is constantly outgrowing itself, changing too rapidly to be described by a sentence or to fit into any conventional mold.

Certain Deep South signs and symbols the visitor does find. If there are no peach trees on Peachtree Street, there are magnolias, camellias, azaleas and gardenias. Who, indeed, would want peach trees in front of his house when he can have the magnolia grandiflora, with its magnificent structure, glossy evergreen leaves and spectacular waxen white blossoms? The "queen of blossoms" an English visitor called them long ago.

Peach trees in full bloom can make a pink paradise of any middle Georgia orchard which eager Atlanta citizens will drive a hundred miles to see. But except in bloom, such trees set sparsely along a city street unfortunately suggest the thought that they would be better in the back yard.

Atlanta's own chosen tree blooms as beautifully in New York's Bronx Park as it does along Peachtree Street. This is the dogwood, and the whole city blossoms white with it in April, usually just in time for Atlanta's annual spring season of Metropolitan Opera.

Although there are no plantations on Peachtree Street, there are many roads branching off Peachtree that lead to other roads and they, in turn, to others that lead eventually to avenues of old cedars or magnolias or moss-hung live oaks. And at the end of these avenues, tall white columns shine like a tourist's dream come true.

The white columns of the old houses are much more than a tourist's dream, of course. They are a part of what has been called "the South's great heyday," a part of that romantic era immortalized not only in Margaret Mitchell's dramatic novel, but also in such stirring poetry as *John Brown's Body*, by Stephen Vincent Benet, which also has a Georgia background.

> "For wherever the winds of Georgia run
> It smells of peaches long in the sun. . . ."

In that era, cotton was truly king and Southern hospitality required a house large enough to accommodate visiting friends and relatives who might linger for a month or a year or a lifetime. On one coastal Georgia plantation, a young couple who came visiting on their honeymoon stayed until their second child was born.

Whether the house was large or small, the welcome was the same. It is a tradition that dies hard, as more than one dweller in a crowded Atlanta apartment house knows unto this day.

Georgia is a state where anything can happen and does. Whatever else may be said, there's never a dull moment. Basically, Georgians are a homogeneous people; early Georgia got most of its education from New England teachers and preachers. But by temperament and achievement, Georgians have always been as individual and diverse as the topography of the state itself.

From Rabun Gap to Tybee Light we have mountains, plain and sea. And to illustrate individuality of temperament and achievement, we have the late Margaret Mitchell, Bobby Jones, Ty Cobb, James Melton, the Talmadges (Eugene and Herman), Coco-Cola millionaires, cotton and cattle farmers, manufacturers, Junior Leaguers, Ku Kluxers, solid citizens, Democrats—even Republicans. All this variety of living gives color to the story of Georgia's old houses.

Since the time Savannah sent the first steamship across the Atlantic and Augusta hailed one of the first steam engines and railroad passenger trains in the country, Georgians have been getting places first in an amazingly varied number of ways.

Recognition has not always settled where due. Too often, the creative urge having been satisfied, individual producers have failed to bestir themselves for a trip to the patent office or to the press agent. This may have been because of the climate or perhaps because in earlier times it was not considered polite to push oneself.

3

FIGURE 1. Sherman watched Atlanta burn from this house—the Neal-Lyon-Neal home, which served as headquarters for General Sherman in Atlanta. Reproduced from *Leslie's Weekly*, December, 1864.

There is the old red brick house in Roswell, once the home of that versatile Presbyterian minister, Dr. Francis R. Goulding, who on the side invented an early model of the sewing machine and also wrote children's books. There is the house in Jefferson, once the home of Dr. Crawford W. Long, whose records show that he was first to use ether as an anesthetic in surgery.

In Athens there is the house in which the first garden club in the world was organized—the Ladies Garden Club, born in Mrs. E. K. Lumpkin's Victorian parlor in the year 1891. The old chancellor's house on the University of Georgia campus, recently razed to make room for a much-needed new library building, was beautiful for its architectural design and interesting for its mellow history as part of the first chartered state university in America. That charter was granted in 1785. It took sixteen years to get around to opening the first classes under an oak arbor with Cherokee Indians gazing popeyed through the branches of neighboring trees. Here again we see the deliberate action of a people who hurry only when there is a war for which they may volunteer. Then Georgia leads the country.

In one old Georgia house, the mother of a president was married in a romantic ante-bellum ceremony. In another, Fanny Kemble, the celebrated English actress, wrote her fateful *Journal of a Residence on a Georgian Plantation*, a journal which helped to end the Confederacy. In another, you cannot admire the beautiful circular stairway for thinking of the twelve Revolutionary patriots hanged over its stairwell by the British.

There never was a "Tara" in Georgia, except between the covers of Margaret Mitchell's book and on the technicolor screen of its film version. But there are many old houses in the state which might have been its prototype and its inspiration.

Romance by candlelight. A breath of scandal. Coffee and pistols at dawn. War and personal struggle. History in the making. It is all here in Georgia's old houses. Even murder.

Architects and architectural writers think well of Georgia's white columns:

"Nowhere did the Greek Revival produce a more perfect blending of the dignified and the gracious, the impressive and the domestic, than in the lovely houses of the (eighteen) thirties and forties in upstate Georgia . . ." says Talbot Hamlin in his book *Greek Revival Architecture in America.*

This "architecture of the south appears upon analysis," he continues, "to have been a much more profound and significant movement than would seem evident at first from the false and sentimental glamour with which an equally shallow and sentimental modern view of the ante-bellum South has enshrined it. Like Greek Revival architecture elsewhere, the Greek Revival of the South stood for the direct solution of practical problems, the frank acceptance of climates and ways of life, the breakdown of the older traditions dating back to Colonial times and the attempt to create a new and American architecture."

"Here," says Howard Major, author of *The Domestic Architecture of the Early American Republic; The Greek Revival,* "we have the individual expression in architecture of the American people; our own great national style without parallel in the domestic architecture of Europe." Mr. Major continues:

"Invariably it has a monumental quality and it is unsurpassed in its restraint. And yet into the monumental quality has been infused a certain charm—an elusive element to secure when it must be combined with such stately character, but undeniably attained. . . . It is high time . . . that Georgia . . . [and other states mentioned] should acquire for posterity some of these Greek Revival buildings which are our only archaeological tradition."

Thirty illustrations of Georgia houses, more than from any other state except New York, appear in Mr. Major's book.

The Greek Revival reached its finest development between 1820 and 1850, the era in which many of Georgia's plantation and town houses were built. Of the three Grecian orders—Doric, Ionic and Corinthian—the Doric was most popular in Georgia. Many fine examples of all three remain. And while they follow the classic pattern, many of them also embody that great variety and individuality which is typical of the Georgia character and personality.

All too often these houses are mistakenly referred to as "Southern Colonial," or houses with "Colonial columns." Colonial columns, of course, are something else again, slimmer, more attenuated, usually one story in height. Such columns, perhaps most plentiful on early New England houses, are also to be seen in Georgia, which was the youngest of the thirteen English colonies.

But it is the Greek Revival column which is the glory of Georgia's ante-bellum houses. Many of these dwellings were planned by Eastern or local architects. Others were adapted from the builders' handbooks current at the time which may still be seen in architectural libraries. Mantels and other hand-carved woodwork were sometimes imported from England or from fine cabinetmakers in New England. More often such work was done locally, perhaps by a traveling cabinetmaker. Sometimes it was the work of slaves who developed great skill as woodworkers, carpenters, bricklayers, etc. Marble mantels were shipped all the way from Italy for Georgia houses, and when plans called for ornamental plaster moldings this was usually the handiwork of Italian artisans.

More than two hundred old Georgia houses—Colonial, post-Revolutionary, Greek Revival and other ante-bellum types—are listed in the "Historic American Buildings Survey" made by the federal government in the early nineteen forties. These houses are considered important enough from an architectural standpoint or historical association to justify the making of photographs and measured drawings which are on file for posterity in the Library of Congress in Washington.

Even this large collection does not include all the interesting old houses in Georgia. Nor can one hope to include them all in a single book. Georgia is the largest state east of the Mississippi—320 miles from north to south—250 miles from east to west. But let's see what we can see——

CHAPTER 2

The Road to the Sea

---

*I*T was one of those days in spring and the car was new. The temptation was to drive off in all directions at once.

If we went south there was ante-bellum Greenwood Plantation, now owned by John Hay (Jock) Whitney. The house there was said by architect Stanford White to be one of the finest examples of Greek Revival architecture in the country.

If we went directly north there was the old house of Chief Joseph Vann, at Spring Place, built when all of North Georgia was Indian country. It was one of the finest houses in that part of the state and one of two brick houses in the entire Cherokee Nation. Slaves owned by Joseph Vann tilled its surrounding acres.

West at Columbus (really southwest) there would be St. Elmo, its twelve Doric columns rising forty feet high. Here Augusta J. Evans, author of *St. Elmo*, was a frequent guest. Thackeray was entertained in this hospitable house and so were two Presidents of the United States, James K. Polk and Millard Fillmore.

East at Savannah, there would be Wormsloe, a plantation dating back to the beginning of the Colony of Georgia in 1733, still owned and occupied by descendants of Noble Jones, who first settled there on a grant from the Trustees of the New Colony.

East, or rather southeast, won, and then the route was to be chosen. That was fairly easy. General Sherman blazed a trail from Atlanta to Savannah back in the 'sixties, and we do mean blazed. Let's follow that, we said. Let's see first the old houses that survived pre-atomic war.

We know that old roads are often lost when new highways are built, but the march to the sea led from town to town. We could still approximate the route.

But it was not as simple as that, unless you could suddenly become quadruplets or develop something like double schizophrenia.

7

Sherman's men, sixty-two thousand strong, fanned out along four different highways from Atlanta to the sea, cutting a swath sixty miles wide. Back and forth and across roamed the foragers, or "bummers" as they were called. In and out, around and about, ranged Kilpatrick's cavalry, striking here, striking there. Now you see them, now you don't.

To oppose this relentless force were three thousand Georgia militia men and Wheeler's cavalry.

In the entire four-year conflict more than a million men were called into service by the North.

The South at no time had more than 500,000 men in the field.

Balancing these against population figures for the two sections, twenty million inhabitants in the North and 5,449,000 white citizens of the eleven seceding states, it is easy to understand why there were few men left in Georgia to resist Sherman. They were fighting outside the state, mainly in Tennessee with Hood and with Lee in the army of Virginia.

Sherman's march through Georgia reached its climax in Savannah. There the beautiful old Green-Meldrim house which was Sherman's headquarters still stands. Let's pause a moment to look backward at Atlanta of the 'sixties, where the march began. During the war years Atlanta's population had grown from ten thousand to eighteen thousand inhabitants.

The city was burned twice. Hollywood found it necessary to make this explanation when filming *Gone With the Wind*.

The first fire took place September 1, 1864, when General Hood's forces finally evacuated Atlanta. The Confederates burned certain buildings containing war materials to prevent them from falling into Union hands. They also burned freight cars loaded with ammunition. The city in general was not touched by these fires.

It was November when Atlanta was burned by Sherman.

The Battle of Atlanta had taken place July 22, 1864. For days beforehand and afterward until September 2, the city had been in a state of siege. Many houses had what were called bombproofs, antedating the underground air-raid shelters of recent wars. Nevertheless, more than a hundred noncombatants were killed by exploding shells.

On September 8, 1864, the triumphant General Sherman rode into Atlanta, then occupied by General Slocum's 20th United States Corps. In Sherman's pocket were the congratulations of President Lincoln for the success of his arms. Sherman was then forty-four years old, red bearded, a bit less spruce perhaps than a West Pointer should be, in his blue uniform and slouch hat, but keen of eye, nervous in gesture and quick in action. Fighting in the last of the gallant wars, he was a realist before his time.

FIGURE 2. Sherman stayed at this American Gothic house of Charles Green in Savannah, now the parish house of St. John's Episcopal Church. This picture shows the battlements, oriels and iron lace.

Soon after General Sherman's arrival, evacuation of Atlanta families began. The necessity for this evacuation of civilian population has often been questioned. General Sherman explained later in his *Memoirs:*

"I had seen Memphis, Vicksburg, Natchez and New Orleans all captured and each at once garrisoned by a full division of troops if not more—so that success was actually crippling our armies in the field by detachments to guard and protect the interests of a hostile population."

Although many families had refugeed before General Sherman's arrival, many remained. The advancing Federal general had been met by Mayor Calhoun and Councilmen Rawson and Wells, with a petition which pictures the confusion and despair of these unfortunates who literally had nowhere to go—the displaced persons of an earlier era.

9

FIGURE 3.   House of Indian Chief Joseph Vann, at Spring Place, built about 1790.
The four wide, vertical cement bands are all that remain of long-gone pilasters.
The dilapidated porch is a later addition.

"Many poor women are in an advanced state of pregnancy—others have young children—their husbands are either in the army, prisoners or dead. Some say I have such and such a one sick at home. What are we to do—we have nowhere to go—I will try to take this or that article, but such and such things I must leave behind, though I need them very much."

The station from which they were evacuated was called Rough and Ready.

During the occupation of Atlanta, General Sherman attended to a great deal of unfinished business in North Georgia, and of the night of November 12 he writes: "With a full staff I started from Kingston for Atlanta . . . sat on the edge of a porch to rest . . . Eddy Van Valkenburg with a portable pocket (telegraph) instrument called Chattanooga. General Thomas's message . . . 'clear road before you'. . . . A few moments later a bridge was burned and the wires were down. . . .

"As we rode on toward Atlanta that night I remember the railroad trains going to the rear with a furious speed, the engineers and a few men about the trains waving us an affectionate adieu. It surely was a strange event—two hostile armies marching in opposite directions, each in the full belief that it was achieving a final and conclusive result in a great war; and I was strongly inspired with the feeling that the movement on our part was a direct attack upon the rebel army and the rebel capital at Richmond, though a full thousand miles of hostile country intervened and that, for better or worse, it would end the war."

General Sherman's own Major Henry Hitchcock describes the burning of Atlanta under date of November 15, 1864:

"This P. M. the torch applied, also sundry buildings blown up by shells inside. Clouds of heavy smoke rise and hang like a pall over the doomed city. At night the grandest and most awful scene. Our headquarters are on high ground . . . half the horizon shows immense and raging fires, lighting up the whole heavens. Probably, says Sherman, visible at Griffin 50 miles off. First, bursts of smoke, dense black volumes, then tongues of flame, then huge waves of fire roll up into the sky. Now and then are heavy explosions and as one fire sinks another rises farther along the horizon . . . a line of fire and smoke, lurid, angry, dreadful to look upon.

"Sherman says, 'This city has done more and probably contributed more to carry on and sustain the war than any other, save Richmond. We have been fighting Atlanta all the time in the past and have been capturing guns, wagons, etc., marked Atlanta and made here . . . and now since they have been doing so much to destroy us and our government, we have to destroy them, at least enough to prevent any more of that . . .'"

Federal Major James Austin Connolly also gives an eyewitness account in a letter to his wife: "Up to about three P. M. this issuing (of supplies) had been carried out, but about this time fire began to break out in various portions of the

FIGURE 4. John Hay (Jock) Whitney's Greenwood in Thomasville stands in the center of a twenty-thousand-acre plantation. The house was completed by an English architect, John Wind, in 1844.

Photo by Frances Benjamin Johnston

FIGURE 5. St. Elmo, in Columbus, has twelve Doric columns, forty feet high. The house was built in 1831 by Seaborn Jones, and has entertained two Presidents of the United States and William Makepeace Thackeray.

city and it soon became evident that these fires were the beginning of a general conflagration which would sweep over the entire city and blot it out of existence. So quartermaster and commissary ceased trying to issue clothing or allot rations. They told the soldiers to go in and take what they wanted before it was burned up. . . . Soldiers found many barrels of whiskey . . . drunken soldiers on foot and on horseback raced up and down the streets while the buildings on either side were solid sheets of flame. They shouted and danced and sang while pillar and dome and roof sank into one common ruin. The night for miles around was as bright as midday. The City of Atlanta was one mass of flame and the morrow must find it a mass of ruins.

"Well, the soldiers fought for it and the soldiers won it and so, I suppose General Sherman thinks, for he is somewhere nearby looking on at all this and not saying one word about preventing it. All the pictures and verbal descriptions of hell I have ever seen never gave me half so vivid an idea of it as did this flame wrapped city tonight. Gate City of the South, farewell."

Sherman watched the fire from the old John Neal home, described by Hitchcock as "Judge Lyon's fine house, large, double brick, very handsome, same headquarters as before." Judge Lyon was a temporary occupant. Both before and after the war the house was owned by Mr. Neal. It occupied the site of Atlanta's present City Hall.

General Sherman writes in his own report: "Colonel Poe, U. S. Engineers, of my staff, had been busy in his special task of destruction. He had a large force at work . . . had leveled the great depot, roundhouse and the machine shops of the Georgia railroad and had applied fire to the wreck . . ."

It was General Sherman's idea to cut off the source of supplies to Confederate forces still fighting in Virginia and other points, according to Tom S. Gray, Jr., in an analytical article, "The March to the Sea." Leaving Atlanta, Sherman divided his army into about equal parts, placing General Howard in command of the right wing and General Slocum in command of the left.

The march to the sea actually began on the morning of November 15, before the torch was applied to Atlanta.

"The right wing and Cavalry followed the railroad toward Jonesboro, General Slocum with the 20th Corps leading off to the east by Decatur and Stone Mountain toward Madison," says General Sherman. "These were divergent lines designed to threaten both Macon and Augusta at the same time, so as to prevent a concentration at our intended destination or 'objective,' Milledgeville, the capital of Georgia, distant about 100 miles. The time allowed each column for reaching Milledgeville was seven days. I remained in Atlanta.

"Outside the city the two wings were subdivided into about equal parts," says Mr. Gray's article, "each of the two columns of the respective wings traveling within 10 to 15 miles of each other on parallel routes. . . . As the army progressed Kilpatrick worked a serpentine across the four columns.

"Thus went down upon Georgia four columns spread over a path approximately 60 miles wide . . ."

In round numbers this army contained sixty-two thousand men.

It was, no doubt, quite a spectacle. In his memoirs General Sherman says: "We had in all about 2,500 wagons with teams of six mules to each and 600 ambulances with 2 horses to each. Wagon trains were divided equally between the four corps so that each had about 800 wagons and these usually on the march occupied about five miles or more of road. Habitually the artillery and wagons had the road, while the men—with the exception of the advance and rear guards—pursued paths improvised by the side of the wagons unless they were forced to use a bridge or causeway in common."

Radio and radar were for later wars. These four divergent marching columns were often able to keep track of each other by the clouds of smoke rising above burning buildings.

Of Sherman's orders, this volume is concerned only with that part which explains the absence of many houses then standing in Atlanta and along the march to the sea:

"The army will forage liberally on the country," he decreed. "Each brigade commander will organize good and sufficient foraging parties under the command of one or more discreet officers who will gather . . . whatever is needed by the command. . . . Cavalry and artillery may appropriate freely horses, mules, wagons, etc. . . . To corps commanders is intrusted the power to destroy mills, houses, cotton gins, etc., and for them this general principle is laid down: In districts and neighborhoods where the army is unmolested, no destruction of such property should be permitted, but should guerrillas or bushwhackers molest our march or should the inhabitants . . . manifest local hostility, then army commanders should order and enforce a devastation more or less relentless, according to the measure of such hostility."

A day later than the main body of the army, General Sherman and his staff left Atlanta. He says:

"About 7 A. M. of November 16 we rode out of Atlanta by the Decatur road. Reaching the hill we naturally paused to look back upon the scene of our past battles. Behind us lay Atlanta, smoldering and in ruins, the black smoke rising high in the air and hanging like a pall over the ruined city . . .

"Away off in the distance on the McDonough road was the rear of Howard's column, the gun barrels glistening in the sun, the white-topped wagons stretching away to the south and right before us, the Fourteenth Corps marching steadily and rapidly . . .

"A spirit of exhilaration runs through the entire army . . ."

Atlanta had fallen and with it the hopes of the Confederacy. Sherman and his army were marching through Georgia . . . to the sea.

And as they traveled, they sang, "John Brown's body lies a-mouldering in the grave . . . but his soul goes marching on."

It still marches.

Like General Sherman, we have looked back. Like General Sherman, let us turn and leave Atlanta (now a city with a metropolitan population of nearly 700,000) by the Decatur road. We will bypass Lithonia, where General Sherman's men spent their first night, with Stone Mountain "a mass of granite in plain view, cut out in clear outline against the sky." We will skim through Conyers and through Covington. "The handsome town of Covington," Sherman called it. We will stop another time. Today we are on our way to historic Burge Plantation.

CHAPTER 3

Up=Country Plantation

"*T*HOUGH Southern rural life has necessarily changed since the Civil War, I doubt that there is in the entire South a place where it has changed less than on the Burge Plantation near Covington, Georgia," wrote Julian Street in his introduction to *A Woman's War-Time Journal,* by Dolly Sumner Lunt (Mrs. Thomas Burge), first published in 1918.

"And," Mr. Street continued, "I do not know in the whole country a place that I should rather see again in springtime—the Georgia springtime, when the air is like a tonic vapor distilled from the earth—from pine trees, tulip trees, Balm-of-Gilead trees (or 'bam' trees, as the Negroes call them), blossoming Judas trees, Georgia crab apple, dogwood pink and white, peach blossom, wisteria, sweet shrub, dog violets, pansy violets, Cherokee roses, wild honeysuckle, azalea and the evanescent green of new treetops, all carried in solution in the sunlight."

Mrs. Thomas Burge, writer of the *Journal,* was the grandmother of Mrs. Louis D. Bolton and Mrs. M. J. Morehouse, who now live at the Burge Plantation—but in separate houses.

There is a legend about the two houses:

Mrs. Bolton, so the story goes, loved the old plantation house. Mrs. Morehouse loved the old garden. In order that each sister might own that part of the plantation dearest her heart, house and garden were divorced. The original house was moved across the road and a new house built on the old site.

"But, of course, I loved the old garden, too," says Mrs. Bolton smilingly. "The facts are that my sister was married to an architect and they both had ideas about the sort of house that should stand in the old garden. And so . . ."

And so the old house was moved to a new site directly across the road. In order to preserve fine old trees the jacked-up house was rolled—five hundred feet or more—parallel with State Highway 142 before the actual crossing was made. Here again it was rolled back of the tree line and from that point up to its new site. In the old garden, directly across the road, arose a more formal house, white clapboard with Corinthian columns, the home of Mr. and Mrs. Morehouse.

Mrs. Bolton's marriage had carried her to Detroit, where her husband was a pioneer in the automobile industry. When he retired and they came South to live, they settled in the original Burge Plantation house. Immediately Mrs. Bolton set about creating a garden for the old house in its new surroundings, a garden now as timeless as the trees that shade it. White against green foliage, the house might have been there from its beginning. Today, as yesterday, cultivated plantation land stretches farther than the eye can reach.

As Mrs. Bolton says, "the house goes around in a circle." Like many up-country dwellings of the period, it started out with rooms on either side of a central hallway and other rooms and wings were added as needed. There are now thirteen rooms, all on one floor. In the late eighteen twenties the up-country was more or less frontier territory. Indians still fished and hunted in near-by streams and forests. Plantation houses, as a rule, were simpler than those along the coast and the Savannnah River as far inland as Augusta.

But this very simplicity is one of the endearing charms of the Burge Plantation house, with its gently sloping roof overhanging a one-story Doric colonnade. Green blinds open against the wide, white horizontal board walls of its front porch.

The house is full of old mahogany and rosewood. Under the oldest tester bed there is a trundle bed. In the living room hangs a gold-framed mirror that belonged to a great aunt's grandmother, Lady Dorothy Vose. There is a plantation desk with its roster of slaves. You see many of these desks in Georgia's plantation houses. Greatly prized at the Burge Plantation are seven splint-bottomed chairs as old as the house itself.

Mrs. Bolton's grandmother, Dolly Sumner Lunt, came down from Bowdoinham, Maine, to teach school at Covington, Georgia. There she met Thomas Burge, a plantation owner and gentleman of the Old South.

She had been brought up in the heart of the abolitionist movement, a relative of Charles Sumner, who was one of the South's bitterest foes. Naturally, she and Thomas Burge—like Romeo and Juliet, children of warring households—fell in love.

They were married and lived happily ever afterward—at least until Thomas Burge's death, less than three years before that difference of opinion between North and South flamed into actual warfare.

Mrs. Burge, living at the plantation with her nine-year-old daughter, Sarah ("Sadai") and a hundred slaves, faced that war as a young widow.

In 1917, when "the world was aghast over the German invasion of Belgium,"

Julian Street was a guest at this same plantation house near Covington. "What must life have been in this part of Georgia when Sherman's men came by . . ." Mr. Street wondered.

"For . . ." he continues, "though Germany's assault was upon an unoffending neutral state and was impelled by greed and military vanity—whereas Sherman's march through Georgia was an invasion of enemy country for the purpose of 'breaking the back' of that enemy and thus terminating the war— nevertheless 'military necessity' was the excuse in either case for a campaign of deliberate destruction—which in the state of Georgia was measured by Sherman himself at one hundred million dollars."

What was life like in Georgia in the eighteen sixties?

Mr. Street found the answer in the journal of Dolly Sumner Lunt (Mrs. Thomas Burge). Sherman and one of the divisions of his great army, marching to the sea, passed directly by the Burge Plantation in November of 1864. But, as Mr. Street discovered, there was plenty of cause for excitement in the neighborhood, long before that time. So interested was he that he prevailed upon Mrs. Bolton and Mrs. Morehouse to allow publication of the journal by the one-time Century Company of New York. Since then the book has been re-issued by Burke of Macon. Permission is given by Mrs. Bolton to reproduce excerpts here:

"I wish," says Mr. Street, in his introduction, "that the reader might sit, as I did, in the very house, in the very room in which the journal was written . . . and read for himself of events which seem, somehow, more vivid for the fact that the ink is faded brown with time.

"I wish that when the journal tells of 'bluecoats coming down the road' the reader might glance up as I did and see the very road down which they came.

"Imagine yourself in a low, white house, standing in a grove of gigantic oaks surrounded by cotton fields. Imagine yourself in a large, comfortable room in this house, in an old rocking chair by the window. From the window you may see the white well-house, its roof mottled with the shifting shadows of green boughs above. Beyond are the garden and the road, and far away in the red fields, Negroes and mules are at work. You look down at the large book resting in your lap and read.

July 22, 1864 [the day of the Battle of Atlanta], Mrs. Burge wrote:

"We have heard the loud booming of cannon all day. . . . Suddenly I saw the servants running to the palings and I walked to the door, when I saw such a stampede as I never witnessed before. The road was full of carriages, wagons, men on horseback, all riding at full speed. Judge Floyd (of Covington) stopped, saying, 'Mrs. Burge, the Yankees are coming. They have got my family, and here is all I have upon earth. Hide your mules and carriages and whatever valuables you have.'

FIGURE 6. Burge Plantation House, near Covington, owned by Mrs. L. D. Bolton, as reproduced from a painting. This house now stands across the road from its original location, which is occupied by a later house.

"Sadai [Mrs. Burge's nine-year-old daughter] said: 'Oh, Mama, what shall we do?'

" 'Never mind, Sadai, they won't hurt you and you must help me hide my things.' I went to the smokehouse, divided out the meat to the servants and bade them hide it. Julia [a servant] took a jar of lard and buried it. . . . China and silver were buried underground and Sadai bade Mary [a servant] hide a bit of soap under some bricks that mama might have a little left. Then she came to me with a part of a loaf of bread, asking if she had not better put it in her pocket, that we might have something to eat that night. And, verily, we have cause to fear that we might be homeless, for on every side we could see smoke arising from burning buildings and bridges. . . .

"Major Ansley, who was wounded in the battle of Missionary Ridge, and has not recovered, came with his wife, sister, two little ones and servants. He was traveling in a bed in a small wagon. They had thought to get to Eatonton, but he was so wearied that they stopped with me for the night. I am glad to have them. I shall sleep none tonight. The woods are full of refugees.

"July 23. I have been left in my home all day with no one but Sadai. Have seen nothing of the raiders, though this morning they burned the buildings around the depot at the Circle [Social Circle, a near-by town]. . . . Just as the sun set Major Ansley and family came back. They heard of the enemy all about and concluded they were as safe here as anywhere. . . . This raid is headed by Garrard and is for the purpose of destroying our railroads. They cruelly shot a George Daniel and a Mr. [Iverson] Jones of Covington, destroyed a great deal of private property and took many citizens prisoners.

"July 29 . . . Sleepless nights. The report is that the Yankees have left Covington for Macon, headed by Stoneman, to release prisoners held there. They robbed every house on the road of its provisions, sometimes taking every piece of meat, blankets and wearing apparel, silver and arms of every description. They would take silk dresses and put them under their saddles and many other things for which they had no use. Our mills, too, they have burned, destroying an immense amount of property.

"August 2, 1864 . . . Just as I got out of bed this morning I peeped through the blinds and there they were sure enough, the Yankees, the bluecoats. The servant women came running in. 'Mistress, they are coming. They are riding into the lot. There are two of them coming up the steps.'

"They said they wanted breakfast and that quick, too. . . . As soon as I could get my clothing on I hastened to the kitchen to hurry up breakfast. Six of them were there, talking with my women . . . passing themselves off as Wheeler's men. . . .

" 'You look like Yankees,' said I.

" 'Yes,' said one, stepping up to me, 'we are Yankees. Did you ever see one before?'

" 'Not for a long time,' I replied, 'and none such as you.' [They were raiders and left after breakfast, taking three of her best mules.]

"August 5, 1864 . . . Mr. Ward [Mrs. Burge's overseer] has been robbed by the Yankees of his watch, pencil and shirt. . . .

"November 8, 1864 . . . Today will probably decide the fate of the Confederacy. If Lincoln is re-elected, I think our fate is a hard one. . . . I have never felt that slavery was altogether right, for it is abused by men. . . . I have often heard Mr. Burge say that if he could see that it was sinful for him to own slaves, he would take them where he could free them. He would not sin for his right hand. . . . I have never bought or sold slaves and I have tried to make life easy and pleasant to those that have been bequeathed to me by the dead. I have never ceased to work. Many a Northern housewife has a much easier time than a Southern matron with her hundred Negroes. . . .

"November 16, 1864 . . . On our way home [from Social Circle where coffee was $7 a pound, Confederate money] we met Brother Evans . . . who inquired if we had heard that the Yankees were coming. . . . Finally settled it in our minds that it could not be so. Probably a foraging party.

"November 17 . . . Have been uneasy all day. Neighbors who had been to town called . . . said it was a large force, moving very slowly. What shall I do? Where go?

"November 18, 1864 . . . Slept very little last night. Went out doors several times and could see large fires like burning buildings. . . . I made a pair of pants for Jack [a slave].

"November 19 . . . Saw Mrs. Laura Perry in the road, surrounded by her children. She said she was looking for her husband [Joe Perry]; that old Mrs. Perry had just sent word that the Yankees went to James Perry's house the night before, plundered his house and drove off all his stock. Before we were done talking, up came Joe and Jim Perry from their hiding place. Happening to turn and look behind as we stood there I saw some bluecoats coming down the hill. Jim immediately raised his gun, swearing he would kill them.

" 'No, don't,' said I, and ran home as fast as I could with Sadai. I could hear them cry, 'Halt, Halt,' and their guns went off in quick succession. Oh, God, the time of trial has come.

"I hastened back to my frightened servants and told them they had better hide, and then went back to the gate to claim protection and a guard. But like demons they rush in. My yards are full. To my smokehouse, my dairy, pantry, kitchen and cellar, like famished wolves they come, breaking locks and whatever is in their way. The thousand pounds of meat in my smokehouse is gone in a twinkling, my flour, my lard, butter, eggs, pickles of various kinds, both in vinegar and brine—wine, jars and jugs all gone. My 18 fat turkeys, my hens, chickens and fowls, my young pigs, are shot down in my yard and hunted as if they were rebels themselves. Utterly powerless, I ran out and appealed to the guard.

" 'I cannot help you, Madam; it is orders.'

"As I stood there, from my lot I saw driven, first, old Dutch, my dear old buggy horse, who has carried my beloved husband so many miles and who at last drew him to his grave; then came old Mary, my brood mare, who for years had been too old and stiff to work, with her three-year-old colt, my two-year-old mule and her last little baby colt. There they go! There go my mules, my sheep and, worse than all, my boys [slaves] . . . forced from home at the point of a bayonet.

"My poor boys. Never have I corrected them; a word was sufficient. Never have they known want of any kind. Their parents are with me, and how sadly they lament the loss of their boys. Their cabins are rifled of every valuable, the soldiers swearing that their Sunday clothes were the white people's and that they never had money to get such things as they had. Poor Frank's chest was broken open [Frank was a slave], his money and his tobacco taken. He has always been a money-making and saving boy; not infrequently has his crop brought him five hundred dollars and more.

"A Captain Webber from Illinois came into my house. Of him I claimed protection from the vandals who were forcing themselves into my room [where the house servants had taken refuge]. He said that he knew my brother Orrington Lunt [a well-known early settler of Chicago]. At that name I could not restrain my feelings, but, bursting into tears, implored him to see my brother and let him know my destitution. I saw nothing before me but starvation. He promised to do this and comforted me with the assurance that my dwelling house would not be burned, though my out-buildings might. Poor little Sadai went crying to him as to a friend and told him they had taken her doll, Nancy . . .

"Sherman himself and a greater portion of his army passed my house that day. All day, as the sad moments rolled on, were they passing not only in front of my house, but from behind; they tore down my garden palings, made a road through my back yard and lot field, driving their stock and riding through, tearing down my fences and desolating my home—wantonly doing it when there was no necessity for it. . . . My heavenly father alone saved me from the destructive fire. My carriage house had in it eight bales of cotton, with my carriage, buggy and harness. On top of the cotton were some carded cotton rolls . . . a large twist of the rolls was taken and set on fire and thrown into the boat of my carriage, which was close up to the cotton bales. Thanks to my God, the cotton only burned over and went out.

"November 20 . . . I had watched all night and the dawn found me watching for the moving of the soldiery that was encamped about us. . . . About ten o'clock they had all passed. . . . A few minutes elapsed and two couriers, riding rapidly passed back. Then presently more soldiers came by and this ended the passing of Sherman's army, leaving me poorer by thirty thousand dollars than I was yesterday morning.

"November 21 . . . Major Lee came down this morning, having heard that I was burned out . . . to proffer me a home. . . . Everyone we meet gives us painful accounts of the desolation caused by the enemy. Each one has to tell his or her own experience, and fellow-suffering makes us all equal and makes us all interested in one another. . . .

"The Yankees found Mrs. Glass's china and glassware that she had buried in a box, broke it all up and sent her word she would set no more fine tables. They also got Mrs. Perry's silver.

"December 25, 1864 . . . Sadai jumped out of bed very early this morning to feel her stocking. . . . She could not believe but that there would be something in it. Finding nothing, she crept back into bed . . .

"April 29, 1865 . . . Boys plowing in old house field. We are needing rain. Everything looks pleasant, but the state of our country is very gloomy. Two armies have surrendered. The President of United States has been assassinated, Richmond evacuated and Davis, President of the Confederacy, put to flight. The old flag has been raised again upon Sumter and an armistice accepted.

[May is full of stories of Confederate soldiers, bitterly returning to their homes and of apprehension of the Yankee troops encamped in the neighborhood.]

"December 24, 1865 . . . My freedmen have been with me and have worked for one sixth of my crop.

"December 25, 1865 . . . Sadai woke very early and crept out of bed to her stocking. Seeing it well filled she soon had a light and eight little Negroes around her. Everything opened that could be divided was shared with them. 'Tis the last Christmas, probably, that we shall be together, freedmen. Now you will, I trust, have your own homes and be joyful under your own vine and fig tree, with none to molest or make afraid."

It is pleasant to know that Mrs. Burge married again—the Reverend William J. Parks. For a time they lived in the dean's house, now the president's house at old Oxford, where the Methodist Episcopal Church had established Emory College in 1836.

Sadai grew up here, pretty and bright and light-hearted, very popular with Emory students. Freshly graduated from Wesleyan College, she went North for a long visit with well-to-do relatives. Perhaps her mother hoped Sadai would choose a husband there. The South's young men were still faced with the job of reclaiming their lands and rebuilding their fortunes. Sadai kept a diary telling all about her wonderful time as she went from one big house to another, but she came home and married a young minister—the Reverend John Davis Gray. With him she went back to Burge Plantation to live. Mrs. Morehouse and Mrs. Bolton were two of their five children. Mrs. Bolton was named Dorothy for the grandmother who wrote the wartime journal.

Unfortunately, both Sadai and her husband died young. The five orphaned children spent a year at Mount Pleasant, plantation of their guardian, Henry L. Graves. There were four Graves children, which made a group of nine in one household. But Mount Pleasant, a house of many gables and many additions, still stands not far from Covington to prove that room was adequate. So was the welcome.

Years later Mrs. Bolton said wonderingly to Mrs. Graves, "Aunt Retta, you seemed so glad to have us."

"I was glad," Aunt Retta answered simply. Retta was short for Henrietta, and she was Aunt by affection. Mrs. Graves had a heart so big there is a tradition her spirit still lingers—watching over the welfare of her descendants—at Mount Pleasant, now owned by her son, Henry L. Graves, Jr.

That Mount Pleasant was all its name implies you cannot doubt as Mrs. Bolton continues, "When our northern relatives came down to take us back with them, we did not want to go.

"Of course, children often shrink from strangeness, but I shall never forget how my two younger brothers hid under the house and stayed there all day long without food or water, hoping they would be left behind. The family and servants looked for them in vain. Finally the old hound dog nosed out their hiding place and gave it away to the searchers."

Years later when Mrs. Bolton returned to Burge Plantation to live, she literally stepped back into the setting of her childhood. She couldn't bear to change anything in the old house—only to add electricity and modern plumbing. And, of course, to cultivate the new garden which so soon took on the character of an old garden.

The problem was what to do with the beautiful eighteenth-century furniture she had accumulated for her Detroit home. She solved this by purchasing the Greek Revival Usher house on Floyd Street in near-by Covington, a house she had long admired and was anxious to see preserved. It all added up to a charming home for her daughter-in-law, Mrs. M. L. Bolton, and two Bolton grandsons.

And so, as Julian Street observed, life has changed little on the Burge Plantation—still lovely in the Georgia springtime, or anytime.

CHAPTER 4

Confederate Girl Spy

ZORA Fair was a Confederate girl spy who lived in Oxford, a mile and a half from Covington. And Jane Conner, whose home was in Covington, led Sherman's army right up Floyd Street, which is perhaps the most Confederate street in Georgia. Two of Newton county's four Confederate generals lived in white-columned houses along this lovely old street which is now a link of State Highway 12. A third, General Anderson, lived at the end of Anderson Avenue which begins at a corner of this same street.

Zora Fair came pretty close to being captured by Sherman. But Jane Conner may be said to have captured Sherman's army. That was the way it looked on a certain day in November of 1864.

Here was the army, passing through Covington on its march to the sea—colors flying and bands playing. And at the head of the column, pretty Jane Conner, stepping lively, or as lively as a young lady could step in hoop skirts.

"This is the way it happened," says Jane Conner's daughter, small, white-haired Mrs. R. R. Fowler, who lives on Floyd Street in the house built about 1900 which replaced the home of her parents, Mr. and Mrs. William T. Wells. "Covington had heard Sherman's army was headed this way," Mrs. Fowler explained. "People stayed in their homes all day long, waiting.

"The next day my grandmother decided the army wasn't coming to Covington after all. She needed some things from town, so she gave her daughter, Jane, a list and told her to see about having the various items delivered. Of course, it wasn't very far to town, as my grandparents lived right in front of the Methodist church.

"So Jane, who later became my mother, took the list and went to town.

25

FIGURE 7. N. S. Turner house at Covington. A carved balustrade connects Doric columns.

Photo by Kenneth Rogers

FIGURE 8.   The old Usher house in Covington, now owned by Mr. and
Mrs. L. D. Bolton, of Burge Plantation.

And," Mrs. Fowler smiled, "when she came back, Sherman's army followed her home. Some of the soldiers broke ranks and followed her right into the house."

Four years earlier, when the war broke out, Jane Conner's trousseau had been all complete and the wedding date set. She and young Mr. Wells decided to wait until the war was over. He told her he would be back before she had a chance to miss him.

Jane's dainty trousseau petticoats were later torn up to make bandages for wounded soldiers when the beautiful old Methodist church became a hospital. Mrs. Fowler shook her head, thinking of all those many stitches put into the many petticoats by hand, the hand embroidery and the laces whipped on. In those days a girl wouldn't think of going anywhere in less than three petticoats.

"There wasn't any trousseau left when my father came limping home bare-footed," she said. "But that didn't delay the wedding. And they settled right here. The whole square [now business property] was once my mother's flower garden."

Pure Southern gallantry, which does not limit itself to the young and fair, inspired the yellow curb in front of Mrs. Fowler's substantial two-story frame house. "The city had the curb painted like that," she explains with proper pride, "so I and my guests would have a place to park."

Mrs. Fowler's son, R. R. Fowler, and his family live on Clark's Hill in a handsome reproduction of an old house that formerly stood on the same site.

General Sherman says in his *Memoirs*, "We passed through the handsome town of Covington, the soldiers closing up their ranks, the color bearers unfurling their flags and the bands striking up patriotic airs . . ."

He explains that he himself rode around by a side street "to avoid the crowd that followed the marching column. Someone brought me an invitation to dine with a sister of Sam Anderson who was a cadet at West Point with me, but the messenger reached me after we had passed the main part of town. I asked to be excused and rode on to a place designated for camp at the crossing of the Ulcofauhachee [Alcovy] river about four miles east of the town."

Zora Fair, the Confederate girl spy, figured in notes made at this camp by Sherman's Assistant Adjutant General, Major Henry Hitchcock, and later included in his book, *Marching with Sherman*.

"Rebel mail captured and brought to General and turned over to me. Only one letter of interest—from a 'young lady' [Miss Izora M. Fair] of Oxford—a little town north of Covington—to Governor Brown, of Georgia, detailing a visit she made to Atlanta recently, disguised as a country negress; face stained with walnuts and hair 'frizzed.'

"She was fired at by our pickets (this before we left Atlanta) then taken to quarters of guard—heard and reports a conversation, etc.

"By another letter, same mail, from a lady in Oxford, it seems Miss F's performance was severely criticized by her female rebel friends.

"The General sent a party to Oxford this P. M. to find and bring Miss Fair to him 'on foot.'

" 'I don't mean to hurt her, but will give her a scare,' he said to me. But she was non est."

The old part of Covington's main street, along which Sherman's army passed, is still very much as it was then, tree-shaded with white-columned houses set back and far apart on either side. It was named Floyd Street in honor of Judge John J. Floyd, who built one of its spacious houses in 1835. This is still called the Judge Floyd house, though it has a street number—308—and has been owned by Miss Hyda Heard for many years.

Of course, all of Covington's ante-bellum houses are not on Floyd Street. And ante-bellum charm is not always the chief attraction when Covington opens its hospitable doors for a house-and-garden tour. Some visitors find themselves more interested in art—because of the murals painted not so many years ago in one old home by a young artist who later became the storm center of one of Atlanta's most sensational murder cases.

Through interlocking romances, most of the houses on Floyd Street are "kissing kin" or have a family "connection." Most of them have fluted Doric columns all the way across the front, white contrasting with green window blinds and fine boxwood and venerable trees. The wide central hallways, big square rooms (some of them twenty-five by twenty-five) and high ceilings create an atmosphere of calm and serenity too often lost in the houses of succeeding architectural periods. Pilastered and corniced doors, windows and hand-carved mantels have a fine solid dignity, enhanced by molded wall cornices and center ceiling rosettes for chandeliers. The old rooms, with their fine proportions, lend themselves to almost any style of furnishings. The most frequent is a mixture of eighteenth century, Empire and Victorian, and the effect is an open invitation to linger.

General James P. Sims grew up at 301 Floyd Street in a Greek Revival house that has since become an apartment building. But it still retains its original fine spiral stair, hand-carved mantels and fanlighted front door.

General Robert Henderson—made a general on the battlefield—was married to a daughter of Cary Wood, who, in 1830, built the house at 302 Floyd, now called Swanscomb. This is said to be the first clapboard house in Covington. After the war General Henderson and his wife lived in this charming house with its six tall Doric columns, but for more than fifty years now the property has belonged to the Swann family. Some in-between owner installed a Victorian stairway. Mrs. T. C. Swann did a re-restoration and has created both within and without an authentic Old South atmosphere.

Not far away at 403 Floyd, Julia Usher came down the wide stairway, with its hand-carved decorations, to be married under the crystal chandelier in the drawing room to Colonel Jack Henderson, son of the General. An Usher sister, Mrs. Floyd, lived in the Judge Floyd house at 308. The old three-story Usher house, with its tall columns and hanging balcony, is given an air of distinction by its crowning balustrade. This house has been owned for a number of years by Mr. and Mrs. L. D. Bolton, of Burge Plantation, and is the home of their daughter-in-law, Mrs. M. L. Bolton.

Back across and down the street at 603 Floyd is the charming "raised cottage" presented as a wedding gift when Judge Floyd's daughter, Fanny, married McCormick Neal in 1858. The deed was registered in her husband's name, because at that time wives could not legally own property in Georgia. Here a one-story, Doric-columned portico extends the width of the house and is supported by a ground floor with a brick foundation laid in pierced design. The large square ceiling and wide central hallway give "the cottage" the same air of spaciousness to be found in more monumental structures of the Greek Revival era. Mr. and Mrs. R. H. Patterson are the present owners.

The classic small house at 1022 Floyd, built about 1845 and restored by Mr. and Mrs. Perino Dearing, has been in the family four or five generations.

Magnolia Terrace, the Greek Revival house of Mrs. E. E. Callaway on Park Circle, crowns a hill facing a green park. The library, the fine collection of paintings and old silver and mahogany—all show Mrs. Callaway's discriminating taste. She not only likes to buy the work of recognized artists, she also likes to discover new ones.

Her breakfast room is decorated with mural paintings by a young French artist, Paul Refoule. This work was done prior to May of 1947, when Refoule's wife, the daughter of an old and socially prominent Atlanta family, was mysteriously murdered.

Conversation of house-and-garden tour visitors usually dies down in the breakfast room of the Callaway house. Here they search the pastoral scenes on the walls as though seeking a clue to what is still an unsolved murder case. They see whimsical pictures of carefree men and maids gathering wild flowers or bearing baskets of fruit on their heads while fanciful animals dance about.

As the visiting sightseers climb back into their cars, conversation breaks out and those in the group who have not heard the story are brought up to date. Of course, it was all in the newspapers at the time of the tragedy.

Paul Refoule first met his future wife in 1936, when she was a student at the Sorbonne in Paris. They were married at a fashionable ceremony in Atlanta a year later and went to France to live.

When World War II broke out, Refoule was called into the French military service. He was captured by the Germans and spent three years in a concentration camp. After his release he, his wife and their young son came to Atlanta to live. Refoule became an instructor in a leading Atlanta art school.

On Wednesday afternoon, May 14, 1947, their son was brought home as usual from school. He could find his mother nowhere in the house, which is situated in a wooded, rather isolated residential section. He did find the current still burning in an electric iron in an upstairs room where the artist's wife apparently had been pressing clothes.

Shortly afterward Paul Refoule arrived and the police were notified. They found Mrs. Refoule's body lying face up in the creek back of the house. According to the official police report "her head was on a rock and . . . she was not as cold as the water in the creek . . . her feet were tied togther with her shoe laces and her throat had a mark around it as if it had been corded with a rope or some object used to choke her . . ."

Apparently no clue led anywhere. Refoule was grilled by the police but no formal charge was ever brought against him. He himself filed suit against the police authorities for $50,000, charging violation of his civil rights. Sometime later he inconspicuously entered an Atlanta hospital where he died of cancer of the lung.

To Mrs. Callaway of Magnolia Terrace the mural paintings in her breakfast room recall a young artist whose pretty wife sometimes came along to watch him as he worked. She remembers their gay laughter. There was nothing then— there is nothing in the finished work—to suggest the later tragedy.

The campsite east of Covington, described by General Sherman, was on the plantation of John Harris, whose handsome town house at 506 Monticello has been owned for many years by the N. S. Turner family. Here tall Doric columns are connected by a carved balustrade which is repeated in the hanging balcony extending almost all the way across the front.

A convalescent Confederate soldier was concealed in the chimney of Clairmont, when Federal troops descended upon Covington. Clairmont, with its fanlighted doors and windows, hanging balcony and Doric columns, is now owned by Editor and Mrs. Belmont Dennis. Among its many antiques is a tester bed as wide as it is long. Old trees, box and a charming garden give the place a dreamy quality of continuity dating from the days when it was known as Carr's Corner.

Dixie Manor, at 607 Pennington, still has its "back house," concealed by garden shrubbery and preserved as an authentic bit of the original scene. It is built of the same brick as the house, and all the brick was imported from England in the early eighteen thirties.

Mrs. J. A. Wright, former owner of Dixie Manor, was a patient who expressed gratitude to her attending physician by willing him her home. Dr. and Mrs. J. R. Sams have fittingly restored both the old Regency house and its garden.

Three square columns grouped at each end of the porch give a charming individuality to the T. C. Meadors home at 1108 Convers Street, which is furnished with Early American antiques, including cupboards of old glass and silver.

Family portraits believed to be the work of Copley hang in the parlor of the R. C. Guinn house, at 109 Davis Street, still called the president's house, because it was here that the president lived when Covington boasted a Southern Masonic Female College. George Washington slept in one of the old beds now at the Porter house at 510 Conyers. The grandfather's clock made in England more than a hundred and fifty years ago has on its dial the letters OLIVER PORTER, instead of the usual numerals.

Many other old houses cherished from generation to generation add to Covington's atmosphere of Confederate charm. Covington is a progressive town, but even its modern houses have learned to live with the past and like it.

CHAPTER 5

The Slave Girl Who Divided a Church

KITTY'S COTTAGE has the romantic sound of a honeymoon retreat. Actually, this one-time home of the slave girl, Kitty Andrew, is a relic of the grim battle that divided the Methodist Episcopal Church into two separate bodies, North and South—seventeen years before the War Between the States.

Eighty-odd years and two wars later—in which North and South had fought as one—the line was still drawn between the two great divisions of that devout denomination founded by the Wesleys. Only in 1937 were they reunited and the words "North" and "South" dropped by their respective governing boards.

Kitty was owned by Bishop James O. Andrew, who lived at Oxford, near Covington. He was president of the board of trustees of Emory College, founded by the Methodist Episcopal Church and chartered in 1836. Here began the great Emory University now in Atlanta. The Georgia Institute of Technology, also in Atlanta, grew out of plans made at old Emory College.

The town of Oxford, founded along with the college, was named for "the seat of learning at which John and Charles Wesley were educated." Even today as the home of Emory Junior College, the old campus, with its great trees, Greek Revival and Victorian Gothic buildings, has an atmosphere faintly ecclesiastical, as though footprints of a century ago might still be found in the dusty, unpaved roads. Old Oxford has been the home of seven Bishops of the Methodist Church, the home of missionaries, of statesmen and of at least one inventor. It was also the home of Kitty Andrew.

Bishop Andrew never bought a slave and never owned any except those few which came to him by inheritance. Among these was a twelve-year-old Negro girl named Kitty, willed to him by a Mrs. Power, of Augusta, "on condition that he bring up and educate Kitty as far as he could and when she reached the

FIGURE 9. Kitty's Cottage, which was moved from Oxford to Salem Camp Ground, near Covington. The cottage was built for Kitty by Bishop James O. Andrew in slavery times. She lived there, a free woman, but gave voluntary service to Mrs. Andrew.

age of 19 she was to be free to go to Liberia, or to remain with the Bishop as a slave, according to her wishes."

When Kitty reached the age of nineteen, in 1841, it was illegal to free slaves in Georgia except to give them transportation to Liberia. Although slavery was forbidden at the time of the founding of the Colony, Georgia eventually followed the example of other states in using the available labor supply. By Kitty's day, Georgia had become one of the great slave-owning states of the South.

Shortly before the Civil War, Georgia's average slave holdings were larger even than those of Virginia or North Carolina and slightly less than in Alabama. The total number of slave owners in Georgia was 41,084 and the total number of slaves was 462,198. These figures are given by Ralph Betts Flanders, Professor of History at New York University, in his book, *Plantation Slavery in Georgia*.

Holdings might range anywhere from one slave to five hundred. In many families each child had its individual slave. In spite of all this, it is estimated that fifteen thousand Georgia farms were operated without slave labor.

This, then, was the situation when Kitty reached the age of nineteen. Kitty had grown up, a fine Christian girl, in the household of Bishop and Mrs. Andrew. The time had come to carry out the final terms of the will.

Bishop Andrew faced his duty conscientiously. He called in two members of the faculty of Emory College to question Kitty as to whether she wished to be freed and sent to Liberia. One of these was Judge Augustus Baldwin Longstreet, author of the celebrated *Georgia Scenes*, who was then president of the college. The other was Professor George W. Lane.

Judge Longstreet's written report of that interview is signed by himself and Professor Lane and dated December 4, 1841.

In order that Kitty might not be influenced by his presence, the Bishop left the room. Judge Longstreet explained to Kitty that the time had come to make her choice:

"And you will do well to think seriously of the matter. If you go to Liberia, you will be perfectly free, as free as I am now. You will be under the laws, to be sure, just as I am, to prevent you from doing anything very bad, but you will have no master, no mistress. You will be, in all respects, just like white women in this country. You will have to work for a living, as all must, but what you make will be your own. . . . If you go, the bishop will send you at his expense. If you stay, the will directs that he is to grant you all of the privileges of a free woman that the law will allow, but you will have to depend upon his character for that and you will still be a slave.

"Now, think of this matter and make your choice for all time to come. If you have had any stories told you about that country that have alarmed you, disregard them. I have told you the truth so far as I know. Now, make your choice."

Kitty said, "I don't want to go to that country. I know nobody there. It is a long ways and I might die before I got there."

Judge Longstreet asked again, "Then I may write it down as your final choice that you remain with Bishop Andrew?"

"Yes, sir, I don't want to go there."

"We certify," the document ends, "that the above is as nearly a literal report of our interview with Kitty as we can make. Not a word was said that could influence her decision which is not here recorded."

Bishop Andrew built Kitty a cottage in the yard near his own home at Oxford and exacted no further service from her. She still gave voluntary service as she chose and tenderly nursed Mrs. Andrew through her last illness in 1842.

Kitty was living in that cottage, a free woman, when the General Conference of the Methodist Episcopal Church met in 1844. Certain Northern delegates felt strongly on the subject of slavery and the meeting was stirred by bitter controversy.

As expressed by the late Bishop Warren A. Candler, "Bishop Andrew was practically deposed from his office for having in his possession a slave which he did not purchase and could not, under the laws of Georgia, emancipate."

The great division of the church followed.

As officially recorded in the *Handbook of All Denominations*, the break "was occasioned by the case of James O. Andrew, a southern bishop, who had become by marriage and inheritance a slave holder . . .

"The General Conference of that year [1844] passed a resolution requesting Bishop Andrew to desist from the exercise of his office so long as this impediment remained.

"Southern delegates presented a protest on behalf of nearly 5,000 ministers and a membership of nearly 500,000 constitutionally represented at the Conference."

This protest was disregarded.

"A plan of separation was adopted.

"After the adjournment of the General Conference the southern delegates met and decided to hold the matter of a separate organization in abeyance until the convention of representatives of all the Southern Conference could be held.

"A convention was called which met at Louisville, Ky., in May, 1845. At this meeting the Methodist Episcopal Church, South, began its existence as a separate body."

Kitty lived on in her cottage until she married Nathan Snell and moved to a home provided by her husband. A little girl was born to them. Later, when Kitty came down with a fatal illness, she commended this child to the care of Bishop Andrew's daughter. Feeling that death was near, Kitty sent for the Bishop and thanked him for the kind care and religious training she had received in his home. She said, remembering the Bishop's wife whom she loved so dearly, "I will soon see Miss Amelia in the better land."

Some years ago the home of Bishop Andrew at Oxford burned to the ground, but Kitty's cottage was not damaged. This comfortable two-room clapboard house was later moved to Salem Camp Ground, near Covington, where Methodists first held camp meetings in 1828. Here, in this stronghold of early Methodism, it is preserved as a relic of Bishop Andrew's fidelity to personal responsibility and its far-reaching results.

Kitty is buried in the small, beautifully kept cemetery at Oxford, where sleep many of the great of old Emory. An impressive monument, "Sacred to the memory of Kitty Andrew Snell," tells the story of the slave girl "who was the cause of the division of the Methodist Episcopal Church in 1844."

CHAPTER 6

The Perfect Mother=in=Law

A STUDENT-PROOF front gate was devised by Judge Augustus Baldwin Longstreet when he lived in the president's house at Emory College. There it may still be seen, but not in front of the house. The old gate, white, with heavily reinforced iron hinges, is displayed as a curiosity in the library at Oxford. Because of its clever construction, the gate could not be removed from its hinges even on Hallowe'en, when prankish spirits run highest on a college campus.

Judge Longstreet came to the college as president in 1841. It was not at all strange that he should contrive a student-proof gate. His father, William Longstreet, had invented a steamboat that sailed up the Savannah in 1807, a mere few days after Fulton's successful tryout in New York. An old letter to Governor Telfair, dated Augusta, September 26, 1790, indicates that William Longstreet might have been first:

"I make no doubt that you have often heard of my steamboat and as often heard it laughed at . . ."

The letter made an appeal for governmental aid in the project. This was not granted and the invention finally was launched through private funds.

Today there is no fence or gate of any kind before the president's house at Oxford, a large white frame structure—Greek Revival with Victorian trimmings—which stands on a vast rolling lawn, shaded by enormous magnolias. The house was begun by Emory's first president, Ignatius Few. Judge Longstreet added the two front rooms, which have an open space between and are connected to the main house by the front porch. The rooms leave free the central section of the porch with its trellised columns and give the effect of a recessed entrance portico.

Judge Longstreet used the room on the left as his study and so did five Bishops who later, in turn, served as president. A sixth, Bishop Ainsworth, boarded in the house as a student. At one time in old Emory's history, everybody "kept boys," even the president.

The president's house is now occupied by Dean Virgil Y. C. Eady and his family. In its spacious, pleasant parlor you may still imagine you hear the notes of Judge Longstreet's glass flute, although the flute itself is in the Smithsonian Institution and the judge lies buried by the side of his adored wife in Oxford, Mississippi, not Oxford, Georgia.

On a certain winter night, after the fireplace embers had turned to ashes, the judge played that flute until the gray dawn peered into the many paned windows. He was accompanied at the piano by his two pretty daughters, Jennie and Fanny. They had been roused from sound sleep in order that the judge might keep his word to a student who periodically went on an alcoholic spree.

Brought before the president at an earlier date, the student had declared that when the evil spirit took hold of him, nothing could free him but the spell of music. Accordingly, Judge Longstreet invited him to report to the president's house when next possessed. There, music would be provided. Next time happened to be a cold winter morning, around one o'clock.

After several hours of a trio performance which must have puzzled the neighbors, Judge Longstreet gave up and chased the young man out again, "still possessed." Although he had lost, Judge Longstreet had kept his word and couldn't have had better publicity.

On another occasion Judge Longstreet overheard certain members of the student body making plans to hide his family carriage in the woods. Shortly before the appointed time he concealed himself in the back of the vehicle. After it had been dragged far from home, the judge rose up, thanked the startled students for the buggy ride and politely requested a return trip. Sheepishly they complied, but with secret admiration.

The judge knew all about college students and college pranks. He had prepped at Professor Waddel's school near Augusta, where students frequently tipped a bucket of water from an upper window onto the head of the professor as he entered the school building. (Professor Waddel cannily provided himself with an umbrella.) Later young Mr. Longstreet attended Yale, where he was presented a pocket knife by a student who claimed to have held the title of ugliest man on the campus until Gus Longstreet appeared. Following his graduation from Yale, Longstreet enrolled at the famous Litchfield Law School, and seven years after he began practice in Augusta he was made a circuit judge.

Actually Longstreet "was of such magnetic personality that he was attractive rather than otherwise," according to John Donald Wade's fine biography, *Augustus Baldwin Longstreet.*

Longstreet's own *Georgia Scenes* and other writings preserve the flavor of

FIGURE 10. The president's house at old Emory College, now Emory Junior College, at Oxford. This is a side view.

a robust frontier humor. A typical bit of comedy from *The Snake Bite* is summarized by Dr. Wade:

"A young man having taken refuge under the bed from the irate father of his beloved, is there pecked so sharply by an old setting hen that—unable to contain himself any longer—he comes sprawling out, shouting, 'I'm snake bit, and I don't care who knows it.' "

As a young lawyer of twenty-seven, Longstreet married a girl who might well have been the inspiration of Melanie in *Gone With the Wind*. A case carried him to Greensboro and there he met the lovely Frances Eliza Parke, who became his wife in 1817. "She had," says Dr. Wade, "a quality altogether apart from physical or mental implications, a quality of spirit that dominated her and everything about her, a certain quietness . . . a calmness and a high serenity of life which nothing could fail bowing to. . . ."

Everybody did bow to these irresistible charms, even her distinguished son-in-law, L. Q. C. Lamar, Jr. His description of Mrs. Longstreet is more than enough to prove she was that practically nonexistent person—the perfect mother-in-law:

"The gentleness of her manners, the grace of her motion, the reserve of her dignity, only served the better to set off the brightness that shone in her conversation and to disclose an intelligence that threw a charm over the modesty of her nature. She was the nonpareil of women, full of warmth and tenderness and depth of feeling—confiding, trustworthy, a lover of home, a true wife and mother, whose hand touched and beautified and sanctified all domestic relations."

Lucius Quintus Cincinnatus Lamar, Jr., who married Longstreet's daughter, Jennie, was one of old Emory's famous graduates. He was a nephew of Mirabeau Buonaparte Lamar, of Georgia, who became the president of the Republic of Texas, in 1838. L. Q. C. Lamar held many important posts in Washington and finally became Associate Chief Justice of the United States Supreme Court. The Lamar School of Law at Emory University in Atlanta was named for him.

Sometime after leaving Emory, Judge Longstreet became president of Mississippi State University. Young Lamar got his political start in Mississippi when he joined his father-in-law and taught law at the university. Longstreet's older daughter, Fanny, married Dr. Henry R. Branham, whose family is still represented in one of the lovely old white houses on the Emory campus at Oxford, Georgia.

For a time, after the War Between the States, both the Longstreet daughters and their husbands, as well as the judge and his wife, lived at Oxford, Mississippi. Though not in the same house, all the family were together, which was the way they liked to be. The judge and Mrs. Longstreet had only one son, who died when a small child. James Longstreet, the Confederate general, was a nephew.

Mrs. Longstreet—that "nonpareil of women"—died in 1868. Before the judge's death, which occurred two years later, he wrote the beautiful epitaph carved on the stone that marks their graves in the cemetery at Oxford, Mississippi:

"He sleeps by the side of his wife of whom he never thought himself worthy and who never thought herself worthy of her husband. In every innocent movement of his life she went hand in hand and heart in heart with him for over 51 years. Death was a kind visitor to them both."

CHAPTER 7

Strange Light—Invisible Guest

HAUNTED house or home of a forgotten scientist—you can take your choice at Orna Villa. This large white frame house with square two-story columns was the former home of Dr. Alexander Means, one of the founders and fourth president of old Emory College, at Oxford, Georgia.

Here in 1857, Dr. Means invented what is claimed to be the first electric light. Edison was a boy of ten at the time.

Here, too, a ghost walks. Mr. and Mrs. E. S. Rheberg, who bought and restored the old house in 1942, are able to explain away most of the strange goings-on, but not all.

More startling than any ghost, seen or unseen, were some of the achievements of Dr. Alexander Means, who often worked late at night in his upstairs study at Orna Villa. His unusual ability was recognized even before he produced the electric light.

In 1851 he was made a Fellow of the Royal Academy of Science in London and was received by the Prince of Wales. While in London he was the house guest of the distinguished scientist, Sir Michael Faraday. At home he enjoyed the friendship of President Millard Fillmore, and when the former President died, Dr. Means was called to preach his funeral.

On June 1, 1857, a group of Atlanta's leading citizens gathered at the old city hall to listen to Dr. Means hold forth on a revolutionary subject. Next day they came back for a remarkable demonstration.

Dr. Means was then serving as professor of chemistry at both the Atlanta Medical College and at Emory College. He never went anywhere without his beaver hat and gold-headed walking stick. Very erect but not tall, he always addressed his students as "young gentlemen."

For this audience of prominent citizens, he omitted the "young," but his subject was his classroom favorite.

"Gentlemen," he said, "I can assure you that electricity, of which we know so little today, can be applied successfully as a motor power. The day will come and it is not very remote, when electricity will supplant steam and will be used for propelling all machinery.

"Notwithstanding what scientists are now teaching—the great English scientist Herbert Spencer is among them in stating positively that electricity cannot be used for locomotion and illumination—I tell you that the time is not far distant when the electric current will be used to light cities and to propel cars.

"Gentlemen, electricity is God's vice-regent in the universe. . . . If," he concluded, "you will honor me tomorrow with your presence in my laboratory at the Medical College, I shall prove to you the truth of what I am saying now."

Dr. Henry Capers, then assistant professor of anatomy, left a record of that demonstration:

"The doctor had his lecture room darkened so that it was as dark as a moonless night. Over his table was suspended a large globe, probably a foot in diameter. Within it he had placed by wires to suspend it a large and long stick of charcoal. Opposite the lower end of this charcoal, two wires came in close contact with the coal.

"Near him was a large electrical machine from which these wires came . . ." (That electrical machine is now at Emory University in Atlanta.)

By hand-turning a large disk which worked against small brushes, frictional electricity was generated. The assembled gentlemen almost leaped out of their seats as sparks began to jump from the disk to the connection for the wires.

Suddenly the spectators saw that stick of dead black carbon glow red, then burst into brilliant light. The darkened room was illuminated by such a brightness that it put to shame the new gaslights of which Atlanta was so proud.

Thus, according to reliable witness, on June 2, 1857, Dr. Means produced the world's first incandescent light.

Green B. Dodd, pioneer Atlanta citizen, one of those present, wrote in a letter, "Never since that remarkable day have I seen a more brilliant light. Nothing in all the phenomena of our wonderful age has ever impressed me more than this exhibition and I can never forget it as long as my memory lasts."

Colonel George W. Adair, C. W. Hunnicutt and Dr. A. G. Thomas were among other reliable eyewitnesses who never forgot—though Georgia and the world apparently did.

Orna Villa—Dr. Means gave it the name—sits back on a slight rise five hundred feet or more from Highway 81. Its four-square-pillared portico gives it the forthrightness of *Gone With the Wind's* "Tara." There are matching pilasters at each corner of the house and smaller ones flank the side-lighted doorway. The

FIGURE 11. Orna Villa in Oxford, the former home of Alexander Means, one of the founders of old Emory College. Here a ghost walks with heavy tread.

heavy, paneled door is three and one half inches thick. A porch added to the right side of the house balances a wing at the left.

Dr. Means was living here when Emory College was chartered in 1836 and the town of Oxford laid out in the forest, about a mile and a half from Covington. Old records show 1,452 acres of land for the college were bought "adjacent to Dr. Means' place." The date the Means house was built is uncertain. When Mr. Rheberg, the present owner, bought the house, he had an ell removed. Workmen found a brand-new 1822 penny in one of the upright studs.

Mr. Rheberg points out that all the heavy timbers—sills, corner posts and plates—were hand-hewn. As a builder, he could easily see that boards for the old part of the house were done with an up-and-down saw, later additions with a circular saw. The door-facings and wainscoting and wide floor boards were all hand-planed, the doors handmade. You can find knife nicks in the carving of the mantels.

When Mr. Rheberg bought the property, a crane still hung in the kitchen fireplace. Mrs. Rheberg furnished the house beautifully in keeping with its architectural era, but she did insist upon a modern kitchen.

The old locks that are still on the doors—but do not keep out the ghost—are original ironmonger's work from England, dated 1791.

The origin of Orna Villa's ghost is explained by a granddaughter of Dr. Means, Mrs. Paul Campbell, Sr., of Atlanta:

"They say it is Uncle Tobe," she declares. "He was a disappointment to grandfather. Grandfather had a struggle getting his own college education. That made him all the more determined that each of his five sons and four daughters should be well educated. When it was time for Uncle Tobe to be thinking about college he told grandfather he'd rather have the money. He wanted to travel.

"Grandfather was horrified. Of course, he wouldn't hear of such foolishness. But Uncle Tobe kept hoping grandfather would change his mind. While he was waiting for this to happen he often paced the back porch. Every time they had a talk, Uncle Tobe tramped up and down afterward.

"Finally, he got tired of waiting and one night he—just disappeared. After he was gone, there were times when the family thought they heard his footsteps on the back porch. But he was never there when they went to investigate.

"By the time the grandchildren were growing up, many people believed the house was haunted. One of my brothers once sat up all night with a shotgun," Mrs. Campbell said. "He swore he would shoot the ghost. But he never saw it. Like everybody else he just heard it. And that's not all. Doors at Orna Villa open and close of their own accord and sometimes you can hear sighing, even though the wind is still."

When Mr. Rheberg bought the Means house, he smiled about the stories of its ghost. He knew about old timbers and the odd noises they produce in changing temperatures. He knew that structural conditions may cause doors to open and close in spooky fashion. Decidedly, he took no stock in ghosts.

Then, on a wintry morning, something happened.

Mr. Rheberg, up ahead of his family for some reason he doesn't remember, got a chill down his spine that had nothing to do with the weather.

Actually, he says, he thought nothing amiss when he first heard the sounds of heavy footsteps, as though someone were pacing up and down the wide back porch.

Glancing at his watch, he told himself that one of his workmen had come by the house to see him about something and had then decided it was too early to knock at the door. No doubt the man was exercising to keep himself warm while waiting for signs of activity inside the house.

"I opened the door, meaning to ask him to come in out of the cold," says Mr. Rheberg. "While I was turning the knob I could still hear the sound of heavy footsteps just outside.

"But when the door opened, there was no one there, and everything was quiet again. Nobody was even in sight."

CHAPTER 8

They All Fell in Love

NOBODY would think of trying on a coffin for size nowadays, but the ready-made article was not so easily available when Edmund B. Walker stored his tailor-made casket in the attic of his home at Madison.

Mr. Walker was a man of strong character and practical viewpoint, accustomed to look ahead and prepare for emergencies. In this particular case, he felt that consideration for others demanded that certain final arrangements be attended to in advance. And so his coffin was made to measure and put away against the time of need.

Years passed and as Mr. Walker gained in weight, he made trips to the attic to satisfy himself that he had not outgrown specifications.

That is the story handed down and vouched for by his great-granddaughter, Kittie Newton. Her cousin, Therese Newton, says that when she was a little girl, she and the other children used to creep up the attic steps of the Edmund Walker home to take a hurried peep at the place where the coffin once rested.

The children told themselves there was space outlined by dust which marked the spot and shuddered deliciously as they tumbled down the steps again.

While neither of the Newton cousins lives in the house where the coffin was parked, they do live in two of the most interesting houses on the old stage-coach road through Madison, which was once the center of a rich plantation section. Many affluent planters lived here in town houses and visited their farms when the spirit moved them. The houses remain to give veracity to historian George White's statement in 1845 that Madison was "the wealthiest and most aristocratic village along the stage coach route between Charleston and New Orleans."

A later visitor wrote on November 19, 1864:

FIGURE 12. Mr. and Mrs. Clarence T. McIntire, passing through Madison, fell in love with The Oaks, and bought this ante-bellum plantation to establish a model stock farm.

"Passed through Madison. Found it the prettiest village I've seen in the state. One garden and yard I never saw excelled, even in Connecticut."

Needless to say, Rufus Mead, Jr., who made this comment, represented that famous type, the Connecticut Yankee. He was indeed Commissary Sergeant of the Fifth Connecticut Volunteers of the Federal Army, marching through Georgia to the sea. Excerpts from his diary and letters are reproduced in the *Georgia Historical Quarterly* of December, 1948.

It is easy to understand how two modern visitors, driving through Madison eighty-odd years later, were likewise impressed. Mr. and Mrs. Chan Horne fell in love with this charming old town of white-columned houses on tree-shaded streets. They decided then and there they wanted to live in Madison. As though it had been waiting for them to walk in and take possession, there was the old Trammel house with its tall Corinthian columns, green lawns and old-fashioned shrubs which they immediately bought.

Mr. and Mrs. Clarence T. McIntire settled in much the same way at The Oaks, a plantation just outside of town. They were driving through Madison—stopped and stayed. The Oaks, with its Doric-columned house, is now a large-scale cattle farm. Miles of trim white fences give it the look of a farm lifted bodily from the Kentucky blue grass.

You realize here and elsewhere in the state how Georgia is changing.

More and more you find these pure-bred cattle and dairy farms. And no matter how you feel about traditional cotton lands becoming pastures, there is nothing to compare with the moment when you are driving along the highway and suddenly the wide fields on both sides are covered thick with crimson clover in full bloom, stretching all the way to the blue horizon. It is beauty on such a lavish scale that you almost feel like accusing Mother Nature of going in for technicolor.

As well as falling in love *with* Madison, many visitors have fallen in love *in* Madison, beginning back when the town had two ante-bellum female colleges, one Methodist, the other Baptist.

Rebecca Latimer, who later became the first woman United States senator, was a student at the Madison Methodist College when William H. Felton, of Cartersville, Georgia, delivered the commencement address. His eyes met hers and he practically tumbled from the rostrum. When that redoubtable lady was in her nineties she still believed in love at first sight. They were married a year after the commencement address and it is said Mrs. Felton helped to write the later speeches which repeatedly sent her husband to the United States House of Representatives. Long after his death she was appointed to fill the unexpired term of the late United States Senator Thomas E. Watson.

Sergeant Rufus Mead, Jr., of the Federal army marching to the sea, might have been writing about any one of many beautiful gardens in Madison. It could have

FIGURE 13. Bonar Hall, in Madison, got its Victorian veranda long after the War Between the States. It is now owned by Mrs. W. T. Bacon.

been the gardens at Bonar Hall, which have their own romantic story of the ante-bellum bride for whom the house was built.

Bonar Hall, now the home of Mrs. W. T. Bacon and her daughter, Therese Newton, is a handsome brick manor house of Georgian architecture. Set two hundred feet back from the old Post Road, it is surrounded by a hundred acres of lawn, gardens and orchards. Originally a brick wall in pierced-diamond design enclosed the lawns and there was a gatekeeper's lodge.

On one side of the house is a brick orangery and on the other an English tea house. At the back a paved court lies between the main house and the quaint two-room brick kitchen. In days gone by a row of slave cabins stood back of the kitchen at the right.

The house was built in 1832, according to the date on the cornice, and at that time it was well outside the town, on the edge of its own plantation acres. Slaves cut the timbers which were soaked in a millpond twelve months to avoid shrinkage. Slaves made the bricks from red Georgia clay for walls which are eighteen inches thick. Doorknobs are of silver and the original roof was of copper.

A hundred years after the house was built, the copper roof blew off in a high wind. "It rolled up like a big sheet of paper and landed in the back yard," says Therese Newton. "I went up to the attic, looked at the sky and prayed it wouldn't rain."

For a number of years Miss Newton has proved that smartness can be much more than clothes-deep. She manages all the varied agricultural interests of the family, which include the raising of beef cattle as well as the direction of numerous farms and peach orchards, spread out over four thousand acres. Her brother, Edward Taylor Newton, who lives with his family in one of Madison's charming old Greek Revival houses, is an attorney, practicing in Atlanta, sixty miles distant.

Bonar Hall was named for Charles Bonar, whose bride, Lady Catherine Whipps, brought with her from England the green fruit plates in the Hepplewhite corner cupboard in the dining room. She was Mrs. Bacon's five times great-grandmother.

Not one single piece of furniture in the old house was bought after the War Between the States. It is furnished entirely with heirlooms, some of them six generations old. The Queen Anne highboy in the upstairs hall came over with the family of Mrs. Bacon's Revolutionary ancestor, Douglas Watson; and the handsome old grandfather clock in the wide central hall actually strikes with an English accent.

The early Sheraton sideboard with amber knobs and six reeded legs was hauled from Charleston, South Carolina, to Georgia in a cotton wagon before the advent of railroads. The 1790 Hepplewhite chest retains its original brasses.

When Sherman went through Burke County (Madison is in Morgan), he and his staff dined from the Sheraton banquet table, with the fourteen carved legs, now in the dining room at Bonar Hall. The table was then owned by Mrs. Bacon's aunt. Against the wall is its matching serving table.

A flint glass sillabub bowl is always the center of Christmas and New Year entertaining. Georgian silver, beautiful French porcelain and fine old glass complete what might easily be called a museum collection for the dining room.

The furniture in the library, like that in the double parlors, is early Victorian. The library mantel clock hasn't missed a tick in a hundred and fifty years and still strikes.

Everything goes double for the double parlors, including a dozen straight chairs, like the sofas and ottomans upholstered in the original black horsehair. There are double fireplaces, of course, and pier mirrors framed in gold leaf. The draperies are of rose and gold brocade and all the cornices are solid brass.

Mrs. Bacon, who graces her house so beautifully, bought the property in 1920. Among necessary restorations was the replanting of 1,100 boxwood plants in the formal garden, which is entirely evergreen.

A divorce for the original owners might have flowered in this garden if John Byne Walker and Eliza Saffold Fannin had loved each other less.

Mr. Walker built the house for his bride, who was only seventeen at the time of their marriage, but she had completed her education in New England. The lovely Eliza came to her husband with a handsome dowry and a mind of her own. The house was one of her dreams come true, but she also wanted a garden planted beyond the brick wall that enclosed the house and lawns. Mr. Walker, a practical man, who is said to have made from $250,000 to $300,000 a year (gross) from cotton, could see this acreage only in terms of the fleecy staple.

He had large plantation holdings in Texas and once a year made a trip west to see them. When he came back from the first of these trips, he found that his bride had planted flowers and old-fashioned shrubs over a considerable space beyond the brick wall.

The flowers bloomed their one season, and when planting time came the garden was plowed under and planted in cotton. Mr. Walker went to Texas as usual. When he came home, he again found a garden on the disputed territory. Again in cotton planting time the garden was plowed under.

It happened three times before Mr. Walker gave up. But he gave up handsomely by engaging an English landscape architect to make his wife's dream gardens come true. The initial outlay totaled $30,000. There are six varieties of box, seven of magnolias and many botanical rarities, including a cork tree, all of them now more than a century old.

Many present-day Madisonians remember "Aunt" Mary Jane Smith, an aged former servant of the J. B. Walker family who lived to a great age and loved to talk about "old times." When just a little girl she was given to "Ole Mistis" and told to stand by to thread needles and bring cool water. There were also eight

FIGURE 14. Boxwood, the home of Miss Kittie Newton in Madison, is a house with two faces. It turns a Greek Revival portico to the old stagecoach road, and a Victorian façade to Second Street.

trained house servants and fifteen others who kept the grounds, horses, stables, etc., in running order.

Like many other old houses, this one passed out of the hands of the Walker family during the Reconstruction period. In the eighteen eighties the original portico was removed and the present lacy white Victorian veranda was added. An old picture shows the house with a small, square front porch, and four white columns.

Invading General Slocum rode his horse up the wide front walk of sparkling sand to that earlier portico. He was met at the door by Colonel Walker, who told him that three of his sons were in the opposing army and he wished he himself were young enough to fight.

General Slocum laughed and the Colonel invited him and his staff inside for refreshments. These were fresh butter, milk and other delicacies stored in the dry well—forerunner of the present-day deep freeze. Mrs. Walker, smilingly gracious, gave more than a thought to the family silver hidden in the boxwood.

Three wars later and many servants less, the old house and its grounds are still beautifully kept. And with the sons of Edward Taylor Newton to look to the future, one can hope they will be loved and cherished over a long time to come.

You leave Bonar Hall reluctantly, but it is easier if the next stop is Boxwood, the home of Kittie Newton, built as a town house in 1851.

All visitors to Boxwood are charmed first by its twin boxwood gardens and next by the hundred-year-old Victorian parlor, the furnishings of which were bought especially for the house when it was new and which remain to form a perfect period piece.

There are two duplicate carved rosewood Victorian "parlor suites" uphol-stered in gold and green satin brocatelle to match the window draperies. These draperies, topped with brass cornices, hang singly because one length of the handsome material was taken down from each window fifty years ago to replace worn seat covers of sofas, chairs and ottomans. The pier mirror and the mirror over the white Carrara marble mantel have matching gold-leaf frames, and the rug is of rose velvet in floral design with a center medallion.

When Mr. and Mrs. Wilds Kolb built the house, they furnished it from top to bottom, brand new. In the beginning there were double parlors, reflecting them-selves in the tall pier mirrors set between end windows. The back parlor is now a library. A long line of Kittie Newton's grandmothers started housekeeping with the mahogany drop-leaf table which is among the furnishings of this room.

The grounds of Boxwood comprise half a city block, and the house, its timbers cut to size and hauled by oxcart from Augusta, is an aristocratic fore-runner of the prefabricated dwelling of later times. It is a transitional house as well, presenting a Greek Revival portico to the old Post Road and a Victorian front to Second Street. The lacy white trim of this latter porch is of cypress, resembling ornamental ironwork.

The doors at both entrances have transom and side lights of ruby glass which bathe the long, very wide hall in a rosy glow. The delicate, winding stair leads upward to spacious bedrooms with spacious chimney-side closets, replacing the armoires or wardrobes of earlier eras.

The kitchen is not a detached building but an added wing. Into this the dining room opens by way of a huge butler's pantry. The kitchen itself is in scale with its six-foot pioneer fireplace. This fireplace now serves as a recess for a large early-model iron cookstove, coldly looking down its nose at a modern electric range across the room.

The servants' quarters and carriage house are screened from the kitchen porch by trees and shrubbery and flanked by an orchard and vegetable garden.

From the first there was running water for the kitchen and for a twelve-by-twelve-foot bathroom. An aqueduct carried this water from two large outdoor cisterns to a big tank still in the attic, where you can also marvel at a twelve-by-twelve-inch ceiling beam cut from a single tree and running the forty-two-foot length of the roof.

Kittie's great-grandfather, Edmund B. Walker, stored his coffin in the attic of the old Peacock house, in Madison, where he lived after giving up his plantation in the country. The plantation house, built in 1825, is now owned by Mr. and Mrs. Paul B. Fraser. From this house, in 1839 or 1840, Mr. Walker set out for North Carolina in a carriage with his fourteen-year-old daughter, Keturah, who was duly enrolled at Salem College, where she remained two years without coming home. It was Keturah's son, John Thomas Newton, who bought Boxwood in 1905 from Louis Pou. Kittie Newton was named for her grandmother, Keturah.

Kittie never knew her great-grandfather Walker. She does know that, with characteristic plantation hospitality, he was always prepared for visitors—even the Last One.

There is a legend that when Sherman's army approached Madison, former United States Senator Joshua Hill rode out on a horse to meet the general and to ask protection for the town.

As it happened, Sherman himself did not come to Madison. His army, divided and subdivided, took four parallel routes and Sherman went by Newborn and Eatonton. General Slocum was in command of the division which went through Madison.

But Senator Joshua Hill, whose white-columned house on the old Post Road is now the home of Mr. and Mrs. Robert Turnell, did have a meeting with Sherman—in Atlanta, before the march to the sea began. Sherman tells about it in his *Memoirs:*

"Messrs. Hill and Foster came into our lines at Decatur, represented themselves as former members of Congress and particular friends of my brother, John Sherman. . . . Mr. Hill had a son killed in the rebel army somewhere near Cassville and they wanted to obtain the body, having learned from a comrade where it was buried. Gave him a note to General John E. Smith at Cartersville requiring him to furnish them an escort and an ambulance for the purpose . . . invited them to supper at officers' mess. Mr. Hill resided at Madison on the main road to Augusta . . . he fully realized the danger of further resistance. . . . I asked him to describe to Governor Brown fully. I had sent similar messages by Judge Wright of Rome and by Mr. King of Marietta . . ."

Mr. Hill, who had been strongly opposed to secession, was the last Southern Congressman to leave Washington. After the war, Georgia sent him back again to the Senate. His rather stern-faced portrait hangs in the home of his granddaughter, Mrs. J. H. Nicholson, who also owns Thurleston, where an old-fashioned tea rose has bloomed every summer since 1819. Madison was founded only ten years earlier.

Thurleston, the former home of Mrs. Nicholson's aunts, the late Misses Bessie and Daisy Butler, is a handsome white clapboard house, Georgian in architecture, with three gables and fluted pilasters, standing in a wide expanse of green lawns and wide-spreading trees.

Everything in the Stokes-McHenry house at 240 South Second Street is just as it was when Mrs. J. G. McHenry, Jr., came there as a bride. Now she is a young great-grandmother, still as becoming to the old house as she must have been from the start.

"Not long ago," she confessed smilingly, "we decided to move an armoire in the upstairs hall. After it was done, we felt like criminals." "We" includes her two daughters, Mrs. Dan Hicky and Mrs. John Shinholser, who also live in the white frame house, built by Judge William Sanders Stokes in 1820.

It is probable the lacy white trim of the front porch was added at a later date. But most of the furnishings were carefully selected and placed by the first generation.

Although occupied exclusively by succeeding generations of the same family, the house was closed for a long period before Judge Stokes's grandson, J. G. McHenry, Jr., brought his bride there to live. The velvet-scroll parlor carpet was carefully rolled in chinaberry leaves and all the furnishings and portraits shrouded by dust covers until the newlyweds took over.

A clue to this blank in the history of the house is given by an oil portrait in the charmingly quaint parlor. There are two little boys and a little girl in the picture, grandchildren of Judge Stokes, whose daughter married J. G. McHenry, Sr. One of the boys, of course, is J. G. McHenry, Jr., late husband of the present

53

owner. Marian, the little girl in the portrait, who might have married and continued to live here, fell in love with Antoine Poulain, who lived in Madison's famous old house known as Snow Hill. Antoine died and Marian went into a decline, as girls sometimes did in those days.

Marian's grandmother decided a trip would help and Marian, suddenly determined, said, "I'm going to get married and live in New York." So they went to New York. There, while sightseeing, grandmother fell down the steps of the Eden Musée. Marian married the attending physician, Dr. Nathan Bozeman, who brought grandmother safely through her accident. Marian lived not only in New York but in Paris.

Of course, Marian was pretty and popular, during her young ladyhood in Madison, as many old invitations show. . . . "Ladies will please not make engagements for the quadrilles."

A pair of white kid dancing pumps remain to show that she had a foot so narrow and so tiny you think she must have been a sprite. There's a closet called the hoop-skirt closet, because it is still full of discarded hoopskirts. There are many other romantic souvenirs to match the lovely old furniture and the five hundred pieces of white and gold china.

Snow Hill, where Marian McHenry's fiancé lived and died, got its name in an unusual way. Lancelot Johnson, who built the house about 1827, invented and patented in 1832 one of the first machines for crushing cotton seeds.

Mr. Johnson painted his house with a combination of cottonseed oil and white lead. He even painted the very steep roof with this mixture, making the place visible for miles. Soon everybody was calling it Snow Hill. The house with its beautiful reeded columns could stand the limelight.

It is said Mr. Johnson was a great believer in personal privacy and that the two wings were built for his sisters, insuring each a completely separate apartment. Still snowy white, the house has an appropriate setting of green lawns, old trees and fine box hedges.

The Doric-columned house of Mr. and Mrs. Charles Candler was also built in 1827. Like many other Madison houses it is furnished with beautiful heirlooms. Mr. Candler, who smiles when he says he is a farmer, raises beagles as a hobby and has a room full of ribbons and trophies.

Among other interesting old houses is Hilltop, the home of Mrs. Roy Lambert, built about 1838, which has a small portico with six fluted Doric columns. The C. R. Mason house, built in 1850, has its original boxwood garden and one of the largest collections of azaleas and camellias in the county. The Kay Tipton house is a fine example of the Greek Revival cottage. It has a pyramidal roof, Doric columns and seven outside doors. A wing at the left is a smaller duplicate of the main house, even to the portico.

There is also the charming raised cottage of Mrs. Mary Barnett Stokes and

Miss Katie Porter Barnett, which still has a cracked panel in its entrance door made by the saber of a Union soldier. At the Cornelius Vason house, the fourteen-inch horizontal wall boards were set so smoothly it was possible, a century later, to apply wallpaper flat against them. There is the old Elijah Jones house, now the home of Reid Manley, which was moved from the center of a block to make room for the new Methodist church. There is the Thomas Baldwin house, originally the Felix Bryan Martin house, with its fine Doric columns. There are the houses of the H. H. Fitzpatricks, the Tom Hollands and ever so many others—all with their treasures, all with their stories of the past.

There is, appropriately enough, a tourist home which was once a stagecoach inn, a fine old house with six columns, two square and four fluted Doric.

Last of all, there is a house—the name of which we will not give—which was lost in a poker game many years ago. It had belonged to the poker player's wife before their marriage. But those were the days when a husband could say, "what is thine is mine and what is mine is my own."

This house—so they say—was responsible for the introduction and passage of the Married Woman's Property Act in Georgia, which made it possible for a wife to own property in her own name. As you can see, Madison, though a romantic town, has its practical side.

CHAPTER 9

Eatonton's Snooty Ghost

I SAW her as plainly as I see you now," declared Miss Alice Wardwell. "The children saw her too."

Miss Wardwell was discussing Sylvia, a well-known ghost in the family of the late Dr. and Mrs. Benjamin W. Hunt, who lived at Panola Hall, one of Eatonton's charming old white-columned houses "on the Avenue."

Miss Wardwell was librarian at Eatonton for many years until her recent retirement. At the time of my visit she had just come in from the garden back of the old Wardwell home, which she shares with her sister, Mrs. J. R. Tweedy. This mellow brick house built on the town square in 1848 was originally the home of the Eatonton branch of the state bank. When the bank was finally dissolved, their father, G. W. Wardwell, bought the building and converted it into a residence with a long Victorian veranda.

Miss Wardwell, gray haired, brisk and definitely forthright, had about her the wholesome outdoor look that gardeners have, even when they have reached retirement age. She was reluctant to talk about Sylvia for publication. The thing had happened but she could not explain it. "I would have thought I was imagining it all, except for the children," she said.

Miss Wardwell paused and her glance swept the long living room in which we sat. Except for a door opening into the old vault, there is nothing now to remind you that this was once a banking room. It has that inviting air which is the sum of so many things, of shiny old mahogany, of family portraits, of books and fresh flowers and of a certain long-time integrity in living.

Miss Wardwell's glance came back to her visitor. Suddenly resolute, she said, "It happened this way," and without further pause and certainly without interruption, she told the story of her strange experience.

56

"I had gone back to the library after dinner for the evening hours. It was summer, and after opening the doors I sat down on the steps to enjoy the coolness while waiting for visitors. Our library building is on a slight elevation directly across the avenue from Panola Hall, the old Hunt home.

"Through the open windows of their living room I could see Dr. and Mrs. Hunt as clearly as though they were on a lighted stage. Mrs. Hunt was busy with some sewing or fancy work and Dr. Hunt was reading.

"At once I was struck by a strangeness about the scene. Dr. and Mrs. Hunt had a visitor to whom they were paying absolutely no attention. The visitor was a beautiful, dark-haired young woman in a white dress, and she stood directly behind Dr. Hunt's chair, as though reading over his shoulder.

"Why, I wondered, were Dr. and Mrs. Hunt ignoring her so completely? They were the most gracious, the most hospitable people in the world. Yet not once did Dr. Hunt raise his eyes from his book, nor Mrs. Hunt look up from her sewing.

"Of course," Miss Wardwell admitted, "I had heard about Sylvia, the ghost at Panola Hall. But," she shrugged, "I had never believed in such things. Anyway, there was nothing spectral about what I saw. It just seemed very odd—this girl standing there and the Hunts acting as though she were not there at all.

"About that time," Miss Wardwell continued, "some children came up the library walk with books to return. 'Children,' I said casually, 'look across the road and tell me what you see.'

"They dutifully turned to look and, of course, said they saw Dr. and Mrs. Hunt. And then one of the girls added, 'They've got company. Look at the young lady standing behind Dr. Hunt.'

"I made sure that each child saw her. This convinced me that even though the girl was a stranger to all of us, she was a real person. Anyway, I naturally would not have put ideas of ghosts into the children's heads. We went on into the library and that was that.

"Next day, Dr. Hunt came in. I said, conversationally, 'I saw you and Mrs. Hunt were having company last night.'

" 'No,' he answered, obviously surprised at my remark, 'we were alone all evening.'

"Even then," Miss Wardwell declared, "I tried not to believe anything out of the ordinary, though I must admit that I felt—odd. I told Dr. Hunt I was sure I had seen someone—a third person—in the living room, a young woman in a white dress.

"He gave me a searching look, and saw that I was serious. 'Alice,' he said, 'it must have been Sylvia you saw.'

"Just like that he said it," Miss Wardwell moved her hands helplessly, her voice echoing an old bafflement. "Dr. and Mrs. Hunt had moved into Panola

FIGURE 15. A ghost named Sylvia was seen here. Panola Hall, in Eatonton, is the former home of Dr. and Mrs. Benjamin W. Hunt—and Sylvia.

FIGURE 16. Sherman waved as he rode by the T. G. Green House in Eatonton.

Hall in 1867," she went on. "The house was old even then and Sylvia was already there. Or so it was said. Every now and then she 'appeared.' The Hunts had learned to accept the situation, but they did not talk about Sylvia to outsiders who might think them queer. But that," declared Miss Wardwell, "was something you couldn't do if you knew the Hunts. They were fine, intelligent, cultured people who meant a lot to Eatonton and Putnam County and Georgia."

Dr. Hunt, Miss Wardwell explained, was a native of New York, a scientist, horticulturist and banker. He is credited with having introduced Jersey cattle into Georgia, after making a personal selection on the Isle of Jersey. His influence was important in the development of the dairy business in Putnam County, of which Eatonton is the seat. Dr. Hunt built Georgia's first silo, developed many plants and new varieties of fig and scuppernong. Mrs. Hunt, the former Louise Reid Pruden, of Eatonton, was an accomplished musician and the author of a book of verse.

Perhaps it was the song, "Who Is Sylvia?" that inspired the Hunts to give this name to the mysterious occupant of one of their upstairs guest rooms. Incidentally, Panola Hall has thirteen rooms and an underground passage leading to a storm cellar in the garden. Miss Wardwell points out that Mrs. Hunt herself wrote a poem about their strange guest who—so the story goes—revealed herself only to those she considered her social equal.

> Sylvia's coming down the stair—
> Pretty Sylvia, young and fair.
> Oft and oft, I meet her there,
> Smile on lip and rose in hair.

It was a damask rose, the poem goes on to say, and at least one guest of the Hunts—who had never before heard of Sylvia—is said to have met her on the stair. He declared afterward that he even smelled the perfume of the damask rose.

He was a Mr. Nelson, Miss Wardwell says, who came to Georgia from Ohio in the interest of a co-operative creamery for Putnam County. Mr. Nelson was a house guest of the Hunts and on his way upstairs late one afternoon he met a young woman coming down.

She was all in hoop-skirted white and there was a rose in her dark hair. Mr. Nelson, with a gallant bow, stood aside on the landing to allow her to pass. She smiled and inclined her lovely head in acknowledgment and floated on down the steps.

Mr. Nelson took for granted she was another guest, and on joining his hosts in the living room a little later was surprised and disappointed not to see her anywhere about. He was hopeful she would reappear when dinner was announced. When he saw the table set for only three, he asked the Hunts about the charming young woman he had encountered on the stairway landing.

Dr. and Mrs. Hunt exchanged significant glances, finally smiled apologetically, then told Mr. Nelson he had been complimented in an unusual way. He was the first of their many guests to whom Sylvia had revealed herself.

That Sylvia is or was a snooty ghost is borne out by another guest of unimpeachable integrity, the late Miss Bessie Butler, who lived at beautiful old Thurleston in Madison and who inherited Panola Hall at the death of Dr. Hunt in 1934.

Miss Butler was interviewed by Mary M. Holtzclaw and her story was published in *The Atlanta Journal Magazine* of December 14, 1941, from which the following is reprinted:

"I had heard about Sylvia for many years," said Miss Butler, "but never expected to see her as I am a practical sort of person and ghosts just don't register with me. It was the afternoon of Mrs. Hunt's last illness [1929]. I went across the hall from my room into a guest room to see if it was in readiness for relatives we expected on the next train.

"The only people in the house at the time were Dr. Hunt and the nurse at Mrs. Hunt's bedside downstairs and the cook in the kitchen. I was the only person upstairs.

"I had walked into the center of the guest room and was taking a swift glance about when, from the corner of the room behind me, came the sound of someone tiptoeing.

"Then a sweet, musical voice called, 'Miss Bessie. Oh, Miss Bessie.' Just that and no more, but it was enough. . . . I ran past the white blur in the corner that I knew to be Sylvia, but I didn't want to see her. . . .

"No, I still don't know who Sylvia is or was in the flesh. . . . There have been many speculations through the sixty years that the Hunts lived at Panola Hall. But this much I do know. Sylvia *is* and she shows herself only to those she considers her social equals. In other words, she is a snooty ghost."

Panola Hall is now a rooming house. When you enter its wide central hall, you are conscious at once of something different in atmosphere from that of most old houses. But it isn't a ghostly atmosphere. It's just that all the doors along the hall are closed for privacy, instead of hospitably open.

At the end of the hall is the lovely stairway, a little shadowy in late afternoon before the lights are turned on. You walk up to the landing, thinking of Sylvia. Perhaps Miss Butler was right. Anyway, nobody has seen Sylvia in a long, long time.

Outside again on Madison Avenue, called simply "the Avenue," you look up and down a charming, wide and shady street, which is a panorama of changing architecture from Greek Revival to fairly modern. It is like many streets in old Georgia towns, houses mostly set back and far apart, surrounded by lawns and flowering shrubs and trees.

Visible from the Avenue, at the end of Wayne, which crosses Madison, are the tall white Corinthian columns of the T. G. Green house, around which legends cluster as well as boxwood.

Thick clumps of boxwood, head high, border the walk leading to a portico that is the perfect backdrop for romance, old or new South. All the garden plantings have the richness of maturity that only time and care can give. The Green house is one of the best preserved of Georgia's ante-bellum mansions.

There is a legend that Sherman mistook the place for a girls' boarding school and for this reason ordered that it be saved from destruction. Since its ante-bellum neighbors also remain, one is forced to conclude this is indeed legend.

As we know, Sherman's official orders were to forage liberally . . . destroy factories, houses, warehouses, mills, gins, barns, supplies, etc. This was done all the way from Atlanta to Savannah over an area sixty miles wide as the four diverging columns of Sherman's army traveled their more-or-less-parallel roads. Depots, stores and courthouses were frequently thrown in for good measure. An Atlanta genealogist has a map on which various blots denote courthouses destroyed. The blots remind her that in these counties she will find no deeds, wills, marriage licenses, tax digests or other family records prior to 1864.

Federal Major Henry Hitchcock of the general's staff wrote, "I think I shall never see a distant column of smoke rising, hereafter, but it will remind me of Sherman in Georgia . . ."

Sometimes, along that flaming march to the sea, fire from the "official" burnings, spread to houses. And it is true that the orders with regard to dwellings were easy to misinterpret. Houses and their occupants were to be unmolested, unless the occupants were "openly hostile."

Certain it is that Sherman himself, who passed through Eatonton on a raw, wintry day in November of 1864, tells of ordering the destruction of the house which sheltered him that night. This house was farther along the road, "about ten miles short of Milledgeville," Sherman records in his *Memoirs*. "In looking around I saw a small box, like a candle box, marked Howell Cobb and on inquiring found that we were at the plantation of Howell Cobb of Georgia, one of the leading rebels of the South and a General in the southern army and who had been Secretary of the United States Treasury in Mr. Buchanan's time. Of course, we confiscated his property. . . . I sent word back to General Davis to explain whose plantation it was and instructed him to spare nothing."

General Cobb's family were at the beautiful old Cobb house (still standing) in Athens, while military visitors were making themselves comfortable at the plantation. General Sherman relates that Lieutenant David Snelling, who commanded his escort, asked permission that evening to make a call on an uncle who lived about six miles distant.

"The Uncle," says Sherman, "was not cordial by any means to find his

61

nephew in the ranks of the host that was desolating the land and Snelling came back, having exchanged his tired horse for a fresher one out of his uncle's stables, explaining that surely some of our bummers would have got the horse had he not."

In view of all this, it is not strange if people along the line of march were sometimes inclined to think their property had been spared by special dispensation. Sherman was teaching in the Louisiana Military Academy when war broke out. To think that he remembered this when he gesticulated toward the children in the garden of an impressive Greek Revival house in Eatonton is, after all, a pretty bit of sentiment and a rare-enough local compliment for the general. Many Georgia children of the 'sixties believed Sherman had horns.

The children in the garden of the Green house, who are said to have inspired Sherman's benevolent gesture, were the numerous grandchildren of Mr. and Mrs. Sidney Reid. Mr. Reid built the house in 1845 and when war came all the family gathered there "for the duration."

In planning his home, Mr. Reid insisted that the foundations be allowed to settle for a whole year before the rest of the structure was added. As a result, the elaborately corniced plaster walls are smooth and uncracked after more than a hundred years.

Sometime in the eighteen nineties the property came into the possession of T. G. Green. The legend that the beautifully preserved house and gardens stand as a monument to a perfect housekeeper is a true one. All of the original white paint retains its pristine freshness, due to Mrs. Green's care that cleaning be done without harsh abrasives.

"Of course," conceded Mrs. Green's daughter, Mrs. Thurston Hatcher, of Atlanta, "servants were more plentiful in mother's day, but it was quite a housekeeping job, I assure you, with eighteen rooms—some of them twenty-five by twenty-five feet square—and ceilings fifteen feet high."

Notable among other Greek Revival houses in Eatonton are the home of Dr. Frederick Griffith, nearer town, and the Bronson and Slade houses. Both of these latter are on the Avenue. The Bronson house has two-story white columns in front and on two sides. The two-story Slade house is built of brick and has an Ionic portico. A wall of the same brick, laid in pierced design, extends from the back around the sides of the yard, with a front section of decorative iron grillework.

Before you reach the far end of the Avenue, the houses stop. Once they stopped even sooner, giving a longer, tree-bordered approach to grounds resembling an English park. In the midst of this park you come upon a great rectangular forecourt of green lawn, level as a ballroom floor, rimmed by a balustrade. This is the frame for a house that might have been lifted bodily from a Victorian novel, its front a series of gables with scalloped trimmings, the whole painted a pale, creamy yellow.

You discover that it is a house with a split personality. While the front is

Victorian, the back is classic Greek Revival. Here Miss Carrie Jenkins, sister of Judge W. F. Jenkins, literally dwells in two eras, though it certainly cannot be said that she lives in the past. The original house was Greek Revival; its long front porch became a cross hall, connecting two architectural periods, when the Victorian front section was added by Miss Jenkins's father. The effect is surprising and wholly delightful.

The old part of the house was at an earlier time the home of Mark A. Cooper, who later established the Etowah Manufacturing and Mining Works, near Cartersville. Sherman used the Cooper furnace as a powder magazine and destroyed it before going on to Atlanta.

Mark A. Cooper is one of many citizens on Putnam's roll of honor. First, of course, is Joel Chandler Harris, who was born in Eatonton in 1848. At Turnwold, the plantation of J. A. Turner, nine miles east of Eatonton, young Harris began his writing career on the plantation newspaper, *The Countryman.* Negroes at Turnwold and their folk tales inspired the stories of Uncle Remus which became famous the world over.

A president for the Republic of Texas, Mirabeau Lamar, was furnished by Putnam County. Also from Putnam came L. Q. C. Lamar, Jr., Associate Justice of the United States Supreme Court.

Something which has been likened to the Pentecost started in Putnam County back in 1827 and its effects are felt in Georgia to this day. An evangelical revival conducted in July of that year by Adiel Sherwood resulted in the addition of sixteen thousand new converts to the Baptist faith.

Sherwood, then living in Eatonton, came south from New York, and he it was who conceived the idea of Mercer University, the plans for which were carried out by Jesse Mercer, mainly with money inherited by Mercer's wife from her first husband, Abraham Simons, of Wilkes County.

Sherwood's famous *Gazetteer of Georgia,* published in 1827, is now a collector's item. In it are listed towns, populations, rivers, post offices, buildings, residence, etc., with all the distances reckoned from Milledgeville, then capital of Georgia.

She Wanted Style—But Got a Broken Leg

*T*HE first, first lady of Milledgeville refused to travel to the governor's mansion in an oxcart. She had her own ideas of what was suitable. Later, it is true, she regretted her choice of conveyance.

Anyway, that first Milledgeville mansion was only a log house on Fishing Creek. Milledgeville's many beautiful Greek Revival houses were yet to be built when Mrs. Jared Irwin arrived as first lady.

For this was the year 1807.

Georgia's capital has been stationary in Atlanta since 1868 but it was pretty portable in its earlier years. Savannah had it first, of course. When the British took over in 1779, Augusta became the seat of government. Military matters got so hot that for one year the capital took refuge at Fort Heard, then went back to Augusta. In 1795 Louisville was selected as the new state capital. It was here in 1803 that Governor John Milledge appointed a commission to seek a site suitable for a "permanent" capital.

There were many fine springs on the chosen site near the head of the Oconee River, and the river itself was important as a means of transportation before the invention of the steam engine.

Milledgeville was literally carved out of the wilderness, on land that had been Indian country until the treaty of 1802. Like Washington, D. C., it is one of the few cities in the country originally planned as a seat of government. Milledgeville's streets are a hundred feet wide. Two of them, Washington and Jefferson, are 120 feet across.

The new town was named for Governor Milledge, but in the meantime he had been elected to the United States Senate and Jared Irwin, president of the Georgia Senate, was appointed to fill the unexpired term.

Mrs. Irwin was like any other woman. It would not be fitting, she told her husband, for the governor and first lady of Georgia to travel to the new capital in an oxcart. A statesman should arrive in state—and his wife, too, of course.

The governor pointed out that she could scarcely expect to ride in one of the official wagons carrying the treasury, public records, etc. (There were fifteen of these wagons, escorted by a mounted troop sent down from Washington, D.C., for the purpose.)

Certainly not, Mrs. Irwin agreed. The governor should buy a gig. They would travel in that. The governor was like most husbands. He bought a gig—"a light carriage with two wheels, drawn by a horse, a kind of chaise," says the dictionary. (Old Georgia tax digests listed such vehicles as "two pleasure wheels.")

On that day in May of 1807, Mrs. Irwin found the new gig so pleasant she declined to leave it even to dine at an inn en route. She demanded curb service. All would have been well except for a white rooster that celebrated the visit of state by mounting a near-by fence and crowing practically in the horse's ear. This so frightened the tethered animal that his wild plunging upset both Mrs. Irwin's tray and the gig. The first lady herself landed on the ground with a broken leg. She was, after all, taken by oxcart to Milledgeville.

Nobody there minded the oxcart, of course.

Things were still a bit primitive in the up-country, as witness the Milledgeville lady who was legally ducked in the Oconee River. She was not a first lady, of course. And though it is well known that she was a common scold, a shrew, she shall be nameless here.

Nobody questioned the sentence, for it had been pronounced by Judge Peter Early, who was noted for the fairness of his decisions.

How was a legal ducking carried out?

The law sat the lady in a sulky—one of those light two-wheeled vehicles still used in trotting races—drove with her out into the middle of the river and dipped her under three times. Maybe the law got a little wet too, but who minded that? Not the watchers on the bank, anyway.

History does not record whether the lady was cured of her shrewishness or merely caught a cold, but Peter Early was later elected governor of Georgia. Only men voted in 1813, of course.

"Milledgeville was born a capital in the fading light of an Indian war dance," says Nelle Womack Hines, historian and writer. "It died as a capital city in the fading light of a burning bridge as Sherman passed on."

What Sherman saw when he arrived in Milledgeville, November 23, 1864, is described by a member of his staff, Major Henry Hitchcock, author of *Marching with Sherman.*

FIGURE 17. Young Captain Henry Ward Beecher knocked at the door of the house of Mr. and Mrs. Richard McAllister Orme in Milledgeville, now owned by Mr. and Mrs. J. O. Sallee.

FIGURE 18. Westover, home of Dr. and Mrs. L. C. Lindsley of Milledgeville, built in 1822, is distinguished by its beautiful fanlighted doors and twin-columned portico.

"Town prettily situated," wrote the Major, "not large, some very good dwellings. State house, arsenal, governor's mansion, all fine. Also hotel, good large building . . ."

Sherman's diverging columns met at Milledgeville for the first time since leaving Atlanta, some sixty-two thousand strong. Kilpatrick was there with his cavalry. It was an occasion. "Colors dipped, cheers, music—all horses scared . . ." Major Hitchcock records . . . his own mount "jumping and rearing like mad, but soon subdued."

After taking over the city, the Federal forces freed all convicts from the state penitentiary and burned that building. At the request of a delegation of citizens, Sherman decided not to burn the many bales of cotton in Milledgeville warehouses, but to confiscate them.

Major Hitchcock writes that he himself was busy drawing up bonds for this cotton and so was not on hand when his fellow Federal officers gathered in the old Gothic Capitol building and held a mock meeting of the Georgia State Legislature.

Sherman wasn't there either. In his *Memoirs,* he notes: "I was not present at these frolics but heard of them and enjoyed the joke."

It had been no joke when Georgia's secession convention was held in this building four years earlier. Already four states had seceded from the Union. Both North and South felt that what happened at the convention of Georgia's legislature would greatly influence other Southern states. Some of Georgia's ablest statesmen were on opposing sides and the contest was long and bitter. But . . . the ordinance of secession was signed in January of 1861.

The War Between the States had been on for four years when Sherman and his army reached Milledgeville in November of 1864.

Four years. And a smart young Federal officer stood outside the beautiful fanlighted door, sheltered by its Doric-columned portico, at the home of Mr. and Mrs. Richard McAllister Orme in Milledgeville.

The door was opened by a frightened butler. Mrs. Orme was just behind him. The young officer announced himself as Captain Henry Ward Beecher and naturally was somewhat startled when Mrs. Orme stepped forward to ask briskly, "Are you Tom's son or William's?" Before he could answer, she added that she had gone to school with both of them. She was a daughter of John Adams, president of Phillips Academy, at Andover, Massachusetts.

The young officer, a nephew and namesake of the famous Henry Ward Beecher, explained in his turn that he was William's son and had been detailed as a guard for Mrs. Orme's house.

Mrs. Orme glanced over her shoulder toward the lovely winding stair. She hoped devoutly that her daughter's husband, Confederate Captain James Alexander, home on leave, had had the good sense to conceal himself somewhere. Anyway, there was nothing to do but invite young Captain Beecher in. This she did graciously, asking him to accompany her to the back parlor to meet a group of ladies who had gathered there for protection.

Today Mrs. Orme's granddaughter, Mrs. J. O. Sallee, who lives in the beautiful old house, may show you the handsome horsehair-covered sofa in the wide hall on which young Captain Beecher rested his sword and his pistols. First he asked permission to do so, explaining gallantly that it would not be becoming to wear arms when presented to a company of ladies.

Federal Captain Beecher, acting as guard for the Orme house, occupied a downstairs guest room. Confederate Captain Alexander, a virtual prisoner, was confined to a dark cubbyhole in the attic. And in the meantime Federal General Gleason, having heard that Mrs. Orme was the former Miss Adams of Massachusetts, called to pay his respects.

Later he reported wryly to General Sherman, "They call her a Yankee, but she's a d—— Rebel."

This Williams-Orme-Crawford-Sallee house, at the corner of Liberty and Washington streets, is one of the "very good dwellings" noted by Major Hitchcock which still stands in Milledgeville. Compiling a guide for a house-and-garden tour, Milledgeville discovered some years ago that forty-four of its notable old houses were built prior to 1860. The oldest dates back to about 1812. In the immediate vicinity are at least twenty others, mostly ante-bellum plantation houses. The majority of these old houses have been carefully preserved. Many are furnished with rare and beautiful family pieces, "handed down," and added to through the years. Here in Milledgeville are many treasures in old silver, old glass and old china.

The Sallee house built in 1822, with its classic pedimented two-columned portico, is more characteristic of Milledgeville and Baldwin County houses than are the spacious porches which predominate in other old Georgia towns. It is doubtful if finer examples of this particular style can be found anywhere than in the exquisitely proportioned porticoes at the Sallee house and at Westover, the home of Dr. and Mrs. L. C. Lindsley, also built in 1822, six miles out of Milledgeville on the Meriwether road.

Each of these houses has exquisite fan- and side-lighted doors, with a matching door opening onto the hanging balcony above. At Westover there are twin instead of single Doric columns at each side of the portico and the triglyph carved entablature extends all the way around the house.

Westover was the plantation home of Colonel Lee Jordan, a power in the politics of his day. The house was enlarged in 1852 and a great banqueting hall added. Westover's gardens, gradually being restored, were among the most elaborately beautiful in Georgia.

That there is a ghost at The Homestead, on Washington and Liberty Streets in Milledgeville, more than one person will testify. Miss Elizabeth Ferguson, who

FIGURE 19. Georgia's governors lived here from 1838 to 1868, when Milledgeville was capital of the state. The old executive mansion was patterned after Palladio's Villa in Italy.

FIGURE 20. Beauvoir, home of Mr. and Mrs. Oscar Ennis, of Milledgeville. It is often called the old Rockwell mansion.

lives there, says that her mother, Mrs. David Ferguson saw the ghost twice and described her as a little old lady in brown who sometimes flits betweeen the box-wood hedges at dusk. She is a friendly ghost, supposed to have followed the Williams family from Wales to New England and thence to Georgia.

The Ferguson house, of transitional style between Georgian and Greek Re-vival, was built in 1818 by Miss Ferguson's great-grandfather, Peter J. Williams, for his bride, Lucinda Parke of Greensboro, Georgia. One of its hand-hewn beams is sixty feet long and twelve inches square.

The Ferguson children, growing up in the old house, heard tales that it was haunted. To reassure them, Mrs. David Ferguson told the children about Aunt Susan and the gold. Shortly before her death, Aunt Susan sold some land and received gold in payment. There was a story that she had buried the gold but nobody knew where. How nice, Mrs. Ferguson suggested, if Aunt Sue's spirit were now trying to tell them where to look for the gold. The children, enchanted with the idea, looked eagerly for the ghost, but never found her.

What about digging for the gold? "Certainly not," says Miss Ferguson. "The old boxwood is much more valuable than any gold could be. It was planted by great-grandmother Lucinda when the house was new." Lucinda also planted the wisteria which more than a century later festoons with purple steamers the great cedar trees. There is much else in this old garden to remind one of Lucinda—pomegranates, crape myrtle, sweet syringa, tea olive, spikenard—much that had reminded Lucinda of her own grandmother's garden.

Perhaps there is a ghost in another old house at Milledgeville. Anyway, a man was hidden there for twenty years after he fought an impromptu duel and was quicker on the draw than his opponent. With the law at his heels, he rushed home and was concealed between two feather beds (mattresses, if you prefer). Search-ers who ransacked the house even looked under the high poster bed in which he was practically suffocating.

Later the fugitive came out for air but never again ventured below stairs. Everybody thought he had escaped to Texas. Servants were forbidden to go up-stairs. The family became strangely inhospitable but were forgiven because of the tragedy. Twenty years of this and death claimed the unhappy prisoner, no longer a young man.

The old house, in giving up its dead, had to give up its secret.

Milledgeville's proudest house is the old executive mansion, home of Georgia governors from 1838 to 1868. Patterned after Palladio's Villa of fourteenth-century Italy, it has a classic portico with four Ionic columns evenly spaced. There is no balcony. But there's plenty of balcony inside, all the way around an upper floor, from which first ladies in hoop skirts, no doubt, took a peep at callers below before sweeping regally downstairs.

As you enter the great front door, you come first into a large square hall and from this into the rotunda, which is fifty feet high with a gilded dome. You spy the circular balcony as your glance descends from this impressive height.

The handsome old stucco building, erected at a cost of $50,000, is sixty feet square. There is a salon sixty feet long, with gold-framed pier mirrors at each end—ten feet tall and six feet wide—and matching mirrors over the twin black marble fire-places. There are, of course, crystal chandeliers.

It is said that the cupola was not a part of the original design for the building, but was added later by a visiting architect from the North, one John Comfort, who liked Milledgeville so much he stayed on and later joined the Confederate army.

There is a legend that a secret underground passage connects the executive mansion with the old state capitol building which is now the home of the Georgia Military College. This tunnel has never been found, but in one of the carved doors you can still see where a passage was cut for the pet cat of some long-gone first lady. This has been stopped up and nobody now knows which mistress of the mansion loved cats.

The eight Georgia governors who lived here were George R. Gilmer, Charles J. McDonald, George W. Crawford, George W. Towns, Howell Cobb, Herschel V. Johnson, Joseph E. Brown, Charles J. Jenkins. For many years now it has been the home of successive presidents of the Georgia State College for Women at Milledgeville.

One of Georgia's present-day statesmen lives on West Montgomery Street in an inviting old house with massive end-chimneys and a Victorian veranda. This is the home of Carl Vinson, member of Congress and chairman of the powerful House Armed Services Committee in Washington. The Vinson house was built in 1832 by Judge Iverson Harris, who also had trees planted to make a shady walk all the way from his home to his office in the business part of town.

Not a first lady, but a great lady, was "Old Miss," born Anne Grantland, who is still the subject of more than one engaging story of Milledgeville's hoop-skirted past.

She was the daughter of Seaton Grantland, early Milledgeville newspaper publisher. At her stepmother's death, Anne became "Young Miss" at Woodville Plantation. The Woodville house was built by Governor John Clark and is one of the oldest still standing in Baldwin County.

Anne married Charles DuBignon, state legislator from Jekyll Island. In time, Anne became noted for the soundness of her political opinions as well as for her many benefactions. She wielded wide influence at the polls in Baldwin County, even though women did not yet have the vote. In time, too, she was no longer "Young Miss" but "Old Miss."

It is related that one of the elderly Negroes at Woodville, greatly disturbed

71

about the Spanish-American War, called on a well-known Milledgeville judge. "Mr. Judge, sir," he asked earnestly, "why don't Old Miss and President McKinley stop this here war?"

One of Atlanta's handsomest present-day houses is named "Woodville." It is the Andrews Drive residence of Mrs. Robert C. Alston, granddaughter of "Old Miss."

Three brides of the present generation have in turn come down the wide stairway to be married at Lockerly, the R. W. Hatcher home on Milledgeville's Irwinton Road. One of the three married Furman Smith, a descendant of Farish Carter, great plantation owner of his day, whose house still stands near Milledgeville, the oldest in Baldwin County. So the old names and the old houses go on together. The Farish Carter house, built in 1806, is described along with Colonel Carter's North Georgia house in the chapter, "More Money Than Carter Had Oats."

Lockerly has a wide front porch and Doric columns extending all the way across its stucco front. The grounds with their great cedars, magnolias, elms and oaks are enclosed by a decorative hand-wrought charcoal fence. Named for the ancestral Hatcher home in England, Lockerly has an authentic ancestral atmosphere of its own—old furniture, many family portraits, old silver and old china. All the children live elsewhere now, including R. W. Hatcher, Jr., but their respective bedrooms are kept in order for impromptu visits. In the nursery, the family cradle is ready for the current grandbaby.

A lady who loved columns was the wife of General John W. A. Sanford, who in the eighteen twenties built the house at Greene and Clarke Streets, now owned by Dr. and Mrs. Richard Binion. It was originally planned with a four-columned portico. "Got to sell another slave," mourned General Sanford, "my wife wants more columns." The finished structure had a porch extending from the front around both sides, and fourteen tall Doric columns.

Evidently Joseph Stovall, who built a house of similar design about the same time, was not superstitious, for this spacious old house, at Wilkinson and Greene Streets, has thirteen columns, supposed to represent the thirteen original states. Here we see a right angle of columns, as the porch extends from the front around one side only. This is now the Charles Conn residence.

In practically every one of Georgia's older towns there is a place called "The Cedars." The one in Milledgeville has a two-columned portico and the not-unusual variation of an upstairs porch instead of a hanging balcony. Originally the house faced Clarke Street and had a circular cedar drive but was later turned around to face Columbia. It is now owned by Mrs. J. I. Garrard.

A fine Ionic portico, the pediment fan decorated, adorns the former home of Governor Herschel V. Johnson. It is named Beauvoir but is usually called the old Rockwell mansion because it was built in 1830 by Colonel W. S. Rockwell. The house sits back on a hill above Allen Memorial Drive; its sweeping lawns are enclosed by a handsome iron fence said to have cost almost as much as the house.

This is now the home of Mr. and Mrs. Oscar Ennis.

At one time the handsome house of the Misses Mary and Kate Cline on Greene Street was used as a temporary home for Georgia's governor while the official residence was being completed. Originally it had only a pedimented Ionic portico. The two-story balustraded porches are a later addition.

The oldest house still standing in Milledgeville was built about 1812 by Major Edward White. Later it was the home of R. B. Moore, father of Jere N. Moore, editor (like his father and grandfather before him) of the Milledgeville *Union-Recorder*.

Erected in 1812, not so long after Milledgeville became the capital, the Brown-Stetson-Sanford house on Wilkinson Street has a stately charm untouched by time. It is a square clapboard structure with one-story square columns and slender Ionic columns above.

Miss Elizabeth Jones, who lives in a delightful old house with square columns in front and a Victorian side porch, on South Liberty, collects rare eighteenth-century antiques. The one-story Greek Revival house of Mrs. J. D. Willis, on the Irwinton Road, shows her love of fine old china and mahogany.

At the Scott home on North Jefferson, built in 1828, the front door is made of a hundred small pieces of wood, a collection from trees grown in Georgia. Records of the Revolutionary War and the War Between the States and many old costumes are among the family heirlooms here.

When Milledgeville ladies stage their house-and-garden tours, their men take equal pride in throwing open the lodge rooms in the old Masonic building, reached by a beautiful but long and dizzy winding stair. Here you may see the high-backed thronelike red velvet chair in which LaFayette sat when he attended a meeting of his brother Masons in the old capital city.

Still looking at houses, if you can call a vault a house, we went to the old Milledgeville cemetery.

"Men have died . . . and worms have eaten them, but not for love," said a certain poet. He should have lived to see this vault:

A prominent Milledgeville citizen, crazed by grief at the death of his young wife, joined her inside, locked the door, put a pistol to his head and ended it all. That's the story, and if you are skeptical, you can peer through the iron grille door of the vault and glimpse the key—still in the lock.

CHAPTER 11

Headstrong Lady

*T*HEY said they would disown her if she accepted the plantation and slaves willed to her by a deceased relative in Georgia.

"They" were ardent abolitionists, living in Massachusetts, and she was their daughter, Sarah Ann Devine, aged eighteen.

Sarah Ann Devine was what might be called headstrong. She came South to take over her Georgia inheritance and to operate Bellevue Plantation twelve miles from Waynesboro in Burke County. Even then, in the early eighteen thirties, it was an old plantation—older than Waynesboro, one of four towns in the United States named for the dashing Revolutionary hero, Mad Anthony Wayne. In modern times Georgia's Waynesboro is better known for its annual field trials of hunting dogs.

The original Bellevue land grant, carefully kept in a fireproof vault by Sarah Ann Devine's great-grandson, Porter Wilkins Carswell, is dated July 7, 1767, and is signed by James Wright, royal governor of the Province of Georgia, for His Majesty, King George III of England. Burke County was then the Parish of St. George.

The house at Bellevue, with its square Colonial columns, was built about 1768. The old "courting parlor," now the dining room, was added in 1850. Other additions, all carefully in character, were made in the eighteen nineties and in 1932, bringing the number of rooms to twenty.

Furnished with heirlooms which delightfully mingle eighteenth-century and Victorian pieces, Bellevue stands in its old garden, its box-bordered walk leading to the gate of a picket fence. Old, old oak trees shade the spreading white wings of the house. Beyond the fence, cotton fields stretch away in all directions, just as they did when Sarah Ann Devine turned her back on New England and came to Georgia to make a home for herself.

74

Though a self-confident young woman, Sarah Ann soon discovered that she needed frequent advice about the management of plantation affairs. Mainly this advice was furnished by her attorney, a tall, dark-haired young man, named John Wright Carswell. They fell in love and were married in the lovely paneled parlor at Bellevue, January 28, 1835, by Bishop J. O. Andrew, of the Methodist Episcopal church.

Nine years later the Methodist Church split into Northern and Southern divisions because Bishop Andrew owned a slave girl named Kitty, whose story is told in an earlier chapter of this book. In 1861 John Devine, the nineteen-year-old son of Sarah Ann and John Wright Carswell, enlisted in the Confederate army to fight his Northern cousins in the War Between the States.

But the eighteen thirties were the great days of the Old South. Cotton was king, the plantation prospered, and though Sarah Ann's parents never forgave her, she and her husband were happy at Bellevue. A rosebush there, still blossoming pink every spring, bears romantic witness to the fact.

John Wright Carswell became judge of the Superior Court of Burke County. After Sherman's march to the sea left so much of Georgia in ruins, Judge Carswell continued to serve without pay. In 1877, when the period of Reconstruction was over, citizens of Burke engraved their lasting thanks on a handsome silver water pitcher which they presented to the judge. This pitcher comes back to Bellevue on high occasions. It is now owned by Porter Carswell's brother, John Wright Carswell, of Savannah, who was named for their great-grandfather.

Near the front porch at Bellevue is the rosebush which was Sarah Ann's special favorite. But ever since a day in 1864 it has been called Sherman's rosebush. Bellevue well remembers that day.

The house was full of women and children who had gathered there for protection. There was skirmishing between the Confederate cavalry of General Wheeler and the Federal cavalry of General Kilpatrick. Fighting overflowed onto the fields of Bellevue. The house was hit several times, and still shows scars left by rifle bullets and minnie balls.

The dent made by a bullet in the hand-carved mantel in the parlor was always of especial interest to the late Mrs. Robert Caldwell Neely, of Waynesboro, as it is to her children and grandchildren today. Mrs. Neely, the former Lillian Wilkins, was one of the Carswell cousins assembled at Bellevue. She was a baby at the time. Little Lillian's mammy nurse, with the child in her arms, stood at a window watching the fighting. Someone in the house called out a warning and mammy moved just as the window was shattered by bullets.

On the day of all this excitement a foraging party from Kilpatrick's cavalry visited the plantation. Officers tied their horses to the tall rosebush by the side of the house.

The only man on the place was Judge Carswell, who was then too old to

FIGURE 21. The parlor at Bellevue, plantation house of Mr. and Mrs. Porter Wilkins Carswell, near Waynesboro. The mantel shows a dent made by a Federal bullet (near diamond).

FIGURE 22. The Shadows, home of Mr. and Mrs. Robert Caldwell Neely, in Waynesboro.

serve in the army. Noticing the rosebush was in danger of being uprooted by the restless horses, he untied the reins and held them while his supplies were taken over, his pigs and cattle slaughtered and his barns and cotton set afire. There was nothing he could do about any of that, but at least he could save his wife's favorite rosebush.

And so we know by this that the love of Sarah Ann Devine and John Wright Carswell grew stronger with the years. What rosebush, symbolizing so much, could fail to do likewise?

John Devine, son of Sarah Ann and the judge, was seriously wounded shortly before the war was over. He was captured and imprisoned at Elmira, New York.

Sarah Ann wrote to her parents in Massachusetts, asking them to use their influence with the Federal government to help their grandson. She found that they had not changed in their convictions about the issues involved. They refused to do anything, pointing out in their reply that her son was a "Rebel."

He was released a year later and walked back to Georgia barefooted through snow and ice, arriving at Bellevue with a severe case of pneumonia. He never recovered his full strength and two years later he died. His son Porter Wilkins Carswell, Sr., was then a year old.

Porter Wilkins Carswell, Jr., now has a son, Porter, III. Both of them inherit Sarah Ann's love of the land. Mr. Carswell, who carries on in the pattern of public service set by the judge, is a gentleman farmer in white linen, supervising operation of six tractors used in tilling Bellevue's three thousand acres. There were many more acres in ante-bellum times—many more than were included in the original land grant to Samuel Eastlake, ancestor of Sarah Ann Devine.

"My husband's family didn't want much land," explains Mrs. Carswell. "They only wanted the land that joined them."

The original house at Bellevue had only six rooms. The kitchen and dining room were in a separate building. In 1918 this latter building was destroyed by a cyclone. On the morning after the storm, the Negro foreman of the plantation remarked fervently, "Last night we sho' found out who was boss around here."

Nothing about the main house was damaged and nothing about it has been changed. It is perfectly preserved, but its age is shown in such details as minor flaws in the blown-glass windowpanes and in the marks of the draw knife used to smooth, on one side only, the wide heart-pine boards used for ceilings and floors. The green window blinds have stationary slats instead of the movable ones which came later. The Crusader paneled doors and window frames all vary slightly in size. Hinges and other hardware are of wrought iron. Only the brass doorknobs and the huge locks were imported from England. Everything else was handmade at home. The hand-hewn timbers of cypress and long-leaf pine were cut as land was cleared for the house. Still to be seen is the pit left when the gray clay was dug from which bricks were made for the massive chimneys.

Bellevue, like most early houses, has numerous outside doors and porches. Mrs. Carswell suggests these porches probably came in handy in winter as convenient places to pile extra firewood.

In the Greek Revival era, Sarah Ann and the judge added the spacious room called the courting parlor. This is now used as the dining room. The crystal chandelier over the English banqueting table high lights old silver and the beautiful molded cornices and center ceiling rosette. The present kitchen ell began in the eighteen nineties as a separate kitchen joined to the house by a covered passageway. When additional rooms were built in 1932, everything was carefully matched with early construction, even the wide floor boards.

Diagonally across the road from the main house at Bellevue is the commissary, presided over for many years by Tom Hughes, who came to the plantation in 1886 as the result of a poker bet.

"When my father was a young man," Mr. Carswell explained, "he was—in addition to his farming interests—engaged in the mercantile business with a Mr. Hopper. When they decided to dissolve the partnership, they divided the stock, but could not divide Tom, the Negro porter at the store.

"They settled the matter of Tom's future employment by playing a hand of stud poker. My father won, as was his life-long habit, and Tom came to Bellevue where he soon made the contract more binding by marrying Winnie Carswell, daughter of former slaves of the family who had taken the Carswell name.

"Tom was foreman of the plantation until he retired at the age of seventy," Mr. Carswell continued. "He was with my father when he was killed many years ago in our cotton gin. After this, Tom seemed to feel the weight of his responsibility more than ever and my family could not have had a better or more faithful friend.

"In 1936 when Tom had completed half a century of devoted service, I gave a barbecue in his honor. A hundred and fifty of his Negro friends were invited, and before the celebration got under way I presented Tom with a new Ford sedan and a gold watch, engraved with his name and the dates 1886–1936."

Former slave quarters at Bellevue have been replaced by tenant houses for Negro employees, sixty of whose children attend the modern plantation school erected by Mr. Carswell. The teaching staff is furnished by the county educational system. Agricultural Burke County's Negro population and schools outnumber its white four to one.

Not far from Bellevue in the overgrown tangle of the old cemetery of Big Buckhead Baptist Church is the grave of one Christian Shultz, a native of Prussia. The marker reads:

"He died a stranger in a strange land, but amidst kind friends."

Sarah Ann Devine must have been reminded of New England when she saw this third oldest Baptist church in Georgia with its four simple square columns rising to the high roof. Built about 1800, long unused and now falling into disrepair as the surrounding wilderness stealthily takes back its own, the old building still has immense dignity.

Here in 1831 was passed the resolution of the Baptist convention to build Mercer University, now at Macon. Here in 1864, during that same cavalry skirmish in which little Lillian Wilkins was narrowly missed by a bullet, the bridge across Big Buckhead Creek was burned. Pursuing horsemen quickly removed pews from the near-by church and used them as a bridge to span the creek. These pews, afterward refinished and replaced, still show the print of the horses' metal-shod hooves on the underside.

As we drove back to Bellevue by unpaved plantation roads cut through wide cotton fields, Mr. Carswell pointed out that many former Burke cotton plantations are now cattle and stock farms. He betrayed a touch of a not-uncommon Georgia nostalgia for the old tradition when he added, "It's the finest cotton land in the world. Naturally, it will grow the best pasturage."

A little farther along he stopped the car in order that we might have a better view of tall crape myrtle trees in front of a tenant house. These were massed with watermelon-pink plumes, and from their branches hung long gray swags of Spanish moss. It was worth lingering to look at, but suddenly there was the quick spatter of a summer shower and all the beauty blurred. Dust began to settle in the road ahead as Mr. Carswell started the car.

"I could enjoy this rain," Mrs. Carswell said, "if it were not so bad for the cotton."

How many times, in how many seasons, I wondered, had this remark been made at Bellevue? Almost, as the fragrant warm dusk closed around, I could imagine it was Sarah Ann whose voice I heard.

Little Lillian Wilkins, that wartime baby of the eighteen sixties, grew up to become mistress of another large ante-bellum Burke County plantation when she married Robert Caldwell Neely.

The town of Waynesboro long ago reached out to include the beautiful old Neely house, which was lovingly restored by the present Mrs. Robert Caldwell Neely. She was Louise Phinizy, who grew up in one of Augusta's charming old houses, and the house at Waynesboro is furnished with heirlooms representing both her own and her husband's family.

Originally the Neely house, with its six tall Doric columns across the front, was called The Pines, but was later rechristened The Shadows because of the beautiful shadow effects created by the tall magnolia trees which are among the handsomest in Georgia. Here too is one of Georgia's loveliest gardens.

The original builder was John James Jones. Later this beautiful home was inherited by his daughter, Mrs. George Pulcher Cox.

Sherman Caught Up with the Joneses

*I*T was hard to keep up with the Joneses back in Colonial times when King George III granted Francis Jones, a Welshman, 66,000 acres of land in what is now Jenkins County but was then a part of the Parish of St. George.

Sherman finally caught up with them in the eighteen sixties. But you can't keep a good Jones down. Today there's both an airplane and a private landing field at Birdsville, the old Jones plantation, and a silver-mounted postillion coach with sliding glass windows in the carriage house.

Both the coach and the carriage house are museum pieces, but the plane goes places and is even handier than a horse for inspecting crops. The landing field is in easy walking distance of the house.

What's left of the plantation, a mere 1,400 acres, is thriving. The family now raises Tennessee walking horses, beef cattle, hogs, grain, peas and some cotton.

The fine old boxwood is still there, and four lanes of live oaks lead to the house that was built by Francis Jones in 1762 and added to by succeeding generations, after the manner of many old English houses which reflect various eras in architecture. The Jones house is worth seeing from any one of its four avenues —white Colonial clapboard with a Greek Revival front and Victorian side porches. The Joneses always had the newest and the best. Which is not to say that they were pretentious, but merely progressive, as befitted a rich and powerful family who played a leading part in shaping the history of Georgia both as colony and as state.

The stagecoach road from Savannah to Augusta passed through the Jones plantation, and in pre-Revolutionary times a small village grew up not far from the big house. Some of these early buildings remain. One is a small clapboard gabled structure which served as a post office and a stagecoach inn.

The postmaster's name was Bird, and in time the place became known as Birdsville, though this name no longer appears on the map. Mail for Birdsville goes to Millen, twelve miles away, and is delivered by rural carrier.

But Mr. and Mrs. Ben Franklin (she was Bessie Jones), who now live in the old plantation house, have an 1835 atlas which shows Birdsville and Waynesboro as the only towns in what was then Burke County. Later a part of Burke became Jenkins County. Birdsville is also listed in that first *Gazetteer of Georgia*, published by the Reverend Adiel Sherwood, in 1827. Even then it was a fairly old place.

Mr. and Mrs. Franklin's son, Ben, Jr., pilots the family airplane and their grandson, Ben, III, is the eighth generation to live at Birdsville. He is a five times great-grandson of Francis Jones.

Old Burke County might well have been the setting for the Georgia scenes in Stephen Vincent Benet's unforgettable narrative poem, *John Brown's Body*. Here were the great plantations, established by settlers who followed the natural course upward from Savannah toward Augusta along the Savannah River.

Here indeed were the endless acres of cotton, the "endless acres of afternoon . . . and a julep mixed with a silver spoon." Here was Georgia of "the careless yield, the watermelons ripe in the field . . . of the mockingbird and the mulberry leaf . . ." In the eighteen sixties, four Jones brothers, descendants of Francis, lived in handsome houses, plantation miles apart, and could share with Benet's Clay Wingate the pleasant feeling that:

> This was his Georgia, this his share
> Of pine and river and sleepy air. . . .

Although Benet wrote that "the house and the courtesy last forever," the Wingate hall of his poem was destroyed by fire from a torch tossed by Union soldiers. They were searching for the buried family silver. Outbuildings caught fire from the torch, then the house.

The same thing came close to happening at Birdsville.

From the J. B. Jones house near Herndon, Sherman went to Millen via the William B. Jones house at Birdsville. Here his foragers overran the plantation, dug for silver, set fire to the house.

The Mrs. Jones of that troubled era at Birdsville had given birth to twins a few days earlier. The twins had died and were buried in the plantation cemetery where founder Francis Jones lies sleeping.

When told the house was on fire, Mrs. Jones refused to leave her bed. She was ill and she was desperately unhappy about the twins, about everything. Her husband, Dr. William B. Jones, was serving with the Confederate army. For all she knew he might have been killed or wounded. Anyway, the cause was lost. She said she would just as soon be dead as have her house burned.

Photo by Carolyn Carter

FIGURE 23. The Greek Revival façade of Birdsville, the old Jones plantation house in Jenkins County, near Millen. It is the home of Mr. and Mrs. Ben Franklin.

A Colonial stair, with hand-carved ornaments, leads to the upstairs hall and the room in which she lay. This and other upstairs bedrooms are low ceiled, as was usual in early houses. Also, as was usual, the Jones house was built above a raised basement and had an attic, giving it four floors in all.

From the back window of her bedroom, Mrs. Jones could see smoke curling upward. Perhaps the foragers thought this would bring her down in a hurry. It didn't. Soldiers themselves put out the blaze.

It is thought the house was fired because the silver had been too well hidden. To ferret out silver had become routine with such visitors. They especially mistrusted newly made graves.

They dug up the little Jones twins.

It was war. But it was a new kind of war then.

As I stood there with Bessie Jones Franklin in the old cemetery, looking down at the small double graves, it did not seem so long ago that all this had happened. And suddenly I found the answer to a question which sometimes seems to puzzle present-day visitors from other sections of the country: Why do we in the South remember so much about this particular war? I realized that the answer is simple.

Invaded countries always remember.

There is so much to remind them. And not the least of these reminders is outside criticism of the thorn crop that follows devastation and a ruined economy, whether or not that economy was basically right. There was no Marshall Plan for the South.

Not until 1949 did Georgia's taxable assets reach a figure comparable to that of 1864. In 1864 the record was $1,612,592,806. On January 1, 1950—allowing for homestead and personal property exemptions—the figure was $1,487,321,566.

It was a long, hard road back.

Federal Major Henry Hitchcock gave some thought to the more immediate angles of the subject in his book, *Marching with Sherman*. While camping at the Herndon plantation of J. B. Jones, one of the four brothers then living in Burke County, he wrote:

"Fine place, large three-story double frame house, wide porch three sides . . . finest house we have seen yet. . . . The General, finding that stragglers yesterday and today had taken all the potatoes and other provisions had a supply for the family sent from our own mess to keep them until we leave and the brave Jones can return and get more."

Hitchcock assumed Mr. Jones was in hiding. As a matter of fact, a daughter of the house was attending boarding school in Savannah. Mr. Jones had gone to Savannah to bring her home before the Federal army reached that city.

Looting of private homes by stragglers and foraging parties continued to trouble Major Hitchcock. He says:

"General S. has told me more than once that for the first two years no man could have done more than he against everything of the sort. . . . His orders explicitly cover and prohibit every such case. But it is the Regimental and Company officers who must carry them out at last. At the same time I don't think the General would take the same trouble now—indeed he admits as much—to hunt out and punish it. Evidently it is a material element in this campaign to produce among the people of Georgia a thorough conviction of the personal misery which attends war and of the utter helplessness of their 'rulers,' State or Confederate, to protect them."

The Jones house, where Major Hitchcock wrote these lines—and which he described as the finest he had yet seen in Georgia—unfortunately burned to the ground in 1910. At one time or another two other ante-bellum Burke County Jones houses, remote from fire protection, were destroyed in the same way.

The house at Birdsville, now owned by Mr. and Mrs. Ben Franklin, is the only one of the four still standing. It is one of the oldest houses in the state. The timbers, hand-hewn with mortised joints, are held together with wooden pegs. Mrs. Franklin points out the beaded weather board of the exterior, no two pieces of which are quite the same.

The old house has changed little since it was given a Greek Revival front in 1847. Actually two large rooms on each floor were built at the front of the house with a recessed porch between. This pedimented porch has two-story Corinthian columns and pilasters and a balcony with an iron-grille balustrade. Bay windows adorn the first-floor rooms and there are triplex windows above.

The Greek Revival rooms are plastered and have ornamental moldings and ceiling rosettes, but the rooms in the older part of the house have walls and ceilings of wide, hand-planed, horizontal boards. The wide fireplaces are framed with beautifully carved Georgian mantels.

Still at Birdsville is the lovely old silver in Colonial fiddle-thread pattern. Greatly treasured are four two-tined forks brought over from England by Francis Jones himself.

While the house is appropriately furnished in old mahogany and walnut, Mrs. Franklin explains that many of the original pieces are now widely scattered among descendants of preceding generations. But everybody, apparently, decided that Birdsville was the place to leave the ancestral spinning wheel. On hand also is the third model of the sewing machine made by Singer. In 1853 the Joneses were still setting the pace.

Generations of Jones girls have practiced scales on the old square piano, from hoop-skirt times on down to the blue-jeans era. There is an old clock, wound once a year at Christmas, which ticked off the years of Dr. Jones's absence with the Confederate army and now ticks off the years for Colonel George Hamilton Franklin, son of the house, serving with the United States Army.

The old basement kitchen at Birdsville is a game room, and Mrs. Franklin points with pride to her modern electric kitchen in the main house.

Add an airplane, and it is clear enough that Birdsville, built in 1762, is right out in front as usual.

CHAPTER 13

Crimson Sash and Black=Plumed Hat

*E*LLA Mitchell was a little girl looking for Sherman. To get a better view she climbed up on the gatepost at her home near Sandersville.

The clatter of hoofs drew nearer. But Ella didn't see Sherman. Instead, she saw Joe Wheeler, the dashing Confederate cavalry leader, who later served as a Major General of the United States Army in the Spanish American War.

They say General Wheeler apparently forgot which war was which when he led the famous charge up Cuba's San Juan hill, for he shouted to his men, "Come on, boys, let's give the Yankees hell."

Camp Wheeler at Macon was named for him in 1917 and Ella Mitchell who saw him in 1864 never forgot him. She gives a delightful word picture of the cocky, bantam-weight general in her *History of Washington County*, Georgia.

At Sandersville, we also have a revealing portrait of General Sherman in a brief interval of relaxation. How did he spend it? Major Henry Hitchcock, of Sherman's staff, tells us. But first, let us return to Ella and her gatepost.

"We were in his [Sherman's] path," she writes. "One of the four routes was the old Louisville road that led directly through Sandersville from Milledgeville to the sea.

". . . we heard the Yankees coming up the Tennille road. Sure enough the clattering of many galloping horses could be heard. I, seated on the gatepost, saw the troops coming. But they were gray!

"Just then a very small, very erect man, dressed in gray, wearing a crimson sash and a large black plumed hat, drew rein and asked my father, who was ill at home [the kick of a horse had punctured his lungs],'Friend, is it true that Sherman's Cavalry had a skirmish with a few Confederates about four miles out?'

"Father saluted and answered, 'Yes, General Wheeler, it is true . . .' "

86

FIGURE 24.   Sherman took a nap here, at the home of R. M. Brown, of Sandersville, and later ordered the business section of the town burned. In 1864 the house was owned by Mr. Brown's grandfather, William Brown.

And that is how Ella Mitchell saw General Wheeler.

Next day she saw much more that she was never to forget.

"We were at breakfast, father lying on a couch, mother, brother and I at the table and the baby in the nurse's arms. We heard firing of rifles and yelling of men, then came a clattering of horses' hoofs and a rain of bullets on the roof. Wheeler's men went dashing by, firing as they went."

Wheeler and his gray-clad Confederate cavalry were in retreat before the advancing Federal army.

Here is Ella's eyewitness account of what happened as the invading Federal army reached her home:

"The road was a mass of blue men," she writes. "The surrounding fields were full of them. In a few minutes our house was filled with the surging mass. In a little while there was not a piece of china, silver or even the table cloth left and the food disappeared in a second. Fences were torn down, hogs shot, cows butchered, women were crying, children screaming, pandemonium reigned. Then the jail, the court house, people's barns and a large factory that made buckets and saddle trees were all ablaze . . ."

The old William Brown house which served as Sherman's Sandersville headquarters still stands. Inside is the desk from which it is said he issued orders to burn the town. Still preserved also is the sofa on which he later took a nap.

But before any of this happened, he and Major Hitchcock, apparently weary of the battlefield, spent several hours in the quiet domesticity of another Sandersville home, chatting with the womenfolk of the family.

Major Hitchcock records their arrival. "General and staff came through square and went to large brick house set back in yard with large garden in front and on both sides. General told H. H. [Henry Hitchcock] to enter. Went up steps—knocked [door locked]—opened by one of our soldiers in hall who had just entered from the rear. Lady in hall, greatly alarmed, begged protection . . .

"General came in presently . . . sat a while on front steps. . . . Told ladies he would protect them but would burn town for people burning bridge and firing in the street. General stayed two or three hours. Mrs. G., at first sharp, got some short answers but no rude ones—afterward General sat in old lady's room with ladies and talked a long time in casual strain. Mrs. G. softened a good deal. General talks 'mighty well'—frank, almost blunt but capital and always to the point and never over-bearing nor rude."

There is no large brick residence on the Sandersville square today, but the two-story frame dwelling of William Brown may still be seen on North Harris Street, though it is almost hidden by a thick growth of shrubbery and trees. The old house, with its wide front porch, supported by slim posts and topped by a balustrade, has a homey, inviting look which, no doubt, appealed to visitors then as now. At any rate, this was Sherman's headquarters. The property is owned by William Brown's grandson, R. M. Brown, who also inherited the desk and sofa used by Sherman. Another reminder of the 'sixties is a bullet hole in one of the carved mantels.

The home of Colonel T. J. Warthen, killed at Malvern Hill, is among other interesting old houses in the Sandersville neighborhood. It is called Forest Grove —square columns gleam through the green of oak trees—and is owned by a grandson of the Colonel, J. L. Wilkerson.

If you should spread a fish-net over the map of Georgia covering the route— three hundred miles long and sixty miles wide—from Atlanta to Savannah, you would then have a fair picture of the zig-zag pattern from town to town followed by the four columns of the Federal army in 1864. Federal General Kilpatrick's cavalry wove its serpentine and raiders from the four columns reached out in all directions. Federal Colonel O. M. Poe made such a map.

Today, in all the towns, the story the old houses tell is much the same.

How did Georgia "take" this destruction of property?

"In Georgia we had to respect the high-toned feelings of the planters, for they yielded with a dignity that won our admiration," declares D. P. Conyngham of the Federal army in *Sherman's March Through the South*.

Hitchcock records a specific example, December 13, 1864. Sherman and his staff were camped beside the Millen road.

"Returning to camp to supper found there Mr. R. R. Cuyler, and his brother, Dr. C., both among the prisoners taken on a train on the Gulf road," says Hitchcock. "Mr. Cuyler is and has been for over 20 years president of the Georgia Central railroad and a leading R. R. man in Georgia. He is a very intelligent man, remarkably vigorous for his age, 69, and takes the terrible destruction of his railroad very philosophically—'fortune of war'. . . . It was very odd to hear Mr. C. ask General S. in the most unconcerned and business-like way what portions of the railroad we had destroyed and to hear the General detail to him step by step how much had been burned, how thoroughly the rails had been torn up, bent and twisted, etc. He is what is vulgarly called a regular old brick—is Mr. C."

CHAPTER 14

Enemies Drink a Toast

*L*EBANON Plantation played a romantic part in the terms of the
surrender of Fort McAllister, clearing the way for Sherman to enter Savannah
as the climax of his march to the sea. Lebanon, ten miles from Savannah, stands
between the fort and the city.

Now the home of Mrs. Mills B. Lane, this beautiful old plantation was then
owned by the Anderson family. Major George W. Anderson was in command
of the two hundred men defending Fort McAllister on the Ogeechee River.

For a week the major and his brave men withstood a concentrated attack
from gunboats and land batteries. Finally both food and ammunition gave out.

What happened then is told by a prominent Savannah attorney, Shelby
Myrick, who as a young man was frequently invited to Sunday dinner with the
late Colonel Anderson and his wife. Mrs. Anderson was a daughter of Senator
John MacPherson Berrien.

"When the delicious dinner had been served," says Mr. Myrick, "Colonel
Anderson would bring forth fine cigars and a decanter of wine of ancient vintage.
After partaking of both with his guests, he invariably became reminiscent and
often repeated the story of his defense of Fort McAllister . . .

" 'But for the fact that we ran out of food and ammunition, we would have
been in there yet fighting until old Sherman gave up any idea of capturing
Savannah,' he always declared.

" 'At length, rather than see my brave soldiers starved to death, I sent forward
to the Commanding General of the assaulting army a request for a cease fire
and a conference for terms of surrender. At that time I did not know the identity
of the Union General. However, when we met under a flag of truce, I was
amazed and delighted to find facing me an old acquaintance and a former comrade-
in-arms, General William B. Hazen.

FIGURE 25.   North and South dined together at Lebanon Plantation, near Savannah, while the war went on. Lebanon is now owned by Mrs. Mills B. Lane.

"'He greeted me most cordially and we clasped hands as old comrades always do. We discussed at length terms of surrender which we could not at first readily agree upon.

"'I then proposed to him that I and my men would capitulate on one condition only—that the General and his staff come to my home at Lebanon plantation, and allow me and my officers to give a dinner in their honor. My men were to march out with the honors of war and be paroled and I and my officers were to retain our side arms and likewise be paroled.

"'My invitation was immediately accepted and I repaired to Lebanon, along with my staff and General Hazen and his staff. My old servants were still about the place, along with some members of my immediate family. Our silver and wines were brought back from secret hiding places and very soon there was what might be considered a real feast for those days. It was enjoyed by Confederates and Federals alike. Toasts were drunk to my defense of Fort McAllister and to the

91

brave men under my command, and the party broke up with an exchange of felicitations from both sides.' "

If such an aristocratic old house could wink with a sly grin, surely Lebanon would do so at the recollection of another visit by Federal soldiers who came uninvited.

In those days a back road connected Lebanon and Saranac Plantations, and when troops passed along the highway, the Lebanon family silver was jockeyed back and forth over the private road from one house to the other for safety.

An old record describes this latter visit to Lebanon of a Federal captain and a detachment of soldiers.

Excited servants brought word of their approach and the butler was hastily dispatched by the back way to Saranac with the silver. An old white mule carried the load.

Mrs. Anderson then seated herself and reached for her knitting. "When the first saber clanked up the steps, no one would have believed there had been hurry or disturbance that day."

The silver was duly demanded. Mrs. Anderson said, ever so sweetly, "My dear Captain, I think you have been misinformed. No silver is here. Look around and take what you will. Some gossip has directed you to the wrong plantation. You surely do not think that with Colonel Anderson away I would risk living with my priceless treasures surrounded as we are by slaves?"

The captain was not put off so easily. He and his men went through the house and, finding no silver, proceeded to the quarters.

"Sitting in the door of one of the cabins was an old wrinkled black woman, her inscrutable face puckered in an expression that might have been a sneer or a smile, the Lord himself would not have known which. The Captain strode over to her and demanded, 'Aunty, where's the silver?'

" 'Fo Lawd, man, missy done sent Joe off with that stuff years ago to Atlanta or New York or somewhere. If I knew, I'd sho'ly tell you. But, boss, ain't you got something for to cure small pox? My children in this cabin all got it, and I's plum run out of medicine.' "

The captain and his men retreated in some confusion.

Later: "Joe led the old white mule back along the rice bank and Mrs. Anderson enjoyed her tea that afternoon as usual out of the big silver pot."

The house at Lebanon was built in 1804 by James Habersham. In 1806 the property was acquired by George Anderson and although it was lost by the Anderson family after the War Between the States, it was bought back again in 1871. In 1916 it was sold to Mills B. Lane by Mrs. George W. Anderson, Jr.

Built above a raised basement and with a two-story gallery extending across the front and around the sides, Lebanon is similar in design to plantation houses in Mississippi and Louisiana. The slim one-story columns of these double porches are set in pairs and connected by a balustrade. A Georgian wing was added when Mrs. Lane restored the original house. One of the state's finest collections of camellias adds to the beauty of the surrounding park, which reaches all the way to the Little Ogeechee River. The house is beautifully furnished with old furniture of its own period.

Mrs. Lane has copies of the original land grants from George II, one to James Devaux for five hundred acres in September of 1756 and one to Philip Delegal for a like number in March of 1758. Even then the property was called Lebanon.

CHAPTER 15

Savannah Outsmarted Sherman

SHERMAN didn't capture Savannah on that December day in 1864. Savannah captured Sherman.

Sherman himself shared the general misconception of the facts. Grandly ensconced in the imposing Gothic Revival house of Charles Green on Macon Street, he dispatched his historic telegram to President Lincoln:

"I beg to present to you as a Christmas gift the City of Savannah with a hundred and fifty heavy guns and plenty of ammunition also about 25,000 bales of cotton."

What actually happened was that General Sherman got something described in unmilitary language as the "runaround."

That's the way it looks when you take the long view, nearly ninety years later. No doubt, that's the way it looked to certain sagacious Savannah citizens of the time. But Sherman was happy about the whole thing and never knew the difference.

Savannah's businessmen, including the great cotton factors of ante-bellum times, "got together" as Sherman's army approached the city. They had had time to think things over and to take a realistic attitude. They knew that Atlanta had gone up in flames. They knew what had happened in Milledgeville and elsewhere along the march to the sea. They had every cause for apprehension, as was proved later, for after leaving Savannah, Sherman's troops made a bonfire of Columbia, the capital city of South Carolina.

The rush problem of Christmas week in 1864 was to save Savannah, Georgia's most important port city. If cotton and other supplies were burned, the whole town might be wiped out. Fort McAllister had been taken. Confederate General William J. Hardee and his small forces had withdrawn across the Savannah River rather than surrender. . . . Savannah was an open city.

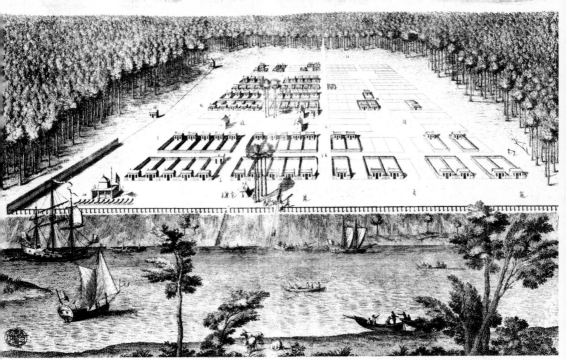

FIGURE 26. This is how Savannah looked on March 29, 1734, with Oglethorpe's tent in the foreground. This lithograph was made from the original in the British Museum for George Wymberly Jones DeRenne in 1876, and was later presented to the Library of Congress.

And so, its businessmen met with Sherman. Knowing he would take the cotton anyway, perhaps burn it, they presented it to him, practically on a silver salver. Charles Green invited the general to use his house as headquarters.

Thus Sherman, to his surprise, was welcomed as a guest; was offered traditional Southern hospitality.

Thus Savannah, exercising diplomatic subtlety with the invaders, also saved face with its own. Mr. Green was not a Southerner. He was a British subject.

The cotton, though confiscated, was saved.

And saved, to charm present-day visitors, was Georgia's beautiful Colonial city, with its lovely old houses which are considered crown jewels in the state's architectural heritage.

Mr. Green gave a New Year party for the general in one of the finest of these houses. With so much military brass in evidence, it was not too noticeable that few civilians were present. General Sherman so enjoyed Savannah that he and his army remained through most of January, 1865, more or less conducting themselves as proper guests, which cannot be said of their stay in any other Georgia town. In his *Memoirs* General Sherman comments on "the good social relations" existing and adds: "I doubt if Savannah either before or since has had a better government than during our stay."

FIGURE 27. Thackeray enjoyed this house in Savannah when he was the guest of Andrew Low in 1856. Today it is the state headquarters of the Colonial Dames. Pictured are house-and-garden-tour hostesses.

Ah, the dear General.

Savannah had put him on the spot. Showing that it expected him to behave as a gentleman, what else could he do? And who, pray, would have created bad "social relations" but the military visitors? Georgia's oldest and proudest city has always been a law unto itself so far as the rest of the state is concerned. The county of which it is the seat of government is known as "the free state of Chatham." But nobody has ever found its citizens lacking in civility.

Savannah simply outsmarted Sherman.

Charles Green, though technically a British subject, had a son in the Confederate army and was himself an ardent Southern sympathizer. His ships ran the blockade all through the war to bring in medical and other supplies from England. He had lived in Savannah since he was seventeen years old. He came over from England as a clerk, remained to amass a fortune in the cotton exporting business and to build one of Savannah's most costly houses. He was the grandfather of present-day writers, Anne and Julian Green, who now live in Paris.

Mr. Green's house, which took eleven years to build, was completed in 1861 on the day Fort Sumter fell. The cost was $93,000. Most of the building material was brought over from England in Mr. Green's own ships.

This impressive American Gothic house with its battlements, oriels and lacy iron verandas is often used by architects as an example illustrating the transition from the classic to the Victorian romantic. Here "the mixture is so frank as to produce a great deal of charm," declares Talbot Hamlin in *The American Spirit in Architecture.*

General Sherman expressed himself as delighted with the "well arranged and well furnished rooms, pictures and statuary." Mr. Green's family was away and Mr. Green explained that he would require only the two rooms over the dining room for himself and his manservant. General Sherman selected "the front room on the second floor to the right of the hall," says Walter Hartridge, Savannah historical writer, who adds that this room was being used at the time by the rector of near-by St. John's Episcopal Church.

"Indignant that a northern general was admitted to the house, the Rev. Mr. McRae made a precipitate departure," Mr. Hartridge records, "leaving in his patriotic haste a marble bust of himself which is still to be seen in a niche in the interior stair well."

Still to be seen in the great formal rooms are the decorative ceiling center-pieces and crystal chandeliers, the white marble mantels with their wide gold-leaf mirrors reaching to the elaborate molded plaster cornices of the high ceilings. Tall pier mirrors, also gold-framed, stand between windows, lightening the effect of carved walnut woodwork. The wide curving marble stairway, with wrought-iron railing, sweeps majestically upward toward a star gleaming in the high dome.

Mr. Green continued to live in the house until his death in 1881, and eleven years later it was sold to Judge Peter Meldrim, one of the South's most distinguished jurists. Here Judge Meldrim entertained President McKinley, Senator Mark Hanna, Major General Fitzhugh Lee and many other noted men of the time.

The judge had four daughters, all attractive, but Sophie was a belle and beauty in the great tradition. Her first marriage to a Yale football star, Ted Coy, was headline news. She is now Mrs. S. M. Shonnard, of New York. Frances married Noble Jones, direct descendant of the Noble Jones who came over with Oglethorpe and founded Wormsloe Plantation, still owned by the family after more than two hundred years. Jane is Mrs. Erastus Hewitt of Cambridge, Massachusetts, and Miss Caroline Meldrim is a leader in that powerful organization which has done so much to preserve historic Savannah—the Colonial Dames.

The Green-Meldrim house, as it is now called, is preserved as the parish house of St. John's Episcopal Church.

If you doubt that Savannah is still one of the most polite cities of modern times, lose your way and ask directions from the first person you meet. Accustomed as you probably are to the pushing, shoving and rude glares common to skyscraper jungles, you receive in Savannah what can only be described as a soothing shock.

In our case, my traveling companion and I, approaching by U. S. Highway

FIGURE 28. Residence of James Barnett, Isle of Hope, Savannah. This antebellum house was built on foundations of the original house, erected in 1740.

80, failed to turn right from Bay Street into Whitaker, which proceeds south into the city of Savannah along an unobstructed thoroughfare. We drove on to Bull Street and soon found ourselves turning first right, then left in order to continue in what otherwise might have been a straight line.

This maneuvering is necessary because of the green, tree-shaded public squares or parks which cut across Bull Street every few blocks. They slow you down—but graciously, for the squares are one of many ingredients in the distilled charm of an old city with a sense of values—a city that has known what to preserve, what to add and what to discard.

The first squares were laid out when the Colony of Georgia was founded by General James Edward Oglethorpe in 1733 and its main street named for his friend, Governor William Bull of South Carolina. Present-day Savannah, a pleasant mixture of mellow old buildings and modern skyscrapers, is one of the few Colonial cities where streets are not a tangle of former lanes and cowpaths. Savannah began with planned streets and a planned economy.

Every now and then business and "progress" raise a hue and cry against the squares, Savannah having become a city with a population of more than 120,000 inhabitants, not counting its many visitors and their automobiles. But happily for the city's scenic heritage, the Colonial Dames stand firm, pointing out that there are plenty of parallel thoroughfares without parks.

Not having taken one of those parallel thoroughfares, we began to feel that it was high time we were getting somewhere, or that maybe we were just going around in circles. And so, at Chippewa Square, with Daniel Chester French's heroic statue of Oglethorpe looming above us, we stopped the car and asked directions. We did not address General Oglethorpe—who was also Sir James—but a colored gentleman, rhythmically engaged with pruning shears.

Sir James himself could not have been more courtly. Straightening up, the interrupted gardener swept off his battered hat and bowed from the waist. "Yes, ma'am," he smiling assured us, "you all goin' the right way. It's just a little piece more along Bull and then you come to Liberty and there's the DeSoto Hotel."

We thanked him and drove on. We could almost see the red carpet spread out in front of the car and there was no doubt that in our hands we now held the keys to the city. In Savannah we lost our way frequently after that. It was always such an agreeable experience.

Savannah has a large Negro population—nearly 50 per cent of its inhabitants. It was one of the first cities in the South to swear in Negro policemen for Negro sections. This is one of many manifestations of Savannah's independent spirit as a city that existed before Georgia became a state. Long after its first skyscrapers were built, Savannah still held to the old Southern custom of shutting up shop in the middle of the day and going home for lunch and a siesta, after which business was resumed as usual. It is said that Savannah ignored with a fine disdain both the national prohibition amendment and the surreptitious speak-easy so common elsewhere.

This self-sufficient spirit is further reflected in Savannah's Independent Presbyterian Church, established in 1755 and at that time a branch of the Church of Scotland. To this day it remains independent of the General Presbytery. Woodrow Wilson married Ellen Axson, granddaughter of one of its ministers, in the old manse, since replaced by an auxiliary building. The present church building, erected in 1889, is famous for the beauty of its architecture, a combination of Georgian with Doric columns and a Christopher Wren spire.

Even John Wesley might have been more popular in Savannah if he had concerned himself less with the daily lives of the congregation of Christ Episcopal Church, which dates from 1733. The beautiful old Greek Revival church of today is the third to stand on the site. Here Wesley organized in 1736 what is believed to be the first Protestant Sunday school in the world. Although he and his brother

FIGURE 29. This old brick house in Savannah was the home of General Lachlan McIntosh, who entertained George Washington and fought a famous duel. Georgia's first legislature met here.

Charles laid the foundations of Methodism, they died members of the Anglican Church.

John Wesley was a great and godly man, but he seems not to have got along very well with his Colonial parishioners, nor yet with the Indians. The course of his love affair with Sophie Hopkey ran no more smoothly. She married another man and Wesley refused her the holy sacrament in church. He had been indicted on ten counts by the civil authorities for "interference in secular affairs" when he hurriedly took ship for England.

Just as Savannah itself is different from any other town in Georgia, so its old houses are different. Many of them are built flush with the sidewalk, their walled gardens shaded by giant live oaks, garlanded with gray Spanish moss. Some of the houses have ornamental iron-grille balconies, and porches which help to create an atmosphere akin to that of Charleston or New Orleans.

Here, in spite of fires in 1759 and 1796, you see more of old England than anywhere else in the state—Georgian architecture, Regency, Victorian. On some streets, blocks of three-story Victorian houses stand in close formation, their high stoops opening onto the sidewalk. Here are Greek Revival houses too, but seldom of the temple type with two-story columns so popular in the up-country.

Many new as well as many old Savannah houses are built of that famous gray brick made of gray clay in the kilns at Hermitage Plantation, just outside the city on the Savannah River, now the site of a paper-bag factory. This gray brick is fought over not only by Savannahians but also by avid builders throughout the state when an old Savannah house is dismantled.

Mr. and Mrs. Raymond Demere spent five years collecting this brick, also the antique paneling and wide floor boards with which to build their beautiful new-old house with its two-story white-columned galleries and "welcoming-arms" double flight of steps. It is called Harrington Hall after the home of Georgia's first Raymond Demere, a captain on General Oglethorpe's staff.

Henry Ford bought the original Hermitage Plantation house in 1934 and used the bricks to build another house on his plantation near Ways, Georgia. The Hermitage, designed in the Regency manner by its ante-bellum owner, Henry McAlpin, was one of the most beautiful houses in the South. Savannah hoped Mr. Ford would reproduce it from the old bricks, but he did not.

Mr. Ford did reproduce two of the Hermitage slave houses which may be seen at Dearborn, Michigan. Hermitage slave quarters are described by a Federal visitor who arrived with Sherman: "There are about 70 or 80 Negro houses, all built of brick and whitewashed, so they look very neat, and rows of live oaks between, making it the handsomest plantation I've seen in Georgia. They keep about 400 hands at work burning brick and made a large fortune at it too." One of the first horse-drawn railroad cars on a flanged track was used by Henry McAlpin for hauling bricks at this plantation.

A fortune in gold was once concealed in the cistern of a McAlpin town house at 230 Barnard Street. This handsome Regency structure with Corinthian columns and double-curved sandstone steps was designed by Henry McAlpin in 1835 for Aaron Champion, a wealthy banker, whose daughter married Mr. McAlpin's son. As Sherman's forces approached Savannah, Mr. Champion cautiously lowered his gold into the cistern. At a later date he drained the cistern and recovered all but one ten-dollar gold piece.

Although the Hermitage now exists only in photographs and in measured drawings in the Library of Congress, you find that suburban life in Savannah may still mean residence on other near-by ante-bellum plantations, perhaps with private hunting preserves. Or it may mean living on an island, with fishing from your own front porch. One of the links with Savannah's delightfully different suburbs is Victory Drive, palm-fringed and azalea-hedged for six miles. Victory Drive and twenty-two-acre Forsyth Park put on their own spectacular azalea show each spring.

Ward McAllister, social arbiter of Newport and New York in the Gay Nineties, who coined the phrase, "the Four Hundred," when he selected that number of guests for a ball given by Mrs. William Astor, grew up in Savannah, which has always had a gay social life. When George Washington visited the city in 1791, he wrote afterward of having met a hundred handsome and handsomely dressed ladies at a dance. An Atlanta bride who married into a prominent Savannah family just prior to World War I says her husband insisted she buy a new gown for each of the seven dances given that winter by the exclusive Cotillion Club.

William Gaston, who never allowed a stranger to stay in a hotel, best illustrates the proud hospitality of Savannah's old houses. Always such visitors were entertained in Mr. Gaston's own home. When John James Audubon came to the city in 1831, seeking subscriptions for his projected book, *Birds of America*, he first went to call on Mr. Gaston. Subscriptions were a thousand dollars each. Gaston not only subscribed but took Audubon to call on other businessmen from whom he obtained six additional subscriptions.

When William Gaston died and was buried far from Savannah, his fellow townsmen erected in his memory the vault that stands near the entrance of beautiful tree-shaded, moss-draped Bonaventure Cemetery. It is a receiving vault, for the benefit of strangers who may happen to die in Savannah.

At the time of Audubon's visit, he and William Gaston made one of their subscription calls at what is now known as the Pink House, so called because the stucco which covers its brick has been turned pink by time. Originally this charming old Georgian structure at 23 Abercorn Street was the home of James Habersham, Jr., who acquired the site in 1771 and built the house in 1789. But when Messrs. Audubon and Gaston walked up the steps of its pillared portico and through its fanlighted doorway, the former residence had become the business house of the Planters Bank of the State of Georgia. Mr. Gaston was one of the directors. It is believed that the portico, window lintels and a new wing were added by the bank sometime after purchasing the property in 1812. The Pink House is now a tea room.

"The most comfortable quarters I have ever had in the United States," declared Thackeray in 1856 in a letter written while he was the Savannah guest of Andrew Low, "of the great house of A. Low & Co., cotton dealers, brokers, merchants, what's the word? They are tremendous men, these cotton merchants."

The word Thackeray wanted was cotton "factor," a term that gave the buildings along Savannah's picturesque water front the name of Factor's Row. The city stands on a bluff above the Savannah River, and these old red brick buildings rising up from river level are approached from Bay Street by iron bridges high above the cobblestone ramps leading to the docks. Savannah's large export business is now more varied and one of the old cotton warehouses has been converted into studios for members of a flourishing art colony.

FIGURE 30. This was the girl-hood home of Juliette Gordon, in Savannah. She later married Willie Low and founded the Girl Scouts. It was built in 1821.

Thackeray came to Savannah on a lecture tour that included most of the important cities of the East and along the Atlantic seaboard. It was his second visit to Georgia and both times he had been a guest of Mr. Low in the latter's handsome brick and stucco, iron-balconied house at 329 Abercorn, built about 1840.

Thackeray describes Savannah as a "tranquil old city, wide streeted, tree shaded." The Regency desk at which the English author handled his correspondence still stands in the drawing room of the Low house. In this same room Juliette Gordon Low founded the Girl Scouts in 1912.

Robert E. Lee was a guest here in 1870, renewing old friendships made when he came to Savannah in 1829, fresh from West Point, to supervise the building of Fort Pulaski, named in honor of Count Pulaski, one of Savannah's Revolutionary heroes.

The Low house, secluded by an old garden and iron picket fence, maintains its character and its dignity as state headquarters of the Colonial Dames.

Juliette Gordon, who went there to live when she married Willie Low, grew up in another fine old house at the corner of Bull and Oglethorpe. This is the former residence of W. W. Gordon, built in 1821, a stucco Regency house with a four-columned Grecian portico and the double flight of steps which distinguish so many Savannah houses. President McKinley and President Taft were entertained here.

Presidents are no novelty in Savannah. George Washington was the first to

FIGURE 31. LaFayette's Balcony. William Jay's combination of Grecian details with Regency architecture is beautifully illustrated in this Savannah house built in 1818 at 124 Abercorn Street.

visit the city, and President Monroe came down in 1818 to take a round trip to Tybee Island on the *Savannah*, the first steamship to cross the Atlantic.

Washington stayed at the Lachlan McIntosh house, which is linked with Georgia's most famous duel.

This encounter between General Lachlan McIntosh and Button Gwinnett, one of Georgia's three signers of the Declaration of Independence, grew out of political rivalry. Early on a May morning in 1777 the two met with their seconds near Savannah's old Colonial Cemetery.

They stood only four paces apart, about twelve feet, and fired at the same time. Each was wounded in the thigh. "Mr. Gwinnett's thigh broke so that he fell . . . the General asked him if he chose to take another shot, was answered yes, if they would help him up . . . the seconds interposed . . . Mr. Gwinnett was brought in, the weather extremely hot . . . a mortification came on . . . he languished from that morning [Friday] till Monday morning following and expired."

Such strong resentment was aroused by Gwinnett's death that McIntosh was tried in court, but he was acquitted. He then asked for transfer to the Northern fighting forces where he served with distinction under Washington.

Although the code duello was outlawed in Georgia in 1809, gentlemen of the state continued for many years to uphold their honor with coffee and pistols at dawn. In time it became the custom for both parties to shoot high and shake hands afterward, according to Thomas Gamble, author of *Savannah Duels and Duellists, 1733–1877.*

The Lachlan McIntosh house, built about 1764, is believed to be the oldest brick house still standing in the state. Georgian in style, with an iron-grille balcony added at a later date, its charm survives though the neighborhood of 110 E. Oglethorpe has changed. Before the Revolution the house was known as Eppinger's Inn; and sometime after the British were chased out of Savannah, it came into the possession of McIntosh. Here, in the "Long Room" of this one-time tavern, Georgia's first legislature met in 1782. Here, in 1791, George Washington was a guest.

Button Gwinnett's charming dormer-windowed house still stands on St. Catherines Island, near Savannah. Because of the rarity of Gwinnett's signature, his name on an old document owned by the State of Georgia has an appraised value of $50,000.

The house in which President Monroe visited is one of Savannah's three best surviving examples of the work of William Jay. This gifted young Englishman who came to visit his sister, Mrs. Robert Bolton, in 1818, and stayed until 1825, left an indelible impression on American architecture, both in Savannah and in Charleston.

President Monroe walked up the steps of a Jay house—Regency with Doric columns—at 111 West Broad Street, as the guest of its owner, William Scarborough. Mr. Scarborough was one of a group of businessmen who financed the building of the steamship *Savannah* and its record-making voyage across the Atlantic in 1819. The President came down for the launching of the new vessel and was taken aboard for a round trip to Tybee Island. Mr. Scarborough's house is now a public school building for Negroes.

Regarded as the masterpiece of all the houses designed by William Jay is the home of the late Miss Margaret Thomas, at 124 Abercorn, overlooking Oglethorpe Square. Miss Thomas's grandfather, George W. Owens, bought the house in 1830, complete with original furnishings and a portrait of LaFayette who was a guest here in 1825. When Miss Thomas died in December of 1951 her will bore testimony that she hoped her home might be maintained "as is," for she left it to the Telfair Academy of Arts and Sciences.

Beautifully illustrated in this house is Jay's method of combining the Regency period with Grecian details, "elaborately, delicately, exquisitely." This, the first of his houses, was built in 1818.

Young Mr. Jay was only twenty-three when he arrived in Georgia, attractive and witty and soon very popular in Savannah society. When Robert Bolton's sister married Richard Richardson, Jay was commissioned to design their house. As a result, the already sought-after visitor became equally popular as an architect.

Now faded a pale lemon color, the lovely old stucco house stands aloof behind its balustrade and screen of shrubbery. In spring the fragrance of blossoming pittosporum floats out as you pause to look before opening the iron gate.

The Ionic portico curves slightly to conform to an arched doorway and is approached by a curving double flight of steps with a delicate outside iron railing. Just above the portico is a fanlighted window and above this a pointed pediment. All the upstairs windows are arched; the cornice of the portico extends around the middle of the house which has quoined corners. The effect is classic simplicity.

LaFayette stood on the side balcony and greeted an admiring public. This balcony, all of cast iron, is one of the most exquisitely elaborate combinations of Grecian detail to be found in America. Composite columns and pilasters support an entablature topped by a cornice adorned with both cresting and pendants. The columns themselves are linked by a lacy iron grille. Spaced directly beneath these four fluted columns rise the balcony supports—four tall acanthus leaves embedded in the wall base of an iron picket fence.

Inside the front entrance hall of the house, a brass-inlaid double stairway is set between gold-capped Corinthian columns. This double stairway leads to the front section of the upstairs hall which is connected to the back hall by a little arched bridge across the stairwell.

Delicate cane-seated Regency chairs, as old as the house, marble-topped consoles with brass mountings and gold mirrors, these and other lovely pieces adorn the parlor downstairs. On either side of the classic white marble mantel are oval niches for books. The ceiling has a Greek key-relief border, rounded at the corners, which have their own fan-shaped plaster ornamentation.

Just the right glow for a room in which LaFayette dined is shed by light strained through a wide amber-lined Greek key fret above a side wall niche in the dining room. Within the niche is a buffet, supported by a single pedestal, on which is displayed some of Miss Thomas's matchless collection of Bohemian glass. It seems just the right room too for LaFayette's portrait, which hangs above the beautiful Duncan Phyfe sideboard against the opposite wall.

The dining room is the largest room in the house and the walls at the fireplace end are curved. Even the wide doors on each side of the black marble mantel follow the arc. The high ceiling has a decorative plaster cornice and the wide polished floor boards alternate dark and light woods.

Another fine example of the work of William Jay stands at 121 Barnard Street. The old Telfair house, with its Corinthian portico and other Grecian detail, is now the Telfair Academy of Arts and Sciences. Most of the original Telfair furniture remains as a setting for a fine collection of paintings, statuary and other exhibits. Thirty guests could sit at the old dining table, and often did

FIGURE 32. Regency Parlor. These and other original furnishings were preserved by the late Miss Margaret Thomas, whose grandfather bought the house at 124 Abercorn Street, Savannah in 1830.

when Alexander Telfair, son of Governor Edward Telfair, presided at its head in the large room where the table still stands.

The oldest Savannah garden which retains its original design and planting still flourishes behind a high brick wall at 119 Charlton Street. Here the house, built about 1849 by William Battersby, has a side-porch entrance flush with the street and two-story galleries overlooking the garden. Camellias, tea olive, Jacqueminot roses and lilac begonia planted by Mrs. Battersby have been cherished by succeeding owners, Julian Hartridge, Mrs. J. J. Wilder, Mrs. Randolph Anderson and now William Murphey.

One of Savannah's most impressive Victorian houses is preserved at 450 Bull Street as quarters for the Oglethorpe Club, an exclusive men's organization. This was once the home of Confederate General Henry R. Jackson, who earlier served as minister plenipotentiary to Austria and to Mexico and was author of the familiar poem, "The Red Old Hills of Georgia."

Two houses illustrating the contrast in homes that succeeded Savannah's first pioneer dwellings are the Giles Becu house at 120 West Oglethorpe Avenue and the Isaiah Davenport house at 324 East State Street. The Becu house is a small two-story wooden structure with chamfered porch posts built soon after the lot was acquired in 1775. Aaron Burr, while Vice President of the United States, visited his aunt, a Mrs. Montmillion, in this house in 1802. Dating from about the same period is the Davenport house, a large impressive three-dormered Georgian structure built of brick brought over from England.

Savannah's very first Colonial residence stood at the site marked by a marble bench in the small park at Yamacraw Bluff on West Bay Street. Oglethorpe pitched camp on this spot after making friends with Tomochichi, chief of the Yamacraws. Mary Musgrove, the half-breed Indian girl who operated a trading post on the Savannah River, acted as interpreter.

Today you marvel at the optimism of Oglethorpe's double-barreled objective, philanthropic and military, to be worked out here in the wilderness inhabited by Indians. With him in the little ship *Anne*, had come thirty-five families, or about 130 persons. Some were men of position, some were handpicked from among the many worthy persons suffering from the unjust debt laws then existing in England. All the men had been grounded in military training. For most of them the colony meant new opportunity. For England the Thirteenth Colony meant a new bulwark against attack by Spain along the southern boundaries of its American possessions.

Soon Georgia attracted various religious groups and other substantial settlers from across the ocean, including a company of Scottish Highlanders, who in 1742 helped to win the Battle of Bloody Marsh at St. Simons Island, ending further threat of Spanish aggression.

Today a colorful restoration project reminds you that the planned economy of the new colony failed, although the colony itself prospered. This is Trustees Garden Village on East Broad Street, named in honor of the English trustees who originally governed the colony. Here the Trustees Garden Club has replanted the experimental garden by which the trustees hoped to establish a new source of spices, wine and silk for England.

Here still standing is the simple frame building from which Sir Hans Sloane sold herbs grown in what he called his Physics garden in Chelsea. Alongside is the old pirate's house, in which Captain Flint is said to have died, gasping, "Darby, bring aft the rum."

All of this would make General Oglethorpe feel right at home, for it duplicates a description given by Francis Moore in his *Voyage to Georgia* in 1735.

"The town of Savannah is built of wood," he wrote. "Some houses are two or three stories high, the boards planed and painted; the houses stand on large lots, 60 feet in front by 90 in depth. Each lot has a fore and back street; the lots are fenced with split pales . . . the streets are very wide and there are four great

Photo by Kenneth Rogers

FIGURE 33. Liberty Street, typical old Savannah.

squares left at proper distances for markets and other conveniences." The squares also served as a place of refuge for settlers in outlying areas in case of Indian or Spanish attack.

From this original Savannah went silk for a dress which Queen Caroline of England wore at court in 1735. But the silk industry itself was soon given up in Georgia as unprofitable.

In time the Thirteenth Colony became a Royal Province with a resident Royal Governor. How he got his walking papers is told by a D. A. R. marker at the corner of Broughton and Whitaker Streets:

"On this site stood in Colonial times Tondee's Tavern where gathered the Sons of Liberty."

Georgia was joining the Revolution.

Georgia was the fourth colony admitted to statehood in the Union. But Savannah was a self-sufficient city with a proud tradition long before Georgia became a state.

Sherman took Georgia, but Savannah took Sherman.

CHAPTER 16

The Great Plantations

*F*ROM the Savannah River to the St. Marys—here were Georgia's great coastal and sea-island plantations of Colonial and ante-bellum times. Some of them remain, some are ruins, some are remembered by old landmarks.

A chapel built because of a plantation duel—the chimney of an old rice mill— a granite marker on a battlesite where the history of the New World was changed —a fashionable golf clubhouse that was once a plantation barn—an old slave cabin. These are a few of the reminders.

As you drive south from Savannah, along the coastal highway, the Golden Isles of Georgia lie off the mainland to your left—"like a string of emeralds, Tybee Wassaw, Ossabaw, St. Catherines, Sapelo, St. Simons, Jekyll and Cumberland." Between these sea islands and the mainland are the quiet waters of the Inland Passage and long stretches of green salt marsh. On their other side is the boundless Atlantic.

There is a persistent legend that the Spanish were first to call them Golden Isles—the Golden Isles of Guale. We know that Sir Robert Montgomery, a Scotsman, described them as golden in a pamphlet he wrote in 1717 when he dreamed of establishing here his New World Utopia, the Margravate of Azilia.

Certain it is that the Spanish had discovered their charm and desirability long before. Pedro Menendez de Aviles, Spanish governor of year-old St. Augustine, traveled up the coast in 1566 with fifty men and was received on St. Catherines Island by an old Indian chief called Guale (pronounced Wally). Menendez wrote that they sat on the beach and ate biscuits and honey.

Here in 1568 was established the first of those Spanish missions in which the cross and the sword went hand in hand—priests to serve as missionaries, soldiers to

FIGURE 34. The house at Wormsloe Plantation, on the Isle of Hope, built on the foundations of the original house. This is Georgia's oldest plantation continuously owned by descendants of the original settler. Noble Jones received his land grant in 1733.

protect the priests from the Indians and to plant the flag of Spain ever farther and farther northward.

Sometimes the Indians went on a rampage and wiped out all evidences of these Spanish settlements—all but the fig trees, ancestors of those that furnish one of Georgia's most delectable fruits today. Sometimes ruins of the missions were left. But always the priests came back, first the Jesuits, then the Franciscans. They came back for more than a hundred years.

There was a time when pirates used the islands as hideouts. Treasure is still buried there.

The last slave ship, the *Wanderer*, landed its then illegal cargo on Jekyll Island in 1858.

And at Eboe's Landing on St. Simons Island is summed up the whole great tragedy of slavery, which ended finally in warfare and that other great tragedy called the Reconstruction Era.

The coastal and sea island plantations naturally were the first to be settled after James Edward Oglethorpe founded the Colony of Georgia in 1733 at Savannah. Among the very first of these plantations was Wormsloe, which was given a name that ties in with the original economic plan of the colony—the raising of silk worms and the manufacture of silk.

Around and about Savannah are other plantations dating back to Colonial times, plantations with such charming names as Laurel Green, Avon Hall, Lebanon, Whitehall, Grove Point, etc. But Wormsloe on the Isle of Hope, seven miles from town, is the oldest plantation in Georgia continuously owned by the same family. At Wild Heron, also near Savannah, stands what is believed to be the oldest plantation house in the state. At Altama, near Darien, is the dower house of Hopeton, one of the South's most famous plantations, visited and written about by various important travelers from abroad in the ante-bellum period.

Near St. Marys is The Refuge, a plantation house built by John Houstoun McIntosh, who at one time was head of the Republic of Florida. He owned other plantations near St. Marys, plantations which are part of a mystery, its answer buried deep by time.

Within the town itself is Orange Hall, a Greek Revival house, dreaming on a wide street that ends at the river docks just before the river joins the sea. St. Marys was an important seaport when the house was built, but there are older houses still standing here. Aaron Burr visited in one of them and the inn was once a smuggler's hideout, so they say.

Just a water jump from St. Marys is Cumberland Island, site of Dungeness, the former Nathanael Greene plantation, now owned by the Carnegie family.

From the Savannah River to the St. Marys, these—and Sapelo—are the most notable of the plantations that remain.

A girl named Mary Jones once held the fort at Wormsloe Plantation when it was temporarily without masculine protection.

She was the daughter of Noble Jones, who came over with Oglethorpe. Noble Jones was captain of a company of rangers stationed at Fort Wimberly on the Wormsloe property to guard the narrows of the Skidaway River.

The original Wormsloe tract, comprising five hundred acres, on the Isle of Hope near Savannah, was granted to Noble Jones by the trustees of the colony in 1733. This grant was later increased to eight hundred acres and confirmed by the Crown in 1756. From 1733 to the present time Wormsloe has remained in the same family. It is now owned by Mrs. Craig Barrow, a direct descendant of Noble Jones.

Fort Wimberly at Wormsloe began as a wooden structure, replaced in 1741 by a tabby building, approximately three hundred feet square with walls eight feet high. This is the fort once held by Mary Jones, according to a story that has come down in the family, a story unfortunately lacking in details. You may still see the embrasures through which Mary fired the cannon.

Mary's brother, named for his father, helped to organize the Sons of Liberty at Tondee's Tavern in Savannah prior to the Revolution. At Fort Wimberly the Liberty Boys broke open a captured British powder magazine and sent a part of the powder North, where it was used at Bunker Hill. Later still in the history of Fort Wimberly, a Confederate battalion stationed here prevented Federal ships from passing along the inland waterway.

The pioneer house at Wormsloe was replaced by a more imposing structure which was later destroyed by fire. The present house rests on the old tabby foundations and its fine marble mantels are ante-bellum. So are its handsome furnishings and the fine family portraits painted by Charles Wilson Peale and Rembrandt Peale.

Wormsloe has perhaps the most impressive grounds of any house in Georgia. Turning right from the highway into a palm-lined drive, you enter through the great arched gateway a mile-long avenue of live oaks leading to a twenty-acre park of these same trees. Here the ground is carpeted with Algerian ivy which twines itself upward around the tree trunks. High overhead the great spreading branches of these trees are draped with streamers of gray Spanish moss. In springtime, color breaks out aloft—the purple of climbing wisteria. To this is added the stately beauty of camellia-japonica trees starred with white, pink and red blossoms and the riotous spectacle of great azalea hedges abloom in mass formation.

This park is the dramatic setting for a beautiful three-story white-columned house which faces the Skidaway River and its private yacht landing. Behind the house is a series of walled formal gardens. There is yet an added enchantment if you can sit quietly on the porch until you yourself become a part of the serenity of your surroundings. Like silence made manifest, deer steal out of the woods to nibble at the ivy.

Although the silk industry soon proved impractical for the new colony, one of the old mulberry trees, planted to furnish food for silk worms, still stands at Wormsloe.

The first Noble Jones became chief justice of the Colony of Georgia, and his son, Dr. Noble Jones, was first president of the Georgia Medical Society. George

FIGURE 35. Wild Heron, near Savannah, is believed the oldest plantation house in Georgia. Built in 1756 by Francis Harris, it is now owned by Shelby Myrick.

Wymberly Jones DeRenne, who was born Jones, decided to adopt a modification of the name of his grandmother, Van Deren, and so the family name became DeRenne.

Mr. DeRenne assembled a fine ante-bellum library at Wormsloe which was destroyed by the bummers in Sherman's army. He immediately set about the collection of another. This was willed by his son, Everard, to the State Library of Georgia. The collector's instinct cropped out again in 1891, when Wymberly Jones DeRenne began one of the state's finest collections of Georgiana—old documents, manuscripts, engravings and other rare historical material. For the protection of this library, as well as suitable display space, he erected a separate templelike fireproof building at Wormsloe. This priceless collection is now at Athens, housed in the University of Georgia library, of which the collector's son, Wymberly Wormsloe DeRenne, is archivist.

What is believed to be the oldest plantation house still standing in Georgia was built in 1756 at Wild Heron Plantation twelve miles from Savannah on the Grove River.

It is a charming story-and-a-half Colonial farm house built above a brick basement. The sloping roof with dormer windows extends over the slim columned porch, which has a flight of steps at each end.

Until bought in 1935 for a country home by Mr. and Mrs. Shelby Myrick of Savannah, Wild Heron Plantation had remained in the same family since 1755, when it was granted by George II of England to Francis Harris.

The original land grant, specifying one thousand acres, more or less, bounded by the Little Ogeechee River, was carried off by one of Sherman's soldiers in 1864. In 1909 it was returned from the North to the postmaster at Savannah, who restored it to Mrs. Robert Hull, a several times great-granddaughter of Francis Harris. Now framed under glass, the interesting old document hangs on the living-room wall of the plantation house.

Francis Harris, according to family records, went back to England and married a rich widow. She it was who named the Georgia plantation after an ancestral English estate. Plantation Negroes slurred the name until Wild Heron became Wild Hern or Wild Horn, and so the place was called for nearly a hundred years. But Mrs. Myrick, delving into Harris family history, discovered the original name and changed it back again.

The Myricks made no changes in restoring the old house except to squeeze in closets and bathrooms. The brick brought over from England, the hand-hewn timbers and most of the wide flooring are still intact.

Special parts had to be cast in order to recondition the huge iron stove, in the basement kitchen, which has St. George and the Dragon over its oven doors. But Mary, the cook, a descendant of former slaves at Wild Heron, declares that her shrimp pilau is better when cooked "slow" on this stove, rather than on the modern electric range which keeps it company. Shrimp pilau is a famous party dish in Savannah and no one excels Mary in its preparation.

The tall palm tree at the southeast corner of the house was planted in 1780 by Elizabeth Harris, first bride of the plantation. The cassina hedges are also old and the snowdrops have been there longer than the oldest servants can remember. The scuppernong arbors still furnish fruit for wine and jelly. Around all this, Mrs. Myrick has built just the right garden for a river plantation house.

About halfway between Savannah and Darien you come to Midway in Liberty County, with its historic old church established in 1752 by Puritans who emigrated to Georgia by way of Connecticut and South Carolina. Puritans though they were, they became slave owners too, as the slave balcony in the church bears witness to this day. British soldiers burned the first church building and the Federal army used the present white frame, steepled structure as a slaughterhouse in the eighteen sixties.

Restored long ago, Midway church is today considered Georgia's cradle of liberty. Two Signers of the Declaration of Independence—Lyman Hall and Button Gwinnett—were among its small flock, as were many of the Liberty Boys. In Midway's near-by cemetery are buried "two Generals of the Revolution, a United States Senator, a commodore, a scientist of world fame and the Georgia ancestors of a president of the United States—Theodore Roosevelt." From Midway, the LeConte brothers went west and founded the University of California.

Darien is next along your route, a seafaring town founded in 1736 by Scottish Highlanders led by John Mohr McIntosh, Hugh Mackay and the Reverend John MacLeod, who immediately established here a Presbyterian church. Margery McIntosh, granddaughter of clan leader John Mohr, married James Spalding. Their son, Thomas, built the great South End house on Sapelo Island, off the coast at Darien, now owned by Richard J. Reynolds and described in another chapter of this book.

At Darien you cross the wide Altamaha River and Butler Island, where English actress Fanny Kemble spent a part of the winter of 1838–39. It was then a rice plantation owned by her husband, Pierce Butler. An old rice-mill chimney, vine covered, is visible from the highway.

One of Georgia's most interesting plantations lies off to the right of this highway, after you leave Darien, traveling south into Glynn County.

This is Altama, which includes within its 6,500 acres the once-celebrated Hopeton and other ante-bellum plantation lands. The Hopeton house no longer exists, but Altama, built as a dower house, still stands amidst its immense solitude.

Hopeton made a profound impression upon the Honorable Amelia Murray, lady-in-waiting to Queen Victoria, when she was a guest here of the James Hamilton Couper family in February of 1855. Indirectly, this trip was responsible for the Honorable Amelia's resignation from her position at court. She wished to publish her *Letters from the United States, Cuba and Canada*. What she saw of the administration of slavery at Hopeton was at wide variance with the stories of abuse she had heard in England. Queen Victoria was known to be strongly opposed to slavery, and in her letters the Honorable Amelia had written frankly. To avoid any embarrassment, she resigned her position as lady-in-waiting to the queen.

The land approach to Altama is by way of a mile-long driveway through a wooded area. The water approach as described by the Honorable Amelia Murray is more picturesque:

"A four-oared canoe-like boat of Mr. Hamilton Couper's had come down [to Darien] from his plantation on the Altamaha. . . . After a very pleasant row of

FIGURE 36. Altama, built as a dower house on the great Hopeton Plantation in Glynn County. The original Hopeton house no longer stands.

about five miles he [Mr. Couper] brought us to his English-like house (as respects the interior) and interesting home, my first resident introduction to plantation life.

"A happy attached negro population surrounds his abode. I never saw servants in any old English family more comfortable or more devoted. It is quite a relief to see anything so patriarchal, after the apparently uncomfortable relations of masters and servants in the Northern states. I should much prefer being a 'slave' here to a grumbling saucy 'help' there, but everyone to their tastes.

"We left the river about a quarter of a mile from the house and came up a narrow canal, between rice plantings, almost to the door. We passed two or three large flat boats, laden with rice, and Mr. Couper took me to see the threshing machine which was at work in the barn; the women putting in the rice just as we do our grain. They were more comfortably dressed than our peasantry, and looked happier. Otherwise (except the complexions), the scene was much the same kind as that at a threshing barn in England."

Both Hopeton and Altama, as well as Christ Church in Savannah were designed by James Hamilton Couper, who for more than forty years managed the two-thousand-acre Hopeton Plantation owned by his father, John Couper, and his father's great friend, James Hamilton. When he inherited his father's plantation, Cannon's Point on St. Simons Island, James Hamilton Couper had the supervision (in the combined estates) of 1,500 slaves.

Mr. Couper took over the management of Hopeton in 1816. An old painting shows that the house erected there was patterned after an Italian villa, with wide galleries overlooking the Altamaha River. This is the broadsweeping tidal river associated with the mystery of the "Lost Gordonia." This is the river which also inspired Goldsmith, in faraway England, to write somewhat inaccurately:

> Through torrid tracts with fainting steps they go,
> Where wild Altama murmurs to their woe;
> Where at each step the stranger fears to wake
> The rattling terrors of the vengeful snake.

The dower house at Hopeton, built about 1855, was given the name used by Goldsmith—Altama. It has an arched portico and bears a family resemblance to the Hopeton house, though it is not so large. Both were built of tabby, that enduring mixture of seashells, lime, sand and water. In later years this and other property was acquired by William DuPont, who used it as a hunting preserve. Later still it was bought by Cator Woolford, of Atlanta, who gave a part of the land to the state for Santo Domingo Park. For a number of years now Altama has been owned by Alfred W. Jones of Sea Island.

Among the many prominent visitors entertained at Hopeton was Sir Charles Lyell. In his *Second Visit to the United States of North America* he records his favorable impressions of Mr. Couper's system of plantation management. At Hopeton, as on other well-run estates, certain slaves were trained as cabinet-makers, carpenters, mechanics, etc., just as some of the women were taught spinning, weaving, sewing and other handicrafts.

"When his mechanics come to consult Mr. Couper on business," wrote Sir Charles, "their manner of speaking to him is quite as independent as that of English artisans to their employers . . ."

Of the plantation-owning class in general, Sir Charles observed:

"There is a warm and generous openness of character in the southerners which mere wealth and a retinue of servants cannot give and they have often a dignity of manner without stiffness which is most agreeable. The landed proprietors here visit each other in the style of English country gentlemen, sometimes dining out with their families and returning at night or, if the distance be great, remaining to sleep and coming home the next morning."

One of the great plantation sports of that time was river-boat racing, with an annual regatta. One year the prize money ran as high as ten thousand dollars.

These racing boats were great hollowed-out cypress logs, twenty-five to fifty feet long, manned by slave crews, who swung the oars in rhythm with the songs they chanted. Usually the plantation owner served as coxswain.

James Hamilton Couper had good news of the 1852 regatta to send his son, then in New York:

"I telegraphed you, mentioning the victory of the Becky. She was the admired of all admirers, her fame is spread far and wide and she deserves her reputation. . . . She made the distance of a mile, less twelve yards, in six minutes, without pressing the crew. She rode the water like a duck with a continuous gliding motion. . . . Her crew of eight was altogether cool and not a false stroke was made. It was a pleasure to sit behind them. The whole regatta has been a brilliant affair and I doubt whether so many fine boats were ever brought together, certainly not in America."

Before he began his plantation career Mr. Couper was graduated with honors from Yale. Afterward he visited his uncle in Glasgow, and from Scotland went to Holland to study diking in order to drain the swamps and deltas of his family's Georgia plantations. Many planters in turn came to Hopeton to inspect the drainage system he installed there.

John Couper, his father, had practiced rotation and diversification of crops at Cannon's Point on St. Simons Island before 1800, and James Hamilton Couper carried these scientific experiments farther at Hopeton. In 1832 he was visited by J. D. LeGare, editor of the *Southern Agriculturist*, who declared Hopeton to be the best plantation he had ever seen. At that time five hundred acres were planted in rice, 170 in cotton and 333 in sugar cane.

Several years earlier Mr. Couper had imported machinery from England for a sugar mill. In 1834 he equipped a cottonseed-oil mill in Mobile. He was, perhaps, the first to extract oil from cottonseed, but this early venture was not a financial success.

Nor were plantation profits ever a certain thing. They might rise to fabulous heights in good years but there were poor years too when the planter was "carried" by his cotton factor—a commission merchant in Charleston or Savannah. At Hopeton, over a forty-year period, the average annual profit, according to *A Social History of the Sea Islands*, was 4.37 per cent.

The mystery of the Lost Gordonia or Franklinia, is much older than Altama.

John Bartram, the famous botanist, and his son William visited Georgia in 1765 and discovered—growing wild in great profusion on the banks of the Altamaha River—a new species of Gordonia. This is a shrub of the tea family bearing a rich blossom somewhat similar to the camellia and gardenia. Bartram carried plants for propagation back to his botanical garden in Philadelphia, naming his discovery Franklinia Alatamaha, for his friend, Benjamin Franklin.

In 1774, the son, William Bartram, again visited Georgia and saw the shrub, growing wild to tree size, in the same general locality

No botanist since that time has been able to spot the Gordonia (or Franklinia) in a wild state in native habitat. All the existing cultivated plants were propagated from the one taken home from Georgia by Bartram in 1774.

What caused the disappearance of the wild Gordonia is one of the mysteries of the botanical world. Certainly its rediscovery would be a botanical sensation. Every now and then specimen plants are sent to Philadelphia for comparison. Always the answer comes back from the experts that the sample is something else—not the Lost Gordonia.

Back on the coastal highway again, you head south for St. Simons Island, turning left onto the long causeway just before reaching the business section of Brunswick.

It's all yours then—that exhilaration described by Sidney Lanier when he wrote about "the length and the breadth and the sweep of the marshes of Glynn."

Here on St. Simons in the golden age of King Cotton were fourteen or more rich plantations, the setting for:

> Oak fringed, island homes that seem
> To sit, like swans, with matchless charm
> On seaborn sound and stream . . .

Now St. Simons is a popular beach resort, with yachting and shooting and fishing clubs, as well as year-round residences and a business section. Much of the Island's original beauty has been retained in hunting preserves and the links of the Sea Island Golf Club, adjuncts of the Cloister Hotel and the cottage colony on adjoining Sea Island. While playing a major part in the development of this section of Georgia, the Sea Island Company has also led in the effort to preserve old landmarks and traditions. At the Cloister, this has resulted in a unique achievement in hospitality, where Georgia's best foot is put forward for visitors much as was the case at Hopeton or at Cannon's Point in plantation times. Oddly enough, all this was the dream of a visitor from the North, who became a Georgia citizen, the late Howard E. Coffin, former vice president of the Hudson Motor Co., who found enthusiastic Southern co-operation when he organized the Sea Island Company and whose work has been ably carried on by his younger cousin, Alfred W. Jones.

Murder was once an invited guest at ghost-haunted Kelvyn Grove Plantation on St. Simons, where a hundred years earlier the Battle of Bloody Marsh had been fought.

Kelvyn Grove was owned by Thomas Cater in the ante-bellum cotton era. And Thomas Cater was killed by his own overseer.

The story is that Mrs. Cater and the overseer were in love and plotted the murder together. The family butler, witness of all that happened, fled with the Caters' baby son to King's Retreat Plantation, where the child was brought up like a member of the family.

The original Cater house is gone, but Thomas Cater who was buried near-by, standing up, is said to walk about the grounds on dark nights, seeking his murderer, perhaps. Nobody knows why two headless children should dance around the pool on moonlight nights as legend says they do.

If ghosts really do haunt Kelvyn Grove, some of them should date back to the time when its marsh ran red with blood.

In the Battle of Bloody Marsh fought here July 7, 1742, the English won an encounter with the Spanish that helped to decide the course of American history.

General Oglethorpe had two forts on St. Simons Island, built to protect the southern boundaries of the English colonies. The ruins of one fort remain at Frederica and the site is part of an eighty-acre national park, in which it is planned to rebuild the town of Colonial Frederica, complete with moat.

On that morning in July, 1742, when the Spanish sailed in with fifty-one ships and three thousand men, Oglethorpe was able to muster about nine hundred men. These nine hundred, according to historian Margaret Davis Cate, included "his regiment of British soldiers, 650 in number, together with the Rangers from Savannah and other places in the Colony, the Highlanders from Darien, Captain Mark Carr's marine company of boatmen and about 100 Indian allies . . ."

That was all. And if the Spanish took St. Simons, they could hope to move on to South Carolina and farther north until they might take over the entire thirteen English colonies.

In spite of the two forts, the invaders made a landing on St. Simons, at Gascoigne Bluff, and two hundred men marched toward Frederica but were turned back by a detachment of the British. Then three hundred Spanish Grenadiers appeared and, greatly outnumbered, the British retreated.

But a little body of about fifty "decided to go back and hide in the underbrush where they might observe the movements of the Spaniards . . ."

The latter, believing the skirmish over, "stacked guns and started to prepare a meal." The small body of Island defenders moved in . . .

"Two hundred of this Spanish force were killed. The wounded tried to escape by running into the marsh which bordered the road and there they died . . ."

The marsh ran red with blood.

After the defeat of their landing force, the Spaniards might not have given up, except for a clever ruse devised by General Oglethorpe. The general sent a letter by a Spanish prisoner to a Frenchman who had enlisted with the British but deserted to join the Spanish. The letter, designed to mislead the enemy as to

FIGURE 37. Orange Hall, a Greek Revival house at St. Marys.

the possibility of reinforcements from South Carolina, went straight to head-quarters.

And so the Spanish were fooled and sailed away. Thus ended their active aggression in North America.

And as Thomas Carlyle wrote of the Battle of Bloody Marsh: "Half the world was hidden in embryo under it—the incalculable Yankee nation itself, the greatest phenomenon of these ages. This too, little as careless readers on either side of the sea now know it, lay involved: Shall there be a Yankee Nation? Shall the New World be Spanish? Shall it be English?"

Kelvyn Grove is now owned by Mrs. Maxfield Parrish, who lives in a house not far from the granite shaft that marks the site of this historic battle. Mrs. Parrish, wife of the artist, is author of *Slave Songs of the Georgia Sea Islands* and is also chief sponsor of groups of Negro singers organized for the purpose of preserving spirituals, "shout songs" and other vocal music, some of which reaches back to Africa.

Songs heard long ago at Eboe Landing on St. Simons Island, and perhaps still echoed in the winds that ruffle the waters of Dunbar Creek, no doubt reach back to Africa. Here is one of the places where slave ships formerly discharged their human cargo.

And here, rather than submit to slavery, a group from the Eboe tribe followed their leader into the water—singing—and were drowned.

No lady's honor, but a boundary line dispute, was involved in a "duel" which resulted in the erection of the Pink Chapel, not far from the old town of Frederica on St. Simons.

It all happened when Fanny Kemble was at Hampton Point on St. Simons and in her *Journal* Fanny says a duel had been arranged.

But no duel was actually fought. Apparently the rift was one that widened with additional provocation, and matters went from bad to worse as friends took sides. When things were at fever heat, the two disputants met accidentally on the steps of the Oglethorpe Hotel in Brunswick. Quickly, one drew his gun and fired, killing the other.

To avoid disapproving glances of neighbors at Christ Church, Dr. Thomas Hazzard, who had fired the shot, built a private chapel on the family plantation at West Point. That is the legend. At any rate, the ruins of this chapel remain, their tabby walls turned pink with time and island moss.

And in the cemetery at Christ Episcopal Church—the church founded by John and Charles Wesley in the early days of the colony—you find a grave, marked by a stone with a broken pediment. This is the grave of John Armstrong Wylly, and the broken pediment symbolizes his life cut short by that shot fired from the steps of the Oglethorpe Hotel.

West Point is now owned by Mrs. Maxwell R. Berry, who built a spacious new house there some years ago. A part of Hamilton Plantation is now the property of the South Georgia Conference of the Methodist Episcopal Church. The original house was long ago replaced by a new one.

At Cannon's Point, the home of James Hamilton's great friend, only the tabby foundation walls of the house remain. Keeping them lonely company is a palm tree planted by Mr. Couper. Cannon's Point was one of St. Simons' most hospitable homes. It was here that the "young couple who came to spend their honeymoon stayed until their second child was born," according to Caroline Couper Lovell.

Aaron Burr, a fugitive from arrest after his duel with Alexander Hamilton, sought and found shelter at Major Pierce Butler's Hampton Point Plantation on St. Simons Island in 1804. He remained, attended by a retinue of Hampton servants, even when his host departed for the Butler summer home in the North.

123

FIGURE 38. Grove Point Plantation, home of George Mercer, Jr. This house, near Savannah, is a reconstruction on the old foundations.

Jekyll Island, once the home of a famous millionaire's club, lies just south of St. Simons. It is now one of Georgia's state parks. Still standing on Jekyll are the walls of the house built in early Colonial times by William Horton, who had a plantation on the north end of the island. Later, for nearly a hundred years, Jekyll was owned by the family of Christopher Poulain DuBignon. In 1886 John DuBignon sold the island to a group who formed the Jekyll Island Club—Rockefellers, Morgans, Vanderbilts, Goulds and other great men of finance who wanted to get away from it all at some private retreat.

Traveling in yachts down the inland waterway, they landed on the western shore of Jekyll Island, where their clubhouse, cottages and the San Souci apartments still stand. Some of them, of course, preferred to come in private railway cars which were switched onto a siding in Brunswick. Although the season lasted only from the middle of January until Easter, when the members and their families were officially in residence, Jekyll's expensive privacy was closely guarded all the year round.

But tastes change with new generations, or perhaps a changing world is responsible for the closing of the Jekyll Island Club, which had its last season in 1941 just prior to the outbreak of World War II. After sixty-one years of ownership by the club, Jekyll Island was sold again in 1947. It is now the property of the State of Georgia.

Back on the mainland in Brunswick, it is doubtful if any traffic officer can direct you to the former Colonial plantation of Plug Point.

The busy city of Brunswick and its streets with old English names had their beginnings in Plug Point in 1771. (Plug Point got its name from the whopping tobacco crop grown there by Mark Carr.) Lacking a plantation house at this late date, any visitor should be willing to settle for Glynn County's old brick courthouse with tall Ionic columns surrounded by a city square of moss-draped oaks. Another sight to see is that other massive Brunswick oak where Sidney Lanier was inspired to write *The Marshes of Glynn*.

About twenty miles south of Brunswick is Refuge Plantation. Just this side of Woodbine, a road turning right leads to this five-thousand-acre tract granted by George III of England to George McIntosh. A son, John Houstoun McIntosh, built the house there about 1765.

This section of Georgia was the debatable land, fought over by the Spanish, the French and the Indians when Florida was still owned by Spain. It may be that this had something to do with the name given the house, a two-story frame structure, with slender free-standing chamfered columns, back of which is a porch with balustrade approached by twin flights of steps. Two dormer windows adorn the sloping gabled roof. The kitchen, with its huge fireplace, is connected to the house by a long covered passageway.

The Refuge is now owned by Mrs. Dan Hebard of Folkston and Philadelphia.

John Houstoun McIntosh owned a plantation on Fort George Island which "became a sort of white house of the Republic" of East Florida, where the leaders got together to confer. He also owned plantations near St. Marys.

On one of these are old tabby walls, standing sphinxlike in a wilderness growth of trees and tangled vines. These impressive ruins are believed by some authorities to be remains of the Santa Maria missions which were established somewhere in the neighborhood by Menendez de Aviles in 1570. Others believe they were sugar mills built by John Houstoun McIntosh more than two centuries later.

The walls, two stories high, enclose a space seventy-five feet wide by 150 feet long. Free-standing columns mark the entrance to the main section, which has a room on each side. There are many small windows in one wall of the second floor. Tall oaks and cedars, which have grown up inside the walls, spread their branches to make a roof.

The leaves whisper in the brooding silence but they give only a part of the answer.

Where is St. Marys? "In a sweet and hidden place among the Saints on Georgia's farthest shores, St. Simons lying not many miles to the North and Point Peter extending against its eastern sky." This was the description given by a delighted New England visitor in 1915. Cumberland Island is offshore from St. Marys, an island on which are both wild horses and the homes of millionaires, Carnegies and Candlers. The old Nathanael Greene Plantation, now owned by the Carnegie family, is described in another chapter of this book.

St. Marys own prize Greek Revival house is Orange Hall, built about 1830 by Horace Pratt, Presbyterian minister. Its four great fluted columns are duplicated in miniature in the balustrade. Orange Hall has especially fine cornices, and carved woodwork, black marble mantels and inside folding blinds for the big recessed windows. It is three stories high and a banquet hall extends all the way across the front of the ground floor.

The Archibald Clark house, of white frame construction, built in 1802, dates back to the time when St. Marys was a flourishing seaport and Major Clark was collector of customs. St. Marys picturesque water front is active enough today with the shrimp fleet and the pleasure craft of hunters and fishermen, but an old painting shows it lined with sixty or seventy buildings, most of which are gone now. A dreamy quality of the past lingers on and you would not be surprised if you rubbed your eyes and found all the old buildings back again.

You would not be surprised to hear the Presbyterian church bell suddenly set up a mad ringing and find a horse in the belfry as happened once upon a time. How did the horse get there? The story is that smugglers hoisted him aloft to distract attention while they landed their loot. The old Inn, said to be a smuggler's hideout (now the home of Miss Kitty Rudulph), still has its secret passage to the third floor.

Aaron Burr, while staying on St. Simons, dropped down to St. Marys and was entertained in the Archibald Clark house, now the home of Captain and Mrs. Alex MacDonell. General Winfield Scott, fresh from the Seminole Wars, was an honored guest of Major Clark. Uninvited guests were British officers who used the house as headquarters during the War of 1812.

French inscriptions on some of the tombs in Oak Grove Cemetery bear witness that a group of the Acadians banished with Evangeline also found their way to St. Marys. Then as now, it was "a sweet and hidden place."

CHAPTER 17

Plantation Ladies

*T*HEY gossiped a bit about the wife of General Nathanael Greene. They said she was fond of Mad Anthony Wayne, who—like her husband—had been a general in the War of the Revolution and had settled near Savannah on one of those plantation grants by which the new state sought to reward its gallant defenders.

And Fanny Kemble, the celebrated English actress, niece of the great Sarah Siddons—what a stir she made! Her marriage to Pierce Butler was not arranged in heaven, though the slaves on his Georgia plantations thought it might have been. Fanny Kemble's *Journal* is credited with diverting English sympathy from the cause of the Confederacy and helping to hasten the Surrender at Appomattox.

Then there was Anna Matilda Page King. Her husband was one of the important men of his day and she was a great lady, a lady of many accomplishments. Mistress of King's Retreat Plantation (now the Sea Island Golf Club), her Sea Island cotton brought the highest prices paid in the days when cotton was king.

Plantation ladies were—as ladies have always been—a law unto themselves, when they had any time to themselves. Usually they were pretty well occupied with producing babies and supervising a large and complicated household which included the "quarters" and the slave hospital. They were in charge of large-scale spinning, weaving and sewing. They also carried the burden of large-scale hospitality at a time when house guests came for a month and sometimes stayed for a year. Plantation ladies were executives, ministering angels, mothers, wives, hostesses or whatever else duty demanded. But they were—as ladies have always been—a law unto themselves. You find this true from the Savannah River to the St. Marys, and anywhere else you may happen to look, no doubt.

Remembrance of a beautiful, spirited woman lasts a long, long time, especially if she happens to take a sidewise glance at a gentleman other than her husband.

So it was with Catherine Greene, wife of General Nathanael Greene, who lived at Mulberry Grove Plantation on the Savannah River just after the Revolutionary War. That house and the Greenes' other thirty-room house, Dungeness, on Cumberland Island, were both laid waste in the War Between the States. There is little trace today of Mulberry Grove, and though Dungeness was rebuilt on the old foundations by the Carnegie family in 1893, it now stands empty, sadly in need of repairs.

But Catherine Greene is still remembered for her beauty and brilliance and for the part she played in the lives of three men.

These were:

Her husband, who had been George Washington's second-in-command and was later placed in charge of the Continental army in the South.

General Anthony Wayne, her husband's fellow officer—called "Mad Anthony" because of his daring military exploits.

And Eli Whitney, who invented the cotton gin in 1793.

Mrs. Greene had been the much-admired Kitty Littlefield of Block Island, when she met and married a handsome young Quaker named Nathanael Greene. "To her distress," says B. N. Nightingale in an article in the *Georgia Historical Quarterly*, "he insisted on forming a company of volunteers who drilled religiously, preparing themselves for the war with Great Britain which all were certain was at hand. . . . Soon Light Horse Harry Lee, Nathanael Greene and Washington were household words . . . the three were not only patriots in a common cause but became firm friends . . ."

When American independence was won at last, various states presented General Greene with large tracts of land in token of their appreciation of his valiant service. He had hoped to settle in South Carolina but sold that property to apply on debts incurred when he gave his personal note in order to obtain provisions and other supplies for the army.

And so the Greenes came to Mulberry Grove, named for the trees that had been planted there to provide food for silkworms when the Thirteenth Colony went all out for a projected silk industry. Mulberry Grove was now a rice plantation. General Greene pronounced the "prospect delightful and the house magnificent."

But it is possible Catherine Greene found plantation days a little dull. She was accustomed to the social life of cities and the admiration of many men. The Revolution had been a stirring time. She had spent weeks in camp with her husband, close to the fighting line. Between battles there were military balls. On one occasion "General Washington had danced for four hours with Mrs. Greene without once sitting down."

FIGURE 39.   The old tabby corn barn at Retreat Plantation on St. Simons Island, now the clubhouse of the Sea Island Golf Club.

"She was one of the most brilliant and entertaining of women," says a history of Savannah River plantations published by the *Georgia Historical Quarterly*. "In addition to beauty," she had "personal charm, intuitive perception and a very acquisitive intellect."

Mulberry Grove is twelve miles northwest of Savannah and the distance seemed greater in 1786. At that time General Anthony Wayne lived "farther up the river" at Richmond and Kew Plantation, his gift from a grateful Georgia government. General Greene and General Wayne were both engaged in rice cultivation and had many interests in common. Mad Anthony was a frequent guest at Mulberry Grove, where he found yet another interest in common with his former fellow officer.

"Hearsay has perpetuated the rumor that about this time the fascinating Catherine fell madly in love with the dashing Anthony. . . . Tradition reports that General Greene was on the verge of severely censuring this mutual attraction when, on June 12, 1786 during a visit to the rice plantation of his wealthy neighbor, William Gibbons, he suffered an attack of sunstroke from which he died."

General Greene was buried with high military honors in Savannah's old Colonial Cemetery, and a hundred years later his remains were moved to Johnson Square, where they lie beneath the imposing Nathanael Greene Monument.

His death was a great shock to the new nation and no doubt also to his wife. Sometime later Mad Anthony was given an appointment by George Washington which took him to the Northwest.

General Greene left five children. As was usual on many plantations, these children received their early education from a private tutor and were later sent to school or college in the East. The tutor at Mulberry Grove was Yale graduate Phineas Miller, who became plantation manager after the general's death and ten years later married Mrs. Greene.

In the meantime, President Washington stopped over at Mulberry Grove when he visited Georgia in 1791. Mrs. Greene herself had made a trip to the East. Returning by boat, she met a young man named Eli Whitney, who expected to take a job as tutor with a Georgia family. When he arrived, he found the position already filled and Mrs. Greene invited him to visit at Mulberry Grove.

This was the year 1793 and cotton was a coming crop. Everybody talked about the need for a machine to separate cotton from its seeds, a long and tedious task when done by hand.

A number of people were struggling with ideas for such an invention, but to Mrs. Greene goes a share of credit for the practical model invented by Eli Whitney. Mr. Whitney seems to have had a hand with gadgets and made himself useful around the plantation. He also perfected a tambour frame for Mrs. Greene's embroidery and repaired her watch. Delighted with these performances, Mrs.

Greene told Mr. Whitney he was just the man to invent the greatly needed cotton machine.

He set to work, but nearly a year passed before he had a working model. Even then there was a vital lack.

"Why, Mr. Whitney, you want a brush," said Mrs. Greene, who thereupon picked up the family clothes brush and removed the lint from the metal teeth of the machine.

"Madam, you have completed the cotton gin," replied Mr. Whitney.

To protect his invention until he could obtain a patent, Whitney's model was closely guarded from outside inspection. Ladies, however, were allowed a look. A certain young man named Edward Lyon, dressed in skirts, took a very good look indeed. The result was that he and his brother John came out with a rival machine.

Phineas Miller became Whitney's financial partner, and sixty long-drawn-out law suits were fought in the effort to sustain their patent. Although Whitney is recognized as inventor of the cotton gin, neither he nor Miller derived any great financial return from the machine that ushered in King Cotton's long and prosperous reign.

Several years before his death, General Greene had acquired a great tract of land on Cumberland Island, off the coast of Georgia at St. Marys. Plans were made for a four-story, thirty-room house to be used as a summer residence. These plans were carried out and the house completed in 1803. Its tabby foundations were six feet thick below the ground and four feet thick above ground. There were twelve acres of gardens, "reaching the marsh in successive terraces . . . eleven miles of oak-lined avenues, seven miles of beach, eight miles of walks and nine miles of open roads." There were orange and olive groves and fields white with cotton.

The house was named Dungeness after a hunting lodge built on Cumberland soon after Oglethorpe settled Georgia. The island, called Missoe by the Indians and San Pedro by Spanish Franciscan priests, had been renamed for the Duke of Cumberland. Dungeness was the name of the duke's county seat, Castle Dungeness, on the Cape of Dungeness in Kent, England.

The Greene family finally lost Mulberry Grove because of debts contracted by General Greene for army provisions during the Revolution. Dungeness became the permanent family residence. Phineas Miller died in 1806 from lockjaw resulting from the stab of a thorn through his hand while he was transplanting orange trees from Florida to Cumberland. Catherine Littlefield Greene Miller died in 1814 at the age of 59, still beautiful, still brilliant and charming. In 1812, when America was again at war with Britain, United States troops were quartered at St. Marys, and Mrs. Miller had the officers to dine at Dungeness. Fortunately she was not there when British Admiral Cockburn landed on Cumberland in 1815 and made himself at home in the great house.

But peace came again to this peaceful isle. Mrs. Miller had willed the place to her daughter, Louisa Greene, who had married James Shaw. Another daughter, Martha Washington Greene, married John Clark Nightingale, and their son, P. M. Nightingale, was on the beach when, early in 1818, a schooner cast anchor and General Light Horse Harry Lee came ashore. Still suffering from old battle wounds, he had sought to regain his health in the West Indies but had given up the struggle.

To Mrs. Shaw he sent word by young Nightingale, "Tell her that I am purposely come to die in the house and in the arms of the daughter of my old friend and compatriot."

Mrs. Shaw and the entire household made him welcome. He was put to bed and everything possible done for his comfort. Terrific pain made him a poor patient at times, and one after another he chased out the servants assigned to wait upon him. Finally Mrs. Shaw placed him in the care of an old Negro woman, Mom Sarah, who had been her mother's favorite maid.

When Mom Sarah, a woman of great dignity, entered the general's room, he ordered her out, and to add emphasis, hurled his boot at her head.

Unused to such treatment, Mom Sarah did not deign to reply, but deliberately picked up the boot and hurled it back at him.

This unexpected response had an unexpected result. The old soldier's face lightened with a smile. From that time until his death, March 25, 1818, Mom Sarah had complete charge of the sick room.

General Light Horse Harry Lee was buried at Dungeness and his grave was visited in later years by his famous son, Robert E. Lee, Commander-in-Chief of the Confederate army. Today the bodies of the two great generals lie in the crypt at Washington and Lee University in Virginia.

In 1893 the Dungeness property was acquired by Thomas Morrison Carnegie, who built a great gabled house on the old foundations. Through long neglect this is now in a state of general dilapidation.

Some few pieces of massive furniture remain. On the day of our visit there were still piles of framed prints and steel engravings lying about, which apparently nobody wanted. In some of the large rooms the wallpaper was peeling.

In the service hall an annunciator for call bells still bore the names of occupants long gone . . . the numbers of rooms long empty. Yet, by its very size, the old house still evokes visions of a bygone splendor—a splendor typical of that gilt and plush era which saw the rise of the great captains of American industry.

Though Dungeness is a picture of desolation, three other Carnegie plantations on the island are maintained in excellent order as part-time residences by members of the family. These keep their original ante-bellum plantation names—Grayfield, Plum Orchard and Stafford. At each the original family burying ground is carefully preserved.

Grayfield is the residence of Mr. and Mrs. Robert Ferguson, who live at Cumberland most of the year and raise purebred cattle. Mrs. Ferguson was named Lucy for her grandmother, Lucy Coleman Carnegie, wife of Thomas M. Carnegie.

The north end of Cumberland was a popular summer resort from about 1880 to the early nineteen hundreds. Here the Howard Candlers of Atlanta have a summer home.

The south end of the island remains intact as the Georgia home of the Carnegie family. Like those who have preceded them, the Carnegies have established at Dungeness their own private burying ground, where modest markers bear dates up to the present time.

In the Greene cemetery the inscription over the grave of Catherine Greene Miller reads:

"Widow of Major General Greene, commander-in-chief of the American Revolutionary Army in the Southern Department, who died September 1, 1814.

"She possessed great talents and exalted virtues."

There were some who said that Fanny Kemble was not really beautiful but there were none to deny that she could charm when she wished to charm. There were none to deny either that she was one of the most brilliantly gifted young English actresses of her time.

When she came to America for a well chaperoned theatrical tour in 1832 dozens of young men fell in love with her. She married a great catch, Pierce Butler, of Philadelphia, and all might have been well except for the fact that Pierce and his brother John owned large plantations in Georgia—Butler Island near Darien and Hampton Point on St. Simons Island. They also owned a large number of slaves.

Fanny visited these Georgia plantations with her husband in 1838, and things were never quite the same between them afterward. A time came in the history of the South when this visit achieved an even wider significance.

Fanny Kemble journeyed to Georgia with her mind already made up about slavery. The very thought revolted her and she was further revolted upon her arrival. Her impressions are vividly recorded in the journal she kept. Many years later, in 1863 to be exact, when England seemed friendly to the cause of the Confederacy, Fanny Kemble—then in London—published her *Journal of a Residence on a Georgian Plantation, 1838-39.*

The book created a sensation little short of that which followed the appearance of *Uncle Tom's Cabin.* English sympathy promptly swung away from the

South and the hoped-for English support was lost. Later the cause was lost. Could it have been partly because of Fanny?

There are none now to defend slavery, if there ever was a defense. The South contended from the beginning that slavery was not the real issue, that it fought for state's rights. Anyway, the part played by Fanny Kemble in the fortunes of the War Between the States will always pose an interesting question.

Sully's portrait shows Fanny Kemble as a young woman of regal poise with large flashing black eyes and soft dark hair twisted in a coronet above her high forehead and falling over her shoulders in long curls. It was said that she resembled her aunt, the great Sarah Siddons, except that she was much smaller in stature.

Fanny left the stage when she married but went back again after her divorce from Pierce Butler. Her Shakespearean readings were so popular that Longfellow was inspired to write a sonnet to Fanny in which he also congratulates the Bard of Avon:

> How must thy listening spirit now rejoice
> To be interpreted by such a voice!

Fanny Kemble and Pierce Butler had two children, Sally and Frances. Sally was about four when the family came to Georgia. Frances was a baby seven months old. The girls grew up to be very different—Sally in sympathy with her mother and Frances with her father. Sally married Owen Wister, Sr., and their son, Owen Wister, wrote *The Virginian, Lady Baltimore*, and other successful novels. Frances married the Reverend James W. Leigh of Stoneleigh Abbey in Warwickshire, England. Their daughter, Alice, married Sir Richard Butler, a distant cousin.

In fairly recent times Alice, Lady Butler, visited Georgia to see the plantations where Grandmother Fanny Kemble Butler wrote her fateful book so many years before. Lady Butler had a double reason for coming. Her own mother, Frances Butler Leigh, also wrote a book. It was called *Ten Years on a Georgia Plantation Since the War*, and began with the experiences of the author and her father, Pierce Butler, when they came south and undertook the operation of Butler Island Plantation with freedmen's labor. The loyalty of former slaves gratified both of them.

Pierce Butler died in 1867 and Frances carried on alone. Then James Leigh came sightseeing from England, carrying a letter of introduction to Frances. They fell in love and were married. He shared his wife's enthusiasm for the plantation and for some time they continued to spend their winters there. What is more, the plantation paid off. These were the ten years "since the war" that Frances wrote about. The two books—like mother and daughter—were very different.

There was nothing much for Lady Butler to see that would remind her of the houses described by Fanny Kemble. An old rice-mill chimney, vine covered, still stands on Butler Island, near Darien, but even this is said to belong to a later day. The ruins of the house were removed when the late Colonel Tillinghast L'Hommideu Huston bought the island. Colonel Huston, who made millions as an engineer and owned half-interest in the New York Yankees, retired to Butler Island in his later years, where he raised fine Jersey cattle and operated a modern dairy farm.

At Hampton Point, on St. Simons Island, there is nothing left from the old days but a magnificent view of the Hampton River. Fanny and Pierce and the children stayed first at Butler Island, the rice plantation, and came to St. Simons for the warmer weather in the spring of 1839, where they lived in temporary quarters. Even then the old house at Hampton Point, or Butler Point as it is also called, was in a sad state of decay. Fanny didn't like the site selected for the new house planned by her husband. You sympathize with her when she writes that it was too far from the Point, "where the waters meet." She didn't like the plans for the house itself. She didn't like much that she found in Georgia, except the food and the scenery and some of the people.

Pierce Butler and his brother were absentee landlords. They lived in Philadelphia and delegated the management of plantation affairs to an agent. More than one neighbor told Fanny Kemble that things were very different on the Butler plantations when old Major Butler was alive.

Major Pierce Butler had come to America in 1766 as an officer in the British army. He was a young man then, the third son of Sir William Butler, and he married rich Polly Middleton of Charleston. Came the Revolution and he was still a major, but this time on the American side. He was a signer of the Constitution of the United States and served as United States Senator from South Carolina. Later he moved to Georgia, where he took his plantation duties as seriously as he did his duties to his new country.

When the major died he willed his property to the sons of his daughter, Sarah, who had married Dr. James Mease of Philadelphia—provided the boys adopted the name of Butler. This they did, but their interest in the plantations was not what the major's had been.

One of the neighbors, whose conversation Fanny records, was John Couper, who lived at Cannon's Point on St. Simons, where the ruins of his house may still be seen. Fanny describes this house as "a roomy, comfortable, handsomely laid-out mansion."

The Couper gardens, from which the Butlers enjoyed fresh fruit, vegetables and flowers, were a delight to Fanny, for the gardens at Hampton were in the same state as the neglected house. Fanny quotes Mr. Couper as saying that "the whole condition and treatment of the [Butler] slaves had changed from the time of Major Butler's death." She describes Mr. Couper as "an old Glasgow man who has been settled here many years. . . . It is curious," she observes, "how many of the people round this neighborhood have Scotch names. . . . Old Mr. Couper spoke with extreme kindness of his own people [slaves] and had evidently bestowed much human and benevolent pains upon endeavors to better their condition."

But Fanny apparently was not much interested in the investigation of plantations such as Mr. Couper's. What seems to have shocked her most at the Butler plantations was the treatment given "lusty women." This, she explains, was the designation for women with child. Three weeks after the birth of a baby, the mother was expected to go back to work, unless obviously unable to do so.

She explains that a doctor was available at Darien when needed. But in those days obstetrics were largely left to midwives. The poor physical condition of some of the women patients Fanny found in slave hospitals was most likely due to the limited knowledge of these midwives, who took the attitude that childbirth was a natural function and that occasional unfortunate after-affects eventually adjusted themselves or were to be endured with fortitude. This was not an uncommon attitude at a time when many pioneer white women were dependent upon midwife care during childbirth.

Finding a willing ear, the people on the Butler plantations took their grievances to Fanny, who in turn took them to Pierce. When she heard that the husband of one of the maids was owned by the overseer rather than by the Butlers and might be separated from his wife if the overseer decided to sell, she was greatly distressed. To please Fanny, Pierce bought the man, but left Fanny to find it out for herself. He was beginning to weary of her dramatics. Even Fanny admits there was a "propensity to lying" on the part of some of the Negroes who came to her but she felt they were justified in using any available means to better their condition.

Fanny also recognized herself as a creature of moods. While on St. Simons Island she wrote: "I suppose one secret of my being able to suffer as acutely as I do without being made either ill or absolutely miserable is the childish excitability of my temperament and the sort of ecstasy which any beautiful thing gives me. . . . As far as I have hitherto had opportunity of observing, children and maniacs are the only creatures who would be capable of sufficiently rapid transitions of thought and feeling to keep pace with me."

She had just described the beauty of "a salt marsh upon a raised causeway that was perfectly alive with land crabs . . . the sides of this road across the swamp were covered with a thick and close embroidery of creeping moss or rather lichens of the most vivid green and red; the latter made my horse's path look as if it was edged with an exquisite pattern of coral. It was like a thing in a fairy tale and delighted me extremely. . . . No day, almost no hour passes without some enjoyment of the sort."

When the Butlers moved the fifteen miles from the rice plantation on Butler Island to their cotton lands on St. Simons, they traveled on the barge *Lily*, which was propelled by eight oarsmen, singing in rhythm with the wide sweep of the oars. All this enchanted Fanny. Describing the approach to St. Simons, she wrote: "You cannot imagine anything so exquisite as the perfect curtains of yellow jasmine with which this whole island is draped; and as the boat comes sweeping down toward the Point, the fragrance from the thickets hung with their golden garlands greets one before one can distinguish them."

Fanny felt that poems should be written to the white mullet of the great Altamaha River. She vowed that she "never tasted such delicious tea as that which we make with this same turbid stream, the water duly filtered, of course. It has some peculiar softness which affects the tea (and it is the same we always use) in a most curious and agreeable manner."

In a letter to her friend, Elizabeth Dwight Sedgewick, of Lenox, Massachusetts, she eulogizes Georgia shad, "a delicate creature, so superior to the animal you northerners devour." The mutton too had a special flavor, perhaps due to grazing on "short wet sweet grass at St. Simons within the sea-salt influence and is some of the very best I ever tasted." There were also wild turkeys, wild ducks and venison to write about when Fanny was in the mood to picture the brighter side.

Fanny dutifully returned calls from neighbors and attended services at Christ Church, in its cathedral-like grove of giant live oaks draped with Spanish moss.

At Butler Island she frequently made trips to Darien by dugout canoe. On St. Simons she rode everywhere, sometimes with her husband, sometimes with a groom, often alone. It was here that she wrote:

"The death I should prefer would be to break my neck off the back of a good horse at a full gallop on a fine day."

But this did not happen. Fanny lived to be eighty-four, a vivacious handsome old lady in dark velvet, surrounded by friends and admirers, many of them noted in the world of literature as well as the theater—Henry James, Edward Fitzgerald and others. Fanny's own literary efforts were not confined to her famous *Journal* and she was celebrated both as writer and actress.

After their Georgia visit, Fanny and Pierce jogged along for some years. They even went to Europe together and spent a season in London where Fanny was presented at court. But they were separated by broad differences in temperament and background and eventually these became too wide to be bridged even temporarily. In 1845 Fanny returned to England—alone. In time, she came back to America but never again to Georgia.

People made long visits in those days. Major and Mrs. William Page, arriving in 1798, spent the better part of a year as guests of Major Pierce Butler in his great house, at Hampton Point on St. Simons Island. While they were there, their daughter Anna Matilda was born.

Anna was the only one of the Pages' twelve children to live. St. Simons seemed to agree with her and because of this—according to Anna's granddaughter, Mrs. Thornton Marye, of Atlanta—her parents decided the island would be a fine place to make their home. Like their host, they owned plantations on the Georgia mainland, and again like Major Butler, they had previously lived in South Carolina. At Major Butler's suggestion the Pages acquired Retreat Plantation (now the Sea Island Golf Club) on the south end of St. Simons Island.

Here from earliest childhood little Anna was trained for the duties she must assume when she became mistress of the plantation. The records kept by Anna, who grew up to become Mrs. Thomas Butler King, show that she received as much as forty-two cents a pound for the famous Sea Island cotton, a price seven cents above that paid to other planters. The high price is said to have been due to her methods of selecting the seed and cultivating the cotton. These records tell many interesting things about Anna herself and her methods of managing a three-thousand-acre plantation and hundreds of slaves.

Anna Page King was a Sea Island lady with patrician features and dark hair piled high on her head, as you can see from her portrait which hangs on a wall of the golf-club lounge. Near by is a likeness of her husband, Thomas Butler King, a gentleman with sideburns and a statesman's face.

The photograph of an elderly, dignified Negro man is among other framed pictures on the walls of the room. This is Neptune, one of the King slaves, born the same day as their son, Captain Henry Lord Page King, who fought in the War Between the States. Neptune went along as body servant, and it was Neptune who brought the body of the young captain all the way back from a Virginia battlefield for burial in the family lot at Christ Church Cemetery on St. Simons Island.

The central section of the Sea Island Golf Club house, with its tabby walls and foundations, was once the combined barn and stables of King's Retreat Plantation. Still standing are the tabby ruins of a much larger building which might be mistaken for the one-time plantation house. This was really the ten-room slave hospital. Two Negro women lived here as nurses and when necessary a doctor was called in. Some distance away stands a tall chimney, all that is left of the big house, which was built of hand-hewn live-oak timbers and put together with wooden pegs.

The mile-long avenue of live oaks draped with Spanish moss is said to have been planted even before the house was built. Anna Page King planted wonderful gardens, so fragrant that their perfume, carried on the breezes, was enjoyed by passing mariners at sea. "The high peaked roof of the cotton barn served as a landmark by which vessels steered through St. Simons Sound before the present light house was built," says Mrs. Marye. "Grateful sea captains brought rare specimens of trees and shrubs and flowers from the four corners of the earth to Retreat. Sometimes these plants in tubs were in transit two years."

Audubon wrote of Mrs. King's gardens when he visited King's Retreat in 1831, while aboard the schooner *Agnes*. "We put back into St. Simons Bay," he says. . . . "This was one of the few put-backs in life of a fortunate kind for me. I made for the shore, met a gentleman on the beach, presented him my card and was immediately invited to dinner. I visited his gardens, got into such agreeable conversation and quarters that I was fain to think I had landed on some of those fairy islands said to have existed in the Golden Age. But this was not all; the owner of this hospitable mansion pressed me to stay a month with him and subscribed to my *Birds of America* in the most gentlemanly manner." The gentleman, of course, was Thomas Butler King, and a subscription to *Birds of America* was a thousand dollars.

Anna Page King was the mother of nine children and she was a very busy person otherwise. Her husband served for sixteen years as a member of Congress and was necessarily away from home a great deal of the time when Anna was in complete charge of plantation affairs. Thomas Butler King was one of the first to advocate the building of a transcontinental railroad. For a time he was collector of the port of San Francisco. During the War Between the States he was appointed a special commissioner to England from the Confederate States of America.

Margaret Davis Cate, Sea Island writer and historian, has photostatic copies of the ledgers, journals and other records kept by Mrs. King.

You may see in these old records where in April of each year a great quantity of ice was brought from the North and placed in the ice house at Retreat. You may see where the piano was tuned regularly—where the doctor was paid each year for his services to family and slaves.

Most remarkable to visitors from the North and East are the entries which show that Mrs. King paid her "people" for whatever work was done beyond their allotted tasks. (Plantation owners always referred to their workers as people, never slaves.) As was customary on all well-operated plantations, Mrs. King also paid her people for "ducks, chickens, eggs, clams, terrapins, baskets, piggins, fanners," etc. Any surplus of these articles they were allowed to sell elsewhere. She lent them money to buy pigs and cows for themselves and their families. All this you find in the record.

Mrs. King also kept vital statistics and so you come to such entries as these: "My good and faithful servant, Hannah, after years of suffering, expired on the night of the 2nd of August, 1854. For honesty, moral character, unselfishness and perfect devotion to her owners, she had not her equal. She died resigned, with a firm trust in her Redeemer. . . . Old Cupid, honest and true to his earthly owners, departed this life at 4 A. M. 29 January 1857 . . ."

One year there was an epidemic of measles at Retreat and you find listed all the names of the children who contracted the disease. Later, of course, it would be important to know who had and who had not had measles. Names of several "infants" are set down as having escaped the contagion.

Anna Page King died in 1859, just before her world crumbled. "A faithful Christian," says the marker over her grave in Christ Church Cemetery, "as daughter, wife and mother, as mistress to her people, a woman loving and gracious, upright, tender and true."

Though King's Retreat has changed since plantation days, it still weaves a special enchantment. The air still has that fine "Mediterranean translucency" described by Thomas Wentworth Higginson, who visited the place in 1863 when the gardens were a ruin. The golf fairway is truly a fairway, with an ocean view on one side and, on another, Sidney Lanier's "beautiful glooms" of the live oaks, "soft dusks in the noon-day fire." Formal plantings include tree-high hedges of oleanders, splashed with spectacular pink and white and red blossoms. Retreat is still like a fairy isle, saved over from some long-gone Golden Age.

CHAPTER 18

Sapelo's Three Millionaires

THREE men of great wealth spent fortunes gilding Sapelo to make it the most golden of the Golden Isles of Georgia.

For each it has been an island empire. Each in his different era and in his different fashion dreamed dreams on a grand scale and made many of those dreams come true.

First of these was Thomas Spalding, heir to the barony of Ashantilly in Scotland, who built "South End" house and operated Sapelo as one of the great plantations of the South's great plantation heyday.

Between Thomas Spalding and the present owner, Richard J. Reynolds of the wealthy North Carolina tobacco family, was the late Howard E. Coffin, former vice-president of the Hudson Motor Co. Mr. Coffin restored South End house and many other island buildings left in ruins by the Federal army in the eighteen sixties.

At Sapelo Mr. Coffin entertained two Presidents of the United States. When Lindbergh and his bride did one of their first disappearing acts into the wild blue yonder they came down on Sapelo's private landing field as guests of Mr. Coffin. The two presidents were successively Calvin Coolidge and Herbert Hoover.

Mr. Coffin himself first came to Sapelo as a guest. In 1911 he attended the Vanderbilt Cup Races at Savannah, which were sponsored by the American Automobile Association and the Automobile Club of America. He was one of the visitors invited by Savannah's mayor and other officials to go shooting and fishing on Sapelo Island, which is near Darien, about fifty miles south of Savannah and twenty-five miles north of Sea Island.

There Mr. Coffin came under the spell of the Golden Isles of Georgia as many had done before him: Carnegies at Cumberland, Rockefellers at Jekyll and, long before that, Oglethorpe at St. Simons. Although Oglethorpe officially founded the colony of Georgia at Savannah in 1733, his only home in America was at Frederica on St. Simons Island, near the fort established for the protection of the southern boundaries of England's colonial possessions.

Always the Golden Isles have inspired dreams. We know that the Spanish dreamed of conquest when they established missions here in 1568, missions antedating those in California. Scottish Sir Robert Montgomery visualized the Golden Isles as a New World Utopia. The Indians dreamed simply of preserving them as a happy hunting and fishing heaven.

Within a year of his first sight of Sapelo, Howard Coffin bought that island and gave his yacht the name *Zapala*, a Spanish version of the Indian name, Sapelo. The old Spalding stables were hastily remodeled as a residence, called Long Tabby, in which the Coffins lived while the main house was being rebuilt.

The foundations and tabby walls of Thomas Spalding's great house, South End, still stood at the south end of the island, which is three miles across at its widest point and has a beach twelve miles long. In the reconstruction of this house the one-time ballroom at the back became a glass-domed indoor swimming pool. Beyond the four Doric columns of the wide-recessed front porch, a tile terrace was laid and beyond this an outdoor pool of decorative design.

Surrounding all this is the lush green of palms, ferns and tropic shrubbery, shaded by great oaks, hung with gray Spanish moss. Surrounding it also is the serenity of complete isolation.

This isolation is dramatized by the approach. You reach Sapelo only by boat or plane. The Sapelo mainland docks are seven miles from Darien, just off Highway 99. Near these docks, automobiles are stored in locked garages and guests transfer to a speedboat which makes the six-mile trip to the island in fifteen minutes through Doughboy Sound and the wide tidal rivers of the inland waterway. From Sapelo Island's own docks the hard-packed oyster-shell road is bordered by a high hedge of oleanders planted by Mr. Coffin. Oleanders give way to the moss-draped live oaks of Thomas Spalding's day, their branches arching high above the plantation road. After about a mile of these, there is the big house.

It has in all sixty rooms, still furnished in the beautiful antiques selected by Mr. and Mrs. Coffin. Mr. Coffin also collected a fine assortment of rare Georgia books for his library. He had a feeling for the history and traditions of the state and an inspired vision of its possibilities. Before the big fireplace in the sixty-by-forty-foot living room, Mr. Coffin and a group of friends dreamed up one of Georgia's finest developments: Sea Island as a resort, including the now well-known Cloister Hotel and the cottage colony.

142

FIGURE 40. South End house, originally built by Thomas Spalding on Sapelo Island soon after 1800. Howard Coffin rebuilt the house more than a century later, and it is now the home of Richard J. Reynolds, tobacco millionaire.

The wing of the Sapelo house formerly occupied by the Coffins is itself a complete apartment, equipped with private kitchen and dining room. Here all the beds had their heads facing north, and not by accident. It is said that even when the Coffins were traveling, beds in hotel rooms must be shifted, if not already so arranged. Certain it is that in November of 1937 when Mr. Coffin's body was placed by that of his wife in Christ Church Cemetery at Frederica, both graves had been dug facing north. All the other graves in the historic old cemetery face east and the rising sun.

At Sapelo, the private wing formerly occupied by the Coffins was converted into a nursery apartment for the six sons of the next and present owner, Richard J. Reynolds, who bought the island in 1934. As a safeguard against possible kidnappers of millionaire offspring, all the windows and doors of this wing were shielded by decorative iron grilles (since removed) which could be opened only from the inside. Four children are sons by Mr. Reynold's first marriage to Elizabeth Dillard. Two are by his second to Mary Ann O'Brien, former Broadway actress.

The first Mrs. Reynolds collected the beautiful Audubon prints which adorn the walls of many of the rooms. But obviously, Mr. Reynolds also likes birds, for the Atlanta artist, Athos Menaboni—famous for his bird paintings—was commissioned to do murals for the walls of the indoor swimming pool, for the ballroom on the top floor and the gameroom in the basement. Mr. Menaboni, with his wife, Sara, spent seven enchanted months on the job. Sapelo, among many other things, is a bird and wild-life sanctuary.

Thus the walls of the indoor swimming pool reflect much of the outdoors. The ballroom has been amusingly converted into a circus tent, its ceiling veiled by a red and white striped awning simulating the big top. Here, Menaboni has peopled the walls with all the circus freaks and performers—snake charmer, fat lady, strong man, clowns, acrobats, aerialists, barkers. French gilt ballroom furniture, boldly upholstered in red, white and blue bunting, adds that final circus touch usually supplied by gilded vans and coaches. It is all as gay and beguiling as it is unexpected.

The ebullient spirit of ballroom and gameroom reappears in the bathroom of a guest suite. Here on the wall above the tub, a Menaboni mermaid is chased by giant fish. Perhaps this mermaid was inspired by the bathroom fittings, which are of white gold. To turn on hot or cold water, you twist the tail of a white-gold dolphin and water gushes from its mouth. The adjoining French boudoir has walls of pale cream satin damask. The huge four-poster bed in the spacious bedroom might have been there since the time of Thomas Spalding.

Thomas Spalding, who built the original South End house soon after he acquired four thousand Sapelo Island acres in 1802, was the son of James Spalding of County Perth, Scotland. James had come to America with the hope of rebuilding his fortunes and returning to Scotland. There, as laird of Ashantilly, he could then recover mortgaged estates originally given to Sir Peter Spalding by Robert, the Bruce, as a reward for his having opened the gates of Berwick Castle in 1318.

But the opportunities of the New World were as golden as the island (St. Simons) on which James Spalding settled, and he soon gave up any idea of returning to Scotland. He established trading houses in Georgia and Florida and became the richest man in Glynn County.

James Spalding married Margery McIntosh, granddaughter of John Morh McIntosh, leader of the clan who came to Georgia from Inverness at the invitation of Oglethorpe and founded the town of Darien. These same Scottish Highlanders helped to defeat the Spanish at the Battle of Bloody Marsh.

James Spalding and his bride lived on St. Simons in the home he built and named Orange Grove. (Later this property became Retreat Plantation and is now the Sea Island Golf Club.) Here at Orange Grove, Thomas Spalding was born March 25, 1774. He was educated for the profession of law, and in 1795, the same year of his admission to the Georgia bar, he married Sally Leake at Belleville Plantation in McIntosh County. Miss Leake had spent three years at school in the East and had a mind as well as beauty.

Sally Leake was an only child. So was Thomas Spalding. They themselves had sixteen children. Three were born prior to their trip to Europe in 1800. Soon after their arrival in England a fourth child was born in Lancaster, and before their return a year and a half later another was added to the family. Between babies they visited Scotland and France, where Mr. Spalding was received by Napoleon who was fresh from his triumph at Marengo.

In London, the trading house with which Thomas Spalding's father had done business in the past lent Thomas Spalding $50,000 on his personal note, which he later repaid. Soon after his return to Georgia he bought all of Sapelo that was for sale—four thousand acres. Before his death he owned the entire island.

Thomas Spalding was his own architect for "the amazingly original, classic and powerfully composed 'South End' house" as it is described by Talbot Hamlin in his book, *Greek Revival Architecture in America*. Mr. Hamlin cites the Spalding house as an example of the fine inventiveness of Southern builders. Roswell King, who later founded the town of Roswell, in North Georgia, directed the actual construction, which was done by slave labor.

The foundations and three-foot-thick walls were of tabby, which is composed of equal parts of oyster shells, lime and sand mixed with water and placed wet in wooden forms after the manner of concrete construction. The house had high ceilings and a flat roof and "was one of the first with high columns to be built in Georgia and one of the very few ever built on the coast," says Dr. E. Merton Coulter in his fine biography, *Thomas Spalding of Sapelo*.

Thomas Spalding built his house to last, and its walls and foundations were still standing when Howard Coffin bought the island more than a century later.

Thomas Spalding expected to found a dynasty. Today some of Georgia's most prominent citizens are his descendants, but Randolph Spalding of Savannah is the last of the direct male line. In 1951 (again quoting Dr. Coulter), "a great-grandson of the great Thomas of Sapelo remained unmarried and when he goes the name Spalding handed down by the lairds of Ashantilly disappears from the earth."

"The great Thomas Spalding" was truly a great man in early Georgia. He helped to frame the constitution of the state which was in force until Georgia seceded in the eighteen sixties. The last official act of his life was a fight for the preservation of the union.

He served in the state senate and in the House of Representatives of the United States. He was president of the Bank of Darien, which in his day was one of the great banks of the country, with branches in Milledgeville, then the state capital, Augusta, Savannah, Macon, St. Marys and at Dahlonega, near the gold mines of the North Georgia hills.

Like his great-grandfather McIntosh, he deplored the institution of slavery, which was forbidden at the time of Georgia's founding. But slavery furnished the labor most easily available and Georgia eventually followed the example of other states. Thomas Spalding accepted the prevailing system "with misgivings." In the course of time he owned as many as five hundred slaves, or people, as they were called by most owners. It was Thomas Spalding's idea to "civilize" his people and better their condition.

At Sapelo a six-hour work day was the rule. When on the task system, Spalding workers might put in even less than six hours. They were allowed to plant their own gardens and crops, raise chickens and pigs for sale and use the proceeds as they wished. Many of them developed unusual skills in handicraft which also brought in a good return.

Thomas Spalding was opposed to white overseers. His second-in-command at Sapelo was Bu Allah, "born in Africa, with a strain of Arabic blood, a Mohammedan, who said his prayers thrice daily, kneeling on his sheepskin rug as he turned his face to the East." Bu Allah lived to a great age, and became an island patriarch, the father of twelve sons and seven daughters.

Writing in an Arabic dialect, he kept a sort of journal at Sapelo which was an object of great interest to scholars a hundred years later. No one had ever been able to decipher it until the manuscript came into the possession of Georgia's State Library. Miss Ella May Thornton, state librarian, submitted photostatic copies to various language experts who were still unable to make a translation.

Finally, in 1939, the mystery began to unfold. Joseph H. Greenberg of Northwestern University took a copy of the manuscript with him to Africa for comparative study and research, though he did not make a translation. In 1945 Dr. Howard W. Glidden, then head of the Near East Section of the Library of

Congress, made both a study and a translation. He agreed with Greenberg's conclusions.

At last the mystery manuscript had yielded up its secret.

But what was it all about?

The contents of the "journal" were things remembered from legal work that had been a part of Bu Allah's student training.

The manuscript was not, as everyone had hoped, Bu Allah's own personal diary of life on Sapelo. It did reveal his original station, and the manuscript was declared by Dr. Glidden, "a great rarity"—the only piece of "American Arabica" in the original known to him.

Certainly Bu Allah's superior character and ability were recognized in life, and long after he was dead Joel Chandler Harris wrote two books based on legends surrounding his memory. They were *The Story of Aaron* and *Aaron in the Wildwoods*.

So much confidence was placed in Bu Allah by Mr. Spalding—so little did Mr. Spalding fear an uprising of his people—that he made Bu Allah a sort of military head as well as overseer of his plantation.

This was during the War of 1812, when the British were a menace to the Georgia sea islands. Thomas Spalding bought muskets which were turned over to Bu Allah with instructions to drill the slaves for the protection of Sapelo.

Said Bu Allah, as recorded by Caroline Couper Lovell, "I will answer for every Negro of the true faith, but not for the Christian dogs you own."

The British did not attack Sapelo, but they did considerable damage on St. Simons and carried off property and a number of slaves from the plantation of John Couper, on that island.

When the terrible hurricane of 1824 laid low many buildings on Sapelo, it was Bu Allah who directed most of the slaves to safety in the plantation sugar mills. Slave houses were tabby buildings of two rooms with a hall between and a loft upstairs for the children. The rooms were furnished with beds, chairs, chests. There was a slave hospital, under the supervision of Mrs. Spalding. Here, as on many plantations, patients often refused to take medicine from the hand of anyone but the mistress. Care of the sick was only one of the many duties of a plantation owner's wife. Though she lived on a golden isle, Mrs. Spalding led no life of gilded ease.

Thomas Spalding's father, James, was one of the first to grow the famous Sea Island cotton. Seeds of this long staple cotton—then cultivated on the Island of Anguilla in the West Indies—were sent to the elder Spalding by Colonel Roger Kelsall, a British Loyalist who had emigrated from Georgia to the Bahamas at the time of the American Revolution. Other Georgia planters received seeds from friends and soon, throughout the ports of the world, the former Anguilla cotton became known as Sea Island cotton.

Thomas Spalding not only grew cotton, he also engaged in large-scale diversification. He raised rice, also great quantities of cane, which was converted into sugar in his own island mills. He wrote articles on these subjects which were in demand by the *Southern Agriculturalist* and other publications of the day. His library, which contained many books on agriculture, was one of the largest in the South.

Says Dr. Coulter: "The planter philosophy of life was dominated as much by a social order as by an economic doctrine. With Spalding and the other coastal planters, it was not all of life to make a living; living itself was a fine art. Owning homes and beautifying them, having friends and entertaining them, meeting them at agricultural and sporting club gatherings, coming together on court days, participating in a considerable amount of political disputation but not much religious excitement, conversing on historical and scientific subjects—all this and more gave content to their living."

Thomas Spalding owned a great deal of property on the mainland. In addition to South End house he also designed a winter residence with a Grecian portico near Darien, which he called Ashantilly. The interior of Ashantilly was destroyed by fire in 1937, but tabby walls and foundations stood firm. This house is now owned by Mr. and Mrs. W. G. Haynes.

Thomas Spalding came back to Ashantilly after presiding over a momentous state convention at Milledgeville, Georgia, in December of 1850. Long before the War Between the States the differences of opinion between North and South developed into issues which threatened their continued union. Thomas Spalding was an old man, full of years and honors, too old perhaps for the duties he assumed with such patriotic zeal.

At the convention he wielded a strong influence; Georgia accepted the compromise of 1850: "the rest of the South fell in line and postponed the Civil War for a decade . . . so long that Spalding was spared the sad spectacle of seeing his country disrupted."

This was December. On the way back to Sapelo, he got as far as Ashantilly, then the home of his son Charles. Here he died shortly afterward, on January 4, 1851, and was buried in near-by St. Andrew's Cemetery. Already sleeping there was Sally Leake Spalding who had been his wife for nearly half a century, "one whose gentle influence was ever felt for good."

Thomas Spalding's own lichen covered epitaph reads: "Earnest of purpose, he relied upon himself alone. What he believed to be right, that he maintained—Nor faltered ever."

Although he owned the whole of Sapelo before his death, Thomas Spalding had neighbors on the island when he bought his first four thousand acres. These were the Marquis de Montelet and the Chevalier de la Horne, who shared the home of the marquis which was called Le Chatalet, soon picturesquely corrupted to "Chocolate" by island Negroes. Mr. Coffin later restored some of the out-build-ings and a slave cabin at Chocolate. But the main house and its separate kitchen remain a faintly pink tabby ruin now overgrown with vines and moss and lichen.

The marquis, who had fled Santo Domingo's bloody slave uprisings, lived in Paris until he came to America. He was a noted epicure and had a superb Negro chef, Cupidon, the envy of all his friends. There was one delicacy the marquis and the chevalier sorely missed. It is said that while taking daily walks about the island they were accompanied by a pig on a leash. They hoped the pig, grubbing for acorns, might discover truffles—a vain hope.

When the marquis died, Cupidon and his wife were freed by the terms of the will which provided for their manumission. But they wanted none of this strange new freedom. Among guests who had been entertained at Le Chatelet there was one whose appreciation of fine food had especially warmed Cupidon's heart. This was Mr. John Couper. Cupidon and his wife immediately set forth for Cannon's Point, the Couper plantation, on St. Simons Island.

Here they were fittingly welcomed. Cupidon not only was placed in charge of the cuisine but was given an apprentice to train in order that his art might not die with him.

The "old marquis," as de Montelet is referred to in some historical writings, was in fact forty-nine at the time of his death, according to the Savannah *Republican*. Before coming to Sapelo, he had lived at the Hermitage Plantation near Savannah, with his bride, Servanne Angelique Charlotte Picot de Boisfeillet. Sometime after her death he moved permanently to his rice plantation on Sapelo, where he died in 1814, "a gentleman esteemed and respected by his friends and acquaintances."

Perhaps the strangest dream ever inspired by the Golden Isles was that of five aristocratic Frenchmen, one of whom had the same family name—De Bois-feillet—as Servanne Angelique, who married the marquis.

Here on Sapelo they proposed to carry out "a most amazing and bizarre speculation," says Dr. Coulter, "the breeding of slaves and selling them through-out the New World. . . . Deaths and dissensions pierced this remarkable bubble."

In addition to Pierre Caesar Picot de Boisfeillet, they were Poulain Du Bignon, Francis Says Dumoussay DeLavauxe, Nicholas Francis Mazone de la Ville Hutchet and Grand Closmesle. All had emigrated to this country at the time of the French Revolution. In 1789 they acquired Sapelo Island from John McQueen.

At a still earlier date the island was the subject of a controversy between Mary Musgrove and the British. When the Indians signed a treaty with Ogle-thorpe, they had reserved Sapelo, St. Catherines and Ossabaw. Mary Musgrove, the half-breed Indian girl who acted as Oglethorpe's interpreter, later married

Thomas Bosomworth and with him the scheme was plotted whereby Mary announced herself as Queen of the Creeks and laid claim to these islands.

To resolve such claims the British government awarded her St. Catherines and sold the other two islands, giving her the money. The Bosomworths lived on St. Catherines for the rest of their lives and are buried there.

Richard Reynolds, like Thomas Spalding, is an active, inventive plantation owner. And like every cattle owner in Georgia, he is interested in raising the stock standard. At Sapelo, the Black Angus is being crossed with hump-backed Brahma bulls. Milk and butter from a fine Guernsey herd are sold on the mainland. About two thousand head of cattle graze in the green pastures on the island. All sorts of agricultural and soil and diking projects are continuously under way.

Sapelo has its own post office and even a small super-market on South End Square. Today six white families and about three hundred Negroes comprise the permanent residents of the island. Some of the Negroes are descendants of slaves owned by Thomas Spalding.

Groups of underprivileged boys are given vacations each year by Mr. Reynolds at a summer camp on Sapelo.

Much of the island's original jungle growth remains to preserve its primeval enchantment for visitors of all ages and to provide a bird and game sanctuary. Here, in one of the biggest rookeries to be found anywhere, are three different kinds of egrets and many other beautiful and rare birds.

A big tree apparently abloom with large white flowers may suddenly be stripped of its spectacular blossoms as you make the startled discovery that the blossoms really are a flock of white herons now in flight. A great bald eagle in a near-by tree also flaps his wings and soars disdainfully away, but not far. The wild turkeys seem to have forgotten there is such a thing as an open season. Even the deer take their time about disappearing into the bush.

Whatever nature failed to provide has been bountifully supplied. Chachalaca, or Brazilian pheasants, were imported by Mr. Coffin as game birds and have reproduced themselves beyond all anticipation. A huge lake has been stocked with fish to make good luck doubly sure for fishermen.

Blackbeard is said to have buried treasure on this island, but archaeologists are more interested in a huge outdoor arena enclosed by a high shell wall which some investigators believe to have been built two thousand year ago. In addition there is the site of what is believed to have been the old Spanish mission of San Jose de Zapala.

CHAPTER 19

The Blood Remembers

*Y*OU could hide a man in one of the secret drawers under the deeply recessed windows.

But not Chief Joseph Vann, who lived in the house, for he was six feet, six inches tall. The chief, half Scot and half Cherokee Indian, was "a man of fine appearance . . . a man of wealth, fond of horses and racing." The legend is that he kept his money hidden in one of these secret drawers.

Chief Vann went to Indian Territory in 1835, but his house still stands at Spring Place in Murray County. It stands on high ground, an impressive red brick structure, companioned by a few ancient shade trees and surrounded by the red Georgia clay of an open field. In the distance is the majestic range of the Cohuttas.

This was one of the finest houses in North Georgia at the time it was built— one of two brick houses in the entire Cherokee Nation. It is now one of the oldest dwellings in its section of the state. You could drive far and not find a more interesting house.

Violence has visited here, forcing a foot through an arched doorway which is dignified by a beautiful fan and recessed side lights. Pistols and muskets were used in desperate combat both above and below the unusual free-hanging balcony of the stairway that leads from the wide lower hall to the second floor and on to the attic. John Howard Payne, author of "Home, Sweet Home," was imprisoned on the charge of sedition in one of the Vann outbuildings, then occupied by the Georgia guard. Chief Vann was dispossessed in spite of the loopholes which made the house a fortress when it was built about 1790.

The Vann house is of modified Georgian architecture, with end-chimneys and a fine modillioned cornice. Its many paned windows have white stone lintels and sills. Four wide, vertical cement bands, evenly spaced across its red brick façade are all that remain of long-gone pilasters. The dilapidated two-story front porch is obviously a later addition.

The front rooms on either side of the wide hall are approximately twenty by thirty feet, with high ceilings and beautifully paneled wainscot. The fine Georgian chimney pieces with overmantels and other carved interior woodwork were imported from England especially for the house. The wallpaper, scraps of which still cling forlornly in high spots, probably also came from England.

But it is the stairway, with its free-hanging, unsupported balcony, midway between the first and second floors, that baffles most visitors. Twenty-three sight-seeing World War II WACs stood on this balcony at one time, and it still held firm.

Unsupported spiral stairways are fairly common in old houses, but this is not a spiral. The walnut staircase, with its carved spandrel ornaments, hugs the side of the wall halfway up to the second floor, then makes a right turn onto an oblong balcony which extends outward upon nothing more substantial than mountain air. From this balcony, the steps do an about face and proceed to the second floor and to the attic, where hundreds of sightseers have left their autographs on its plastered walls.

On the second floor you may turn left at the head of the stairs into the room where Spencer Riley's blood was spilled in the gun battle for possession of the house after the Vanns were served an eviction order. The bloodstains are gone from the wide scrubbed floor boards, but you—like the WACs—are impressed with the solidity of the old house. Try as you will, you cannot produce a creak.

Those floors, resting on huge, heavy wooden beams and sills, are as firm as the firmest pavement of a city street. You cross the hall to another spacious bed-room and look out at the wooded mountains. In spite of its hectic history, you realize there is an innate calm about the old house, like the calm of the neighboring hills. You begin to understand how it could survive so many years of shifting and sometimes shiftless tenancy, yet still retain a certain dignity and some of its original beauty.

A contractor named Robert Howell is said to have built the Vann house and also the house of David McNair across the line in Tennessee, the first brick houses in the Cherokee Nation. Many conflicting stories have been told about the bricks used in the construction of the Vann house and whether it was built for James or Joseph Vann. There were two Jameses, father and son, also a son named Joseph Vann. This is according to old records collected by Dr. J. E. Bradford, who bought the Vann place in 1920 and lives "a cornfield away."

It has been said the bricks for the house were brought over from England, that they were made in Philadelphia, that they were made in Savannah, that they were hauled to Spring Place by mule or Indian back.

"The truth is that the bricks were made about four hundred yards from the

Photo by Carolyn Carter

FIGURE 41. Free-hanging stairway of Chief Vann's house at Spring Place. Here a gun battle for possession of the house took place.

house," declares the Reverend William Jasper Cotter, Methodist minister, in his autobiography dealing with life in the Cherokee Nation from the time his family moved from Hall to Murray County in 1832. "I have seen the old brick yard where they were made," he stoutly affirms. Mortar was mixed by having mules and oxen tramp back and forth across the mud.

Joseph Vann was in possession in Mr. Cotter's day. "He owned quite a number of slaves," Mr. Cotter continues. "Vann's quarters were four miles out at Mill Creek. He was fond of fine stock, particularly fine horses. . . . The wealthy mixed bloods could have what they wanted and that of the best from Philadelphia or Washington City."

In the eighteen thirties Joseph Vann had eight hundred acres under cultivation. "He often had as many as twenty or thirty plows running in one field."

Joseph Vann was one of the five hundred young Cherokee braves who fought with Andrew Jackson in the famous battle of Horseshoe Bend in 1814. In seven hours of bloody fighting and blood-curdling war whoops on the banks of the Tallapoosa River in Alabama, all but a handful of the opposing thousand Creek warriors were killed. None surrendered. Many were drowned trying to escape.

Vann was also a member of a delegation appointed by the Cherokee General Council in 1832 to plead its nation's cause in Washington . . . against removal west. Some years earlier the Cherokees had adopted a representative form of government, and elected John Ross as their head.

John Ross, Principal Chief of the Cherokee Nation, was one of the "wealthy mixed bloods," son of a Scottish father and of an Indian mother whose father was a Scotsman. He was educated at Kingston, Tennessee. The Ross home, a two-story white frame house, stood at the head of the Coosa River, in what is now the city of Rome. Judge John Martin, treasurer of the Cherokee Nation, owned a plantation (now Carter's Quarters) on the Coosawattee River, about fifteen miles south of the Vann house. These are a few of the Cherokees described by Mr. Cotter as "wealthy mixed bloods." Major John Ridge, also a Cherokee chief but not of mixed blood, lived in a house called The Chieftains, on the Oostanaula River not far from the home of John Ross. Enlarged and improved, the Ridge house is still known by its Indian name.

Usually the white men who married into the Cherokees were of good stock, younger sons from Scotland or England, very different from the squaw men of the western tribes. The Cherokees themselves were a superior nation among North American Indians, greatly interested in education and other advantages of civilization. They lived in cabins or houses, tilled their fields, raised cattle and hogs, ran trading posts, hunted and fished and were in the main peaceful and law-abiding. When there was trouble, it was often traceable to the white man's fire water.

Near the turn of the eighteenth century, when the Moravians decided to establish a mission in Georgia, they were invited by James Vann to use a site near the Vann trading post at Spring Place. The mission, built like a blockhouse, was opened in 1802 and for many years—according to official records at Winston-Salem, North Carolina—the Vanns helped support various Cherokee students at the mission. A number of Indian boys were sent from the Cherokee Nation to the foreign mission school at Cornwall, Connecticut.

While the State of Georgia was still waiting for the federal government to carry out its long overdue agreement to move the Indians west, the Cherokee lands were divided into counties and the land lots distributed by public lottery. Tickets drawn entitled holders to buy specified property. Where the property was still occupied, the law required the ticket holder to wait a certain length of time until the place was vacated. This did not always happen.

It did not happen at the Vann house.

Joseph Vann received an eviction notice February 23, 1835, but he and his family were allowed to remain temporarily in one room. Spencer Riley of old Cass County (now Bartow) had been a boarder, occupying an upstairs bedroom in the Vann home since the preceding October. Having seen service as a constable, Mr. Riley was prepared to fight for legal procedure.

"It was March 2, 1835 when the outrage hereinafter related took place," says Mr. Riley in a statement published later in the Milledgeville [Georgia] *Journal.*

Captain W. N. Bishop, with a detachment of the Georgia Guard, "resolved to clear the Vann house and put his brother, Absalom Bishop, in possession," according to Mr. Riley.

From the free-hanging balcony of the stairway, Mr. Riley insisted that he would go peaceably if Captain Bishop, in the hall below, would acknowledge he had taken possession of the house by force.

Captain Bishop refused, and the battle was on.

"They fired upon me and fell back; I then fired too," Mr. Riley says. "Their shot slightly wounded me in my hand and arms, and immediately after ten or twelve muskets were fired at me, but being protected by the stairs, the shots did not take effect . . . they aimed at the spot they supposed I was and shot the banisters to pieces."

One of the guard threw a firebrand onto the stairs to force Riley down, but this was quickly removed in order to protect the house.

"I then presented a gun in sight to deter their further approach," Mr. Riley continues. "A rifle was fired by Absalom Bishop; the ball struck my gun and split, one part of it striking glancingly on my forehead . . . fragments of it wounding me on several other places on my face. . . . Several more muskets were fired at me . . . wounding me severely . . ."

Mr. Riley, bleeding, dropped on the bed in his room at the head of the stairs, from which he was rushed forty-five miles through a snowstorm to jail, charged with assault with intent to murder. His wounds, he says, were attended to next day when he was able to get word to friends.

Joseph Vann did what is called making the best of things. He accepted compromise—pay from the federal government for his "property improvements" and transfer to Indian Territory, now Oklahoma. He left behind the only home he had ever known and the lands he loved.

But—though the mind accepts—the heart remembers. The blood remembers.

More than a hundred years later the blood remembered when Neal Vann—wearing the uniform of a United States World War II army officer—made a pilgrimage to Spring Place, just to see the Vann house, the home of his ancestors.

Back of the violence at the Vann house was the larger struggle which had begun when the first Indians were removed west from Eastern states many years before. Little progress had been made along this line in Georgia.

In 1802 the state had renounced her claims to original charter lands in what became Alabama and Mississippi, and in return the federal government had agreed to do two things: It would make a settlement with the Cherokees for the lands they claimed in Georgia and would move them to territory beyond the Mississippi. In Georgia, as elsewhere in the country, the Indians were wards of Uncle Sam. No one could settle on Indian lands without a permit from the Indian agent.

(Colonel Return Jonathan Meigs was one of the early Indian agents for the area including the Vann house, and seems to have been generally popular. The quaint story of how he got his name is included in official records of the Moravian mission. His mother, a Quakeress, said "no" when his father proposed. Just before her suitor was beyond earshot, she called out, "Return, Jonathan." Their first-born's name attests the happiness they found together.)

Weary of the long delay in carrying out federal plans for the removal of the Cherokees, Georgia's Governor George R. Gilmer in 1830 requested that United States troops be withdrawn from Indian lands within the state. This was done and the Georgia Guard took over. In the meantime federal enrolling agents were making a canvass of all Indian residents, offering to reimburse them for property improvements, and to furnish transportation west, where new lands would be given in return, as well as a year's support. Many Indians accepted and were sent to Indian Territory.

Because the mountain fastnesses of the Cherokee country had long been a refuge for lawbreakers, Georgia passed an act requiring all settlers on its Indian lands to take an oath to uphold the constitution and the laws of the state. At that time an organized gang of robbers and murderers called the Pony Club, preyed upon frontier settlers and travelers along the old Federal Road. This was the first white man's road through the Indian country, and led from western Tennessee into North Georgia and on down to Augusta and Savannah. This way

Photo by Kenneth Rogers

FIGURE 42. Original Indian-time cabin near Atlanta, built of hewn logs.

came the cattle and hog drovers, fur trappers, farmers and others with produce to sell in the cities, from which they returned with new purchases and cash. It was "the darkest and most dangerous place in the old Cherokee Nation," according to the Reverend W. J. Cotter.

After paving the way for law and order, the state divided the Cherokee lands into counties and land lots. The distribution of lands by public lottery began in October, 1832.

Gold had been discovered in the North Georgia hills in 1829. The federal government later established a mint at Dahlonega. DeSoto and his followers had hoped to find treasure here when they visited this section in 1540. Now, everybody hoped to draw a lot with a gold mine. The gold lots contained forty acres, the regular land lots 160. (Every Cherokee head of a family was allowed a reservation of 160 acres, but no title was given.) "Lottery tickets were placed in a large hopper, the crank of which was turned by the Rev. J. B. Payne . . ." says Mr. Cotter. "The fortunate drawer, whether a poor widow or an old soldier, had an equal chance to buy the richest gold land or the richest farm land."

The Cherokee who fought hardest against removal to Indian Territory was John Ross, Principal Chief of the Nation. Among those finally willing to compromise were Cherokee Chief Major John Ridge, his son, John Ridge, and his nephew, Elias Boudinot.

Boudinot was editor of *The Phoenix*, published both in Cherokee and in English at New Echota, the capital of the Cherokee Nation near Calhoun, Georgia. He lost that job in 1832 and later lost his life because of differences of opinion with Ross.

Printing a newspaper in both languages was made possible by Sequoyah's famous alphabet which he invented in 1828. Using this alphabet, members of his race were able to read and write with only a few lessons.

When Sequoyah was middle-aged, an English spelling book had come into his possession, and although he could neither read nor write, he was able to use some of the English letters in working out symbols for his own alphabet.

These letters he scratched laboriously on tree bark, the job consuming twelve years in all. His wife was no different from many with paler faces. She thought he was wasting his time. One day in a fit of marital pique she pitched the whole business into the fire. The result of twelve years of patient effort blazed merrily. Whatever Sequoyah's immediate reaction, he soon began his job all over again. Fortunately, transcription from memory required a much shorter time.

Elias Boudinot, one-time editor of *The Phoenix*, had attended the mission school at Cornwall, and later had been a student at Andover. His Indian name, Kill-kee-nah, is translated as The Buck and is said to have been an apt description of his appearance. While in school, he had asked and been granted permission to adopt as his own the name of the president of the American Bible Institute, Elias Boudinot. When he returned to the Cherokee Nation with his new name, he also brought his bride, the former Harriett Ruggles Gold, daughter of a well-to-do white family of Cornwall. Both expected to become teachers. They had several children; a son later fought in the Confederate army. Harriett Boudinot died and is buried at New Echota, not far from the monument which marks the site of the old capital of the Cherokee Nation.

Boudinot and the two Ridges, father and son, were among those who met at New Echota with representatives from Washington and signed the treaty of December 29, 1835, by which the Cherokees finally accepted settlement for their lands east of the Mississippi.

By the terms of this treaty the Nation received five million dollars and new lands in the west. Individual Indians also received pay for property improvements, were given transportation west, a year's support and were granted new lands in Indian Territory.

According to the law of the Nation it was treason to sign away lands except by act of General Council. Principal Chief John Ross and other high council members did not attend the meeting at New Echota, hoping to block a quorum, but business went forward anyway.

It was a time of great unrest and bitterness. Andrew Jackson, the old Indian fighter, was President of the United States. "If I had known Jackson was going to drive us from our homes, I would have killed him that day at the Horseshoe," declared Chief Junaluska of the western North Carolina Cherokees.

Like Joseph Vann, Boudinot and the two Ridges went to Indian Territory in advance of the general migration. There, after the great body of Cherokees finally arrived, revenge caught up with them. Both the Ridges and Boudinot were brutally murdered on June 22, 1839.

It was three years after Joseph Vann and his family were evicted from the Vann house at Spring Place before the last of the Cherokees were removed from Georgia in 1838, under General Winfield Scott.

Their slow progress westward, six hundred to seven hundred miles in nearly five months, has been called "The Trail of Tears."

Such a mass movement in pioneer times entailed many hardships at best and there are some historians who say that the federal government did not make adequate preparations. Groups of the Cherokees were confined overlong at concentration points and meantime the seasons changed.

Some of the delay seems to have been due to management of affairs, in their later stages, by John Ross himself. Bowing at last to the inevitable, he asked and was given the privilege of leading his people into exile. It turned out to be a bigger job than he anticipated. Apparently it was a bigger job than anyone anticipated.

Certain it is that the movement was by that time inevitable. And certain it is too that of some fourteen thousand Cherokees who started out on the journey from Georgia, the Carolinas and Tennessee, four thousand died en route, among them the wife of John Ross. These deaths were due to everything from common colds and simple heartbreak to a scourge of cholera. At the point along the route where cholera struck, a local doctor who worked night and day ministering to the ill was himself among the many casualties.

"I had a part in all this tragic scene," wrote the Reverend W. J. Cotter, from the vantage point of the Vann house neighborhood. He believed the government did everything possible to handle the situation humanely.

"Everything for their comfort was considered," Mr. Cotter insisted in his book. "The mildest time of the year was chosen. From General Scott down every soldier and every citizen looked upon them with an eye of pity.

"Col. W. J. Howard, the quartermaster, boarded with us. . . . I hauled the first corn for their horses and perhaps the last. . . . Fort Gilmer was near the Carter place. . . . The situation required a dozen or more military posts.

"On a mild May morning two men stood at our gate. Dismounted from his large raw-boned white horse, his bridle rein on his arm, stood General Winfield Scott, with White Path, an Indian, for whom White Path Gold Mine was named. There was neither a white man nor an Indian there—only two old soldiers who had fought together at the Battle of Horseshoe Bend. White Path exhibited a medal that General Jackson had given him for his bravery in this battle . . .

"After all the warning and with the soldiers in our midst, the inevitable day appointed found the Indians at work in their fields. It is remembered as well as if it had been seen yesterday that two or three dropped their hoes and ran as fast as they could. The men handled them gently, but picked them up in the road, in the field, anywhere and carried them to the post. . . .

"When a hundred or more families had been collected, they were marched to Ross's landing [now Chattanooga]. It was a mournful sight to all who witnessed it—old men and women with gray hairs walking with the sad company. Provisions were made for those to ride who could not walk. . . . The young Indians and children were as merry as larks."

Mr. Cotter helped to haul household effects from the abondoned Indian cabins to be sent after their owners. "Chickens, cats and dogs all ran away when they saw us. Ponies under the shade trees fighting the flies with the noise of their bells, the cows and calves lowing to each other; the poor dogs howling for their owners; the open doors of the cabins as we left them—to have seen it all would have melted to tenderness a heart of stone. And in contrast, there was a beautiful growing crop of corn and beans."

Some of the Cherokees, who fled into the mountains, remained behind and as a result we have today the Cherokee Reservation in North Carolina. The right to remain was dearly bought for these fugitives whose chief was Utsali.

As the story comes down—and it is not a pretty one—the wife of an elderly Indian, named Charley, was a bit slow on the march to the fort where Indians were assembled before starting the trip west. To hurry her, a soldier did some prodding with his bayonet.

Whether old Charley and the male members of his family exchanged words in Cherokee, or whether they merely acted with one accord, it all happened in a flash. Each seized a soldier and wrestled for his gun. One of the guns exploded and a soldier was killed. During this commotion the small group of Indians got away.

General Scott felt certain they would join the Utsali fugitives. So he sought to make a bargain with Utsali. Word was sent through William H. Thomas, an honest Indian trader, greatly respected by the Cherokees. General Scott would cease his efforts to capture Utsali and his group—he would even petition Washington to allow them to remain—if they would surrender Charley and his relatives.

When the terms were relayed to old Charley, hiding with his family in a cave in the Great Smokies, he said, "I will come. I don't want to be hunted by my own people."

For the attack on armed authority, General Scott decided that he must make an example of the offenders. Old Charley, his brother and two elder sons were shot. By military order the execution was carried out by fellow Cherokees.

It has often been said that John Howard Payne, author of "Home, Sweet Home," was imprisoned in the Vann house, at Spring Place. But Payne's own story states that he was lodged by the Georgia Guard at Spring Place in "a small log hut, with no window and one door."

Payne came to Georgia in 1835 looking for material to publish in a projected magazine. Here two unrelated and unforgettable adventures happened to him.

He fell in love with an Athens, Georgia, girl.

He got into trouble as an Indian sympathizer.

In the Cherokee country, he immediately became suspect when he interviewed John Ross in a cabin just across the Tennessee line. Ross had taken refuge there when his Georgia home was his no longer. By this time Ross's resistance to removal west was a sore subject with the Georgia Guard.

In his own statement, John Howard Payne says that his interest was in certain historical material about the Cherokees which had been turned over to Ross by a predecessor, Charles R. Hicks. Payne made a transcript of this material for his proposed magazine. Unfortunately, he also made some notes in which he said the Georgia Guard looked less like soldiers than like banditti.

This did not help when the same Georgia Guard crossed the Tennessee line, arrested Ross and his guest, seized all papers and brought their prisoners to Spring Place. Music may have its charms, but one member of the Guard, who happened to hum "Home, Sweet Home," seems to have been more charmed by the fact that he had the author of that poignant ballad under his thumb at the moment.

Payne and Ross were charged vaguely with being abolitionists and plotting an uprising of blacks and redskins against the whites. Ross was freed after nine days and succeeded in getting word back to Payne that his "friends had not forgotten." Apparently everybody from the President on down was petitioned in Payne's behalf, but news traveled slowly and it was twelve and a half days before he was given his freedom.

John Howard Payne had brought with him to Georgia letters of introduction to various prominent men of the day. One of these was addressed to General Edward Harden. The general invited him to be a guest in the Harden home in Athens, where he met the general's pretty brunette daughter, Mary, with whom he promptly fell in love. He later gave her a number of Indian relics, which have come down in the Harden family. Other romantic mementos are an autographed copy of "Home, Sweet Home" and a letter, dated July 18, 1836, in which John Howard Payne laid his heart and hand at the feet of the Georgia girl, entreating her to "smile upon his suit."

What Mary said is still her own private affair. But she did not marry Payne. She did not marry anyone. And the composer of "Home, Sweet Home," died in the consular service in Morocco in 1852—still a bachelor.

CHAPTER 20

More Money Than Carter Had Oats

*E*VERYTHING he touched turned to gold."

This was often said of Farish Carter, Georgia's richest ante-bellum plantation owner, who as a boy ran away from school to make his fortune and did.

There was another old saying used to describe a rich man—"he had more money than Carter had oats"—which is said to have been inspired by Farish Carter himself. Wealth beyond calculation is the way it added up in the days before adding machines were invented.

Colonel Carter's two ante-bellum homes are still owned by his descendants. One house is at Scottsboro, near Milledgeville, which was the state capital in Farish Carter's time. The other is at Carter's Quarters and was originally the home of an Indian chief.

Carter's Quarters stands in what was once the heart of the old Cherokee Nation, now Murray County in North Georgia. The house was there before Murray was drawn on the maps and before the town of Chatsworth was founded nine miles north. Built sometime around 1800 as a two-story white frame dwelling, extensive additions have since been made, but this original house remains intact as a wing of the present handsome structure.

Carter's Quarters is the largest plantation in Georgia which has come down to the present time "undiminished in area from the old feudal days." It was divided in recent years but all the fifteen thousand acres are still owned by Carter descendants. The house and its surrounding fifteen hundred acres are now the joint property of five great-grandchildren, who take turns using it for vacations and weekends. They are W. Colquitt Carter, Mary McDonald Barnett and Samuel Carter Barnett of Atlanta and Mrs. George Hamilton and Mrs. Henry Hamilton of Dalton.

Colonel Carter first saw the house when it was the home of Judge John Martin, treasurer of the Cherokee Nation. The colonel was making a trip through North Georgia to Tennessee by way of the old Federal Road and he spent a night en route as Judge Martin's guest. Judge Martin, one of the wealthy "mixed bloods" of the Cherokees, owned eighty slaves. His plantation was then called Coosawattee, after the river that flows through its green valley.

Colonel Carter was greatly impressed with the beauty of the Coosawattee Valley and the great Cohutta mountains. Later, when the Cherokee lands were ceded to the federal government and plans agreed upon for the removal of the Indians, he bought Coosawattee Plantation.

This was an achievement, even for a man of Colonel Carter's means and influence. In 1832 the State of Georgia divided the Indian lands into lots of 160 acres each, except in the gold section around Dahlonega where lots were limited to forty acres each. These were numbered and the numbers drawn by prospective purchasers. Colonel Carter bought up all the lots drawn by others until he had the entire fifteen thousand acres of the Coosawattee Plantation. By that time he had spent $40,000, which was a considerable sum in the eighteen thirties. The change of the plantation's name to Carter's Quarters seems to have come about gradually, inspired perhaps by the quarters of the slaves, "in sight of the old home . . . a little village kept clean and neat."

Colonel Carter and his family continued to live in the house near Milledgeville and used the North Georgia plantation as a summer home. A gang of cutthroats made three attempts to murder the Colonel at Carter's Quarters, believing he had a fortune stored there.

Each time the bandits failed, for a very good reason. "The dogs were set upon them by the Negroes at the house who supposed that some animal was skulking in the bushes." When the gang was finally caught, one of its members confessed they had killed and robbed wealthy men from Virginia to Florida, and having heard that Carter was extremely wealthy, had selected him as another victim.

On one of his trips to North Georgia, Farish Carter happened to stop over in a town which was in process of getting itself named. He jokingly suggested to the city fathers that they might use his name, which they did.

And so, as you travel north from Atlanta to Carter's Quarters, you come about midway to Cartersville, named just like that for Colonel Carter. There you turn right into U. S. Highway 411 and drive through farmlands and vineyards past Pine Log Mountain and on to the beautiful valley of the Coosawattee River.

At this point the highway follows the route of the old Federal Road, the first white man's road from Kentucky and Tennessee through the Indian country of North Georgia down to Augusta and Savannnah. It was a dangerous road in the old days and even now, as you travel north, it gives you the feeling that you are entering a remote mountain fastness.

Photo by Carolyn Carter

FIGURE 43.   Original house of Indian Chief John Martin, Treasurer of the Cherokee Nation. It was built around 1800 near Chatsworth. Note the hand-carved
scallop trim and irregular spacing of windows.

Off to the left of this historic highway, screened by the green leaves of many trees, is the white plantation house, Carter's Quarters. It stands on a grassy knoll in the midst of spacious tree-shaded grounds that remind you of the parks surrounding old English country houses.

Additions to the house were made as needed when Colonel Carter bought the property. These created a somewhat heterogeneous effect, and in the nineteen thirties they were removed. Today the old house has a twin—a duplicate end-wing—and these are joined by a central section with a long white-columned porch. The beautiful effect of architectural balance is enhanced by rich plantings of boxwood, great oaks and elms and by two ancient cedar trees standing directly at center front of the porch and rising twice as high as the two-story house.

This is the view you get as you enter the grounds. Follow the driveway around to the front and step back to Judge Martin's day. Here the original one-story front porch, with its slim chamfered columns and a quaint scalloped cornice carved by skilled Indian craftsmen, overlooks a wide, sloping expanse of green, at the foot of which is Rock Spring, a landmark of other days around which the Indians are said to have held ceremonial rites.

Doors from the porch open into each of the two downstairs front rooms with their white painted walls of wide horizontal hand-planed boards and polished floors of slightly narrower heart pine. Fire places have beautiful hand-carved Georgian mantels, and from the room on the right a graceful stairway, with carved decorations, leads to the second floor. These four large rooms are just as they were when the house was built. No doubt, there were the usual shed rooms at the back, torn down along with the early Carter additions.

From rear windows you can see the separate building which housed the old kitchen and dining room. These are still furnished with tables and cupboards put together with wooden pegs. Iron pots hang on a crane at the huge kitchen fireplace. The old one-room plantation office building also still stands in the side yard.

Judge Martin, for whom the house was built, is described as being five feet, ten inches tall, blond and weighing about 170 pounds. "He had two wives at one time," according to the autobiography of the Reverend Mr. Cotter.

"These wives were sisters, Misses Lucy and Nellie McDaniel, who had about the same amount of Indian blood John Martin had. He had good homes for them both, about 15 miles apart, one on the Saluquay river, the other on the Coosawattee . . .

"I was there in 1834 and saw Susannna (the grown-up daughter at Coosawattee) sweep their house for the last time," Mr. Cotter writes. "She burned the broom for good luck, walked down the steps and got into the carriage. With a sad heart they left their old home and started on their long journey to the West."

The date, 1834, is probably a misprint. John Martin still lived in his house in 1835, according to a letter written by Governor Wilson Lumpkin and reprinted

Photo by Carolyn Carter

FIGURE 44. Carter's Quarters near Chatsworth. Farish Carter, Georgia's richest ante-bellum plantation owner, bought the John Martin house and used it as the left wing of this house.

in volume one of his book on the *Removal of the Cherokees*. The letter, dated February 10, 1835, is addressed to Colonel William N. Bishop of the Georgia Guard and says in part: "I am glad to have it in my power to inform you that our friend, Colonel Carter, without hesitancy, wrote to Judge Martin informing him that he might continue to keep his place the present year . . ." Eighteen thirty-five to 1838 was the time officially set for the removal.

Sad as it was that Judge Martin had to give up his home, he himself was one of the Cherokee leaders who believed that only the removal of the Indians could solve the situation then existing in North Georgia, parts of the Carolinas and Tennessee. He received pay for his Georgia property and was granted new lands west of the Mississippi, where he became the first chief justice of the supreme court of Indian Territory—now Oklahoma.

When Farish Carter acquired this great North Georgia plantation, he was living at Scottsboro, five miles from Milledgeville, in a house which is now the oldest residence still standing in Baldwin County. It was built by General John Scott (of the state militia) in 1806, and the settlement which grew up around it was called Scottsboro. Farish Carter bought the Scottsboro Plantation and Bona Vista, the old Mills place, on the Oconee River in 1815.

In 1811 he had married Eliza McDonald, whose brother, Charles J. McDonald, was later governor of Georgia. To insure themselves congenial neighbors at Scottsboro, Colonel Carter presented building lots to a selected group of friends. He also built extensive additions to his own residence, among these "a double breezeway, which forms a cross-passage though the house." The porch extends around two sides of the house and its eaves and slender columns are draped with wisteria. Great oaks provide further shade and coolness.

Near-by Milledgeville was then the capital of Georgia, and much entertaining was done by the Carters. It is said that there was never a time when guests were not coming and going, or more likely coming and remaining for an indefinite time. There were twenty house servants.

Farish Carter's home life seems to have been somewhat like that later depicted in *Life with Father*. Although a shrewd businessman as well as a planter, he was generous with his family, his friends and his wife's numerous kin. Many boys and girls—some from Murray County—were educated at his expense. But Mrs. Carter could never be completely happy because her husband was not a church member. She herself was a praying Baptist and all their married life Mrs. Carter not only used prayer but every known maneuver to get her husband into the fold of the Baptist Church.

He held out for forty-eight years, but finally, in his old age, was baptized in 1859, two years before his death.

Farish Carter's "career fits exactly into the period of the old South, for he was born [November 28, 1780] two months after the British laid siege to Augusta and died two months after the firing upon Fort Sumter [June 17, 1861]." This apt observation is made by Ralph B. Flanders, author of *Plantation Slavery in Georgia*.

Farish Carter's father, Major James Carter, lost his life in the siege of Augusta. "It is reasonably certain that he was descended from the Carters of Virginia," says Dr. Flanders. (Farish Carter visited relatives there in 1802.)

When Mrs. James Carter remarried, there was stepfather trouble, and Farish ran away from the school of the Reverend Hope Hull in Washington, Wilkes, to make his fortune.

"It was during the war of 1812 and the subsequent trouble with the Indians and Spaniards that Carter laid the foundation for this fortune," Dr. Flanders explains. "In the capacity of United States Army contractor for the State of Georgia he received amounts during one year alone which totaled $57,000.

"Everything he touched turned to gold. Although he never held public office, the leading attorneys, representatives, senators and governors were his intimate friends and many of them were indebted to him for their success in life.

"His name was to be found among the directors of the leading banks; he possessed a fortune in stocks and bonds; most of the water power of the state was under his control; his steamboats plied the Ocmulgee, Oconee, Altamaha, Tennessee and even the Mississippi river. Other interests included a cotton factory, a woolen mill, a marble quarry, a cigar factory, innumerable stores, corn and flour mills and ferries. As a planter he accumulated enormous holdings in lands and slaves and at the time of his death his property was located in Georgia, Florida, Alabama, Mississippi, Louisiana, Arkansas, Indiana and Illinois."

Business took Farish Carter to Havana, New York, Washington, Mississippi, Louisiana and many other points. His wide interests are reflected in the fact that he subscribed to fourteen out-of-town newspapers. His many books remain on the library shelves at Scottsboro, "works on theology, science, philosophy, politics, a set of American state papers." Many of the original rich furnishings also remain in the house, which is now owned by John R. L. Smith, whose late wife was a great-granddaughter of Farish Carter. Their son, Furman Smith, lives in Atlanta.

During Colonel Carter's frequent business trips, Mrs. Carter managed the Baldwin County plantations. A son, James, directed a plantation in Macon County, Alabama. Another son, Samuel McDonald Carter, was in charge of the plantation at Carter's Quarters, while still another son, Benjamin F. Carter, directed the cigar factory in near-by Dalton which turned out two thousand cigars a day.

In the eighteen fifties, Farish Carter considered selling his slaves and investing this enormous capital otherwise. "Such a decision at that time, heretical to say the least, shocked his family and friends and at the earnest solicitation of his wife, the idea was abandoned."

Perhaps Farish Carter, astute businessman that he was, saw the shape of things to come. At any rate, he died just at the right time, in 1861, at the end of his era, just before his world was destroyed by the war which began with that first fatal shot, fired at Fort Sumter.

CHAPTER 2 1

Bride of Bulloch Hall

*R*OSWELL King reined in his horse and paused on the banks of the
the Chattahoochee River to enjoy the view. He was en route from Darien to the
government mint at Dahlonega, where gold was being mined in the North Georgia
hills and coined into spending money practically on the same spot.

Roswell King was manager of the great Pierce Butler plantations on Butler
and St. Simons Islands, where Pierce Butler's wife, Fanny Kemble, the famous
English actress, wrote her journal of life on a Georgia plantation, as described
in a previous chapter. He was also an influential citizen of Darien and had come
to North Georgia on a mission for the then powerful Bank of Darien. This was
in the early eighteen thirties, and there was no means of rail transportation, so
he made the trip on horseback into a section of the state still largely inhabited by
Cherokee Indians.

The spot at which he paused is now the town of Roswell, twenty-one miles
from Atlanta. For in that brief glance around him Mr. King saw more than the
beautiful natural scenery. He saw sites for summer homes of coastal residents.
He saw mills operated by water power. He saw lands cleared for cotton.

And so a group of spacious houses blossomed white in the green up-country
wilderness of North Georgia as the result of one man's dream. These old houses,
with their tall white columns, still lend an atmosphere of romance and charm to
the town which bears its founder's name—an atmosphere that has an authentic
background of solid fact.

In Bulloch Hall, one of the three most impressive of the old houses—the other
two are Barrington Hall and Mimosa Hall—Mittie Bulloch was married to Theodore Roosevelt in December, 1853. Their son, also named Theodore, became
President of the United States. Another son, Elliott, was the father of Eleanor,
wife of President Franklin D. Roosevelt.

Photo by Frances Benjamin Johnston

FIGURE 45. The mother of a President married here at Bulloch Hall in Roswell.

Roswell King and his son, Barrington King, bought large tracts of land in this section, and building sites were presented to relatives and friends. In the late eighteen thirties a Boston architect was commissioned to build houses and the beautiful Presbyterian church.

Those original settlers—Kings, Bullochs, Dunwodys, Smiths, Pratts, Hands—found life in Roswell so pleasant they soon gave up any thought of return to the coast, and the houses became permanent residences. Other families soon joined the colony and built homes.

Roswell King died in 1844 and Major James Stephen Bulloch did not live to see his daughter married. Grandfather-to-be of a President, he was himself the grandson of Archibald Bulloch, Revolutionary governor of Georgia, who played such an important part in shaping the destiny of the state.

The John Dunwodys of Phoenix Hall (now Mimosa) naturally were among Roswell guests at Mittie Bulloch's wedding. They were aunt and uncle of the bride, who had been christened Martha. Mrs. Dunwody was the former Jane Bulloch. Guests came from far and wide and stayed for days to enjoy the many parties given by family and friends for the bride and bridegroom. In those days newly married couples did not rush off immediately after the wedding.

Barrington King's daughter, Eva, was one of Mittie Bulloch's bridesmaids. Many years later she described the wedding in an interview given to Margaret Mitchell which was published in *The Atlanta Journal Magazine*, June 10, 1923. Miss Mitchell was for four years a member of *The Journal Magazine* staff.

At the time of the interview Mrs. W. E. Baker, the former Eva King, was eighty-seven years old and still living at Barrington Hall.

" 'Of course, Mittie Bulloch's wedding was a very fine affair,' Mrs. Baker told Margaret Mitchell. 'For days beforehand all the girls visited each other to have icing parties. That was the way we iced our cakes,' she explained. 'All of the girls got together and iced cakes at each other's houses.

" 'The wedding was at night and everything was very sweet for the ceremony. The dining room at Bulloch Hall was decorated with flowers and vines, but, of course, not so elaborately as houses are decorated now. Mittie wore a white satin dress and a long veil that became her beautifully, and we bridesmaids wore white muslin dresses made with full skirts and tight basque waists.

" 'We carried flowers too and came down the wide stairway with the trailing clusters in our arms. The ceremony took place in the dining room and we grouped ourselves just at the folding doors. Everything was beautiful.

" 'When the wedding was over, everybody crowded around congratulating the Roosevelts and kissing them and shaking hands. You could even see the servants peeping out of the back hall and beaming around corners . . .

" 'There were long mahogany tables covered with refreshments. On one table there were all kinds of baked and roasted meats. . . . On another table were cakes of every conceivable kind, with the bride's cake large and white and frosted in delicate designs rising in the center.

" 'We had ice brought all the way from Savannah to make the ice cream and no one there was more astonished at it than Mr. Roosevelt's parents. It was their first trip South . . . and they were pleased by the elegance of everything. . . . We sat at little tables and the servants served us. There is no such service now, because then there were so many servants and so much time to train them.

" 'After the wedding there were parties for some days and then Mr. Roosevelt took Mittie away to New York. . . . She came back to visit several times but I never saw President Roosevelt until he visited Roswell [in 1905] after his big African trip. He had heard so much about the town that he was anxious to see it.

" 'As his mother's old friend, I invited him and his party to breakfast with me, but it seemed that that was an unprecedented thing, so he ate in his private railway car. The man who was his secretary, or at any rate who arranged his engagements—did not want him to come out to my house for some reason.

" 'This secretary sent word to me that I could see the President at the reception at the church.' Here Mrs. Baker drew herself up and folded her hands firmly in her lap. 'I sent word,' she continued in positive accents, 'that if President Roosevelt didn't care enough to come to see his mother's old friend, I certainly would not go to see him.

" 'That very morning I had a lovely visit from the President and his wife,' she continued with triumph and dignity struggling in her voice. 'I met them at the door myself and showed them in instead of sending the maid . . .

" 'We all talked very pleasantly. I told him of his mother and her girlhood and her marriage and he sat and listened. He liked the South . . .' "

Even a President of the United States should have been a bit impressed as he and his party moved up the box-bordered walk to the wide front door of Barrington Hall.

The big white house is set amid spacious grounds steeply terraced. Something about the approach on foot to one of these old houses, the fluted Doric columns of its wide portico rising two-stories high in front and on both sides, definitely dwarfs the ego. Perhaps this is not so strange when we remember that this particular architectural style is an adaptation of the Greek Parthenon.

Barrington Hall, on the southern side of the square around which the town was built, is the first of the old houses seen on the left as one enters Roswell when driving from Atlanta. It is now the home of the Misses Evelyn and Katharine Simpson, nieces of Mrs. Baker. This is the only one of the three Halls still owned and lived in by descendants of the builder. Among its furnishings are many interesting family heirlooms.

Farther over to the left on a slight rise at the end of tree-shaded Bulloch Avenue is Bulloch Hall, where the famous wedding took place. It is classic Greek

Revival with pedimented roof and four tall Doric columns across its wide front porch.

On one of the many visits of President and Mrs. Franklin D. Roosevelt to Warm Springs, Mrs. Roosevelt drove up to Roswell to see the home of her Georgia grandmother. She was welcomed by Mrs. J. B. Wing, the present owner, into the wide central hall with its lovely columned arch and graceful stair.

Mrs. Roosevelt was shown the spacious double parlors on the left and the library on the right, which opens into the dining room. In this latter room, Mrs. Roosevelt, smiling, stood on the exact spot on which Mittie Bulloch said her vows so many years before.

Mimosa Hall, the third of Roswell's three original halls—now the home of Mr. and Mrs. Granger Hansell—is the dream realized for everybody who loves old houses. Perfectly preserved and exquisitely furnished in traditional style, it is a setting for modern hospitality rivaling that of ante-bellum times.

Mimosa's four tall Doric columns are first glimpsed through green leaves as you turn into the long flagstone driveway leading to the flagged court in front of the house. Ivy, so old that it blooms, climbs over the columns and onto the stucco walls. There is lavender wisteria in season and a rambling Lady Banksia rose blossoms yellow from a chaste tree at one side of the broad front porch.

You half expect to be met by a hostess in hoop skirts, for time has lingered here in stately calm, perhaps because all the various owners of the house have loved it. Only a short distance from the business center of town and a half hour's drive from Atlanta, Mimosa Hall still rests serene in its own century and the seclusion of its rolling green lawns, towering oaks, magnolias, mimosas, cedars, pines and other trees.

Mrs. Hansell suggests that it is really a sort of heritage house, with visible evidence of the affection it inspired in all its owners.

John Dunwody, its builder, loved his house so much that when it burned on the night of the housewarming, he immediately had it rebuilt. Originally, the house was white clapboard, almost a twin of Bulloch Hall. Bricks for its rebuilding were made on the place by slave labor and covered over with stucco blocks. Because it had risen from the ashes, Mr. Dunwody christened the new structure Phoenix Hall.

Shortly after the War Between the States, the property was acquired by Confederate General Andrew Jackson Hansell of Marietta, great-grandfather of Granger Hansell, the present owner. Mr. Hansell, an Atlanta attorney, also had a great-grandfather on "the other side." That general visited the South with General Sherman, liked what he saw and came back to settle after the war.

But it was the Southern great-grandfather who settled at Roswell. Today Sally and Granger Hansell can enjoy the fragrance of lilies of the valley planted in their garden three generations earlier by a great-grandmother. This is true, in

Photo by Harold Haliday Costain

FIGURE 46.   In its setting of green, Mimosa Hall, at Roswell,
stands like a Grecian temple.

spite of the fact that the house has changed hands more than once between Hansell ownership.

In 1899 it was bought by Mrs. Barrington J. King, widow of a descendant of the founder of Roswell. She planted additional mimosa trees and renamed the place Mimosa Hall.

One of the South's most gifted architects bought the property in 1918. The late Neel Reid designed many of the houses which have won for Atlanta its reputation as a city of beautiful homes, but chose an old house, an "original," for himself.

Mr. Reid tore out the partitions separating double parlors at Mimosa Hall and made one long beautiful paneled drawing room with twin fireplaces. In the spacious hall are three block-printed grisaille side-wall panels which Mr. Reid brought back from Europe. The larger of these makes an effective background for a handsome mahogany console, a signed piece by Lannieu, whose shop was near that of Duncan Phyfe in New York. This is one of many beautiful old pieces of mahogany with which the Hansells have furnished their house.

Mrs. Hansell insists there are no formal gardens at Mimosa Hall but they are very lovely just the same, like outdoor living rooms, green-velvet-carpeted, walled by green hedges of flowering shrubs and tall trees. The gardens are separated from the paddock by a long allée—a tree-bordered walk for cloistered meditation.

They have lovely names too, these gardens. There is the weeping garden, so named because of the weeping cherry and weeping willow trees that dominate its planting. There is the lily pool garden, and a swimming pool, overlooked by a flagged terrace, shaded with English laurel, mimosas and crape myrtle. And there are, of course, a rose garden and a cutting garden.

Mimosa Hall truly counts no hours but those that are serene.

The very first of the fine old houses, planned by that Boston architect whose name nobody remembers, is the Doric-columned white frame house owned by Mr. and Mrs. Nap Rucker. This house is set apart from the others by a hand-turned balustrade which encloses its front garden. Built for Roswell King's daughter, Mrs. Eliza Hand, it was also for a time the home of Mr. King himself.

Nap Rucker, for ten years a star pitcher for the Brooklyn Dodgers, is one big-league baseball player who knew what he wanted to do when he retired. He continued as a scout for the Dodgers, but he also operated a picturesque gristmill at Roswell. Unfortunately the mill burned while he was away on one of his scouting trips. Mr. Rucker is now superintendent of the Roswell water works, but keeps an eye on his native Crabapple. This small North Georgia town, three miles from Roswell, has produced a surprising number of big-league baseball players, including Nap's nephew, John Rucker, who was an outfielder with the New York Giants.

Dr. Francis R. Goulding, Presbyterian minister, inventor of an early-model sewing machine and author of the beloved children's classic, *The Young Ma-rooners*, spent his last years in Roswell and is buried in one of its old cemeteries. He lived in what is now known as the J. G. Wright house, a large red brick dwelling with massive columns remodeled since Dr. Goulding's day.

There are many legends as to why Dr. Goulding failed to patent the sewing machine he invented and which was in use in Georgia a year ahead of the Howe model. One of the legends is that the Goulding model was stolen and in the meantime another inventor had obtained a patent. Another story is that Dr. Goulding's model fell out of his buggy when he was crossing a river and was lost. He did receive credit while living for his popular juvenile stories, and a new edition of *The Young Marooners* was published in fairly recent times.

Great Oaks, used as the manse when Nathaniel A. Pratt served as Roswell's first Presbyterian minister, is built of bricks, handmade by slaves. Very handsome they are now, weathered a mellow wine red. Mr. Pratt married Roswell King's daughter and the house is still "in the family," as the home of Mr. and Mrs. Emmett Rushin. Mrs. Rushin is a great-granddaughter of the Pratts.

A fine example of the "raised-cottage" type of architecture in Roswell is the old Robert A. Lewis house, built about 1847 and now owned by Mr. and Mrs. Robert Sommerville. Although called a cottage, this white-columned house has large formal rooms with beautiful marble mantelpieces. Its brick "basement" is really a ground floor, originally planned for use as kitchen, dining room, schoolroom, office, etc.

Roswell, a town much visited by Atlantian's with guests from above the Mason and Dixon line, has placed markers which guide sightseers to these and other charming old houses, churches, cemeteries and historic spots.

The old covered bridge across the Chattahoochee River, which made such a romantic approach to Roswell, was replaced long ago by a wide, modern span. But Roswell itself is still Atlanta's most romantic approach to an ante-bellum past.

CHAPTER 22

Stagecoach Inn

*T*URN your back on your car for a moment and you can easily imagine you have just stepped out of a stagecoach.

Before you is Traveler's Rest, a stagecoach tavern built in 1775 shortly before the Revolutionary War. Those small round openings under the eaves and in the end-chimneys are loopholes through which guns were fired at attacking Indians who, nevertheless, wiped out the original owners of Traveler's Rest.

Less than five minutes ago you were speeding along Highway 123 half a dozen miles or so above Toccoa, your horizon bounded by the beautiful Blue Ridge Mountains. Time is still racing along 123 and all the other highways. But you took a left turn into an up-and-down unpaved road and then a right turn and suddenly time stood still.

There was the old tavern—like a flash back in a movie, but real. Tucked out of sight on a green tree-shaded hill overlooking the broad Tugalo River Valley, Traveler's Rest greets you with an atmosphere of welcome which is as much a part of the simple two-story frame building as the low-columned porch extending one hundred feet across its front. This is probably the oldest house still standing in Northeast Georgia, never painted but well preserved, nothing about it changed, inside or out. Even the original furnishings remain, down to the last musket on its convenient wall rack. The house has twenty rooms and today is the home of only one person, Mrs. Mary Jarrett White, granddaughter of Devereaux Jarrett, who bought the property about 1800.

What a welcome sight Traveler's Rest must have been to stagecoach passengers after a long day of jolting over rough mountain roads through mud or dust. It was a stopping point just this side of South Carolina, with the Tugalo River as the dividing line between the two states which were colonies when the inn was built. Jarrett's Bridge spanned the stream.

A visit by a stagecoach to Traveler's Rest in August of 1837 is described by G. W. Featherstonhaugh, English scientist and a Fellow of the Royal Society of

FIGURE 47.　Traveler's Rest, old stagecoach inn near the Georgia-South Carolina border, was built in 1775 shortly before the Revolutionary War. It is now the home of Mrs. Mary Jarrett White (pictured), descendant of an early owner.

London, who came to America to gather specimens of mineral deposits. The title of his book, *Canoe Voyage*, was inspired by a trip to the headwaters of the "Minnay Sotor" (Minnesota). In Georgia he inspected the regions around Dahlonega, where gold was discovered in 1829. From that point he set out by stagecoach for Fort Hill, South Carolina, to visit the celebrated statesman, John C. Calhoun, spending a night en route at Clarksville. Next morning at five o'clock the journey was resumed.

"Twelve miles from Clarksville," writes Mr. Featherstonhaugh, "I went up a narrow ravine to see the very pleasing water fall of Toccoa . . . the height of the cascade is about 200 feet and the breadth about 30 feet. . . . It is one of the prettiest things I ever saw and is in a lovely retired place shut in by hills on both sides . . .

"We now proceeded for eight miles at a rapid pace down the steep southern slope of the mountains through beautiful woods and dales to Jarrett's on the Tugalo, a main branch of the Savannah. Here I got an excellent breakfast of coffee, ham, chicken, good bread, butter, honey and plenty of good new milk for a quarter of a dollar.

"The landlord cultivated an extensive farm and there was a fine bottom of good land near the house. He was a quiet, intelligent, well behaved man and a great admirer of Mr. Calhoun and seemed anxious to do what was obliging and proper more from good feeling than for the poor return he chose to take for his good fare. What a charming country this would be to travel in if one was sure of meeting with such nice clean quarters once a day. The traveler does sometimes, but unfortunately they stand nearly in the same proportion to the dirty ones that the known planets do to the fixed stars."

Traveler's Rest continued as a popular mountain resort long after railroads succeeded stagecoaches and Charles K. Jarrett succeeded his father as landlord, carrying on the tradition established by Devereaux Jarrett, who so favorably impressed Mr. Featherstonhaugh. (Charles K. was Mrs. White's father.)

In fairly recent years Mrs. White decided that the name Traveler's Rest was inappropriate for a private residence and changed it to Jarrett's Manor. This is the name on the marker placed in the front yard by the D. A. R. But now that Toccoa plans to promote the historic old building as one of its many tourist attractions, she says she half regrets the change.

A gracious, vivacious lady of eighty-two, she declares humorously, "Everything about the place is old but me. Grandfather owned all the land hereabout— including what is now Toccoa—thousands of acres. I have only six."

She was the last of the babies to be rocked in the hand-carved swinging cradle which still stands in one of the big bedrooms. Here, like the babies before her, she was feather-cuddled in a hollowed-out pine log, suspended from a crossbar supported by wooden framework. On each side of the cradle are cut-out hand holds for swinging it back and forth. Mrs. White grew up as "Baby" Jarrett. At Lucy Cobb Institute in Athens, fashionable finishing school of its day, she answered to the name of Mary Elizabeth for the first time. Today in Toccoa everybody blithely hails her as "Miss Baby."

"They say this is where grandfather kept his gold nuggets," she said, moving from the cradle to the hand-carved mantel above a fireplace big enough for a five-foot log. The cross paneling of the mantel is adorned with tiny knobs which serve for more than decoration. Each opens a secret drawer.

The nuggets are gone, but in the drawers of old mahogany secretaries are love letters stored by Mrs. White's grandmother and other ladies of the house. Faded ink comes alive today in high-flown language, threatening suicide if the fair one withholds her favor.

FIGURE 48. In spite of loopholes (marked by arrows), the original owners of Traveler's Rest, Jesse Walton and family, were massacred by Indians.

Gentlemen seemed to know their minds in those days. Mrs. White's father took one look at beautiful Elizabeth Lucas of Athens and said, "There's the girl I'm going to marry." He hadn't even met her then but lost nŏ time about that small technicality. And they did marry.

Jarrett brides left their own memorials at Traveler's Rest—old-fashioned shrubs planted in the yard from which twin flights of shallow stone steps lead to the cedar-shaded porch. Here, in days gone by, coming events sometimes cast their shadows before them, for Traveler's Rest was a favorite meeting place of Georgia's political leaders.

It was a favorite of Joseph E. Brown—later war governor of Georgia—who brought his bride to Traveler's Rest. The room in which they spent their wedding night is pointed out by Mrs. White. Like most of the other bedrooms it has a huge mahogany four-poster bed, dresser, chest, wardrobe, washstand and towel rack. Bedrooms here are strictly bowl and pitcher. Thanks to rural electrification there are electric lights everywhere and modern refrigeration as well as running water for the kitchen and for Mrs. White's own living quarters.

There is no central hallway at Traveler's Rest. Six front rooms, their locks bearing the English royal crown and crest, open onto the long front porch and into each other and into slightly smaller back rooms. One stairway extends upward between two rooms directly from the porch. The other stair, with hand-carved spandrel ornaments, is in the big "public room" where travelers signed the register long ago. Opening from this room to the left is the spacious dining room and just below this is the basement kitchen, with huge fireplace and flagstone floor and an adjoining wine cellar. In the side yard stand the ruins of the old smoke-house with huge troughs (hollowed-out logs) which once held the meat supply.

Rooms on the second floor follow the pattern of those below, opening onto a front hall instead of a porch. Here you may see the attic steps on which the original owners made their last stand before marauding red men.

Although the marker in the front yard says 1786, the *Georgia Guide* maintains that Traveler's Rest was "built in 1775 by Jesse Walton. Soon afterward the Walton family, with the exception of one member, was massacred by the Indians. The house was then bought by James R. Wylie, who sold it to Devereaux Jarrett about 1800. It has since remained in the possession of the Jarrett family . . . records of the family real estate and business transactions bear the names of George Walton, Robert Toombs, Alexander Stephens and Jefferson Davis."

Not only has Traveler's Rest, or Jarrett Manor, remained in the same family since 1800, but three fine old ante-bellum houses built by Devereaux Jarrett for his children are still owned by his descendants.

Best known of these is the lovely white frame Greek Revival Prather house on Prather Bridge Road, several miles out from Toccoa. Its wide porch extends from the front around both sides of the house and tall, square white columns taper slightly as they reach upward two stories. Above the Palladian front doorway hangs a delicate balustraded balcony. Still furnished but unoccupied, surrounded by silence, the deserted house sits brooding in its ruined gardens high above the Tugalo River, its stone foundations firm but its wooden porches rotting away. It is like a house in a dream, or an old lady who was once a belle, now sitting alone, lost in the confusion of her many memories.

First mistress of the house was lovely Sallie Jarrett, who went there from Traveler's Rest as the bride of Joseph Prather. It is now owned by Mrs. J. D. Prather, who lives in Charleston with her son Joseph Prather.

Several miles distant on the unpaved river road and set amid green acres of farmland is the large Georgian house of handmade bricks built for Devereaux Jarrett's son Robert, and now occupied by a great-grandson, Robert Jarrett, a widower who lives there alone.

Looping back toward Traveler's Rest—or Jarrett Manor—you come to a third fine old house. This also is built of handmade bricks and was originally the home of son Thomas Patton Jarrett. It is now owned jointly by his granddaughters— who are great-granddaughters of Devereaux Jarrett—Miss Henry Turnbull and Mrs. Jimmie Pierce.

Sometime ago their nephew, Augustus Turnbull, heard the call of the land all the way from Chicago and came back to live in the old house and to operate the farm. Today you find blue ribbons from poultry and cattle shows hanging casually in the living room and children romping through the wide hall and out into the old-fashioned garden.

Devereaux Jarrett is long gone, but Traveler's Rest remains, and the fifth generation of his descendants lives in the green valley of the Tugalo

CHAPTER 23

Wisdom's Wild Ride

*T*HEY spread a red carpet from carriage to doorstep for the bogus Lord Beresford when he was a guest at beautiful Doric-columned Thornwood in Rome.

But the family butler, serving dinner, forgot his careful coaching as to the proper way to address nobility. Instead of "My lord," he said, "My God, have a biscuit."

Or so the bogus Lord Beresford declared in a book which he later found time to write in jail.

Certain it is that he did come to Rome sometime in the gay 'nineties, representing himself to be an English peer and the agent of large "interests" with money to invest in mining or other properties in the South. Certain it is too that he was suave and handsome and that he did have an English accent.

Apparently he tipped his hand when he drew a check for two thousand dollars on a London bank. But before the check bounced back, Beresford had received a traditional welcome not only at Thornwood but in many other aristocratic homes in this hospitable city of seven hills.

Rome didn't get its name because of the seven hills, except accidentally, and it wasn't named for Rome, Italy, though Mussolini chose to think so when Italian rayon mills were added to other industries in this flourishing North Georgia city.

Mussolini added his own flourish by presenting to Rome, Georgia, a replica of the Capitoline wolf mother suckling the infants Romulus and Remus. This piece of statuary stood in front of Rome city hall until World War II, when the city fathers decided that at last they had a legitimate excuse to remove it from public view. In the meantime the rayon mills had changed hands and were no longer controlled by "foreign" interests.

Actually, the name Rome was picked out of a hat by four men who selected the site for the town in 1834. No doubt this accidental winner was suggested by the beautiful wooded hills and the rivers—the Etowah and the Oostanaula, which come together here and form the Coosa.

At that time these hills and rivers made a sylvan setting for the white frame houses—one of which still stands—of two of the most powerful Indian chiefs of the Cherokee Nation. They still make an effective setting for the many beautiful houses of modern Rome, where life is pleasantly regulated by the old town clock in the red brick tower which has stood high on Neely Hill since 1871.

Handsomest and perhaps most historic of Rome's old houses is Thornwood, built in 1848 by Colonel Alfred Shorter, who founded Shorter College in 1877. Just southwest of town on one of Rome's lesser hills, Thornwood faces the Alabama Road, now Shorter Avenue—a big two-story white frame house with a one-story four-columned Doric portico in front and long colonnades at each end.

From this vantage point Thornwood saw John Wisdom gallop past in his spectacular dash to warn Rome of Federal Colonel Abel D. Streight's approach in May of 1863. Both Thornwood and Rome well remember Confederate General Nathan Bedford Forrest, because he "got there first with the most." Not the most men, but the most strategy, and sixteen-year-old Emma Sanson perched behind him on his horse for a part of the way.

Thornwood, surrounded by its great oak trees, was a welcome sight to Streight's advance scouting detachment of two hundred men commanded by Captain Milton Russell. They decided to make themselves at home and did.

Thanks to John Wisdom, they did not take over the bridges at Rome or carry out other advance objectives. Such a barricade of cotton bales had been rolled out and such a fine show of preparedness put on that Captain Russell decided to wait at Thornwood for reinforcements.

The sixty-seven-mile dash of John H. Wisdom, who carried the warning to Rome, completely outdistanced the more famous eighteen-mile ride of Paul Revere in Colonial New England. Mr. Wisdom, a rural mail carrier, forty-three years of age, living in Gadsden, Alabama, had just returned from his day's round when he learned that Streight had passed through Gadsden, headed for Rome. It was then three-thirty in the afternoon. Mr. Wisdom, still in his buggy, grabbed up the reins, urged his horse forward and set out with the most important message he would ever carry.

Twenty-two miles later, at Gnatville, his horse exhausted, he changed to a lame saddle pony which he rode five miles to Goshen where he obtained a fresh mount. In all five horses and one mule supplied his transportation and he reached Rome shortly before midnight. He had made the trip of sixty-seven miles in a little less than eight and a half hours. The pony express couldn't have done better.

Rome later presented Mr. Wisdom with a silver service and $400 in money

FIGURE 49. At one time a red carpet was spread for visitors at Thornwood in Rome, built in 1848 by Colonel Alfred Shorter, now owned by Mr. and Mrs. W. A. DuPre.

and also sent $400 to the Widow Hanks at Gnatville, who had lent him the lame pony when no other mount was available.

The morning after Wisdom's wild ride, Federal Captain Russell and his advance detachment took over Thornwood. Streight and his main body of troops were still in Alabama, hotly pursued by Forrest's cavalry. After crossing Black Warrior Creek, Streight ordered his men to burn the bridge. The bridge was still flaming when Forrest rode up and drew rein.

And this is when Emma Sanson stepped into history—Emma who lived with her sister and widowed mother in a near-by farmhouse. Emma knew of a trail about two hundred yards above the bridge, "where the cows sometimes crossed at low water."

There was no time to saddle a horse for Emma. At General Forrest's request and over her mother's protests (people might talk about Emma riding with the soldiers that way), the girl swung up behind Forrest and they were off. Emma sat sideways, of course.

FIGURE 50. Thornwood's stairway is divided by two parallel balustraded balconies. At the first balcony, one flight turns left and ascends to the front hall; the other continues straight ahead to the second balcony at the back.

As they neared the ford, they dismounted in order to be less conspicuous. Nevertheless, Emma's long, full skirts were ripped by a bullet fired by a Federal sharpshooter.

After marking the site of the ford, Forrest escorted Emma back home, warned the ladies to seek temporary shelter elsewhere and returned to his men, guiding them across the creek. Before moving on, he took time to write a note of thanks to Emma. It was dated May 2, 1863.

Streight, believing he had left Forrest high and dry, relaxed at the Lawrence plantation near Gaylesville, Alabama, about twenty-four miles from Rome. While he and his forces were enjoying breakfast, Forrest closed in and fooled Streight into thinking the woods were full of Confederate cavalrymen.

Streight and Forrest met for a parley but the Union general refused to surrender unless it could be demonstrated that he was surrounded by greatly superior forces. Forrest had thought of that.

As they talked, Forrest's cavalry wove in and out among the hills until the Federal commander was completely confused as to their number. In the same way, two Confederate cannon were maneuvered so deftly that Streight counted them as fifteen. "Name of God, how many guns have you got?" he ejaculated.

And so he surrendered himself and his fourteen hundred and sixty-six men to General Forrest, whose superior forces numbered six hundred. The later capture of the detachment which had visited Thornwood brought the total close to seventeen hundred.

Rome gave Forrest a jubilant reception in the old Choice house, now the site of the General Forrest Hotel. And they do say it is a wonder he wasn't completely scalped, what with all the ladies clamoring for a lock of his hair.

Mrs. Daniel Printup, "one of Rome's most regal and aristocratic dowagers had him in charge . . . a man of austere and rather forbidding appearance, he was subdued as no Yankee gun had ever been able to subdue him . . . meekly submitting as she snipped from his head locks of his hair which she bestowed upon his eager admirers," says an article by Maud H. Yancey.

Forrest had no formal military training, but military leaders have come all the way from Europe to study his tactics, just as they have the tactics of Lee and other great Confederate generals. Forrest had accumulated more than a million dollars when he entered the war as a private at the age of forty. He came out a lieutenant general, with little left but his plantation lands in Mississippi. Twenty of his former slaves, who had volunteered to serve under him as teamsters during the war, went back with General Forrest to rebuild those lands.

Forrest couldn't have said "fustest with the mostest," according to his biographer, Robert Selph Henry. He "would have been totally incapable of so obvious and self-conscious a piece of literary carpentry." What he actually said is recorded verbatim by several miltary contemporaries. First of these was General Basil Duke, to whom Forrest said, recalling a successful operation in Tennessee, "I just . . . got there first with the most men." That was his military credo—"first with the most." The dialect trimmings were added, no doubt, as the legend grew. And now, as Mr. Henry observes, quoting the Baltimore *Sun*, "We probably shall never hear the 'lastest' of them."

Some of those who welcomed Forrest to Rome, May 3, 1863, were still alive when the town erected a monument to the great cavalryman on Rome's truly Broad Street. They knew it was "first with the most." No doubt, Rome also remembered Emma Sanson when it dedicated the first monument in the South "To the Women of the Confederacy."

Colonel Alfred Shorter, who built Thornwood, was perhaps Rome's wealthiest ante-bellum citizen. His wife, the former Miss Martha Harper, widow of John Baldwin, also brought him a fortune, which he characteristically enlarged by wise investment.

They moved to Rome from Monticello in 1847 and soon afterward selected a homesite on a wooded rise above Horseleg Creek, where they built a spacious twelve-room house with a big detached kitchen. Hawthorn grew thick on the place and this suggested the name given the house, Thornwood.

Like many Greek Revival houses, Thornwood's long central hall leads to a rear portico exactly like the one in front. Doric columns are supplemented by matching pilasters and the frieze of the entablature carries the classic triglyph decoration. Beautiful hand-carving adorns the interior woodwork, and the wide pine floor boards were rift-cut to length for the big rooms.

Thornwood's most unusual feature is its stairway, which is divided by two parallel balustraded balconies. On the first balcony one flight turns left and ascends to the upstairs front hall. The other flight goes straight ahead to the second balcony at the back, which is on a level with the upstairs front hall. Here the stairs take a left turn and proceed to the attic.

Colonel and Mrs. Shorter had no children, but adopted Mrs. Shorter's nephew and niece, Charles and Martha Harper. Martha married D. E. B. Hamilton, a Baptist minister, and after Colonel Shorter's death in 1882 they moved to Thornwood. Three generations of the Hamilton family lived here before Thornwood was sold to Mr. and Mrs. W. A. DuPre in 1944.

The DuPres added a kitchen wing at the right of the house, careful to maintain character and balance. Along with Thornwood they inherited a lot of autographs to vouch for Federal occupation, also a few nicks in the Doric columns made by Federal sabers. The autographs are in the attic. Those on other walls were long ago painted or papered over.

Thornwood was twice occupied by Federal troops. Sometime before the arrival of Streight's advance detachment, Colonel and Mrs. Shorter had gone to their plantation in South Georgia, leaving Thornwood in the care of a niece-in-law, Mrs. Alexander Thornton Harper of Cave Spring. Mrs. Harper's husband was in the Confederate army and she was alone in the house with four small children and the servants.

Informed by Federal Captain Russell that she would have to vacate, young Mrs. Harper firmly refused. But when she saw the grounds overrun with blue-coats and was told that the house and all of Rome would be in ashes by night, she accepted a military escort to Cave Spring. Forrest and Wisdom and Emma Sanson saved the town that time but a little more than a year later Sherman burned the business and industrial sections, and quite a few houses when the flames spread.

It is said that Sherman planned his march to the sea on the drop-leaf table at Rose Hill, the Charles H. Smith home where he established headquarters in November of 1864. He and his staff were photographed sitting around the table. Major Charles H. Smith, then an officer in the Confederate army, became famous for his humorous writings under the pen name of Bill Arp. His house was long ago replaced by the Gordon Hight residence.

At a still earlier time in Rome's history, Major John Ridge, Cherokee Indian chief, lived at what is now 80 Chatillon Road. The house, altered and enlarged, is still called The Chieftains, and in the attic you may still see the huge hand-hewn beams. A contemporary account (the diary of W. R. Grahame, February 2, 1832),

FIGURE 51. The Chieftains at Rome still carries its name of 1832, when the central section of the house was the home of Cherokee Indian Chief, Major John Ridge. The grounds were once a tribal meeting place.

describes The Chieftains as a two-story frame structure "52 by 28 feet . . . and there are many others of handsome design which show the wealth and civilization of the owners." Among these were the homes of Chief Joseph Vann and Judge John Martin, Treasurer of the Cherokee Nation, which still stand near Chatsworth and are described in other chapters of this book.

The Chieftains today is a gracious two-story white house with one-story wings, surrounded by green lawns and shaded by great oaks. At one side the lawn slopes down to the Oostanaula River, where Major Ridge had his trading post and ferry. Ridge received his commission from Andrew Jackson in 1814 at the Battle of Horseshoe Bend in Alabama, when five hundred Cherokees joined with Federal forces to rout a much larger number of warring Creeks. Major Ridge's son, John, was a college graduate and his daughter, Sallie, went to finishing school.

The grounds at The Chieftains were a tribal meeting place, and a marker shows that one of the great oaks is called treaty oak, because negotiations were completed here for the final treaty of December 29, 1835, signed at New Echota, near Calhoun.

The terms of that treaty are outlined in the chapter, "The Blood Remembers."

As we know, Major Ridge gave up The Chieftains, and with his son, John

Ridge, and his nephew, Elias Boudinot, went west to Indian Territory. And there, in 1839, they were executed, "in accordance with the tribal law that inflicted the death penalty for the sale of lands without full consent of the Nation."

At the head of the group who did not sign the treaty of 1835 was Principal Chief John Ross, whose house stood about a mile south of The Chieftains, near where the Oostanaula joins the Etowah to form the Coosa. Whether or not the Ross house had a name, John Ross dated all his letters and other documents, "Head of Coosa." The Ross house is long gone, but The Chieftains is preserved as official residence of the local manager of the Celanese Corporation of America. Mr. and Mrs. W. E. Crooks, who live there, cherish all its traditions.

Colonel Daniel Randolph Mitchell, one of Rome's founders, built himself a fine square-pillared house in 1850 which replaced his earlier dwelling. This later house still stands at the corner of West 11th Street and North Fifth Avenue. The surrounding Mitchell plantation acres were long ago divided into city lots.

It is said that the first piano in Rome stood in the Mitchell's parlor. With five daughters, no doubt somebody was always practicing scales. As was usual on many plantations, each of these girls had her personal Negro maid. Each of the three sons had his individual body servant.

Colonel Mitchell who was a lawyer as well as a planter, organized the Rome bar. He was also a surveyor and laid out the town's first streets, including Broad Street, which is 136 feet wide. Indians were among its early pedestrians, and the late Mrs. Robert Battey recalled witnessing the Green Corn dance at The Chieftains when she was about seven years old, according to George Battey's *History of Rome and Floyd County*.

Colonel Mitchell it was who dropped the prize-winning suggestion into the hat and gave to Rome its name in 1834. The other founding fathers were Major Philip Walker Hemphill—whose former plantation house is incorporated in the Darlington School—Colonel Zachariah B. Hargrove and Colonel William Smith.

Woodrow Wilson is said to have proposed to Ellen Axson on a love seat which is one of the family heirlooms at Coligni, the old Dean home on the Martha Berry Highway. The romance that began here ended when Ellen Axson Wilson died in the White House in Washington. President Wilson brought her body back to Rome to be buried at beautiful Myrtle Hill Cemetery. The funeral was held at the First Presbyterian Church, where Ellen Axson's father had been pastor many years before.

Another antique at Coligni is a handsome four poster bed sold along with the house because it was "just too large to move." The house has changed hands only once since it was built in 1856 by Dr. H. V. M. Miller, a great admirer of the French Huguenot leader, Coligny. Around 1868 Coligni became the property of

FIGURE 52.   Oak Hill, in Rome, home of Martha Berry, who founded the famous
Berry schools for mountain boys and girls at Rome.

Dr. Sidney Pryor Smith. One of his daughters, Agnes, married Linton A. Dean
and eventually the house became known as the Dean place.

Coligni is, of course, French in architectural feeling. A wrought-iron lyre-
pattern balustrade outlines its second story gallery. The downstairs windows are
twelve feet high and six feet wide. There are fourteen rooms and the original
Toile de Jouy wallpaper is still on the walls. Coligni stands on its own hill from
which are visible most of Rome's seven hills and also the winding Oostanaula
River, which borders the Dean farmlands on the east. The old house is now owned
by five Dean daughters, who use it as a summer home—Mrs. David G. Anderson,
Mrs. William N. Randle, Mrs. Lee D. Temple, Mrs. Pennington Nixon and Mrs.
George W. Miller.

Martha Berry highway was, of course, named for the founder of the famous

Berry schools and college at Mount Berry, near Rome, which are visited every year by fifteen to twenty-five thousand sightseers.

Martha Berry was born in 1866, just across the road from the schools, in the big house, Oak Hill, which was the home of her parents, Captain and Mrs. Tom Berry. The idea for the Berry schools was born in a log-cabin playhouse where Martha Berry first read Bible stories to under-privileged mountain boys and girls. From this she went on to Sunday school and day school and finally to an agricultural and industrial boarding school where students, working their way through, could learn both mental and manual skills and to appreciate the cultural things of life.

Miss Berry died in 1942, but not before she had seen the number of school buildings grow to nearly a hundred, the campus to thirty thousand acres and the student body to more than a thousand boys and girls, many of whom still "work their way."

How did Martha Berry accomplish all this?

She had a vision and made others see that vision. Mr. and Mrs. Henry Ford gave the handsome group of stone Gothic buildings that house the girls' school. There have been many other big gifts but, as Miss Berry always said, it was mostly the little gifts that added up.

She herself gave everything she had to the school, including Ionic-columned Oak Hill, which she inherited from her father. There were eight boys and girls in the Berry family and all the girls were considered beauties. One of the Berry girls exchanged Rome, Georgia, for Rome, Italy, when she became the Princess Ruspoli by marriage. But Martha Berry never found time to think of matrimony.

Scattered between Rome and Cave Spring—and in Cave Spring—are a number of interesting old houses. You come upon them unexpectedly, around a turn of the road. The white frame Alex White house, with its carved woodwork, is one of the pleasant surprises. Farther along is the home of Miss Fannie Gibbons and her brother, Charles Pitner Gibbons, built of mellow handmade bricks above a raised basement and adorned with an Ionic portico.

North at Dalton are other fine old houses. Here also is the former home of the late Robert Loveman, who wrote the famous "April Rain":

> It is not raining rain to me,
> It's raining daffodils.

Still farther north at Chickamauga is the handsome Doric-columned brick house built about 1850 by John Gordon, whose grandson, Gordon Lee, served in the United States House of Representatives from 1905 to 1927.

You come upon the old houses unexpectedly and always there is a challenge to the imagination—the challenge of the past living on into the present.

CHAPTER 24

Sherman's Georgia Romance

CECELIA STOVALL got a big rush when she went up for the dances at West Point Military Academy in 1836. The young cadet who fell hardest was William Tecumseh Sherman, roommate of her brother, Marcellus A. Stovall.

Cecelia, a dark-eyed belle and beauty, was the daughter of Pleasant A. Stovall, wealthy cotton merchant of Augusta. At West Point she met young Sherman's romantic advances with a bit of plain talk:

'Your eyes are so cold and cruel," she told him. "I pity the man who ever becomes your foe. Ah, how you would crush an enemy."

And Sherman said, "Even though you were my enemy, my dear, I would ever love and protect you."

The story of Sherman's Georgia romance—which had a dramatic sequel—is a famous one and moreover a true one. Its details are recorded in the *History of Bartow County* by Lucy J. Cunyus and by several other Georgia historians.

Young Marcellus Stovall resigned from West Point in 1837 on account of ill health and made the Grand Tour of Europe. Cecelia Stovall also went to Europe that year and in London saw the coronation of Queen Victoria.

In 1845 young Lieutenant Sherman, who had given Cecelia such a rush at West Point, was assigned to detached duty in her home town of Augusta. But by that time Cecelia was so interested in another West Point graduate—Richard B. Garnett, then stationed at the United States Arsenal in Augusta—that her father packed her off to visit relatives in South Carolina. There was nothing wrong with Dick Garnett except his salary, which Mr. Stovall considered inadequate. No doubt, he would have felt the same about Lieutenant Sherman.

In South Carolina Cecelia met Charles T. Shelman, of old Cass, now Bartow County, Georgia. They fell in love. Her father approved and they were married in 1848.

Charles Shelman later built a beautiful white house with six tall Doric columns on a hill above the Etowah River in Bartow County. It was called Shelman Heights, and many of its handsome furnishings were selected in Europe by Cecelia and her father. Here the Shelmans were living when North and South went to war in 1861.

And here Cecelia's old beau, William Tecumseh Sherman, came to call on a day in 1864. It was not a social call. He was Major General Sherman now at the head of an invading army.

A fellow officer called Sherman's attention to the big white house on the hill. It was a bit off the line of march but was nonetheless swarming with bluecoats.

The two Federal officers rode up to the gate, where they were attracted by the lamentations of an elderly Negro man. Shaking his white woolly head, he was mumbling, "I sho'ly is glad Miss Cecelia ain't here to see it with her own eyes."

"Miss Cecelia?" echoed General Sherman. "Not Miss Cecelia Stovall?"

But it was, of course, only she was now Mrs. Shelman.

The general, preparing to send in his name, was informed that Captain Shelman was in the Confederate army and that Miss Cecelia had refugeed. The house was in the care of this aged family servant.

So Sherman left a written message, still preserved among Stovall family mementos. And before riding off, he sternly issued orders that everything taken from the house was to be replaced. Guards were detailed to stand by until the army had passed.

To Joe, the faithful family retainer, General Sherman said, "Say to your mistress for me that she might have remained in her home in safety; that she and her property would have been protected. Hand her this when you see her."

And here is what the general wrote:

"You once said that I would crush an enemy and you pitied my foe. Do you recall my reply? Although many years have passed, my answer is the same. 'I would ever shield and protect you.' That I have done. Forgive all else. I am only a soldier.

Wm. T. Sherman."

Shelman Heights burned to the ground on New Year's day in 1911. An old photograph reproduced in the *History of Bartow County* shows it white and beautiful and well preserved to the last. Captain Shelman died there in 1886 but Cecelia lived on until 1904, witty and charming and the center of attention to the end of her days.

Very different from General Sherman's romantic note was an official report filed in the same general neighborhood by Federal Brigadier General Milo S. Hascall, encamped near Etowah Cliffs, the home of William Henry Stiles. Etowah Cliffs is one of several fine old houses still standing along or near the Etowah River

FIGURE 53. Etowah Cliffs, near Cartersville, was built by William Henry Stiles, overlooking the Etowah River.

—old houses which reflect a bygone glamour faintly tinged with the pomp and glitter of foreign courts.

William Henry Stiles, owner of Etowah Cliffs, had been United States Minister to Austria. Confederate General P. M. B. Young, whose home was at Walnut Grove, later served as United States Consul General in Russia. Valley View was the ante-bellum home of Colonel J. C. Sproull, whose grandson, Sproull Fouche, spent many fairly recent years as American charge d'affaires in Romania.

And, of course, there was Glen Holly, home of "the iron king of Georgia," Mark A. Cooper. Near Kingston was Woodlands, the fabulous castle of Godfrey Barnsley, whose fleet of ships carried his cotton to England from Savannah and other Southern ports. There was the brick house copied from his family home in Virginia by Benjamin Reynolds, who owned a gold mine in Habersham County. There was Spring Bank, the Charles Wallace Howard home, and many other handsomely furnished houses in which fine paintings, rare books, bric-a-brac, silver, china and old wines were conversation pieces collected on European travels. Indians had lived on these lands until 1838, but in 1861 old Cass County (now Bartow), was the home of a cosmopolitan group who made a fine art of living. The houses which remain, though inspired by the Greek Revival, are all very different in appearance and offer an interesting study in architectural contrasts.

From this neighborhood then—from Etowah Cliffs to be exact—Brigadier-General Milo S. Hascall, commanding the second division of the U. S. 23rd Army Corps, wrote on May 23, 1864:

"I consider it my duty to call the attention of the major general commanding the corps to the terrible state of things that exists in different parts of the grand army under Major-General Sherman, so far as the wanton destruction of private property and works of art is concerned. It has not been my fortune to march a single day during the last week without being compelled to witness sights which are enough to disgrace and render worthy of defeat any army in the universe.

"I have seen as many as half a dozen houses and barns on fire at one time," he continues, "and in too many cases the wanton destruction of fine paintings and other works of art and culture has been reported to me, and also come under my own observation. . . . While I am willing that everything shall be taken that will be of service to our army or beneficial to the enemy, if done in an orderly manner, I have no desire to serve with an army where the fundamental principles of civilized warfare are so shockingly violated at every step of our progress . . ."

Many of the treasures at Etowah Cliffs had been sent for safekeeping to Savannah, the former home of Mr. Stiles, but his fine library was destroyed.

The mission which brought Mr. Stiles to North Georgia in 1838 was something of an adventure. He was appointed by the federal government to make payment in gold to the Cherokee Indians for lands ceded before their removal west.

Mr. Stiles was so charmed with the mountains, rivers and valleys of the up-

FIGURE 54. "I'll be a major general or in hell in half an hour," said General P. M. B. Young, as he led a Confederate charge. This was his home, Walnut Grove near Cartersville . . . It is now the home of his niece, Mrs. John Cummings.

country that he accepted lands in payment for his services. Here, not far from the town of Cartersville, he built Etowah Cliffs, which started out as a frame structure to which extensive brick additions were made. The fine view of the river may still be enjoyed from a two-story porch with slim columns which follows the line of the house around a projecting pedimented center section. A diamond-design balustrade connects the second-story columns and adds a pleasing finish.

All the bedrooms have dressing rooms and all the mantels and window sills on the lower floor are of Viennese marble. When Mr. Stiles came back from Austria—he was United States minister from 1845-1849—he brought along many of the rich furnishings he had collected for the legation. The mahogany dining table seated twenty, and there were two complete sets of Willow china, one in blue, one in yellow, also a 144-piece set of Bohemian glass with the Stiles monogram blown into each piece.

197

The three-tier epergne from this set and various other family heirlooms are now at Malbone, the home of Mr. and Mrs. Robert M. Stiles, near Etowah Cliffs.

Robert M. Stiles is a great nephew of Henry and of Robert Mackay Stiles, who built Malbone in 1867. A large brick house with inset square-columned entrance and wide-arched bay windows on each side, Malbone faces a broad sweep of lawn with Stiles Mountain rising in the distance. Both houses are off the Euharlee Road and are approached by an osage-lined driveway which leads left to Malbone and right to Etowah Cliffs. At this writing, Etowah Cliffs is used as a tenant house.

Peacocks now strut on the lawn at Walnut Grove just as they did when Pierce Manning Butler Young went away to war in the eighteen sixties to become the youngest major general north or south of the Mason-Dixon line. Walnut Grove is built of handmade bricks and has a two-story portico, supported by square columns. The long gallery is at the back of the house.

Besides the general and the peacocks, Walnut Grove is famous for its boxwood and its great walnut trees. Some of these trees were cut and carved for the handsome interior woodwork. Others were fashioned into furniture. The Metropolitan Museum wanted the piecrust table at Walnut Grove, a rare example of the cabinetmaker's art, but Mr. and Mrs. John Cummings, the present owners, wanted it too. Mrs. Cummings is a great niece of the general, whose father, Dr. R. M. Young, built the house about 1840.

General Young was a very dashing soldier and a handsome one. He resigned from the West Point graduating class of 1861 and later took part in the attack on Fort Sumter. On two occasions he was seriously wounded in battle. On another, when he was warned by an aide that the charge he led was almost certain suicide, General Young's reply was, "I'll be a major-general or in hell in half an hour."

Just as he was in the thick of battle from the first, so he was at the last. General Young assisted in leading the Confederate troops out of Savannah before all escape was closed by Sherman's army and the Union navy. Two days after the war was over he was still fighting at Augusta.

General Young served Georgia for many years in the United States House of Representatives and later was appointed consul general to Russia by President Cleveland. Later still he served as American minister to Guatemala and Honduras.

Both Mrs. Cummings's mother and grandmother were married in the spacious parlor where she and Mr. Cummings stood to take their vows. Their young son is the fifth generation to live in the house. Polled Herefords and forage crops have succeeded cotton on Walnut Grove's broad plantation acres.

There's a certain spot on the wide square-columned back porch at Valley View that wasn't a safe place to stand, once upon a time.

Driving out from Cartersville along the Euharlee Road, you come to the stone gateposts that mark the entrance to Valley View. The driveway leads through a deeply wooded area and eventually to the gate of an iron-grille fence enclosing the box garden and the house, which overlooks a broad valley.

Free-standing Ionic columns guard a wide porch extending from the front around two sides of the house, which is built of handmade bricks. You feel that there is something a little odd about the hanging balcony which also extends around two sides. The answer is that the balcony is minus its original decorative iron balustrade. This was removed by Federal troops in the War Between the States and taken to Mark A. Cooper's iron foundry where it was melted up and molded into cannon balls.

Mrs. Sproull Fouche, who lives at Valley View, spent many years with her late husband in Romania where he was American charge d'affaires. An affectionately inscribed photograph of beautiful Queen Marie and other gifts from the Romanian royal family are reminiscent of a storybook era which, like that of King Cotton, is gone forever.

When Mr. Fouche's grandfather, Colonel J. C. Sproull, moved his family to Valley View from Abbeville, South Carolina, in 1839, he brought them in a stagecoach bought especially for the journey. Tied to the back of the coach were the root beginnings of the handsome boxwood and cherry laurel now so abundant at Valley View.

Daughter Rebecca Sproull, who later married Major Robert Fouche, kept a diary all through the War Between the States. The family stayed on at Valley View from the start in 1861 until 1864, and left only when they could hear the noise of cannon fired at near-by Cassville, a town which did not exist when the Federal army had passed.

Federal General George W. Schofield occupied Valley View for three months. Mrs. Fouche's rosewood desk was a piano when he took possession. When the family came back they found the keyboard and strings of the piano had been ripped out and the case used as a trough in which to feed horses. It was a time when the South was making the best of things, and the best, in this case, was to salvage the piano by converting it into a desk.

There were a great many autographs on the interior walls of Valley View, but these were painted over and only one remains today in a closet on the second floor.

> Newton Westfall
> Co. C 4th Ind. Cav.
> Sept. 7th 1864

Photo by Thomas Spencer

FIGURE 55. Valley View, near Cartersville, is the home of Mrs. Sproull Fouche, friend of the late Queen Marie of Romania. The iron balcony railing was removed by Federal soldiers to mold bullets. This is a side view.

Equally interesting is the mark made by the slave great-grandfather of the present gardener. He left his fingerprints on one of the bricks used in the walk in front of the house. It was not an accident. Like Newton Westfall, he sought to leave some permanent record of his existence. In a way, each signed his work.

The rooms at the back of the house at Valley View extend around a U-shaped court, and all open onto a square-columned gallery. Bullet holes in one of the square columns on the back porch have been stopped up to prevent bees from establishing residence inside.

"A federal soldier was standing right there where you are now," says Mrs. Fouche, "and then . . . he wasn't. He was shot by a Confederate sniper," she explains. "The bullets that killed him made these holes in the column."

You move away a bit hastily, glancing up at the big oak tree that shades the court and wondering if the sniper could have been concealed in its leafy branches. For a moment, the whole thing seems very real. But only for a moment. Colonel Sproull built too well for anything short of complete destruction to affect the character and atmosphere of a house that is today, as yesterday, a gracious home.

A famous Bartow County house that isn't there any more was Glen Holly, home of Mark A. Cooper, iron king of Georgia. But the unique friendship monument which Mr. Cooper erected to prominent Georgians who helped him through a financial crisis still stands. It was the only bit of property left intact at the Etowah industries when Sherman passed on.

Mr. Cooper, formerly an Eatonton attorney, developed the Etowah Manufacturing and Mining Co. in 1845. Iron from his foundry was shipped to England to be made into steel. Several barrels of flour from his flour mills were sent as a gift to Queen Victoria. Also at Etowah were a blast furnace, rolling mill, nail factory, two sawmills and two gristmills. Sherman used the furnace as a powder magazine and later blew up the works.

Mr. Cooper's house, Glen Holly, situated some distance from the plant on the Etowah River, survived until recent years when Uncle Sam decided to build the great Allatoona Dam on the Etowah south of Cartersville. The knoll on which the house stood is now a small green island in the big lake above the dam. At high-water mark the island disappears entirely.

Mr. Cooper bought out a couple of partners just before the panic of 1857. He needed $200,000 to tide him over. Leading businessmen, all his friends, rallied around. Mr. Cooper made a profit of $20,000 the next year and by 1860 was in the clear. His lasting gratitude is expressed in the friendship monument which some years ago was moved to the city square in Cartersville:

> This monument is erected by
> Mark A. Cooper
> Proprietor at Etowah
> as a grateful tribute to the
> friendship and liberality of
> those whose names are
> hereon inscribed, which
> prompted them
> to aid him in
> the prosecution
> and development of
> the interests at
> Etowah.

Long before Sherman came to old Cass County at the head of an army, he visited in one of its homes near Cartersville. He tells about it in his *Memoirs:*

"In 1844 when a lieutenant in the Third Army I had been sent from Charleston, S. C., to Marietta, Ga. . . . after completing the work at Marietta our party was transferred to Bellefonte, Ala. I had ridden the distance on horseback and had noted well the topography of the country, especially that about Kennesaw, Allatoona and the Etowah river. On that occasion I had stopped some days with a Colonel [Lewis] Tumlin to see some remarkable Indian mounds on the Etowah river usually called the Hightower. . . . I therefore [in 1864] knew that the Allatoona pass was very strong and resolved to move instead from Kingston to Marietta via Dallas."

The fourth generation Lewis Tumlin is now living in the house at Glen Cove Farms where Sherman was an invited guest in 1844. It is a tall, twelve-room white frame dwelling with brick pillars. The stairwell ceiling in its central hall appears to be about forty feet high.

The Etowah mounds mentioned by Sherman were long since explored by archaeologists and pronounced among the most important in the United States.

A letter that left its mark in Georgia history was written at The Oaks, a great weathered frame house which stands about midway between Spring Bank, the old Howard house, two miles north of Kingston, and Barnsley Gardens, four miles farther along.

The architecture of The Oaks is somewhat unusual in that the recessed portico is placed at the left front, instead of center, of a façade that appears to be about a hundred feet across. The portico has a pointed pediment and is supported by free-standing Doric columns. Smaller columns support the second-story balcony.

This spacious fourteen-room house was built in the early eighteen forties by Senator Oliver Prince, who with the Reverend James H. George conducted a boarding school here.

In 1861, at the start of the War Between the States, James Harris of Harrisonburg, Virginia, looking for a safe place for his large family, bought The Oaks. After the surrender, an uncle, Dr. Alexander Harris, came for a visit and died in the house in November of that year. His son, a young soldier just back from the war, wrote a letter asking Alexander Stephens, former Vice President of the Confederate States, to lend him money to complete his education. After writing the letter, the former soldier waited days until he could obtain pennies to buy stamps. Stephens did lend the money and the young letter writer, whose name was Nat Harris, later became governor of Georgia and was one of the founders of Georgia Institute of Technology in Atlanta.

A house built around a former Indian cabin is the picturesque log home of the late Corra Harris, about twenty miles from Cartersville. Mrs. Harris, author of "A Circuit Rider's Wife," published in *The Saturday Evening Post* in 1910 and later in book form, wrote many novels, short stories and articles which appeared in leading national magazines. In 1911 she was sent to Europe by the *Post* and again in 1914 as the first woman war correspondent.

She was also one of the first of the new school of realists among Southern writers, succeeding the period of moonlight and magnolias. "A Circuit Rider's

Photo by Wilbur G. Kurtz

FIGURE 56. Benjamin Reynolds owned a gold mine, and built this house near Kingston in 1846, after the fashion of his native Virginia architecture.

Wife" not only created a literary sensation but made Mrs. Harris a target for bitter criticism by certain dignitaries of the religious denomination formerly served by her husband. Hollywood came to North Georgia in 1951 for an on-the-spot filming of the story under the title of *I'd Climb the Highest Mountain*.

In 1913 Mrs. Harris bought several hundred acres of farmland near Pine Log in Bartow County. Standing on a hill overlooking a broad valley rimmed by distant mountains was an Indian cabin, dating from the eighteen thirties. This small dwelling became the nucleus of a residence which finally contained around twenty rooms. Mrs. Harris named the place In the Valley, and here she entertained some of the country's most celebrated men and women. She did her writing in a small separate cabin.

Mrs. Harris died in 1935 and is buried under the floor of a stone chapel not far from the house. This chapel, designed by Ralph Adams Cram, architect for the Cathedral of St. John the Divine in New York, also contains an under-glass exhibit of the author's nineteen books, many magazine articles and other mementos of her writing career. In the Valley is now owned by Mr. and Mrs. Elbert Smith, Jr.

203

One of Bartow's handsomest old houses is the home built southwest of Kingston in about 1846 by Benjamin Reynolds. It is constructed of handmade bricks and has the dignity of line and the tall chimneys typical of Mr. Reynolds's native Virginia. Four tall free-standing Doric columns support the pointed pediment of its portico. The spindle balustrade of the hanging balcony is topped by a decorative wheat-sheaf railing. A detached kitchen was at one time connected to the main house by a long covered passageway. The house, which has twelve spacious rooms, was used as a hospital during the War Between the States. It is owned by Mrs. B. B. Branson, widow of a descendant of the builder, but the gold mine owned by Mr. Reynolds in Habersham County has long since passed out of the family.

One of the several Georgia houses occupied by the Reverend Francis Robert Goulding during a long pastorate of various Presbyterian churches stands near Kingston. His Bartow County residence is now owned and is being restored by Mr. and Mrs. G. C. Phillips, who also own Barnsley Gardens (described in the chapter, "Murder at Ghost Castle"). The Howard house, near Kingston, is described in the chapter, "Mystery of the Murchison Sisters." There are a number of other interesting old houses both in Kingston and in Cartersville and scattered about over the county.

Murder at Ghost Castle

*M*URDER came to Barnsley Gardens November 5, 1935, when the great-grandson of the builder of this ruined "ghost castle," six miles from Kingston, shot and killed his brother.

There is a legend that the great-grandfather himself, Godfrey Barnsley, fought a poison duel with his brother, Gartrelle. They loved the same girl, so the story goes, one Chessie Scarlett.

At the request of the two brothers, a "disinterested" friend privately poured two glasses of wine and placed in one a lethal dose of poison. Neither Godfrey nor Gartrelle had any way of guessing which glass. The color of the wine still seemed the same.

Each brother picked up a glass and drank. Godfrey Barnsley lived.

It turned out that the girl loved the brother who died.

Mrs. Addie Baltzelle Saylor, mother of the two great-grandsons of Godfrey Barnsley, last of the family to live at Barnsley Gardens, accepted the story as nothing more than romantic tradition. Godfrey Barnsley, she pointed out, married the beautiful Julia Scarborough of Savannah, and loved her all his life. Mrs. Saylor, who died in 1942, had in her possession a "spirit" letter bearing witness to this unwavering devotion. That letter is among a small collection of Mrs. Saylor's family keepsakes now on file in the rare books and manuscripts division of the Emory University Library in Atlanta.

Julia was the daughter of William Scarborough, one of the rich cotton factors who financed the building of the *Savannah*, which in 1819 set a record as the first steamship to cross the Atlantic.

Godfrey Barnsley, an English younger son, came to Savannah from Derbyshire, England, when only eighteen and amassed a fortune in the cotton exporting business. He sent the first baled cotton from Savannah to England and eventually his own fleet of ships plied between his warehouses in Savannah, Mobile, New Orleans and Liverpool.

Julia Scarborough and Godfrey Barnsley were married in 1828, and the first of their eight children was born while they were on a visit to England.

The Barnsleys gave a fancy-dress ball in Savannah in 1837 which set such a high mark in that city's social history that some doubted it would ever be equaled. This function took place in the old William Scarborough house, still standing at 111 W. Broad Street, a handsome columned house designed in 1818 by the brilliant young English architect, William Jay. Here Mr. Scarborough had entertained President Monroe, but the Barnsley ball—celebrating the return of prosperity after a depression—seems to have eclipsed anything before or, perhaps, since.

And when Godfrey Barnsley later built a house in what was then the North Georgia wilderness, it wasn't just a house; it was a castle, complete with tower. There were twenty-six rooms in all and the whole elaborate structure was built of handmade bricks. Old sketches by Mr. Barnsley indicate that he had his prospective Georgia castle in mind while he was traveling in Europe. One of these sketches shows the ruins of Fountain Abbey in Derbyshire.

Mr. Barnsley fell in love with North Georgia scenery when he made a trip into the mountains in the eighteen thirties. Through the Reverend Charles Wallace Howard, he acquired ten thousand acres of land near Mr. Howard's own plantation, Spring Bank, in old Cass County, now Bartow. The house at Spring Bank, a weathered frame structure with dormer windows, may still be seen as you drive over the hilly unpaved road to Barnsley Gardens.

Originally the Barnsley place was given the name of Woodlands. All the old family correspondence refers to it by this name. But as the fame of its gardens grew, the public gave it another name, which gradually supplanted the old—Barnsley Gardens.

These gardens, with their oval boxwood maze, great lawns, English and Japanese yews and other fine old trees, are still green after more than a hundred years. Red Louis Phillipe roses bloomed there bravely on the day of our visit and other flowers too.

But the big house, facing this garden, is a roofless brick shell, a gaunt ruin on an acorn-shaped hill, surrounded by the green isolation of valley farmlands and wooded mountains.

Cottonwood trees, growing up through the rotted floors of the spacious rooms, push their branches out through empty window arches. The bare inner brick walls are covered with the pale green tapestry of flattened wisteria leaves on vines which have wandered far from their gnarled roots outside the house. Gone from the wide hall is the grand stairway under which a vault for valuables was built. There is no sign now of the huge tank in the tower from which pipes carried water to the many bedrooms, water warmed by the heat of chimney flues.

Actually three houses were built and still stand. One of these was a frame cottage at the left to be used as a dwelling while other construction was under way. This cottage was to be replaced by a detached brick wing similar to the one standing at the right of the ruined structure. This latter so-called wing is really a well-preserved brick house with slim columns and dormer windows. It has a dining room of banquet size, two kitchens and a group of bedrooms. The stove in one kitchen is large enough to take care of dinner for a hundred guests.

Godfrey Barnsley's castle was still unfinished when the South went to war in 1861. The exterior of the house, with its tall tower, wide overhanging roof, arched doors and windows, presented a fine and finished appearance, as shown by old photographs. But there was still some interior work to be completed and many of the furnishings imported from Europe were still to be unpacked.

It was as though the clock stopped at Barnsley Gardens on a certain day in 1861—a gold clock that had once belonged to Marie Antoinette. Perhaps it was not a lucky clock. Workmen laid down their tools and picked up tools of a grimmer sort. They never came back to Barnsley Gardens.

Godfrey Barnsley's great fortune was swept away by the war. In 1906 a tornado took off the roof of the castle. Time and the elements have had their way with it since then. Perhaps a cycle of misfortune was completed in 1935 when brother shot brother in the living room of the detached dormer wing which had become the family residence.

Long ago people had begun to call the big house a ghost castle and to say that the place was unlucky because Godfrey Barnsley had built on the site of an Indian cabin. The Indians had already been removed west, of course, when he acquired the property in the late eighteen thirties.

The first of the misfortunes was the death in 1845 of Godfrey Barnsley's wife, his beloved Julia, who never lived to see the castle planned for her. Mr. Barnsley went to New Orleans for a time and took the children along. But he was back at his North Georgia home in 1861. His ships had been turned over to the Confederacy and two of his sons were in the Southern army, Lucien and George.

Harper's Weekly of July 2, 1864, carries a drawing of Barnsley Gardens which shows a cavalry battle fought on the grounds in front of the house May 18, 1864. This drawing was made by *Harper's* staff artist, Theodore Davis, who went along with Sherman on the march to the sea.

But it was Federal General James B. McPherson—not Sherman—who spent a night at Barnsley Gardens.

The house was staffed with white servants, after the manner of Mr. Barnsley's

FIGURE 57. Both ghosts and murder walked here at Woodlands, better known as Barnsley Gardens, near Kingston. This photograph shows the ruins of the house, after the roof was blown off by a tornado in 1906.

native England. The housekeeper, Mary Quin, was Irish and expressed herself in characteristic fashion when she said that General McPherson was "a gintleman in low company."

Mary, it seems, had engaged in a battle of her own with the enemy and had won—with the general's assistance. This encounter is described by Frances Thomas Howard, daughter of the Reverend Mr. Howard, in her book, *In and Out of the Lines*, a record of the war experiences of the Howard family and their neighbors.

Various depredations had got Mary's Irish dander up—priceless china wantonly smashed, a raid on the wine cellar and the disappearance of the fine linen sheets from the bed in which the general had slept. But the final straw was the theft of Mr. Barnsley's watch.

A Federal soldier had inquired the time and when Mr. Barnsley—then nearly sixty—took out his watch, the soldier snatched it and ran.

Mary gave chase and caught up with the culprit in the basement. "And where are yez goin?" she demanded.

"I'm going to burn this old secesher's house," he told her, taking a shovel full of red hot coals and making for the scullery with Mary still right behind him.

There was a scuffle. Mary was knocked down by a blow from the soldier's clubbed musket. He got away but a letter dropped from his pocket as he ran. Mary found it after she had cleared out the coals. Entirely on her own, she set out next day to walk the six miles to General McPherson's headquarters in Kingston.

The general, who was later killed in the siege of Atlanta—Fort McPerson in Atlanta is named for him—granted Mary an interview. Mary stated her grievance and presented the soldier's letter. General McPherson read the address and ordered that the man's entire company be lined up so that Mary might identify the watch stealer.

Mary assured him there would be no trouble about that, and there wasn't. She had scratched the thief's face good and proper and the marks were still eloquent evidence against him.

The watch being duly restored, Mary related that General McPherson then said, "The man that strikes a woman is not fit to live. Shall I have this fellow shot?"

"No, no," Mary protested, "I don't want no more of his dirty blood on me hands than I got there yesterday."

The General laughed and said, "I think we'd better enlist you. At any rate, this scoundrel shall go to Chattanooga to work on the fortifications there till the war is over."

Not until the autumn of 1864 did Barnsley Gardens, Spring Bank and the other old houses in Cass County see the last of Federal troops.

Italian statuary planned for the gardens at the Barnsley home were the cause of several raids by army stragglers. Workmen who hauled the heavy packing cases to the house and stored them in the basement were sure they contained Mr. Barnsley's gold brought up from Savannah for safekeeping. The word got around. Federal visitors prospecting for gold were annoyed when they discovered statuary instead, and expressed this resentment by various acts of vandalism.

Godfrey Barnsley went to New Orleans again after the war to try to rebuild his fortune but died there in 1873 at the age of sixty-eight. His body was brought back for burial in the family cemetery near Barnsley Gardens. It is said that voodoo practitioners later dug up his corpse and cut off the right hand. Talk of ghosts at the castle took a fresh start.

Superstitious Negro field workers had long avoided a lonely grave at the back of the house. A marker shows this to be the last resting place of Colonel R. G. Earle, C. S. A. Colonel Earle had ridden to Barnsley Gardens to warn the family of the approach of Federal troops. This act of gallantry cost him his life, for he rode from the house right into a detachment of Federal soldiers. Surrounded, he tried to shoot his way out, but was himself riddled by bullets.

Tragedy struck again at Barnsley Gardens in 1866 when Captain James Peter Baltzelle (Mrs. Saylor's father) was killed by falling timbers while supervising the rebuilding of a bridge burned by the army. He had come through the war without a scratch.

Godfrey Barnsley's sons were among the Irreconcilables—those Southerners who could not accept defeat when the war was over. Some of the Irreconcilables went to the West Indies, some to Central and some to South America, where their descendants live to this day, speaking Spanish or Portuguese fluently and English with a foreign accent, but keeping their Georgia, Alabama and South Carolina names. George Barnsley joined the Confederate colony in Brazil, and old correspondence regarding his power of attorney indicates that his brother Lucien was there also. George came back to Barnsley Gardens in the eighteen nineties to claim a share of the art treasures and other furnishings of the house. These he shipped to New York and sold at a great sacrifice, according to his niece, Mrs. Addie Baltzelle Saylor.

Mrs. Saylor and her family were living at Barnsley Gardens in 1906 when a tornado blew the roof off the main house. Furnishings were hastily transferred to the two smaller houses. Then, before the Saylors were able to raise money for necessary repairs to the main house, Mr. Saylor died. Mrs. Saylor was left with three children to bring up, a girl and two boys. The wing with the dormer windows became the permanent family residence, its great dining room converted into a living room.

Mrs. Saylor believed that Barnsley Gardens was haunted by more than the memories of its past tragedies. She wrote a series of articles for *The Atlanta Journal Magazine* which were published shortly before her death in 1942, and in one of these she said that she had often seen her long-dead grandmother, the beautiful Julia Scarborough, walking in the gardens at Barnsley. Every afternoon at a certain time, Mrs. Saylor said, she also heard her grandfather push back his chair in the library, just as he had done in life.

She believed that George Barnsley appeared at the front door of the house on the day of his death in South America.

Mrs. Saylor's younger son, Harry, answered the door when a loud knock was heard. He came back, his mother said, looking very odd. She asked for an explanation.

"Uncle George was there," Harry told her, "but he disappeared." They went back to the door. It was a gloomy, rainy day, but there were no muddy footprints on the floor of the porch.

Harry tried to laugh it off. Next day they received the cablegram telling of George Barnsley's death in South America at the exact time Harry answered that summons at the front door.

Mrs. Saylor's daughter grew up, married and moved to another state. From earliest childhood the two boys dreamed of restoring the house built by their great-grandfather. But it was a job of mammoth proportions and there was never enough money. Bartow County is rich in mineral deposits—barite, bauxite, manganese, ocher, iron, brick clays, shale, talc and limestone. There was always the hope that the mineral rights at Barnsley Gardens might restore the family fortunes.

The Saylor boys were very different in temperament, according to an old family friend. Preston, the older brother, achieved some success in the prize ring, using the professional name of K. O. Duggan. Harry was the quiet type. He gave all his time to affairs at Barnsley Gardens.

On November 5, 1935, the morning of his death, Harry discussed plans for certain structural repairs with his mother and said, "It won't be long now, mama."

But the house that Godfrey Barnsley never finished was not to be finished by his grandsons.

For sometime there had been bad blood between Harry and his older brother, Preston Saylor. As so often happens, disagreements about property rights had engendered ill feeling. But an even more serious complication had developed.

Preston Saylor suffered injuries in the prize ring which, it was alleged, temporarily affected his mind, and he had been committed to the state hospital for the insane.

Then on March 13, 1935, he escaped. He went back to Barnsley Gardens but did not stay.

It was said he blamed his younger brother for his commitment. It was also said that when he returned to Barnsley Gardens in November of that same year, he hid in one of the outbuildings for a time.

And then, on the morning of November 5, 1935, he appeared suddenly in the living room of the house and shot his brother.

Harry fell, a bullet through his heart, and died in his mother's arms.

"Preston was not himself," Mrs. Saylor cried in her dark extremity. And later she wrote, "I love my older son too."

Preston Saylor was convicted of murder but recommended to the mercy of the court. On November 27, 1936, he was sentenced to life imprisonment. In January, 1943, he was paroled and subsequently given his full freedom.

After Mrs. Saylor's death in 1942 the remaining estate of two thousand acres was sold to Mr. and Mrs. G. C. Phillips of Birmingham and Kingston. They also bought the large collection of books and old papers that made up the Barnsley library. All the rest of the handsome furnishings were sold at auction.

A tenant farmer and his family now live in the house built for Godfrey Barnsley's white housekeeping staff, a long one-story brick building on the slope near the big spring. Children not of Barnsley blood play among the ruins of the main house and chase butterflies in the old garden.

And so ends the story of the Barnsleys at the great house planned in the North Georgia mountains by a young Englishman for the girl he loved—a dream castle that became a ghost castle.

That Godfrey Barnsley loved Julia all his life is shown by his touching effort to communicate with her in New Orleans through the medium of spiritualism. Among the small collection of Mrs. Saylor's keepsakes now at Emory University library is a transcript of a purported message to Godfrey Barnsley from his deceased father-in-law, William Scarborough.

"My dear Julia is with me and when she has proper control, she will have something to say which will send home conviction of spiritualism," Mr. Scarborough's spirit is quoted as saying.

But Godfrey Barnsley seems to have been skeptical. Apparently he asked the spirit of William Scarborough to describe the mortal Scarborough and received this reply:

"If I should ask you to describe your minute physical appearance and features as they were 20 years ago, could you do so?" The "spirit" then assured Mr. Barnsley that "you shall in good time be reasonably convinced."

Unfortunately that is the end of the transcript.

CHAPTER 26

Mystery of the Murchison Sisters

NOBODY knows to this day why the Murchison sisters were sent to a federal prison in Louisville, Kentucky, as a result of their call on the Reverend Charles Wallace Howard family at Spring Bank, two miles north of Kingston.

There was never any charge, never any trial, but one of the girls had given up her life before the incident was closed.

Spring Bank, a weathered frame structure with three dormer windows, reflects New England in the steep pitch of its roof. (It is said that Southern and Eastern branches of the family broke off all relations during the War Between the States.) Originally the wide central hall of the Howard house was open at each end, dogtrot or breezeway fashion. There is a story that the ends were closed and doors installed after hounds and hunters literally chased a fox through the hall one night. The house formerly had extensive wings—the gallery of the east wing was seventy feet long—but one wing burned and the other was torn away in later years.

The Reverend Charles Wallace Howard, who built the house, was at one time pastor of the French Huguenot church in Charleston, South Carolina. In 1850 he opened a prep school for boys at Spring Bank. It was, in a way, co-educational, for his six daughters were also pupils. When all the boys, including Mr. Howard's son, went away to fight for the Confederacy, Mr. Howard himself organized a company of soldiers, the 63rd Georgia. He was then fifty-two years old and was affectionately called by his men "the old Captain."

Two of the Howard daughters, Frances and Jane, were sitting in the parlor of the house at Spring Bank when they looked out and saw the Murchison sisters riding horseback across the lawn. It was five o'clock of an afternoon in the spring of 1864.

The Howards rushed out to great their guests who explained that they had been on the way since nine that morning. The Murchison family (sometimes spelled Merkerson) lived in a house on the Etowah River only about five miles from Spring Bank.

There was, of course, a reason why the trip took so much time. Frances Thomas Howard includes the story in her book, *In and Out of the Lines*, written in 1870. At the time it was published in 1905 by Neale of New York, it was not proper for ladies' and gentlemen's names to appear in print. But the copy of Miss Howard's book at the Georgia State Library contains a typewritten key. From this we know that the two characters designated as Rose and Julia McDonald were really the Murchison sisters.

At the time these two girls visited Spring Bank, a large Federal force was encamped at Kingston. All was quiet, but Federal Colonel Sampson, commandant of the post, refused to give the young women a pass through the lines. He also told Julia that unless she pulled off her Confederate gray jacket, he would do it for her.

Angry at what they considered an unnecessary insult, the girls determined to make their trip to Spring Bank even without a pass. This they did by flanking the pickets, in a wide detour. It was a lark; something to tell their grandchildren.

After leaving Spring Bank they reached home safely enough, "passing the pickets at a gallop." But there at the Murchison house an armed guard waited with an order for their arrest.

Rose, the survivor, tells their story. First they were sent to Nashville, Tennessee, and then to Louisville, Kentucky, to Barrack 1, "where for six weeks we endured a living death. We slept on the bare floor without a pillow, blanket or bedding of any kind and were never alone—day and night an armed guard was with us. I could not sleep. . . . We had not once a change of clothing, for our trunk had been rifled on the way and when it reached us was empty. At last we were removed to the Female Military Prison, but here as in the Barrack, there was no bedding. . . . Measles broke out . . .

"It was during my illness that I first saw the anomalous creature that was put over us for our sins, and I remember lying in a half stupor and wondering what the thing was. The dress was that of a man, but the braided hair and skinny, shrewish features were those of a woman. Bitter experience soon taught me to know this thing well, for it was a woman—the prison doctor. If ever a fiend in human guise walked this earth it did in that woman's body. The white guards pitied us and occasionally did us a kindness and for this reason she had them removed, Negroes being substituted."

Rose sewed stripes on the uniform of one of the Negro guards and he paid her twenty-five cents for the service. She spent the money for a broom with

Photo by Beverly M. DuBose, Jr.

FIGURE 58. Two girls made a fatal call here in 1864—Spring Bank, the old Charles Wallace Howard house near Kingston. The house formerly had extensive wings and porches.

which to sweep her cell. The doctor took the broom away. Later Rose saw it in the kitchen and reclaimed it with the result that:

The doctor "walked across the floor and slapped my face with all her strength. The instant she struck me, my fears vanished. A bar of iron that we used as a poker lay on the hearth near me, and I picked it up.

" 'Doctor,' I said, 'if you touch me again, it will be the last move you'll ever make.' I was still weak from my illness but at that moment passion gave me strength."

But the doctor had the last word. Rose was dumped into the dungeon by the Negro guards—"a room underground, cold, damp and dark . . . the snow was knee deep outside.

"Some ladies in Louisville promised us a Christmas dinner and every day we talked of it over our scanty meals. At last the long-wished-for day arrived. . . . The doctor furnished each room with a loaf of bread and a pitcher of water and locked up the inmates for the day. She alone knew what became of the Christmas dinner. . . .

"Some Confederate prisoners were marched past our windows, and Julia and I and others waved to them. The doctor saw us. We spent the rest of Christmas in the dungeon . . .

"She wished constantly to dose us but we had no confidence in her and refused to submit to her experiments."

215

(Official records show that at this time twenty Southern women and fourteen children were imprisoned in Louisville and that a "doctress" was on duty.)

Rose was released April 21, 1865, after ten months' confinement. (Lee had surrendered April 9.) The release was signed by Brevet Brigadier General L. D. Watkins, military commander, and Lieutenant George Shane, superintendent.

"We were put out without food, transportation or money," Rose records. "I went to the office and asked for transportation for the party. It was given us to Chattanooga, but still we had no money; so I applied to the Masons and they gave me funds. With it I paid our expenses from Chattanooga to Dalton. I walked the remaining 50 miles home."

And what of Julia, she who had worn the Confederate gray jacket?

In the preceding winter Julia had contracted a cold and a deep cough which prison conditions made worse. "We thought she had consumption," Rose later told Frances Howard. "The ladies of Louisville who visited us advised her to take the oath (of allegiance) so that she might leave the prison. By taking the oath she would be compelled to go to Ohio. We had great difficulty in persuading her, but at last she consented and went away. I heard from her constantly. She could not stand the severe climate and made up her mind to disguise herself and go south through Louisville.

"For a long time I heard nothing from her but at length I received a letter from a physician in Tennessee, telling us of her death. She had passed safely through Kentucky but in Tennessee she was shot and left for dead in the road. This gentleman found her, wounded and dying, and he carried her to his own house, where she lived long enough to write a farewell letter."

Mrs. Howard and the Howard daughters remained at Spring Bank through most of the war. From May of 1864 until November of that year they literally lived "in and out of the lines." The opening chapters of Miss Howard's book describe the retreat of the Confederate army as it passed the house, with her father, Captain Howard, and her brother, Lieutenant Jett Thomas Howard, stepping out of General Hardee's Corps long enough for a word with the family.

Next day came a Federal general whose name, oddly enough, was also Howard (General O. O. Howard). He and his staff stopped at Spring Bank. Both the general and Frances Howard record their meeting. Was he one of the Northern relatives no longer acknowledged by the family? Miss Howard does not say. But cousins fighting cousins were no novelty in a war which frequently brought brothers—and sometimes fathers and sons—face to face on opposing battlefronts.

Anyway, Miss Howard had excellent reason for saying as little as possible to a Federal general. Here is her summary of their conversation:

" 'Did you say the whole of Johnston's army passed on this road yesterday?'

" 'I did not say so,' was my reply.

" 'Ah, no,' he continued, 'it was the corps to which your father belongs.'

"Receiving no response he continued, 'To what corps did you say your father belonged?'

" 'I did not say he belonged to any corps,' I answered.

" 'If he is in the army, he must belong to some corps,' he replied impatiently.

" 'It would seem probable,' was my answer.

General Howard "sprang from his chair and with flushed face exclaimed, 'Madam, when you meet a gentleman, treat him as such.' "

On several occasions Federal soldiers overran the Howard house, helped themselves to valuables and one time smeared a mixture of lampblack and lard over the inside walls. These marauders were chased out by Federal officers, who placed guards on duty to protect the premises. Federal Colonel B. D. Dean, who succeeded Colonel Sampson as commandant of the post at Kingston, was invariably considerate and kind, according to Miss Howard.

In the autumn of 1864, Federal General Steadman ordered that all "Rebel women" in that area be sent a distance of "not less than three miles from the railroad." A rail had been removed from the track near Calhoun and a train wrecked as a result. As all the men had gone to war, women were suspected of this sabotage.

The Howard ladies were invited by Godfrey Barnsley to stay at his Georgia castle, then called Woodlands, four miles distant. But they were back at home when Confederate General William T. Wofford and Federal General Judah met in the parlor at Spring Bank to arrange terms for the peaceful surrender of seven thousand Confederate soldiers on May 12, 1865—the last armed Confederate forces in Georgia.

Miss Howard writes of looking out of an upstairs window on that day and seeing Prince Felix Salm-Salm, an Austrian, who had come to America to fight the South in one of the regiments of German soldiers hired for service with the Federal army.

Later, for a brief period during Reconstruction, Prince Salm-Salm was United States Military Governor of Atlanta. He and his wife, the flamboyant Agnes, lived lavishly in the old Lawshe house which then stood on downtown Peachtree Street.

Later still this adventurous pair turned up in Mexico with the Emperor Maximilian and it is said Salm-Salm would have been executed by Juarez along with Maximilian except for the timely intervention of Agnes. (You can read all about it in *The Phantom Crown* by Bertita Harding or in Agnes's own story, *Ten Years of My Life*.)

At Spring Bank, on that morning in May of 1865, Prince Salm-Salm thanked Mrs. Howard "in tolerably good English for the tremendous big breakfast he had eaten."

Miss Frances Thomas Howard was at one time resident teacher at Oak Hill, the home of Captain and Mrs. Thomas Berry, near Rome. Martha Berry, who grew up to found the famous Berry schools, was a pupil. So was Eugenia Berry, who became the Princess Ruspoli through marriage.

Miss Howard later established a select school for girls at Spring Bank. "Aunt Fanny's theories of teaching the young were not conventional," according to a niece, Mrs. Roger Noble Burnham of Los Angeles. "Not a spelling book, but the dictionary, not a reader but the classics . . . 'Mr.' Pineo's rules of grammar . . . mathematics, I don't recall any." And, of course, art, music . . . how to enter a drawing room.

Mrs. Bulow Campbell of Atlanta, next to the youngest of the Berry children, was also a pupil there. She remembers Spring Bank as a place where life was at once simple and elegant and charming to look back upon. Miss Fanny's mother was by that time an exquisite old lady in black silk dress and lace cap. She had seen the coronation of Queen Victoria when she went to England with Mr. Howard, who was sent on a special mission for the State of Georgia. Manners taught at Spring Bank School were almost as formal as those at court. Every afternoon a frugal tea was served but in high style and from the handsome family silver service. A girl was really getting somewhere when she was allowed to pour.

But the girls made their own beds and learned other useful things and were adequately prepared for finishing school or college. Miss Fanny knew that a world could change.

And yet, not even Miss Fanny could ever figure out why the Murchison sisters were dealt with so severely for their innocent call at Spring Bank on that afternoon back in 1864.

CHAPTER 27

How the World's Richest Girl
Got Her Start

THE mother of the world's richest girl grew up, a belle and beauty, in one of Macon's white-columned houses. She was Nanaline Holt, who married James Buchanan Duke, tobacco millionaire. Their daughter, Doris Duke, inherits her "Rebel" blood from a captain of Confederate cavalry.

Like many other fine old ante-bellum houses in Macon, the former Holt home has held its ground and has kept its looks in spite of the city's constant business and industrial expansion. Still a part of the modern scene, these houses reflect—today as yesterday—Macon's own enviable zest for living, its own whole-hearted hospitality.

No doubt, Nanaline Holt often stepped out onto the graceful hanging balcony of the Doric-columned Holt house to glimpse young men at the door below and to decide whether or not she would be "at home." She could take her choice and did. She married not one but two rich husbands.

"Nanaline Holt was the prettiest thing you ever saw," says an old friend. "And anything she wore looked lovely on her. This was fortunate, because the Holts, like so many of us, were not as well off as they had been before the war.

"Was she a blonde? Of course not, she was a brunette, or rather she had black hair and gray blue eyes and very fair skin. She was an Irish type. And she had charm, of course. Young men fell over themselves falling in love with her."

Nanaline Holt first married Will Inman of the pioneer Atlanta family and they had a son. Mr. Inman died, and sometime afterward she met James Buchanan Duke, in North Carolina. He was much older, but they were married. It is their daughter, Doris, who came along to inherit the Duke tobacco millions and to carry the title today of the world's richest girl.

The Holt house in Macon, at 1129 Georgia Avenue, was built in the eighteen forties by Judge Thaddeus Goode Holt. It was designed by Elam Alexander who was responsible for so much of the fine local architecture. Originally the columns extended only across the front, but were carried around the Orange Street side at a later date.

Judge Holt's son, Captain T. G. Holt, Jr., of the Confederate cavalry, also became a judge. He was the father of Nanaline. Her generation was the last of the family to live in the old house which is now owned by Mrs. A. M. Peeler. It is beautifully furnished and has the air of gracious serenity which sets apart old houses of its era.

A modern apartment dweller could only sigh wistfully at the prodigality of space when Mrs. Peeler's niece, Mrs. Carling Schatzman, indicated one of the big upstairs bedrooms and said fondly, "That's where she keeps her hats." Hats are Mrs. Peeler's hobby.

It seemed just the right touch, somehow, for a house in which a belle and beauty had grown up.

Many of Macon's old homes have their memories of Sidney Lanier, the South's great poet, who was given a niche in New York University's Hall of Fame some years ago.

"This nice old place with the columns was his uncle's home. And this one is where he met Mary Day, the girl he married. And here, at the old Wesleyan conservatory, is where he taught music."

So the conversation runs, up hill and down, along Macon's pleasant streets with their handsome shade trees to match the handsome old houses set back on rolling box-hedged lawns.

You decide that the quaint Gothic Victorian cottage at 935 High Street looks just exactly right as the birthplace of a poet. This was the home of Sidney Lanier's grandparents and here he was born in 1842.

Here today is a framed copy of that beautiful likeness of the young Sidney Lanier, in which he himself looks exactly as a poet should, dark and handsome his hair a bit long. He had grown up playing any instrument he could lay his hands on and songs were eternally singing themselves in his head, but he tried desperately to become a good lawyer, to please his father who was a successful attorney.

You are saddened to think of this and of all the young men who still must go to war. For Sidney Lanier hurried away in the eighteen sixties to serve as a blockade runner for the Confederacy—was captured and, while imprisoned, contracted tuberculosis from which he never recovered.

FIGURE 59. The mother of the world's richest girl lived here. Now the home of Mrs. A. M. Peeler of Macon, it was formerly the residence of Nanaline Holt, who married James Buchanan Duke and became the mother of Doris Duke.

But you are cheered, too, to remember that success came to him while he still lived, success both as a musician and as a poet. He played his beloved flute with the Peabody Symphony Orchestra in Baltimore. He was lecturer on English literature at Johns Hopkins University. He wrote the cantata used in the opening ceremonies of the Philadelphia Centennial and so his fame began. All his poetry has that singing quality—"The Marshes of Glynn" . . . "The Ballad of Trees and the Master" . . . "How Love Looked for Hell." Most Georgia school children first learn about the Chattahoochee River from his poem:

> Down from the hills of Habersham,
> Through the Valleys of Hall,
> I hurry amain, to reach the plain,—
> Run the rapid and leap the fall . . .

221

He lived like a poet and he died like one, writing his last lines on his deathbed with his temperature at 104. His wife, Mary Day, dedicated her life to helping him fight the battle to regain his health. They tried everything. Finally, on his doctor's recommendation, they were living in a tent on a hillside in North Carolina. They were there alone when, in September, 1881, the pen literally dropped from his fingers.

Eneas Africanus, a Georgia literary phenomenon, was written by Harry Stillwell Edwards at Holly Bluff Plantation just outside of Macon. The place is noted for its many beautiful holly trees, and Mr. Edwards loved it so much that he said, shortly before his death in 1938, "I shall not journey farther than I can dream my way back."

Eleven thousand acres of the plantation became Camp Wheeler at the time of the First World War, but the family reserved ten acres surrounding the rambling weathered frame house which is now the home of Mr. and Mrs. Rosser Smith. Mrs. Smith is a granddaughter of Mr. Edwards. Leased again by the government during World War II, the entire tract is now back in the possession of the family, but is still called Camp Wheeler after Confederate General Joseph Wheeler, who won added distinction with the United States Army in the Spanish-American War.

Mr. Edwards, at one time editor of the Macon *News*, did most of his later writing in a retreat near the house called Kingfisher Cabin. Here he entertained Henry Ford, Harvey Firestone and many other friends. After Mr. Edwards's death, Mr. Ford wanted to buy the cabin for his Dearborn Museum, but the Macon Rotary Club felt it should be kept at home and the small house was moved to the campus of Wesleyan College at Rivoli.

Mr. Edwards won a $10,000 prize in 1896 for a novel *Sons and Fathers*, that he wrote in forty days. This book is now out of print and much of his other writing is lost in newspaper columns.

But the golden legend of *Eneas* remains.

Eneas Africanus, a long short story by Mr. Edwards was first published in book form in Macon in 1920. It sold 1,500,000 copies in no time at all. Later an illustrated edition was brought out by a national publishing house and there have been innumerable reprintings. *Eneas*, still selling, is well past the three-million mark, and through translation has become a citizen of the world.

Mr. Edwards never admitted that the tale is fiction. And perhaps it isn't. Certainly Eneas had his counterpart in many families. Certainly his story is the classic of all the legends about what happened to the silver when Sherman came through.

Eneas, a trusted servant in the family of Confederate Major George E.

Photo by Drinnon

FIGURE 60.   Sidney Lanier was born here in 1842 in the Gothic cottage of his grandparents, which still stands on High Street in Macon.

Tommey, wandered for eight years over seven Southern states, trying to find his way from the Tommey stock farm in North Georgia to the plantation, Tommeysville, near Louisville in Washington County in the Southeastern part of the state.

In 1864, as Mr. Edwards tells it, Major Tommey's family caught the last train out of Floyd County before Sherman destroyed the railroad. Eneas followed, driving Lady Chain, a blooded mare hitched to a farm wagon in which a trunk of silver was hidden under forage. Among the silver was a bride's cup, handed down in the Tommey family since 1670.

Eneas was well supplied with Confederate money for his expenses, but he had never made the trip alone from North to South Georgia and he got lost.

223

FIGURE 61. Thackeray described this house in 1856 when it was being built by Mr. and Mrs. William B. Johnston, in Macon. It is now the home of Mr. and Mrs. P. L. Hay. The architecture was inspired by the Johnston's honeymoon in Italy.

As time went on, the Tommey family, believing he had been murdered and robbed, gave him up for dead.

In 1872, eight years after Eneas set out on his journey, Major Tommey wrote a letter, asking that it be published in the Macon paper, and requesting that "other papers please copy." His daughter was soon to be married and he hoped the letter might bring information leading to recovery of the bride's cup which had been packed with the silver entrusted to Eneas.

Replies came from various points. Eneas, with his engaging character, his stories of the affluence of Major Tommey—stories that got bigger with each telling—had left an impression in many places. The letters revealed that Eneas had married again and had begotten several children. Lady Chain had produced a colt. With this wonder colt and his own ready tongue, Eneas had become a horse-racing preacher.

Everybody had been anxious to help Eneas along the way, but the names of plantations, towns and counties he sought were similar to many others and usually he was helped along in the wrong direction.

Nevertheless, Eneas, well heeled with track winnings and everything intact, got back to Tommeysville just in time for the wedding. Slavery was long over but Eneas made the major a present of the new family acquired on his travels.

This is the bare outline of the story. It should be read in the original for the charm of Mr. Edwards's telling. He himself was a charming gentleman. Nobody who met him ever forgot him, certainly not the children who were around when he won that $10,000 prize. He bought bicycles for his own children, for their friends and the friends of their friends. He bought thirty in all.

Thackeray commented on Macon's "pretty houses" when he gave a lecture there in 1856, which he says was attended by the "young ladies of Wesleyan" (oldest chartered woman's college in the United States, founded in 1837).

In a letter to his daughters, Anne and Harriett, in London, Thackeray tells how their friends, Mr. and Mrs. William B. Johnston, were at that time building themselves a house in Macon "and meanwhile living in one of their Negro houses in an uncommonly nice big room on the ground floor, in which I felt I could instantly write novels. I must have a ground floor room on a garden and instantly write novels.

"Mr. Johnston keeps a shop here," he continued. "Almost everybody keeps a shop. He is very rich though and has left the shop to his brother. . . . They all have pretty houses a little way from their businesses." Mr. Thackeray is impressed with the fact that he himself is about $500 richer by the week . . . says he thinks "Little Dorritt" is "capital as far as I have read" . . . wonders how much Dickens is worth.

It seems too bad that Mr. Thackeray could not have seen the finished and furnished twenty-four room Italian-style house at 934 Georgia Avenue, which for richness rivals anything in Vanity Fair. This house was under construction from 1855—a year before Thackeray's visit—until 1860. Perhaps it isn't strictly accurate to say it was finished even then.

Mr. Johnston had heard the superstitious saying that an old man who builds a house seldom lives to enjoy it. He was only forty, but he was taking no chances. One section of the decorative iron fence was never hung. This was the unfinished detail by which he hoped to beat the jinx. A resident of Macon says she remembers, as a child, seeing this piece of fencing in the basement of the old William B. Johnston house and hearing the story of why it was there.

Mr. Johnston built the house for his bride, Ann Tracy, on the site of her former home. They had honeymooned in Europe, fallen in love with Italian architecture and brought back plans and furnishings for a house that had everything—ballroom, art gallery, conservatory, elaborately carved interior woodwork, nineteen Cararra marble mantels, and a five-hundred-pound front door with solid silver hinges. A niche on the stairway landing revolves to disclose a secret room. Mr. Johnston served as depositary for the largest share of the Confederate treasury this side of Richmond. Perhaps the money was stored in this hidden room.

After Mr. Johnston's death his daughter, Mary Ellen, and her husband, Judge William H. Felton, continued to live in the house. Mr. Johnston, it should be added, reached the ripe old age of seventy-eight.

Mr. and Mrs. P. L. Hay, who have owned the house for many years, find it a perfect setting for collected art treasures. Mr. Hay added the one thing lacking, an elevator.

Almost always in Macon you are taken first to 988 Bond Street to see Overlook, the home of Mrs. B. P. O'Neal—who some years ago tried to give it away without success. This is one of Macon's most impressive houses and occupies the town's most commanding site on the very peak of Coleman Hill, with the rest of Macon spread out in bright panorama below. Parthenon-like, with its surrounding Doric colonnade and triglyph frieze, the old house is shaded by mammoth magnolia trees, and vast green lawns drop away on all sides.

It was a natural choice for Federal General James H. Wilson, who, it is said, lived here during the military occupation following the War Between the States. With its spacious parlors and beautiful free-hanging stair, the old house also made a beautiful setting—when the grim days of Reconstruction were over —for the german given in honor of Winnie Davis, daughter of the President of the late Confederate States of America. Overlook was then owned by S. T. Coleman. His daughter, Miss "Birdie" Coleman, was hostess at that memorable party.

FIGURE 62. Overlook, the B. P. O'Neal house in Macon, built in 1836, was the scene of a brilliant ball given for Winnie Davis, daughter of the Confederate President.

It must be said that General Wilson captured the city of Macon after the war was over.

General Lee had surrendered to General Grant on April 9, 1865 at Appomattox Courthouse.

This news had reached Macon, but as late as April 20 it still had not reached General Wilson. April 20 was the day the city fathers heard that General Wilson was headed toward Macon from Columbus, where he had just burned 100,000 bales of cotton.

FIGURE 63. Architects admire the Ralph Small house in Macon, which is often cited as a fine example of the beauty and variety achieved within the classic mold.

Macon's home defenses had been disbanded. Hurriedly, under flags of truce, messengers were sent out along all the roads leading into the city from the west. Meanwhile 2,500 barrels of corn whisky were emptied into the gutter to forestall any Federal celebration that might get out of hand.

When finally reached, fourteen miles from Macon, General Wilson tossed his hat into the air and shouted "peace!" But he had set out to capture Macon and capture it he did.

That first night he and his staff "registered" at the old Lanier Hotel, which still stands. In spite of Macon's precautions, Wilson's soldiers burned two blocks of business property on Mulberry Street. But things settled down and General Wilson stayed on to enforce military rule. In later years he was invited back and was entertained at The Cedars, another fine old Macon house, which was then the home of Judge Emory Speer.

Jerry Cowles, who built Overlook in 1836, came down from New York as a young man to try his fortune in Macon. His quick rise to prosperity may still be measured by his two houses.

In 1829 he built for himself, his young wife and their baby, a charming Greek Revival stucco cottage on Walnut Street, with lawns extending all the way to the Ocmulgee River. Six years later, Overlook, the more ambitious residence, was begun.

Today we find that the Greek Revival cottage has been widely copied by architects. (An Atlanta version was so beloved by its owners that they took it down in sections and carried it along when they moved to Virginia.) On the other hand, Mrs. B. P. O'Neal—according to a news story in the Macon *Telegraph*—has offered to deed the big house to any suitable foundation or organization which will preserve it "in perpetuity." All of this is easily understood, the scarcity of domestic service and the upkeep of big houses being what they are.

So far, sad to say, there have been no takers for Overlook, but when business and bulldozers threatened the very foundations of the Jerry Cowles cottage, young Mr. and Mrs. Alfred Sams had a talk with Mrs. Sams's architect uncle, Elliott Dunwody. The house was just what they wanted but they wanted it in a proper setting, plus modern conveniences. Under Mr. Dunwody's supervision the old house was carefully dismantled, each piece numbered and all put together again at Rivoli, six miles distant.

This much-copied house has an Ionic portico and fanlighted door. Though a cottage, it is spacious and has elaborate molded cornices and ceiling centerpieces, carved woodwork and mantels with gold-leaf medallions.

From the wide hallway, with its central arch, two rooms open on either side and there is an added wing. Twin end-chimneys are joined by a parapet to make a graceful roof line. Rejuvenated, the house stands again in the midst of rolling green lawns and tall trees. Once again, it has furnishings that "belong."

Whether or not a house may be called a belle and beauty, it is certain that the home of Ralph Small, has a stag line of architectural admirers.

Originally this white frame house faced Vineville Avenue and was approached by a double avenue of cedars. But, like several other old Macon homes, it was turned about in adjusting itself to the city's growth and now graces 156 Rogers Avenue.

Talbot Hamlin, in his book *Greek Revival Architecture in America*, uses it to illustrate the great variety of detail possible in the classic pattern. "Perhaps the most refined of the characteristic Georgia examples," he writes, "is the exquisite Ralph Small house in Macon."

The square columns at each end of its long porch, flanking Doric columns, "were in many cases used for esthetic reasons only," he points out. Instead of a

FIGURE 64. Godey's *Lady's Book* published the building plans of the R. J. Carmichael house in Macon, erected in 1846. It was designed in the shape of a Greek cross; the porch was rounded in later years.

pediment, "raked blocking courses, sometimes richly decorated with anthemions and scrolls, were frequently used to mark the center of long horizontal roof eaves, as for instance in the Ralph Small house." (In less technical terms, a raked blocking is a sort of parapet, sloping off from mid-center. Anthemions are stylized honeysuckle blossoms.)

All in all, Mr. Hamlin concludes, this Macon house could have been designed by the noted New England architect, Elias Carter, who is known to have done

Photo by Talmadge Veal

FIGURE 65. The Alfred Sams residence at Rivoli, suburb of Macon, was built in 1829 by Jerry Cowles of New York, who later built Overlook. It has spacious rooms, elaborate molded cornices, ceiling centerpieces and carved woodwork.

some work in the South. "Many good architects came South in that lush era of prosperity," he observes.

Another detail of the Small house is the frieze of inverted laurel wreaths, not so common elsewhere in Georgia but used effectively on several Macon houses. A notable example is the old Hugenin-Proudfit house at 1261 Jefferson Terrace, beautifully restored by Mr. and Mrs. Buford Birdsey.

The Small house and three others in Macon are used by Howard Major to illustrate—in addition to variety of detail—the striking individuality often achieved within the Greek Revival style. The other three—Elam Alexander designs—are the O'Neal, R. J. Carmichael and Sanford Birdsey houses. Mr. Major cites all four as choice examples in his book, *The Domestic Architecture of the Early American Republic*.

Godey's *Lady's Book* is said to have printed the plans followed in 1846 in building the Carmichael house at 1183 Georgia Avenue. The design is that of a modified Greek Cross, with rooms branching off in four directions from an octagonal hall. A free-hanging stairway sings itself upward to a cupola high above the second story.

Originally the Ionic-columned front porch followed the line of the house between the arms of the cross. Later it was given a rounded front. The interior of the house, with large bay window recesses at the end of each room, no doubt, presented a major problem in decoration. Happily, its various vistas are enhanced by exquisite eighteenth-century mahogany furnishings and an over-all effect of unity heightened by just the right fabrics and colors.

The Cedars, the Sanford Birdsey home at 2056 Vineville, also has an unusual floor plan. It is built in the form of an H, giving the front porch a U-shaped colonnade.

Another variation of floor plan is found in the Asa Holt-Canning house at 856 Mulberry Street, built in 1853 and still "in the family" as the home of Mrs. Kate Martin Roberson.

The columned porch extends all the way across the front of the house, but the long hall is at the side, which places the entrance at the end of the porch. This style is sometimes called a single house.

The Asa G. Holt home was one of the few Macon houses damaged in the War Between the States. General Stoneman "raided the state almost to the gates of Macon," and a shell from one of his batteries struck the sidewalk in front of the Holt house, July 30, 1864. The shell bounced against a porch column, went through the parlor wall and landed in the hall—unexploded.

There are many other delightful old houses in Macon. Some few of them, like the Lanier cottage which is now a tea room, have had to adapt themselves to changing circumstances. The classic Callaway house, designed by Elam Alexander, is the entrance building of the Macon hospital, but its exterior is unchanged. The only New York type town house ever built in Macon is the Emerson-Holmes-Massee building, today occupied as a photographic studio.

CHAPTER 28

Confederate WACs Won Their Only Battle

GEORGIA'S Confederate WACs won their only encounter with the Federal army—but not by force of arms.

This company of trained girl soldiers, who preceded the Woman's Army Corps of World War II by eighty years, were the Nancy Harts, of LaGrange. Their name was inspired by the Georgia Revolutionary heroine who captured six British officers and men and shot two who didn't believe she would pull the trigger.

The Nancy Harts of LaGrange were also ready to shoot to kill. At least, that's what they said and certainly they all became expert markswomen. Actually they only killed a cow owned by Judge Orville Augustus Bull, father of two of the girls—Andelia, Third Lieutenant, and Sallie, Second Corporal. This fatality, of course, was an accident. In their first practice sessions the Nancies just shut their eyes and banged away.

As to actual military encounter, what could the girl soldiers do when the Yankee colonel at the head of invading troops practically surrendered before they could draw a bead? He was Colonel O. H. LaGrange, whose name, oddly enough, was the same as that of the town.

And so to the Nancy Harts goes the credit of saving the many beautiful Greek Revival houses in LaGrange. Of course, the business section was burned, but that was routine. Colonel LaGrange stationed guards at the houses and there was none of the usual "foraging." In return for his gallantry, the LaGrange ladies fed his entire troop. The colonel, it should be added, later married a Georgia girl.

Photo by Kenneth Rogers

FIGURE 66.   A Confederate WAC lived here—Mrs. Peter Heard, First Lieutenant of the Nancy Harts. It is now the home of Mrs. Ethel Dallis Hill at LaGrange.

The Nancy Harts, organized in 1861, soon learned to handle firearms, but none of them ever forgot the day one of the girls hit a hornet's nest instead of the target.

"The hornets responded to the attack," said Mrs. James Allen Morris, former First Corporal Leila Pullen, of the Nancy Harts, in a paper she read in 1902 before the United Daughters of the Confederacy in Atlanta. This paper, "Personal Recollections of the War," is now in the possession of her daughter, Mrs. Robert M. Crumley of Atlanta.

Mrs. Morris tells how the LaGrange girls organized themselves as a home guard with the determination to protect the town from Federal raids. Every able-bodied young woman, married or single, was enrolled. The captain, Mrs. Brown Morgan, outranked her husband who was a first lieutenant in the Confederate army.

FIGURE 67. The Oaks, boyhood home of artist Lamar Dodd, and still the residence of his mother, Mrs. Francis J. Dodd, in LaGrange. Note the widow's walk and unsupported balcony.

The Nancies had no uniforms, because cloth and brass buttons were needed for the fighting men. Wearing dresses with long full skirts, they were drilled twice a week by Dr. H. C. Ware, who was barred from field service by physical disability.

Target practice took place at Harris Grove. Guns included any firearms not already in use by the Confederate army. "It was an open question," Mrs. Morris declares, "whether the muzzle or the breach was the more dangerous. I have yet a feeling of how the flint lock fowling piece of my grandfather got in its vigorous kicks. But we soon became expert and didn't mind shooting."

Their day of battle was a long time coming. Meanwhile the Nancy Harts continued target practice and staged a military march twice a week to inspire the homefolks with confidence in their ability to defend the town. But their major activity was serving as nurses in the hospitals filled with wounded sent back from the fighting lines.

Then on April 16, 1865, came rumors that put the girl soldiers on the alert.

Actually, the war was over, but nobody in southwest Georgia then knew that General Lee had surrendered to General Grant in Virginia on April 9. In fact, the news traveled so slowly that the last land engagement of the War Between the States was fought nearly a month later at Palmetto Ranch, near Galveston, Texas, on May 13, 1865. The Confederate cruiser, the *Shenandoah*, continued to war on Union whaling ships in the far-off Pacific and Arctic Oceans until July. When the fatal news finally reached Captain Waddell and his crew they did a twenty-thousand-mile detour to avoid capture, sailing around the Horn and surrendering finally to British authorities in the neutral port of Liverpool in November.

The Nancy Harts were uncomfortably close to the two very last land engagements east of the Mississippi. These took place just south of LaGrange at Columbus, forty-eight miles distant, and at West Point, only fourteen miles away.

On the afternoon of April 16, General James H. Wilson's army began its attack on Columbus. Colonel LaGrange and a brigade of cavalry were already engaged with a flanking movement at West Point.

Battle scars on the old white square-columned Griggs house at West Point show that it was directly in the line of fire. The remains of Fort Tyler may be seen on the hill just behind the house. In charge of the hastily mustered Confederate forces at West Point was General R. C. Tyler, then on crutches because of the loss of a leg at Missionary Ridge. He was one of the day's many casualties. By this time the South's very young boys were fighting, as well as men beyond the military age of fifty-five. Few of them had uniforms or training.

Here at West Point, Federal Colonel LaGrange displayed a fine humanitarian spirit, according to Clifford L. Smith in his *History of Troup County:*

"Finally as the enemy came over the parapet, the small Confederate forces remaining clubbed their muskets and still fought desperately. Colonel LaGrange, a gallant Federal officer, on finding the helpless condition of the defenders and no white flag, called upon them to surrender and ordered his men to cease firing upon such brave men. He was amazed to find that he had been fighting a little company of 64 men all day."

It was the following afternoon that Colonel LaGrange swept into the town of LaGrange. And here Mrs. Morris, née Corporal Pullen of the Nancy Harts, again takes up the story:

"We were standing in front of my house when we saw coming down College Hill a body of blue coats rushing upon our defenseless city. . . . As this body approached we saw it was a regular brigade of Federal Cavalry, having in charge the Confederate soldiers captured at Fort Tyler. . . ."

FIGURE 68. Residence of Mr. and Mrs. John Wilcox, LaGrange. Note the fine Palladian doorway in this ante-bellum story-and-a-half home.

FIGURE 69.   Bellevue, former home of Benjamin H. Hill of LaGrange, is now
being restored as a clubhouse for the LaGrange Woman's Club.

The cavalry came to a halt in front of the Nancy Harts. First Corporal Pullen observed that Confederate Major R. B. Parkman, a prisoner of war, was riding beside the Federal Colonel.

"I said, 'Major, I regret to see you in this plight.'

"The Colonel inquired, 'Miss, is this your sweetheart?'

"I replied indignantly, 'Yes, he is.'

" 'Such honesty deserves reward,' the Colonel said. 'I will give him a parole and let him spend the evening with you.'

"Both officers dismounting, Major Parkman then introduced us. 'Colonel LaGrange, I have the pleasure of introducing you to a regularly commissioned officer of the Nancy Harts.'

"The Colonel very pleasantly replied, 'I should think the Nancy Harts might use their eyes with better effect upon the federal soldiers than their rusty guns.' "

Major Parkman then drew First Corporal Pullen aside to ask whether it would be agreeable with her mother if she invited Colonel LaGrange and two other Federal officers to her house for refreshment. They had been very kind to him, he explained.

So the Nancies broke ranks, more introductions were performed and a group of the girl soldiers went along with the Yankee officers for tea at the home of First Corporal Pullen. Nancy Hart officers, in addition to those already mentioned, were Mrs. Peter Heard, First Lieutenant; Alice Smith, Second Lieutenant; Augusta Hill, First Sergeant; Pack Beall, Second Sergeant and Mrs. John T. Gay, Third Corporal.

At the Pullen home they found the servants missing and soon it became apparent there had been a general walkout. The ladies of LaGrange spent the night in the big kitchens of those white-columned houses, cooking food for Federal troops and Confederate prisoners.

Next morning Federals and Confederates set out to meet General Wilson in Macon. There they learned the war was over. Prisoners were released and began the return trip to LaGrange and near-by points.

First Corporal Pullen closes her paper with the romantic note that Colonel LaGrange, who remained in Macon for some time, took one of the city's "fairest daughters" North with him as his bride. Of course, it would have made a better story if he had captured one of the Nancy Harts. In fact, there is a legend that he married Second Corporal Sallie Bull. On the contrary, that young lady was joined in wedlock to a former Confederate officer, Major John Park.

First Corporal Pullen didn't marry her Confederate beau, after all. She said, "I will" to a gentleman from the North, James A. Morris of Morristown, Pa. They met after the war was over in the home of Confederate General and Mrs. John B. Gordon in Atlanta.

Photo by Lee Stietenroth

FIGURE 70. Cloverland, one of the oldest frame houses in Troup County, is the plantation home of Mr. and Mrs. Tom Hutchinson, near LaGrange. The columns were a later addition.

Sutherland, the Gordons' large white-columned house, formerly stood in Kirkwood, then a suburb of Atlanta. Mrs. Gordon was the lovely Frances Haralson of LaGrange, and though she was not a Nancy Hart, she was equally militant. She literally went to war with her general. He was five times wounded at the bloody Battle of Sharpsburg, in Virginia, giving up only when he fell unconscious from his horse. Mrs. Gordon's careful nursing saved his life.

A quaint anecdote about Mrs. Gordon's camp following is told by the general's niece, Miss Loulie Gordon Roper, of Kingston.

Apparently the war had been on for some time when Confederate General

Jubal Early, seeing a carriage drive into camp, inquired as to the occupants. "That's Mrs. Gordon's carriage, sir," he was told.

"Humph," General Early remarked drily, "if all my men kept up as well as Mrs. Gordon does, there would be no stragglers."

Three of the loveliest old houses in present-day LaGrange were the homes of Nancy Harts. Doubtless there are others which could claim this honor, for LaGrange, now a city of thirty-five thousand inhabitants, still has dozens of these white-columned houses, most of which maintain their ante-bellum atmosphere of serenity within a protective grove of oaks and elms or an old-fashioned box-hedged garden.

When LaGrange had only eleven hundred inhabitants, the town was graced with around a hundred houses of classic design. Indians still dropped in occasionally to do a bit of scalping when the first of these was built. LaGrange was founded in 1828 on lands ceded by the Creeks only three years earlier. The name of the town was a compliment to LaFayette, who visited Georgia in 1825 as a guest of Governor Troup, for whom the county was named. LaGrange was the name of the French estate of the marquis.

In 1861 Mrs. J. Brown Morgan, captain of the Nancy Harts, lived in the house at 305 Broad Street. It is one of the oldest in LaGrange and has been owned for many years by the Pinckard family. The handsome columns were added sometime after Vines Harwell built the house for his bride, Mary Lane. The town had not yet been incorporated when their twin sons, Henry and John, were born there on Christmas Eve of 1827.

Third Corporal of the Nancies, Mrs. John T. Gay, was born Caroline Ware in the white house with six Doric columns at 311 Vernon Street. Here two ancient camellia bushes have grown into tall, thickly foliaged dark green trees and stand on either side of the front door like quaint, formal set-pieces against the white of the classic old house. So charming is the effect, especially when the pink and white camellias blossom out in waxlike perfection, that the present owner, Mrs. R. T. Segrest, is quite accustomed to having people stop and stare.

Young Mrs. Peter Heard, first lieutenant of the Nancy Harts, lived in the stately white house with tall Doric columns on three sides, standing far back from the street among its elms and oaks at 206 Broad. Massive hedges of box-wood on either side of the walk were planted in 1861 and are the perfect approach for a house still filled with treasures of the long ago. A delicate hanging balcony extends all the way across the front of the house, which was built in the eighteen thirties and has been owned for more than sixty years by the family of Mrs. Ethel Dallis Hill, who lives there with her daughter, Mrs. M. J. Crayton.

This house is one of several in LaGrange included in Howard Major's

Domestic Architecture of the Early American Republic, as distinguished examples of the variety achieved within the classic mold. Others are the houses of Mrs. Francis J. Dodd at 1103 Vernon Street, Ben H. Hill on McLendon, Miss Kate Wilkinson at 301 Vernon and Wiley Reeves at 523 Greenville Street.

From one of these old houses came an artist whose work now hangs in the Metropolitan Museum. Other fine paintings by Lamar Dodd—head of the Fine Arts Department of the University of Georgia in Athens—may be seen here in LaGrange at The Oaks, the home of his mother, Mrs. Francis J. Dodd. This house, with its six massive Doric columns, was built in 1845 by Philip Hunter Greene. It has a hanging balcony, a widow's walk, a huge conservatory and one of the loveliest curving stairways in LaGrange, framed by the central arch of the wide hallway.

Great disillusionment as well as great honor came to Confederate Senator Benjamin H. Hill at Bellevue, the handsome white frame house with tall Ionic columns, now used as a meeting place for the LaGrange Woman's Club. This was one of three Georgia homes of Senator Hill.

McLendon Street in LaGrange was formerly the juniper-lined driveway of Bellevue, the grounds of which originally included twelve hundred acres.

Mr. Hill entertained Confederate President Jefferson Davis and many other distinguished visitors in the great double parlors of the house, which are formal enough for state apartments. Their wide recessed windows and double doors have elaborately carved cornices capped with gold. Equally elaborate are the ceiling decorations. The mantels are of black Cararra marble.

Here at Bellevue, Senator Hill was arrested by Federal soldiers and taken away on ten minutes' notice. As a member of the Georgia legislature he had opposed secession but later gave it his support and was so closely associated with the President of the Confederacy that he was regarded as his spokesman.

When the war was over, Mr. Hill again adapted his policies to altered circumstances, counseling acceptance of reconstruction rule. This lost him the support of his constituents in Troup County.

In 1869 he said good-bye to Bellevue and moved his family to Athens, to the equally handsome house at 570 Prince Avenue, now the official residence of the president of the University of Georgia. There in 1875 he was elected to the United States House of Representatives and in 1877 to the United States Senate. A brilliant orator, he is credited with influencing President Hayes to withdraw Federal occupation troops from the South, which was done in 1877.

Still standing in Troup County is the boyhood home of Mr. Hill, the sturdy two-story plantation house of his father, John Hill, at Long Cane.

The fine details of workmanship that went into LaGrange's old houses is illustrated in the one-and-a-half-story home of Mr. and Mrs. John Wilcox on Hines Street, built in 1833. It has a beautiful Palladian doorway with leaded

Photo by Kenneth Rogers

FIGURE 71. Nutwood, near LaGrange, is the plantation house of Mr. and Mrs. A. E. Mallory. Built in 1833, it has its own private lake for fishing. It was called Nutwood because the first pecan tree in the county was planted here.

fan- and side lights. The star medallions centering the capitals of the four Ionic columns are repeated in the pilasters. A carved balustrade, connecting the columns, creates an effect of intimacy which gives the house unusual charm.

The rich variety of these old houses is perhaps best illustrated in their balconies. Some extend all the way across the front as at Bellevue and at the house of Mrs. Ethel Dallis Hill. In the beautiful old Atkinson house, at 207 Broad, now the home of Mr. and Mrs. George Forrester, the balcony includes the bedroom windows on each side of the upstairs door. This house, with its Ionic columns, was originally built in the country and later moved into town. The Alvin Smith house, near LaGrange College, has a small square balcony that extends outward to connect the tall Corinthian columns. The Ward house at 401 Vernon has a two-story veranda all the way across the front.

One of the oldest frame houses in the county is Cloverland, built three miles from LaGrange by surveyor Samuel Reeves and now owned by Mr. and Mrs. Tom Hutchinson. Spring is the time to drive down its long avenue of graceful pecan trees. It is like passing between lines of ballet dancers, all wearing chartreuse green dirndles, gayly fluttering in the breeze. Surrounded by a box garden and old trees and the broad acres of a cattle farm, the carefully restored house is typical of its era, two rooms up and two down, with a wide steep stairway and a hall between and shed rooms in the back. The massive Doric columns were added at a later date.

As you turn into the crape-myrtle-bordered avenue at Nutwood on the Big Springs Road you catch your first delightful glimpse of a classic white pedimented house with Ionic portico set behind a wide circle of green box and framed by unusually fine magnolia and oak trees.

Nutwood, the home of Mr. and Mrs. A. E. Mallory, is a four-hundred-acre farm with a private lake for fishing. The house was built by Joel D. Newsome in 1833 and got its name from the fact that the first pecan tree in the county was planted here. Visitors later came from all around to take a look. More interesting today is the original smoke house, still standing in the back yard, stocked in traditional manner with hams, sausage and other home-cured meats.

The most marrying house in the county is now the home of the Misses Tommie and Lena Martin, who say they didn't buy it with any matrimonial plans in mind. This stately old house with free-standing Doric columns was built in 1833 by Graves Swanson, who had eight daughters, all of whom were duly married off. It is said they used the hanging balcony as a lookout when beaux were expected. Then, tilting their hoop skirts in order to navigate the narrow stairway from the second floor, they would come down, prettily surprised at finding guests.

Among many other lovely old houses in and around LaGrange—and on into

Photo by Snelson Davis

FIGURE 72. Hills and Dales, famous Ferrell gardens at LaGrange and the house that replaced the old Ferrell residence. This is now the home of Mr. and Mrs. Fuller Callaway, Jr.

Greenville and Columbus—is the Ionic-columned Nathan Van Boddie house, seven miles from LaGrange. Built in 1836, it has a dining room forty feet long and twenty feet wide, which occasionally doubled as a ballroom.

Gardens are usually designed for houses, but the Fuller Callaway house at LaGrange was built to fit the setting of its famous ante-bellum Ferrell gardens which spread out over five acres of formal terraces. It is a handsome Georgian Italian villa, designed by Neel Reid, which gracefully crowns the wide, level hilltop and gives accent to an ever-expanding pattern of loveliness, set in 1841 by the late Mrs. Blount Ferrell who planned the gardens.

An open-air church and a series of gardens which work out religious and heraldic mottoes in boxwood are among the many unusual features of The Terraces, now known as Hills and Dales.

Three women have made a career of these gardens. Mrs. Ferrell planned the six broad terraces, the walks with their magnificent tree plantings, their flowering shrubs and the bowers at the end of these shaded walks. She utilized boxwood

245

creatively, not alone to outline colorful beds of flowers and to form artistic designs, but also to spell out words and to give her gardens an atmosphere of religious tranquillity.

Sentinel boxwood, eighteen feet high and eight feet thick, line the walk to the church garden, where pulpit, pews, organ, harp, collection plate and other furnishings are carved from tree-box. A benign "God Is Love" was the first of Mrs. Ferrell's many evergreen mottoes in dwarf boxwood. Its companion piece, "Fiat Justica," was planted for her hubsand, Judge Ferrell. She and the judge had spent sixty-one years together here in their rambling white frame house when Mrs. Ferrell died at the age of eighty-six in 1903. The judge was ninety-two at the time of his death in 1908.

There was a bit of local speculation as to what changes might be made when Fuller Callaway, Sr., bought the estate in 1912 (eighty acres then, now fifteen hundred).

Sometime after taking possession, Mr. Callaway—sitting in a sequestered spot —overheard an interesting conversation between two old gentlemen of LaGrange who were taking a walk through the grounds.

"Well," one of them said, "what do you think of the place since Fuller's fixed it up?"

His companion said it didn't look so very different to him.

The other one remarked thoughtfully, "It's a funny thing to me that he'd buy all those statues of himself to put up around here and not a damn' one of 'em looks like him!"

Mr. Callaway had placed antique statues of Greek philosophers in some of the bowers at the end of the walks.

Another entertaining story about the late Mr. Callaway, who founded the great Callaway Mills, concerns his revision of the family coat of arms when Mrs. Callaway decided to transfer its mottoes to the garden. These were to be "St. Callaway" and "Ora Pro Novis" (Pray for Us). Mr. Callaway humorously told his wife he needed concentrated prayer for himself, and so in the garden the motto reads, "Ora Pro Mi" (Pray for Me).

Under Mrs. Callaway's supervision the gardens continued to grow in beauty, and now Mrs. Fuller Callaway, Jr., carries on with the same inspired devotion. A sunken garden and a pool at the foot of the terraces and a fountain framed with evergreen on the topmost level have been happily incorporated into the original design. Add the color and fragrance of Confederate jasmine, wisteria, climbing yellow Lady Banksia roses, magnolias, banana shrub, tea olive, azaleas, camellias—all the Old South favorites and all the new ones—plus a complete rose garden and large greenhouses and you still have to see the gardens to believe their beauty.

CHAPTER 29

Southern Charm and the Hell Bomb

SOUTHERN charm in the middle of a squeeze play. . . .

This is the drama that began in Augusta when Uncle Sam decided to locate a hydrogen-bomb plant immediately across the Savannah River.

Already Augusta was bounded on the west by Camp Gordon and on the northwest by the mammoth Clark Hill dam project, both of which brought a tremendous increase in population to the general neighborhood. Now on the east loomed the fantastic activity of what is casually called the Savannah River Operation Office (of the Atomic Energy Commission)—literally a billion, nine-million-dollar plant to brew fuel for the hydrogen bomb. Here was another census jump, beginning with thirty-five thousand construction workers and their families. On the Augusta outskirts a mushroom growth of houses sprang up in all directions.

Business would boom, of course, but would Augusta ever be the same again? Would congestion displace comfort and courtesy? Some of the old guard feared Augusta would become another Atlanta.

A population figure of seventy-one thousand seemed just about right in a town where businessmen still like to go home for a leisurely lunch that is really dinner in the middle of the day. Augusta's design for living, which really places the accent on living, long ago made permanent residents of many visitors first attracted by the town's advantages as a winter resort.

But a slower, more graceful tempo doesn't mean slower thinking, as some sharp gentlemen from the outside have ruefully discovered when they tried to put over a fast one in a business deal. Augusta started out as a trading post and it is still a trading center, one of the most important in the Southeast. Scotch, English and French settlers did a flourishing business here with the Indians even before

Oglethorpe founded Georgia at Savannah in 1733. Officially, Augusta became Georgia's second oldest city when it was established as Fort Augusta in 1735.

Augusta's historic old White House, where thirteen American patriots were hanged in the well of the beautiful spiral stairway in 1780, is only one of the city's well-preserved pre-Revolutionary houses. Another is Meadow Garden, home of George Walton, one of the Georgia signers of the Declaration of Independence. Still another is the house of a thousand crystal chandeliers, built as an inn in 1761, carefully taken apart in 1929 and re-erected on "the hill," Augusta's most beautiful residential section.

In the King Cotton era, Augusta shipped cotton to all the ports of the world, first via the Savannah River to the seacoast and later by railroad. The first locomotive-drawn passenger train in the Western Hemisphere operated between Charleston and Hamburg, terminus point just across the Savannah River from Augusta. Laying of the tracks began in February of 1829. Tobacco was also an important crop. The very first Augustans who sought summer coolness on the Sand Hills three miles from town—now called simply "the hill"—crossed an old tobacco road, along which casks, drawn by horses, were once rolled to market in Augusta.

When Augusta built a canal in 1845 from the Savannah River to furnish water power for industry, city fathers took for granted that these industries would always be carefully selected. But in 1951 Augusta faced the problem of adjusting to mammoth new enterprises not of its own choosing which were, nonetheless, received with traditional hospitality. Augusta had become the center for three vast government projects. World War I had brought a population increase of forty thousand to Camp Hancock, but that was temporary. World War II brought Camp Gordon. Later the great Clark Hill Dam was begun. And then—the hydrogen bomb.

What would happen to Augusta's way of life, its especial brand of Southern charm?

Only the future could tell for sure, but in Augusta's past there was more than a hint of the answer.

Time was when the Savannah River periodically overflowed its banks into some of Augusta's fine old homes. There was an emergency technique for this, recalled by an Augusta grand dame. "We jacked up the piano, installed the milk cow and chickens on the back porch and retired to the second floor . . ."

Levees long ago took the river under control. Augusta will, no doubt, control its new industrial inundation.

Augusta businessmen have never lost their traditional interest in hunting and fishing—though sometimes the hunting may be limited to tracking down golf balls at the Country Club or the Augusta National Golf Course. But also—as early

Photo by Guy Hayes

FIGURE 73. Thirteen American patriots were hanged over the stairwell in Augusta's old White House in 1780. One of Georgia's authentic Colonial structures, it was built as an inn in 1750. During the Revolution it was McKay's Trading Post, and is now preserved by the Richmond County Historical Association.

as 1808—Augusta had a Thespian club and the state's first medical association, which in 1828 founded the Medical Academy of Georgia—later the University of Georgia School of Medicine. The Augusta Library Society was organized in 1827, and by 1848 the Young Men's Library Association had begun to bring in foreign lecturers, including William Makepeace Thackeray.

Augustus Baldwin Longstreet, author of the celebrated *Georgia Scenes*, was born in Augusta. His father, William Longstreet, taking time to tinker with mechanical gadgets, came up with a steamboat which plied the Savannah River in 1807, the same year of Fulton's successful tryout on the Hudson. Charles Colcock Jones wrote his inclusive historical works at Montrose, the beautiful old Greek Revival house on "the hill," which is still owned and occupied by his descendants. Also on the hill is the charming Sand Hills cottage which was the home of poet Richard Henry Wilde, who wrote "My Life Is Like the Summer Rose."

Other poets have been inspired by the felicitous atmosphere of Augusta, as shown by the Poet's Monument on Greene Street—a lovely old street with central parks and a parade of monuments not far from the business section and Augusta's very Broad Street. Two of these poets were James Ryder Randall, best known for "Maryland, My Maryland"; and Father A. J. Ryan, poet-priest of the Confederacy, who wrote "The Conquered Banner":

> Furl that banner, for 'tis weary,
> Round its staff 'tis drooping dreary. . . .
> . . . Once ten thousand hailed it gladly. . . .
> Swore it should forever wave. . . .

Paul Hamilton Hayne, "the Tennyson of the South," and Sidney Lanier, who wrote "The Marshes of Glynn" and other poems singing the beauties of his native Georgia, are also honored by the Poet's Monument. Lanier's home was at Macon, but the other three lived in Augusta at one time or another.

The writing tradition continues in Augusta, led today by Berry Fleming, a native son, whose active interest in Georgia politics was reflected in his Book-of-the-Month-Club novel, *Colonel Effingham's Raid*. A one-time winter resident who now has a permanent home in Augusta is Edison Marshall, big game hunter and producer of annual best sellers.

The Augusta pattern of hospitality is illustrated by the late Judge J. C. C. Black, whose two daughters, Miss Katherine Black and Mrs. Thomas D. Carey, live on in the big brick Victorian house on Greene Street.

"Father felt that winter visitors staying in our hotels should also have the opportunity of knowing what life is like in Augusta homes," explained Miss Katie Black, "which meant that we had a great many dinner guests."

Among these guests were President William Howard Taft, John D. Rockefeller, Sr., Nicholas Murray Butler, William Lyon Phelps and others, whose framed photographs adorn a wall in the library of the Black home.

Judge Black himself is included in a group photograph of the Conversation Club, composed of prominent winter visitors and Augustans who formerly met at the Bon Air Hotel at ten o'clock every morning during the season for an hour of discussion. No doubt, these sessions would have made a fine television program.

As daughters of their father, Miss Black and Mrs. Carey felt a personal responsibility when World War II filled near-by Camp Gordon to overflowing. Local newspapers urged everybody with an extra bedroom to make it available for military occupation.

"But, of course, we couldn't take money for rooms," said Miss Black, raising aristocratic eyebrows.

Photo by Kenneth Rogers

FIGURE 74. The Augusta National Golf Club house was an ante-bellum dwelling, famous for its Fruitlands nursery, which set the pattern for so many Georgia gardens. The great Masters' Golf Tournament is played on the course here each spring.

So the rooms were made available without charge. And so also the broad stairway's "inclinator" (installed for the judge in his later years) has ever since been called a scooter, the name given it by delighted young military guests.

Today, as always, Augusta feels its responsibility to visitors. If spring rains muddy up the lakes at the Augusta National Golf Club just before the annual Masters' Tournament, what does the management do but dye the lakes blue? It doesn't hurt the fish and, of course, that's important too—General Ike Eisenhower is chairman of the fish committee. Just the same, the club must look its best for the Masters'.

This is the club dreamed up by Atlanta's Bobby Jones, grand-slam master of golf, and this is the fabulous tournament which brings all the greats of golf and many other important visitors to Augusta each spring, and to a clubhouse which was once an ante-bellum mansion.

FIGURE 75. Meadow Garden was the Augusta home of George Walton, the Signer, until he built a mansion on The Hill. It is preserved by the Daughters of the American Revolution.

Traveling out the Washington Road, these visitors turn into one of the longest magnolia avenues in the country. It is a perfectly straight driveway, with the trees forming practically a green wall on either side, and at the end shines a big-white-columned house.

The old house, which couldn't be more suitable, is a square, two-story structure crowned with a cupola and surrounded by tall square white pillars and a wide two-story gallery. Like many houses of the period it has a wide central hallway and is built above a raised basement—an early form of air conditioning which assures summer coolness for the ground floor.

This house goes even farther with its weather insurance—its thick walls are of cement, which keeps out the cold in winter and the heat in summer. Dennis Redmond, who started the house in 1854, had a theory borne out by the years, that this was the way to build for Southern comfort in a day when central heating was unheard of.

FIGURE 76. House of a thousand crystal chandeliers. It's done with mirrors at the home of Dr. A. J. Kilpatrick in Augusta. Mirrors which face each other from opposite ends of the double parlors reflect the iridescent prisms over and over.

P. J. A. Berckmans, Belgian horticulturist, bought the place in 1857 and converted cotton acres into the famous Fruitlands Nursery. Shrubs and trees from this nursery set the pattern for many of Georgia's lovely old gardens. With such a start it is not strange that Augusta itself should have become known as the garden city, and surely in Augusta one realizes there is a certain charm that only age can give to a garden.

Incidentally, Mr. Berckmans set a scenic pattern for the golf course laid out nearly a hundred years later at Fruitlands by Bobby Jones and Alistair McKenzie. Each of the eighteen holes of the Augusta National is named for the shrub or tree which predominates in the nearest planting—camellia (tree size), dogwood, firethorn, azalea, etc.

That guests who expect Southern hospitality also owe their hosts a certain consideration is wittily set forth by Judge Henry C. Hammond, distinguished

253

Augusta jurist, whose originality and independence of expression once shocked some of the visiting ladies at a garden-club convention dinner in Augusta. The judge is what is nowadays called a personality, and any visit which includes a glimpse of Augusta's delightful social life must convince the guest that personality is the chief ingredient of that city's charm.

At the garden-club dinner, held at the Bon Air Hotel quite a few years ago, Judge Hammond launched on its long career that famous story about the lady gardener and her choice of a birthday gift from her husband. As speaker of the evening, he first told the ladies that in his opinion the garden-club craze was taking all the romance out of matrimony.

"Why, just the other day, one of my friends asked his wife what she would like for a birthday present," he said, "and what do you think she wanted?"

Judge Hammond paused and the ladies leaned forward expectantly. "A load of well-rotted cow manure!" he exploded.

The judge's feelings about guests are expressed in an advertisement which he runs in the Augusta *Chronicle* and *The Herald* every year. In spite of his remarks about lady gardeners, he is a highly successful grower of camellias and azaleas which in spring transform the pine grove around his brick house on Walton Way Extension into a spectacularly beautiful park.

Since nearly everybody comes to see his camellias anyway, the judge now announces the peak blooming season ahead of time in the newspaper advertising columns, inviting both "friends and enemies" to attend. "Bring small children and dogs on a leash," the ad says. "Leave all bad children at home."

They say if you stand on the circular stairs at the old White House, at 1822 Broad Street, in Augusta, and count to thirteen, you will hear a groan. This writer heard something—though it may have been a creak of the curving stair rail.

Certainly there were groans inside the house and out on a day in September, 1780, when Colonel Thomas Browne, an Augusta Tory, took his terrible vengeance here.

Browne had been chased out of town by the patriots but he was happy to come back with the British when they took Fort Augusta. Colonel Elijah Clarke and five hundred American soldiers laid siege; and the British, barricaded in the old White House for four days, were without rations and ammunition and ready to surrender when reinforcements arrived from Charleston.

Colonel Clarke was forced to retreat, leaving behind twenty-eight wounded soldiers and one officer, Captain Ashby. The Tory Colonel Browne, wounded also, lay on a bed in a back room of the White House which commanded a fine view of the spiral stairway. It was his suggestion that thirteen of these men be hanged over the stairwell—one for each of the thirteen states—while he himself looked on and enjoyed the gruesome spectacle. The other sixteen prisoners were turned over to the Indians, who put them to death by slow torture.

One of Georgia's authentic Colonial structures, the old White House was built about 1750 as an inn. At the time of the Revolution it was known as McKay's Trading Post. It is of white clapboard, with a gambrell roof, fine end-chimneys and a square-columned recessed porch all the way across the front. Delicately carved spindles make the banister rail of the porch, and the cornice has a dentil decoration.

This is the oldest house in Augusta and one of the oldest in the state. It is preserved by the Richmond County Historical Association as a shrine to the memory of twenty-nine brave men who died here for American freedom.

The all-time tops in Southern charm was an Augusta belle—Octavia Walton LeVert, granddaughter of George Walton, the Signer. "For years she was the best known woman in the social life of America," declares Lucian Lamar Knight, late state historian. So celebrated was she for her beauty and intellectual brilliance that prominent visitors from abroad felt that they could not leave the country without an introduction.

When she traveled in Europe she was received by all the important royalty in a day when royalty still had its storybook glamour. She was presented to Queen Victoria in 1853 at a state ball, an unusual honor. Here she delighted the Italian, French and Spanish ambassadors by conversing with each in his respective language. In Rome the Pope was equally pleased to discover that she spoke Italian, and they enjoyed a long and discursive chat which she records in her *Souvenirs of Travel*, published in 1857.

The Waltons were living in Mobile when Octavia met, fell in love with and married Dr. Henry LeVert.

By executive appointment she represented the State of Alabama as commissioner at the Paris Exposition in 1855. She wrote the oration delivered in 1856 by Charles Dreux when the monument to her friend, Henry Clay, was dedicated in New Orleans. Due credit was given in the newspapers of the day. Both these honors were then signal recognition for a woman.

The unpublished letters of Madame LeVert show that Henry Clay was only one of the many distinguished men who were her friends. A remark by DeLamartine, the French poet, historian and orator, seems more than ever timely now. He said to her, "Your country, madame, has the most precious manuscript in the world—the signed Declaration of Independence. Do not your people make pilgrimages to see it?"

The granddaughter of one of the signers of that document inherited much of his intellect. Her education was received largely from her mother and grandmother Walton. Her father, one of four almost contemporary George Waltons in the family, was at one time acting governor of the territory of east Florida, and it was here that Octavia first began to mingle in official circles. She assisted in translating her father's foreign correspondence, and when a name was to be chosen for the capital of the new state of Florida, Octavia's suggestion was selected—the beautiful Indian name—Tallahassee.

George Walton, the Signer, was named for his uncle, George Walton. Both had sons who were given the same name. The Signer, a superior court judge, was accordingly addressed as Judge Walton. He fought in the Revolution, helped to frame the federal constitution and served as governor of Georgia and as United States Senator. Both the judge and his son, George, lived at Meadow Garden.

The broad meadows that gave the place its name long ago became business property. At Nelson Street, between Thirteenth and Fifteenth, the house is now hemmed in by a coal and ice plant and a lumberyard. But its immediate grounds are enclosed by a white picket fence. and once you enter the gate, you are in a garden-close and another century.

The white frame house is a charming one-and-a-half-story structure with three dormer windows and a recessed porch with slim posts all the way across the front. Filled with antiques and relics of historic interest, Meadow Garden is preserved by the Daughters of the American Revolution.

Judge George Walton, the Signer, was among the first to build on "the hill." But Walton Way, the principal street from town, once a plank road, does not lead directly to his house, which is at 2116 Wrightsboro Road. In an old letter written by Judge Walton (recorded in the Richmond County deed book for 1794), he says, "Having completed a mansion of my own at this place and removed my family, you will please take possession of Meadow Garden place as trustee of my sons under the deed of Thomas Watkins, esq. for that purpose . . ."

This letter indicates that he planned to use the new house as a year-round home. In this he anticipated most of the other residents who originally built cottages on the Sand Hills for summer quarters only.

Judge George Walton's white frame house, with its delicate spiderweb banisters outlining the two-story front porch, has been cherished through the years and is now the home of collateral descendants, Mr. and Mrs. A. W. Harper. All the original hand-carved interior woodwork is intact. The central hall has a fine arch and a lovely spiral stair.

Octavia Walton was born in neither of these houses but at Bellevue, present site of St. Joseph's Academy. Judge George Walton, the Signer, narrowly missed living in another historic Augusta house which still stands. This is the old government house at 432 Telfair Street, built in 1790 when Augusta was capital of Georgia. Judge Walton was governor in 1789. Edward Telfair occupied the new state house as chief executive and welcomed there the first President of the United

Photo by Morgan Fitz

FIGURE 77. Montrose, in Augusta, is one of the South's best-preserved ante-bellum Greek Revival houses. Built in 1849, it was the home of Colonel Charles Colcock Jones, Georgia historian, and is now owned by his descendants.

States when George Washington took his famous tour in 1791. A square stucco structure with wings, the old house is furnished in traditional style, preserving much of its original stately atmosphere. A row of old-fashioned service bells hangs across the top of the back porch.

Another Augusta charmer was Cecelia Stovall, who was given an epic rush by a young lieutenant, William Tecumseh Sherman, when she visited her brother, Marcellus Stovall at West Point in 1836. (See chapter, "Sherman's Georgia Romance.")

Sherman was later stationed on detached duty in Augusta. Could it have been

257

because of the beautiful Cecelia that he bypassed that city on his march to the sea?

Or was it because he knew the strength of the Augusta Arsenal, then in Confederate hands? Five days after Georgia seceded from the Union, United States Captain Arnold Elzy went through the formality of surrendering the arsenal to his former West Point classmate, Colonal W. H. T. Walker. Colonel Walker later became a Confederate general and was killed in the Battle of Atlanta. Fort Walker at Grant Park is named for him.

Two handsome old Greek Revival houses at the Augusta Arsenal still serve as official residences. Originally established on the Savannah River in 1819, the arsenal was moved to the hill in 1829.

Natchez may have its annual ball in the house of a thousand candles but Augusta has a two-century-old house lighted all the year around by a thousand crystal chandeliers. It's done with mirrors at the home of Dr. A. J. Kilpatrick on Comfort Road in Forrest Hills.

Built as an inn in 1751, the house formerly stood on downtown Greene Street, but was moved to the hill in 1929. Each piece of material was carefully numbered as taken down so that everything could go back in its proper place. Even the brick walk in front was laid just as it had been on Greene Street.

But something was lacking in the new location. There were no magnolia trees on the broad lawn in front and somehow the house didn't look the same without them. Young sapling magnolias wouldn't do, of course. And so great trees of mature vintage were transplanted and flourished here, completing the effect so happily you would never dream that either house or trees had not stood here all the time.

In 1825 LaFayette addressed a large gathering from the Doric portico at the front, which is approached by graceful horseshoe stairs with decorative iron railings.

Actually, there is only one crystal chandelier in each of the double parlors. But gold-framed pier mirrors which face each other from opposite ends of these spacious rooms reflect the iridescent prisms over and over until you have the illusion of gazing down a brilliantly lighted corridor stretching away into infinity. The mirrors are hung between windows and the gold frames of the mirrors extend out as cornices over these windows, which, like the chandeliers, are reflected endlessly. The twin mirrors over the Carrara marble mantels also match the pier mirrors and join in creating the illusion of rooms lighted by myriad crystal chandeliers—an enchanting spectacle.

One of Augusta's finest Greek Revival houses is Montrose, also on the hill and set far back from the street in the middle of a broad sweep of lawn at 2249

Walton Way. The combination of line and color—tall white Corinthian columns against the yellow clapboard walls of a spacious house with wings at each side—achieves an unusually dramatic effect.

Directly in front of its high steps is an old cannon that saw service in the Revolution at Fort Morris, which was defended by valiant Scottish highlanders. When the British demanded surrender of the fort, Colonel John McIntosh, leader of the highlanders, tersely replied, "Come and take it."

Many years later the cannon was presented to Colonel Charles Colcock Jones, who produced his vast historical and other literary works at Montrose. Colonel Jones's library, one of the finest in the South, overflows into the wide central hall. Even the stairway landing is lined with shelves of books. The twin marble mantels in the double drawing room at Montrose are among the many fine features of a house built in 1849 which has been kept in perfect repair by succeeding generations. Now living at Montrose with their families are two granddaughters of Colonel Jones, Mrs. Earl Waller and Mrs. Harcourt Waller, sisters who married brothers.

A lady's secret and a gentleman who weighed 450 pounds add interest to the handsome house at 915 Milledge Road, the home of Miss Nan Langdon and her brother, Paul D. Langdon.

The lovely garden here was begun in 1826 and the house replaces an older structure, but fits its setting perfectly. Here again is a large frame house painted yellow. This one has a recessed two-story gallery with white columns and balustrade.

It was Judge Henry C. Hammond who gave us the secret of Miss Langdon's ingenious device for avoiding unnecessary demands upon her time. (Inside the house are portraits of ancestors which the judge shares with the Langdons.)

At the top of the high front steps Judge Hammond paused and gave a yank to an almost invisible length of twine fastened to the left column. Through the open upstairs hall window came the clear tinkle of a bell. It is, according to the judge, a private bell which announces to Miss Langdon that the caller is an intimate friend or relative. The regulation doorbell may or may not bring results. Anyway, the judge disregarded it completely.

In no time at all, the front door opened and a Negro maid in crisp gray and white smilingly invited us to enter. The July weather was warm, but the spacious, high-ceilinged house was cool. Iced lemonade in tall glasses, topped with mint, made it seem even cooler. Miss Langdon fits her house as the house fits the garden.

Among the many treasures in the Langdon home is a mahogany dining table which came over from England not long after Georgia was settled, and which has now been retired to the drawing room. The central section serves as a reading table; and the ends, which have tilt tops, make a pair of graceful background pieces. Joined together, the three become a banquet board which Miss Langdon says "seats twenty, comfortably."

This exquisite example of the cabinetmaker's art was "rafted" (says the judge) up the Savannah River in 1788, through the wilderness to Augusta to grace the home of Ann Clay, who married Thomas Cumming.

Whether or not this table had anything to do with it, one of their sons, Alfred, came to weigh 450 pounds. Avoirdupois evidently did not interfere with his political activities. Like his father, he served as mayor of Augusta—intendant, they called it in those days—and later was governor of Utah.

The early houses on the Sand Hills, built in the late seventeen hundreds and early eighteen hundreds, were for the most part summer cottages, and what is now The Hill was called Summerville. These houses, which shared certain main characteristics, are today referred to by architects as the Sand Hills' cottage type. They have an inviting simplicity of line—dormer windows in a sloping roof above a story-and-a-half house which usually rests on a raised brick basement. There is a porch across the front with slim posts, a wide central hall and spacious rooms, with delicate hand-carved woodwork.

The simplicity of these houses was always an elegant simplicity, for wnen Summerville became a part of the city and the houses year-round residences, they made a perfect setting for old Sheraton, Hepplewhite, Duncan Phyfe and other fine furnishings.

The Sheraton sideboard at Sandy Acres, the Sand Hills cottage of Mr. and Mrs. Rodney Cohen, for instance, is one of the finest in the country. The Metropolitan Museum has long coveted this sideboard, as well as Mrs. Cohen's exquisite collection of old glass, but Mrs. Cohen cannot visualize her house without them.

Mrs. Cohen first saw the house at 2150 Battle Row when she came to Augusta as a bride. It was love at first sight, but years passed before Editor Thomas Loyless decided to sell. The Cohens were given first choice because Mrs. Loyless wanted the house to have an owner who would cherish it as she had.

The Rodney Cohens later inherited High Gate, a larger house with a fine old garden and walks made of sunken millstones. High Gate is, in fact, two houses, joined together by a one-story connecting room to make a unique and handsome effect. High Gate was a temptation, but Mr. and Mrs. Cohen found that their love of Sandy Acres had grown along with its own beautiful garden, and there they decided to remain.

The body of a poet was buried in the back garden at the Verdery cottage, which is the home of Mrs. James Verdery and her mother, Mrs. Craig Cranston. Richard Henry Wilde, who wrote "My Life Is Like the Summer Rose," once lived here. The family graveyard, then in the back garden, was later moved to a

Photo by Morgan Fitz

FIGURE 78. Sand Hills cottage of Mrs. Charles I. Mell, on The Hill in Augusta has the elegant simplicity of many of this type built in the late seventeen and early eighteen hundreds.

cemetery. The Verdery cottage, built before 1800, was given an engaging Victorian trim when this was the vogue.

Other happy versions of the Sand Hills cottage type include the old house at 1016 Hickman Road, now the home of Mrs. Charles I. Mell, Sr.; Azalea cottage, at 2236 Walton Way, the home of Mrs. Thomas Barrett, Jr.; and the Chafee cottage, 914 Milledge, home of Mr. and Mrs. Lombard Fortson.

The Sand Hills cottages were mixed in with more ambitious houses. One of the latter is the J. A. Setze place at 635 Gary Street, a white frame house with fluted columns, built soon after the Revolution by John Milledge, who was elected governor of Georgia in 1802. He built his house on a hill so that he could look out over his five-thousand-acre plantation. For a better view of Augusta he topped the trees. Effects of the topping are still visible.

Also noteworthy are the house now owned by Mr. and Mrs. William Groat and the Frank S. Dennis cottage, which was for thirty of its early years the home of Colonel John Forsyth, governor of Georgia and Secretary of State under Andrew Jackson. As minister to Spain, Colonel Forsyth persuaded Ferdinand VII to sign the treaty of 1819 ceding Florida to the United States. The former home of Colonel Forsyth was given a new front in 1857.

Built in 1826, the Cumming-Langdon-Weiss house, at 819 Milledge Road, is of Georgian architecture with a wide front piazza. The beautiful white-columned Scott B. Appleby home at 2260 Walton Way is one of many other fine old houses which remain to merge Augusta's past with its present. Augusta not only likes a long lunch hour—in many old houses there were originally both a winter and a summer dining room. In some of these houses the summer dining room, overlooking the back garden, is still used as such.

An interesting study in architectural contrasts is offered by former residences now preserved for use as clubs, libraries, art museums, etc., in the older "downtown" section of Augusta. The Phinizy house at 519 Greene Street, a handsome Georgian building with pink marble floors on the ground floor and a graceful horseshoe stair leading to the second-story porch, is now the Elks Club.

Ware's Folly, at 506 Telfair, built in 1818 at a cost of $40,000, a fabulous sum in those days, is also Georgian with Adam influence. It is now the Gertrude Herbert Institute of Art. At 540 Telfair is the Young Men's Library—now the Augusta Library and Museum. Of Tudor design with Gothic trimmings, it was formerly the old Richmond Academy. The beautiful Greek Revival building which housed the first medical academy in Georgia might have been lost to posterity except for the vigorous campaigning of Mrs. Rodney Cohen, who helped to make it the Garden Center of Augusta.

Richmond County, of which Augusta is the seat, started out as St. Paul's Parish. The present St. Paul's Episcopal Church stands on the site of the original church built in 1750, which served as a fort during the Revolution.

CHAPTER 30

Lost Gold of the Confederacy

WHAT became of the lost gold of the Confederacy?

Does it lie at the bottom of the Savannah River? Was it captured by Federal raiders? Is it a forgotten fund on deposit somewhere in a foreign bank? Or was it buried near Washington, Georgia, called "Washington-Wilkes" by old-timers, who added the name of the county to distinguish this charming ante-bellum town of white-columned houses from "Washington City," the national capital?

A bag containing $5,000 in gold coins was tossed over the fence into the garden of the Washington-Wilkes home of General Robert Toombs, Georgia's "unreconstructed rebel." General Toombs promptly turned the $5,000 over to Confederate authorities to be used as pay for returning soldiers. But this was only a small part of the fund which was largely composed of gold sovereigns obtained as a loan from England.

Half a million dollars in gold, silver and bullion—all that was left of the treasury of a hotly pursued government-in-flight—started out under heavy guard from Richmond on April 2, 1865. An additional two hundred thousand dollars from Richmond banks was also entrusted to the treasure train.

This train was the last to leave Richmond before the Confederate capital was evacuated by Southern troops. It followed directly behind the special train that carried Confederate President Jefferson Davis and his cabinet.

For more than a month the boxes and chests containing this money were on the move, sometimes in railroad cars, sometimes in wagon trains. Twice the treasure was taken to Washington-Wilkes before it came back for a final visit. Always it was just one jump ahead of capture by Federal forces.

Captain William Harwar Parker and his corps of midshipmen, detailed by Secretary of the Confederate Navy Stephen R. Mallory to transport the treasure to safety, were determined to do just that. Captain Parker had been an officer of the United States Navy for twenty years. When Virginia seceded he resigned his commission and became a blockade runner for the Confederacy. Later he was placed in command of the *Patrick Henry*, floating naval academy for Confederate midshipmen. Captain Parker told of his adventure with the treasure train in a book published many years ago by Scribner, *Recollections of a Naval Officer, 1841–1865.*

"So far as I know," wrote Captain Parker, "there was about half a million dollars in gold, silver and bullion. At least that is what the senior teller informed me. I saw the boxes containing the treasure many times in the weary 30 days that followed but I never saw the coin." The additional $200,000 was in charge of Richmond bank officers who traveled with the treasure train for safety.

Captain Parker was determined to deliver the Confederate treasure to President Davis in person. This became increasingly difficult since the former President was himself a fugitive. Lee surrendered to Grant on April 9. Sherman and Johnston had their final conference on April 26. The war was over but Northern newspapers clamored for the arrest and execution of Davis and other Confederate leaders—including Robert Toombs—as "traitors." Northern troops, still fanned out in all directions, were on the alert to take these leaders into custody. Chief prize, of course, was Jefferson Davis, who had been United States Secretary of War before he became President of the Confederate States of America.

What finally happened to the Confederate treasure can be answered only in part. Secrecy was all-important at the time and there was danger on every side. Captain Parker's account shows that his train stopped at Danville, Virginia, and at Greensboro, North Carolina, and narrowly missed being captured by Stoneman's raiders at Salisbury, North Carolina.

In Charlotte the treasure was turned over to Confederate officials at the mint. In the meantime Stoneman took Salisbury and it was decided the money should be moved farther south, so boxes and chests were loaded back into the train. Here Mrs. Davis, wife of the president, and her children, joined the party.

At Chester, South Carolina, the treasure was hastily transferred to wagons and a wagon train formed. Mrs. Davis and the children traveled in an ambulance which frequently got stuck in mud, at which times—baby in arms—Mrs. Davis waded through mire above her ankles.

From Chester the wagon train moved to Newberry and then to Abbeville, South Carolina. Here another wagon train was formed and set out across country for Washington, Georgia. Bad news got worse by the minute and Captain Parker "lightened ship" as they moved along, throwing away records, books, etc., and even loads of Confederate paper money.

"I left guards at every bridge ready to burn it to check pursuit," says Captain Parker. "I never allowed anyone to pass us on the road and yet the coming of the treasure was known at every village we passed through."

FIGURE 79. The South's unreconstructed rebel, Robert Toombs, lived in this house in Washington. One bag of the lost gold of the Confederacy was tossed into the Toombs garden.

FIGURE 80. The M. H. Barnett house in Washington was the home of Dr. Allen Tupper, grandfather of Mrs. George C. Marshall, wife of the former Secretary of Defense.

When the wagon train reached Washington, Georgia, there was no news of President Davis. Instead Captain Parker heard that Macon had been captured April 20. He decided to take the treasure to Augusta by railroad train. En route they met another train and learned that Lee had surrendered April 9. This was confirmed at Augusta, where Federal forces were expected. The treasure train was guarded in the railroad yards overnight and next day turned back toward Washington, Georgia. Here the treasure was again loaded into a wagon train and sent back to Abbeville, South Carolina, where it was unloaded and placed in a warehouse.

Hearing there that President Davis was expected, Captain Parker had the treasure loaded into railway cars with a locomotive ready under full steam. When the presidential party arrived, Captain Parker was instructed to turn the funds over to the Acting Secretary of the Confederate Treasury who in turn placed them in the care of General Basil Duke.

On May 2, exactly a month after he had taken the treasure under his protection, Captain Parker disbanded his gallant crew of midshipmen. But the adventures of the treasure continued.

At Abbeville the boxes and chests were transferred from the railroad car to the cavalry-guarded wagon train of the Confederate President and started to Washington for the third time. A rider was sent ahead to make sure the town was free of Federal troops. Safe for the moment, Jefferson Davis held his final brief cabinet meeting here on May 5 in the old Georgia branch bank building, and Washington has ever since been called the last capital of the Confederacy.

But safety was short-lived. Federal General Upton was on the march to take over the arsenal in Augusta. Davis and his party accordingly left Washington. Mrs. Davis had gone on ahead but was with her husband when he was captured May 10, 1865, at Irwinville. Davis was taken to Fortress Monroe, where he was held in chains for two years. Cornelius Vanderbilt, Horace Greeley and other prominent Easterners signed the $100,000 bond which obtained his release in May of 1867.

What happened to the Confederate gold? By the time the treasure arrived in Washington for the third time in 1865, various amounts had already been paid out on official orders for military provisions, soldiers' pay, etc. There were, too, of course, the heavy traveling expenses of the treasure train itself.

Thirty-five thousand dollars had been turned over to the presidential party at Danville, soon after the train left Richmond. This was to be used as government expenses, and when Jefferson Davis was captured, $25,000 of this was still in hand. As a safety measure, it had been divided among various members of his party, who then separated into two groups, one of which avoided capture. Of the money saved by the second group, about $6,000 was supposed to be turned over to Mrs. Davis for herself and the children. Fifteen hundred dollars is known to have reached Jefferson Davis at Fortress Monroe.

Of the remaining treasure in official hands, old records show that a fund of $86,000 was placed in the care of a bonded Confederate naval officer for transfer to some foreign port and deposit to the credit of the Confederate government. The plan was to conceal the $86,000 in a false bottom of a carriage and thus smuggle it to Savannah or Charleston for shipment.

But the Confederate government was rapidly falling apart. The South was in the hands of a conquering army. The woods were full of raiders. It is too late now to look down the long road of the years and hope to discover what happened to that carriage.

But to this day the legend persists that Confederate gold is buried in or around Washington, Georgia.

The day after Jefferson Davis was arrested at Irwinville, Federal troops appeared at the home of General Robert Toombs in Washington, armed with an order from Secretary of War Stanton demanding the arrest of Toombs.

How the Confederate general eluded his would-be captors and became an exile in Europe for nearly two years is one of those romantic stories that couldn't happen but did. Perhaps it couldn't have happened this time, except for young Charles E. Irvin, late lieutenant of the late Confederate army.

General Toombs, a man of fine appearance and magnetic personality, was one of the South's leading attorneys, a brilliant orator and a United States Senator at the time the war began. He was a firm believer in states' rights and a leader in the fight for secession. He was chosen Secretary of State for the newly created Confederate States of America, but preferred service in the field, where he distinguished himself at the Battle of Antietam. This preference seems natural enough for the son of Major James Toombs, of Virginia, a veteran of the Revolution who settled in Wilkes County, where Robert Toombs was born in 1810.

Both his friends and his political enemies agreed that Robert Toombs was a man of the highest integrity. "I would rather be buried at the public expense than leave a dirty shilling," he said. Toombs had a fierce pride to match this integrity. At the University of Georgia he had rebelled against the too-strict discipline of the time and had not been allowed to graduate. There is a legend that he delivered an address under an oak tree outside the chapel, attracting more visitors than the commencement exercises inside. The tree, now dead, was ever afterward called the Toombs Oak. Toombs was later graduated from Union College in New York and studied law at the University of Virginia. Many years later the University of Georgia offered him a degree which it was his pleasure to decline.

He also declined to give up his individual liberty, perhaps his life, to Federal troops after the war was over. When in May of 1865 General Wilde and his detachment of soldiers came to arrest him at the beautiful old Toombs house in Washington, General Toombs fortunately saw them first.

This house, like many other ante-bellum structures, is built on a raised basement. General Toombs happened to be in his office on the ground floor when bluecoats swarmed all over the front garden and up the high steps of the broad front porch with its four massive Doric columns. One of the soldiers, a Negro, flourished a bayonet on which was impaled a photograph of General Toombs. This was the sight that met the eyes of Mrs. Toombs and the Toombs' daughter, Sallie—Mrs. Dudley DuBose—when they answered a preemptory summons to the front door.

General Wilde demanded that Mrs. Toombs produce her husband. Mrs. Toombs, with great dignity, informed him that her husband was not at home. She spoke truly, for she knew the General had escaped through the back way leading to the stables. To give him as much time as possible, she invited General

FIGURE 81. The South's most famous refugees slept here—Mrs. Jefferson Davis, wife of the Confederate President, and her daughter were guests in the Rochford Johnson house in Washington after the fall of the Confederacy.

Wilde into the house, where she and Mrs. DuBose entered into a lively conversation with him.

But Southern charm could not long divert General Wilde and he was soon threatening to burn the house unless Toombs was forthcoming. All the Negroes on the place, newly freed slaves, had seen General Toombs leave and knew that he went first to his overseer's house, but none of them told. A neighbor, the Reverend Henry Allen Tupper, finally convinced General Wilde that his search was useless.

It was an easy matter to get word to General Toombs when the son of a neighbor appeared, young Lieutenant Irvin, and asked to be of assistance. His first commission was to obtain money, clothes and the general's horse, Gray Alice, which had been his mount all through the war. Lieutenant Irvin also obtained for the general the parole papers of Major Luther Martin.

For seven long months the general and the young lieutenant played a game of hide and seek with the Federals. At Oglethorpe in Macon County they rode straight through a Federal garrison without being recognized. General Toombs,

269

one of the best-known men in Georgia, had countless friends and was given shelter at one large plantation after another, though the penalty for his hosts would have been great had this been discovered. One of the houses at which he stayed a week was the beautiful old Prather home on the Tugalo River, described in the chapter, Stagecoach Inn.

Young Lieutenant Irvin endeavored to arrange for General Toombs to leave the country through the port of Savannah, but this was not considered safe. Eventually they made their way to Alabama and from Mobile by river steamboat to New Orleans. When a fellow passenger showed too-obvious interest in the general, Irvin took over the job of discovering whether the man was friend or foe. If foe, he was to be pitched overboard. Fortunately this drastic measure was unnecessary as the passenger turned out to be an admirer of the general, ready to join forces in helping him escape.

At New Orleans the faithful young aide saw the general safely aboard ship for Cuba and they said good-bye. This was November and they had started out together in May.

From Havana, General Toombs sailed for Europe where he remained until the spring of 1867. He owned extensive plantation lands in Alabama and Texas as well as in Georgia and some of this land was sold to defray his expenses abroad. The price was low in the lean days following the war—$5 an acre. General Toombs greatly mystified his new friends by asserting that he ate an acre of dirt a day.

Mrs. Toombs joined him in his exile, but she was called home in November of 1866 because of the fatal illness of their daughter, Sallie. The general followed his wife home early the next year. "The worst that can happen to me," he wrote Mrs. Toombs, "is a prison and I do not see much to choose between my present condition and any decent fort."

In Washington, D. C., he stopped by to see President Andrew Johnson with whom he had served in the Senate, and was allowed to proceed to Washington, Georgia, without interference. Asked by Senator Oliver P. Morton why he did not petition for a pardon under the general amnesty act, he snorted, "Pardon for what? I haven't pardoned you all yet." On another occasion he declared, "I shall not be the first of my name to accept the stigma of a pardon." He remained until his death in 1885 Georgia's "unreconstructed rebel," the last citizen of the Confederacy.

Although he could no longer vote in national elections, he took great interest in the political affairs of the state and also wielded a powerful influence in framing a new constitution for Georgia. His renewed law practice flourished.

The ready wit of General Toombs is best remembered by the things he opposed, as shown by Pleasant A. Stovall's interesting biography. General Toombs

FIGURE 82. The Colonel A. T. Colley house in Washington. The dining room, which extends the width of the house, has been the scene of grand-scale entertaining.

disapproved of prohibition, declaring humorously that "Prohibitionists are men of small pints."

When the town sought to build a hotel, he went all out against it. "If a respectable man comes to town, he can stay at my house. If he isn't respectable, we don't want him here at all."

His scorn of political dishonesty expressed itself in another characteristic remark. "I hope the Lord will allow me to go to Heaven like a gentleman. Some of these Georgia politicians I do not want to associate with."

Of the degeneracy of the times and political chicanery in general, he said, "I expect when a man is 70, he ought to go. He knows too much for other people's convenience."

The Toombs house was built in 1794 by Dr. Joel Abbott. Robert Toombs bought it in 1837, remodeled and enlarged it and added the tall Doric columns. It has remained in the family ever since and is now owned by two great nieces, Mrs. Kenneth Boyd and Miss Kathleen Colley.

The gold-patterned wallpaper in the front parlor was selected by Mrs. Toombs, the former Miss Julia DuBose, whom Robert Toombs married in 1830 when he was twenty and freshly admitted to the Georgia bar. The wrought-iron chandeliers were brought down from Washington, D. C., when he resigned from the United States Senate in 1861. These chandeliers were lighted with gas from his own private plant, the first in Washington-Wilkes.

In the spacious library on the left of the wide central hall are the hand-carved bookshelves on which many of Robert Toombs's books remain. Most of the original handsome furnishings also remain to preserve that atmosphere of serenity which was the background for an active and sometimes turbulent public career.

Persian lilacs, delicate sweet syringa, old-fashioned roses, still bloom in the garden planted long ago by Mrs. Toombs. The path worn in the herring-bone brick walk is eloquent of the hospitality of this fine old house.

U. S. Highway 78 from Atlanta to Augusta becomes Lexington Avenue as it nears Washington-Wilkes and then Robert Toombs Avenue as it passes through town, where it takes on a decidedly ante-bellum air. Many of the old houses, built long before the Greek Revival era, had their white columns added in the eighteen thirties. The town was laid out in 1780.

It is nice to know as you drive along Lexington Avenue that young Charles E. Irvin, postwar aide to General Toombs, was able to buy back, in the eighteen eighties, the old house which was the family home until after the War Between the States. It stands far back from the road, tall white Corinthian columns gleaming through the dark green leaves of magnolias and oak trees, and is now the home of Mr. Irvin's daughters, Mrs. C. H. Orr and Mrs. A. F. Hill.

One of the handsomest of the many old houses on Toombs Avenue was the home of Dr. Henry Allen Tupper, who came to the aid of Mrs. Toombs when Federal General Wilde attempted to arrest her husband. Dr. Tupper was the grandfather of Mrs. George Marshall, wife of the former United States Secretary of Defense. Dr. Tupper moved to Washington from Charleston because he said people in Washington valued fineness and beauty more than they did money. He served for twenty years as pastor of Washington's Baptist church and sent his entire salary to the Baptist mission board. The old Tupper house, now owned by Mr. and Mrs. M. H. Barnett, is surrounded by a two-story Doric colonnade approached by a graceful double flight of steps. A delicate iron balustraded balcony hangs above the fanlighted front door.

When Mrs. Jefferson Davis arrived in Washington, along with the treasure train, she and her children were guests in the white, square-pillared house at 303 Alexander, now the home of Mr. and Mrs. Rochford Johnson. This is really two houses, one in front of the other, joined together by a wide hallway. What is now the front was originally a plantation house, dismantled about 1851, moved eight miles into town and re-erected on the present site.

This marriage of two houses was engineered by Dr. Fielding Ficklen. His son, Boyce, who was born here, never forgot the calm and poise of Mrs. Davis

272

FIGURE 83. This is the town house of the Pembroke Popes in Washington, which has a forty-acre garden. Mr. Pope raises Hereford cattle on his five-thousand-acre farm "in the country."

when she was a house guest and one of the South's most famous refugees. She slept in one of the front bedrooms, on the right of the upstairs hall, and Mrs. Johnson still keeps it as a guest room, furnished much as it must have been long ago, with a huge four-poster bed, old mahogany bureau and other family pieces.

Here, as in many other old houses, you not only step back into the setting of the past, but you also step back into its traditional hospitality. On a certain Sunday in early fall this writer was the only non-relative at midday dinner when twelve sat down at the long mahogany table in the spacious dining room of the Johnson home.

It was a meal to remember, but routine for the long-time family cook. The damask-laid table was set with old family silver and white and gold bone china —the gold decoration painted on by Mrs. Johnson's mother years before. Flanking the silver bowl of early pink camellias were small cut-glass dishes containing watermelon-rind pickles and fig preserves.

273

First came a fresh fruit cocktail which included the sweet almondy bitter of late Georgia peaches. Was there rum in it too? Then, baked hen and dressing passed on a garnished silver platter, followed immediately by another great platter of baked Wilkes County ham. The invariable Southern combination of chicken (fried, baked, broiled or otherwise) with baked country ham is a marriage most surely made in heaven. Rice and gravy are always served with them of course, and every grain of rice must stand apart. (Every grain did.)

Vegetables were all fresh from the host's early fall garden. Tender young butter beans. Small pods of okra cooked in butter. Corn soufflé. Candied sweet potatoes. A salad of curly green garden lettuce and tomatoes. Two kinds of hot bread, of course—feather-light rolls and corn-meal egg bread.

Finally, tall glasses of sillabub, that airy mixture of milk, cream, sugar and sherry, always made in a special churn at the very last moment before serving. Coffee.

Well, we all stayed on to late tea. In between we went calling at other old houses and everywhere had some refreshment, coffee or tea or wine and cake. At one stop we had scuppernongs which we picked fresh from the vines on the old arbor back of the house.

Two of the biggest dining rooms in Washington are at The Cedars on Sims Street and at 343 Toombs Avenue, the old home of Miss Maria Randolph, now owned by Colonel A. T. Colley.

Miss Randolph was descended from Pocahontas and very proud of the fact. She was "six feet tall and every inch a lady." The house in which she entertained on a grand scale has a two-columned Doric portico with a triglyph frieze that extends across the façade. The pilastered front door, with its transom and side lights has a duplicate door above, opening onto an iron-railed balcony. Two large front rooms open from each side of the wide entrance hall downstairs, and this hall opens into a dining room extending the entire width of the house.

The Cedars, a delightful rambling old house of twenty-eight rooms, has triple furnishings in its huge dining room. There are three tables, three sideboards, side tables, china cabinets and heaven knows how many chairs, and the room still isn't crowded. Two sets of furnishings were added by members of the family who moved back home after living elsewhere.

In one of the large bedrooms there is a four-poster bed seven feet wide. A downstairs sitting room contains a collection of family war mementos dating from the Revolution. One of these is a silver knee buckle given an ancestress of the family by Cornwallis. His soldiers had stolen her pet calf, which he ordered restored, adding the buckle as a consolation prize. On the walls of the room, old portraits of bearded fighters look down the years at framed photographs of World War II veterans, including WACs and WAVEs.

The Cedars was owned in 1818 by Francis Colley whose descendants live there today, Mrs. T. J. Barksdale, Mrs. Bessie DeVaughan and Mrs. Latimer.

Georgia's first woman newspaper editor lived in the two-story white clapboard house at 315 East Toombs Avenue. When David Hillhouse died in 1803, his widow, Mrs. Sarah Hillhouse, succeeded him as editor of the *Monitor*. She built the house about 1814 and lived here until her death in 1831. Gabriel Toombs, brother of Robert, bought the place in 1869, and it is now the home of his granddaughter, Mrs. Hardeman Toombs Wood. In 1849 Gabriel Toombs owned the house at 319 East Robert Toombs Avenue, and the present owner, is his grandson, Gabriel Toombs.

Among other lovely old houses on Toombs Avenue is the home of Mr. and Mrs. Pembroke Pope, which has a Doric colonnade, a widow's walk, and a forty-acre garden. When Mark A. Cooper's daughter, Susan, married into the Pope family, she installed the graceful stairway which was made at Glen Holly, her father's ante-bellum plantation in Bartow County. Pembroke Pope, the present owner, collects old furniture, especially Pembroke tables. He has a five-thousand-acre farm in the country on which he raises Hereford cattle.

The original hand-hewn log smokehouse is still in use at the home of Mrs. E. B. Cade. This is an impressive Doric-columned house on a hill at 120 Tignall Road. The original slave quarters also still stand.

One of Washington's first brick houses was built in 1808 by William and Felix Gilbert, who first camped on the site while traveling to Georgia from Virginia. They liked it so well they decided to settle there. Descendants of Felix Gilbert still find it a pleasant place to live. They are Mrs. J. G. Wright and Miss Charlotte Alexander. What was a virgin site when the house was built is now 312 North Alexander Avenue.

One of the most impressive houses in this charming old town is the residence of Mrs. J. T. Lindsey at 212 Liberty Street. It is surrounded by a Doric colonnade and has a beautiful hanging balcony which also extends around the house. Its interior woodwork and molded plaster cornices are especially fine.

The old workshop of Eli Whitney, inventor of the cotton gin, may be seen at Mount Pleasant Plantation, seven miles southeast of Washington. This building of hand-hewn logs formerly stood on the adjoining plantation of Miller and Whitney, later the site of a textile mill. The plantation house at Mount Pleasant is a two-story frame structure built in 1790 by the Talbot family and sold to Thomas P. Burdette in 1857. It is now owned by his son J. L. Burdette.

On the old Augusta Road, about nine miles southeast of Washington, is the Abraham Simons house, also built about 1790, by Captain Abraham Simons, a Jewish officer who fought in the Revolution. With its deserted ballroom and elaborately decorated ceilings, this is definitely a house that has seen better days.

Simons married Nancy Mills, who survived him. His grave stands on a hill beyond the house. He was buried standing up with his musket at his side. If he met the devil, he wanted to be prepared to shoot him.

Unlike the lost gold of the Confederacy, there's no doubt about what happened to the fortune left by Abraham Simons. His wife's second husband was Jesse Mercer, one of Georgia's great Baptists. With her full approval, he used the money to help found and endow Mercer University, originally at Penfield, now at Macon.

CHAPTER 31

World's First Garden Club

*I*T all started in Athens and many husbands have wondered where it would end.

Twelve ladies, gathered in the ante-bellum home of Mrs. E. K. Lumpkin at 973 Prince Avenue, organized the world's first garden club in January of 1891. The name they chose was typical of its era—the Ladies' Garden Club.

Since that time, garden clubs have changed the face of the earth. Organized into city, state and national federations they have become a power in the land, fighting for the conservation and development of natural beauty, for scenic city planning and for more fragrant politics in general.

There may have been times when some garden-club husbands have felt that enthusiasm was carrying the ladies a little far from the home front. Other husbands have simply stepped in and beat the ladies at their own game with men's garden-club shows of the biggest dahlias, the finest roses, the most prolific camellias, the most spectacular iris, the most exotic orchids. Men seem to go in for the more showy specimens and to make them even showier.

And it is all such good clean fun that doctors often prescribe gardening as a curb for neurotic tendencies and a build-up for the sagging ego as well as the sagging sinew.

The twelve Athens ladies really started something.

To be sure, their claim as "first" was disputed for a time. But the ladies had documentary evidence and finally in 1939 official recognition and tribute were paid by the National Council of State Garden Clubs. That same year work was started on the beautiful Founders' Memorial Gardens sponsored jointly by the Garden Club of Georgia and the Department of Landscape Architecture at the State University.

Old records in the possession of charter members still living in 1939 show that the Athens Ladies' Garden Club was, from the first, a club with duly elected officers and that its sessions were conducted by parliamentary procedure. Each member specialized in the study and cultivation of some particular flower and vegetable. Printed programs, saved as souvenirs, record flower and vegetable shows held in the club's second year and judged according to present standard regulations.

The old stucco house in which this historic first garden-club meeting took place has a wide veranda all the way across the front adorned with lacy ironwork. It was built in 1848 and is one of a number of old houses with ironwork trim which add a French and Spanish touch to the many white columns of Georgia's classic city.

For Athens lives up to its name. It was founded as a seat of learning and most of its fine old houses were built at the height of the Greek Revival era in architecture. Set back from tree-shaded streets and surrounded by old gardens and wide lawns, these white-columned houses still dominate their Victorian and modern neighbors and give the town a charm which was officially recognized by Uncle Sam when the new Post Office was carefully designed to fit right into the Old South atmosphere.

Though the college has played a large part in making Athens a city with a lively interest in music and the other arts, Athens is more than a college town. It is a manufacturing and trading center for an area fifty or more miles wide. Yet most of its menfolk can shake off the frustrations of downtown traffic within a few minutes and a few quick turns and be home to lunch in the quiet of residential seclusion.

Carved from the wilderness, the town came into being as the site of America's first chartered state university. The charter date was 1785, but the college did not open its doors until 1801, when the first classes were conducted under great oak trees with curious Cherokee Indians as onlookers. Athens was then the farthest north of any town in Georgia and the Indians were its nearest neighbors.

The old James Camak house, built in 1830, was the first white man's residence erected beyond the original limits of the town. For its first eight years— until the Indians were removed west in 1838—this house technically stood within the borders of the Cherokee Nation. Facing what became Meigs Street, it is a handsome brick house with iron trimming and beautifully carved interior woodwork. Since 1949 it has been the Masonic Temple, but for five generations it was the home of the Camak family.

The town of Watkinsville, near Athens, was originally considered as a home for the state university, but was turned down because it was feared the tavern there might prove a disrupting influence to students.

Old College, the first permanent building which still stands on the campus,

FIGURE 84. The world's first garden club was organized here in the E. K. Lumpkin house in Athens, in 1891. The Ladies' Garden Club, in its second year, held flower and vegetable shows which were judged by today's standards.

was copied from Connecticut Hall at Yale, alma mater of Abraham Baldwin, one of the founders of the University of Georgia. Josiah Meigs, the first active president, was a former Yale professor of natural philosophy.

When Georgia's mammoth football stadium was dedicated in 1929, the Yale football team "broke precedent" by traveling south for a game with the Georgia bulldogs. (Georgia won 15–0.) But the biggest day at the university stadium is when Georgia meets on home grounds its ancient rival from Atlanta, the Yellow Jackets of the Georgia Institute of Technology.

Georgia has had many famous graduates. Two students who were roommates at the university were later selected as the state's two nominations for Statuary Hall in the national capital. They were Dr. Crawford W. Long, who performed the first operation in which sulphuric ether was used as an anesthetic, and Alexander H. Stephens, Vice President of the Confederacy, United States Representative and Governor of Georgia.

The old Long residence on Chase Street, just off Prince Avenue, was badly damaged by fire in 1951. Dr. Long lived in Jefferson, Georgia, eighteen miles north of Athens, when he painlessly removed two small tumors from

FIGURE 85. "The most superb of all" is the President's House in Athens. Formerly the Ben H. Hill house, it is now the official residence of the president of the University of Georgia.

the neck of James M. Venable, after first administering ether on a towel. The date was March 30, 1842.

"Ether frolics" led to Dr. Long's discovery that the drug could produce an insensitive state. He himself tried inhaling ether for its exhilarating effect. Others tried it with such hilarious results that the experiments were called ether frolics. Dr. Long saw a scientific truth shining through the merriment.

Athens is the only city in the world which has a double-barreled cannon, a tree that owns itself, and a fire engine that burned up.

The fire engine, let us hasten to explain, belonged to the early volunteer fire department and had been more or less retired. The double-barreled cannon was designed for use in the War Between the States but Union troops came

FIGURE 86.   The Corinthian columns of the President's House in Athens, as seen from the hanging balcony of this ante-bellum home on Prince Avenue.

to Athens only for the period of military rule following the surrender. The unused cannon now rests in peace on the grounds of the commodious house built by James Tinsley in 1830, which is today the home of the Athens Regional Library.

The tree that owns itself was so called because of a deed executed many years ago by Colonel W. H. Jackson, conveying to the said white oak "entire possession of itself and of the land within eight feet of it on all sides." That venerable tree was uprooted in a high wind in 1942 but today it has a son which has inherited the site. The young tree grew from an acorn of the old tree, planted by the late Miss Moina Michael, herself known to fame as the Poppy Lady, because she originated National Poppy Day for the benefit of disabled war veterans.

Although both the university and the town of Athens started off with a New England look, both soon realized the suitability of the classic pattern.

Athens is "filled with fine specimens" of Greek Revival architecture, according to Fiske Kimball, author of *Domestic Architecture of the American Colonies and of the Early Republic*. "The most superb of all," he declares, is "the Hill house, with its peristyle of tall Corinthian columns." The Hill house is now the official residence of the president of the University of Georgia.

Pretty hoop-skirted co-eds, dressed for a "formal," feel quite at home in Athens, for many of them live in sorority houses built as private residences more than a century ago. Though a great many old houses are still occupied as homes—sometimes by fourth- and fifth-generation owners who give a special graciousness to traditional Athens hospitality—many others which might have been lost have survived as fraternity and sorority houses and some have been converted into clubs or other civic buildings.

The Hill house, now the President's House, at 570 Prince Avenue, was built in 1855. Its fourteen tall Corinthian columns, extending from the front around two sides, overlook a formal box garden, green with all the old-time favorites—dwarf and clipped tree box, cherry laurel, magnolias and cedars of Lebanon. Here too are all the fragances of romantic legend, cape jessamine (gardenia to you, perhaps), sweet syringa, tea olive, lilacs, flowering quince, pittosporum, sweet shrub, old-fashioned pinks and many others. Smooth lawns are laid like a deep-piled carpet at each side of the house and the Doric columns at the back overlook another garden and a charming early cottage.

Perhaps no other house in Georgia has more elaborate interior plaster cornices and ceiling centerpieces than the President's House. Crystal chandeliers hanging from these centerpieces in the double drawing room are reflected in the gold-framed mirrors over twin white marble mantels.

Although strongly associated with the memory of Benjamin H. Hill, who moved to Athens in 1869 from another fine old house in LaGrange, the Presi-

Photo by William Columbus Davis

FIGURE 87. The cornices and crystal chandelier of the President's House in Athens are perhaps the most elaborate in Georgia.

Photo by Kenneth Rogers

FIGURE 88. Henry Grady, spokesman of the New South, lived in this Doric-columned home in Athens. The thirteen columns are said to represent the thirteen original colonies.

dent's House was built by John Grant, who came to Georgia from Virginia. From 1888 it was owned by Captain James White and subsequently was inherited by his daughter, the late Mrs. W. F. Bradshaw. From this estate it was acquired by the university.

Mr. Hill, a leading Southern statesman of his day, came to Athens an embittered man. His home constituency had turned against him because he counseled the acceptance of Reconstruction rule following the War Between the States. While living in the house on Prince Avenue in Athens, he was elected to the United States House of Representatives and later to the Senate. He is credited with influencing President Hayes to withdraw Federal occupation troops and military rule from Georgia, thus ending the Reconstruction Era in 1877, a dozen years after the war was over.

Columns present a united front on Prince Avenue all the way from the President's House to the former home of Henry Grady. These two houses are linked by the twin Doric-columned homes built by Simon and M. G. Michael at a much later date, but of authentic Greek Revival architecture. The Hill

Photo by Kenneth Rogers

FIGURE 89. In ante-bellum times this was the home of Confederate General Howell Cobb in Athens. General Cobb was Secretary of the United States Treasury under President Buchanan.

and Grady houses are linked also by the fact that Henry Grady picked up where Senator Hill left off.

Grady was the spokesman for the New South, a brilliant orator, with a witty, homespun, philosophy, popular in the North as well as the South. Winning his way into the hearts of his hearers, he helped to heal the wounds of war and to reunite the two sections. As managing editor of the Atlanta *Constitution*, he made that newspaper one of the best known in the country, and through its columns fought for the development of neglected opportunities in a section still struggling to rebuild its ruined economic system.

Grady lived in the house at 634 Prince Avenue while a student at the university, where the School of Journalism is named for him. It is said that the thirteen columns of the Grady house represent the thirteen original colonies. Symbolically too, these columns are staunchly joined together by a railing of iron grillework.

Prince Avenue is not only one of Georgia's loveliest streets of white columns; it is also a sort of Who's Who of the state's history. Georgia's first chief justice of the Supreme Court, Joseph Henry Lumpkin, built (in 1842) the beautiful house

Photo by William Columbus Davis

FIGURE 90.   Kappa Alpha Theta Sorority, of the University of Georgia in Athens, selected the old A. P. Dearing home as its chapter house. This red brick dwelling was built in 1856.

with Doric columns at 248 Prince Avenue. Judge Lumpkin was co-founder of the Lumpkin Law School at the university.

Both Confederate Generals Howell Cobb and Thomas R. R. Cobb owned fine Doric-columned houses on Prince. The Howell Cobb house, built in 1835, stands at the head of Pope Street, one block back from Prince. Originally, Pope Street was the driveway leading to the Cobb house. The grounds then extended all the way to a broad Prince Avenue frontage.

General Howell Cobb's later house at the corner of Hill and Harris Streets was begun by him in 1850, shortly before he became governor of Georgia and is similar to the house just off Prince. Both have delicate hanging balconies and both have tall Doric columns. Howell Cobb served as Secretary of State under President Buchanan and was a staunch supporter of the Union during the trying times that culminated in the compromise of 1850. But in the 'sixties he spoke out in favor of secession and took up arms to fight for his principles.

At 194 Prince is the old home of General Thomas R. R. Cobb, brother of General Howell Cobb. Thomas R. R. Cobb bought the house in 1845—it was built about 1830—and added the interesting octagonal wings.

John B. Cobb, another brother, owned a house on Milledge, which was moved some years ago to 575 Harris Street. While the other Cobbs went in for colonnades, John Cobb built his house with a Grecian pediment supported by four Doric columns.

Like a picture typifying all the romantic legends of the Old South, is the Upson house, with its tall columns and magnificent magnolias at 1022 Prince Avenue. Many of the original ante-bellum furnishings are intact. This was a plantation house when built in 1840, and the old smokehouse and other buildings still stand in the back. The Upson house is still presided over by a member of the family, Mrs. Bradford Foss.

Milledge Avenue, named for Governor John Milledge, who gave the land for the university, is also a street of many white columns. Three of its fine old houses were built by members of the Dearing family. Perhaps the most beautiful is the A. P. Dearing house at 338 South Milledge, built in 1856 of red brick, with a Doric colonnade extending from the front around both sides. This house remained in the family until 1938, when it became the home of the Kappa Alpha Theta sorority.

William Dearing built two Doric-columned white frame houses, one at 225 and one at 387 South Milledge, which are still occupied as private residences.

One of the oldest houses in Athens is still owned and occupied by descendants of Mrs. Stephen Harris, who bought the place in 1831. This is the home of Miss Mary Harris Brumby, at 343 Hancock Avenue. It was built in 1818 and was the residence of Moses Waddell, president of the university from 1819 to 1829.

The house is of Post-Colonial design and formerly had a stoop with small columns at the front. This was replaced some generations back by the present porch supported by square posts. The house is filled with old books, lovely old furniture, silver and some choice Waterford glass. The Sheraton sideboard is particularly fine.

A secret stair and a dry well are among the unique attractions at the Greek Revival house of Mr. and Mrs. M. G. Nicholson at 298 Hull Street. This house too is filled with family heirlooms, among them a portrait by the

FIGURE 91. A secret stair and a dry well, the forerunner of the deep freeze, are unique features at the M. G. Nicholson house in Athens, which was built in 1825. The Doric-columned façade was added in 1845.

French artist, Saint-Memin. Some of the furniture bears witness to the fine craftsmanship of slave cabinetmakers. The secret stair from the first to the second floor provides an unsuspected outside entrance and exit.

What appears to be a summer house in the side yard turns out to be a dry well, used for deep storage of foodstuffs in days when the deep freeze was undreamed of. A dizzy flight of steps leads down into the well, which the family butler still uses as a watermelon cooler.

The older part of the house was built about 1825 as a dining hall for university students. The Doric-columned front section was added in 1840 by Thomas Wray, and the place was bought in 1867 by the father of the present owner. Here the traditional cherry laurel in the old garden is supplemented by Grecian laurel as fitting garnishment for a Greek Revival house.

288

FIGURE 92. Iron lace and an unusual porch roof at the old Hunnicutt house in Athens, on North Milledge Avenue.

Photo by Kenneth Rogers

FIGURE 93. The old Phinizy house in Athens has a two-story porch adorned with lacy ironwork. The house was built in 1857.

Photo by William Columbus Davis

Photo by Kenneth Rogers

FIGURE 94. Miss Mildred Rutherford, Georgia educator and historian, lived in this quaint Athens house.

The old Gerdine house with its massive Doric columns, standing opposite the Post Office in downtown Athens, was built in 1834 and for many years has been the home of the Linton family. Among its furnishings is a fine old plantation desk.

Lending variety to the old houses in Athens are those with fine ornamental iron grillework. Among the most noteworthy of these is the house at 325 North Milledge Avenue, built in 1865 and owned and occupied by the Hunnicutt family since 1871. Especially charming is the old Ferdinand Phinizy house at 250 South Milledge, built in 1857, with a two-story porch adorned with lacy ironwork. This is now the home of a granddaughter, Mrs. Robert Segrest.

The old Mell house at 897 South Milledge is an interesting example of the Victorian superimposed upon the Greek Revival style. The floor plan follows the classic pattern, and the columns, though greatly attenuated, are two stories high and extend all the way across the front. They are connected by an iron-work rail and at the top by sinuously carved Victorian ornamentation.

The Delta Tau Delta fraternity house at 125 North Milledge, built in 1859 and formerly the Joe Hodgson home, is another interesting old house with iron-work decoration.

The home of Alpha Delta Pi sorority, formerly the J. S. Hamilton home, at 150 South Milledge, has wide verandas on three sides supported by ironwork shipped from England in the last vessel to complete the trip before the blockade of Southern ports was brought on by the War Between the States. The house of palest stucco is French Colonial in design, with solid stone walls twelve inches thick. There are eleven beautifully carved mantels.

The M. S. Hodgson home, at 749 Cobb Street, with its three Gothic gables and ironwork trim, is both charming and quaint. It was built in 1853.

A porch one hundred feet long at Lucy Cobb Dormitory is lavishly trimmed with this iron lace in a design as intricate as that of the lace which adorned the many petticoats of its ante-bellum girl students. Founded in 1858, Lucy Cobb Institute was for many years Georgia's most fashionable school for girls. Some-time after the university became co-educational, the building was converted into a dormitory. Grandmothers of present-day students, remembering their own strictly chaperoned days at Lucy Cobb, are always fascinated by the sight of boys and girls now mingling so freely on the university campus.

One of the most impressive houses preserved by fraternities is the old Ross Crane home at 247 Pulaski Street, built about 1842, now owned by Sigma Alpha Epsilon. This has tall square columns, and a beautiful hanging balcony with a railing in wheat-sheaf design. The fine boxwood and magnolias which were a part of one of the South's finest gardens still attract garden-club visitors from all over the country.

On Milledge, Prince and other Athens streets, many of the old houses bear Grecian emblems above their wide doorways, designating them as homes of fraternities or sororities. Some fraternities and sororities, building new houses of their own, have also followed the classic pattern. After all, what could be more suitable for Greek letter societies in a college town named Athens?

Some of the town's finest Greek Revival buildings are to be found on the campus, notably the old Chapel, with its Doric portico, built in 1831. Here, too, newer buildings fit in with the classic pattern, so that the campus is a continuous colonnade. Old houses, absorbed for university use as the campus enlarged, add to the pleasant scene—the Bishop cottage, with its two white Doric columns and pilasters, the Lustrat house, Strahan, Lucas and Reed houses, and the old stone house which was the home of Governor Wilson Lumpkin, father of Martha Lumpkin Compton, for whom Atlanta was first named Marthasville. There are various others. The Department of Landscape Architecture is housed in a former residence and here are the beautiful gardens which memorialize the world's first garden club.

The Mummy That Came to Life

*M*ISS ELBERTA was a mummy for a dozen years but when she returned to miraculous life, she really made history.

All this began in a beautiful old house in Marshallville. It happened long before the first of the now-famous camellia shows given annually by this charming town of a thousand inhabitants and five thousand camellias. Every February, Marshallville has a one-day population jump of at least twelve thousand, as visitors arrive from all directions to view the camellias and the town's fine old Greek Revival houses.

That should be enough for one town. But Marshallville was also the birthplace of Miss Elberta, the glamour girl who gave Georgia the title of Peach State and Georgia girls the name of Georgia peaches.

How Miss Elberta became a mummy, how she was kissed awake like the sleeping beauty . . . well, it couldn't have happened, of course, if Miss Elberta hadn't been a peach herself.

Her story begins at the Lewis Rumph home, some miles out from town, now owned by Edwin Rumph. This story is also part of a complicated family connection.

You get your first glimpse of the lovely old white-columned house at the end of a vista of box and tall trees. Seen like this, there is something about the house and its setting—something that gives you the feeling that you yourself may be caught up in a spell if you venture too near.

This is only your imagination, of course, helped along by thoughts of a sleeping beauty in one of the big upstairs bedrooms. The atmosphere promptly changes as you hear more about those bedrooms.

Originally there were only two rooms upstairs. Others were added when

by Library of Congress

FIGURE 95.   Lewis Rumph home, in Marshallville, now owned by Edwin Rumph.
A mummy came to life here.

Lewis Rumph, a widower, with five children, married Maria, Mrs. Benjamin D. Plant, a widow with three children. In order to keep boys and girls separate, no doors connected the new rooms with the old. Two stairways led upward, one to each separate section of the second story.

Nevertheless, Samuel Rumph, Lewis's son, married his stepsister, Caroline Plant. They had a son named Samuel Henry Rumph. (Keep your eye on him.) Meanwhile, the senior Rumphs had produced three children of their own, one of whom was named Lewis Adolphus Rumph. Young Samuel Henry Rumph later married a sister of the wife of Lewis Adolphus and in addition to being a half-nephew on both sides of Lewis A., he then became his double uncle's brother-in-law.

In 1857, Increase Cook Plant of Macon, brother of the senior Mrs. Rumph's first husband, sent her second husband an assortment of budded peach trees from a Delaware nursery. These included the Chinese Cling, Early and Late Crawford, Nixon Free, Stump of the World and Tellitson. Mr. Rumph set them out in the family orchard where they eventually blossomed and bore fruit.

293

Of all the varieties produced by this assortment, everyone agreed that the Chinese Clingstone was superior. Mrs. Rumph saved some of the seeds of this fruit, dropped them in a work basket and there, completely forgotten, they stayed for at least a dozen years.

When Mrs. Rumph's grandson, Samuel Henry Rumph, grew up and became interested in making experiments at his own near-by plantation called Willow Lake, she remembered the peach seeds, hunted them up and presented them to him.

The year was 1870 when Samuel H. Rumph planted these mummified peach seeds of the Chinese Cling, seeds saved by his grandmother when he himself was a child.

Much to everyone's surprise, the seeds sprouted and green shoots appeared. But it was the fruit, borne about five years later, that proved this a "miracle planting."

When Mrs. Rumph presented the seeds to her grandson, it is doubtful if either of them gave a thought to the fact that these were produced by a tree which had stood among an assortment of other peach trees, all their varied blossoms subject to the usual processes of pollination.

Cross-pollination, as practiced by horticultural experts, is a fine art. But the honeybees and the vagrant breezes of a long ago springtime had blended an even more subtle magic. For the fruit of these seedlings was a new delicious golden peach. It was not a clingstone, for it could be broken in half with the hands—a peach firm enough for shipment to Eastern markets.

And that is how the commercial peach industry was born in Georgia.

Samuel H. Rumph named the new peach Elberta, for his wife. He designed a new type of container for shipping and invented a refrigeration process which completely revolutionized peach marketing. As a necessary by-product, he also found himself in the nursery business, eventually shipping as many as ten thousand trees to a single customer. Today the sedate yearbook of the United States Department of Agriculture recognizes the Elberta as the leading commercial peach in the country.

Uncle Lewis A. Rumph and Roland Hiley, who also planted some of the mummified seeds, named their peaches respectively Georgia Belle and Hiley Belle. All are well known varieties today.

The thousands of acres of peach orchards planted in middle Georgia, as a result of Miss Elberta's miraculous awakening, stage their own prodigal pink blossom festival every spring. It is a sight worth traveling far to see, especially as you approach Marshallville where State Highway 49—leading through all this loveliness—is bordered for four miles with crape myrtle trees, interspersed with camellia bushes.

This spectacular planting is a memorial honoring the founders of Marshall-

FIGURE 96. John Donald Wade House. The town of Marshallville occupies a part of its former plantation acres. The large dining room indicates the extent of ante-bellum hospitality.

ville who built the fine old houses and planted the first of the town's many camellia bushes when they moved to Georgia from Orangeburg, South Carolina, in the eighteen thirties. These early settlers also planted the oak trees which now form a green arch over Main Street.

Marshallville's early camellias were lumped together under one designation as "japonicas." Nobody then was harassed by the question of whether camellia rhymed with "I feel you" or "I tell you." (You is given the sound of "yuh," of course.) Nobody bothered about botanical names. Even today the inclination is to identify varieties by the names of original Marshallville growers. If you insist upon being technical, the Dollie Rice, the Lizzie Ware and the Emma Lester are, respectively, the Mathotiana Alba, Rubra and Rosea. It's that way about all of them, and if you've ever been to Marshallville, that's the way you want it.

Today's camellia bushes in Marshallville are ten and twelve feet high and eighteen and twenty feet across, starred from early fall through late spring with the almost-too-perfect blossoms—in white, pink, shades of red, variegated. Some bushes, through grafting, produce all four. These camellias grow in old gardens along with fragrant banana shrub and tea olive, azaleas and magnolias—old gardens with "box-bordered walks, euonymous hedges and clipped cloisters of laurel." Here is enchantment from which some visitors never quite recover.

A plantation house that became a town house, when some of its own plantation acres became the town of Marshallville, is now the home of Dr. and Mrs. John Donald Wade and their daughter, Anne. Dr. Wade, former professor of English at the University of Georgia, is the author of two fine biographies, *Augustus Baldwin Longstreet* and *John Wesley*. His house was built by a great uncle, Daniel Frederick, who married Caroline Rumph and moved to Georgia in 1832. Just as everybody in Marshallville grows camellias, an astonishing percentage of its citizens are kin to the pioneer Fredericks, Rumphs and Murphs.

The Wade house, with tall square columns and hanging balcony, looks just as it should, completely charming, in an old garden facing Main Street and an intersecting street which was once a plantation road. Here the extent of ante-bellum hospitality may be measured by the dimensions of the dining room, which is eighteen by thirty-two feet. As Dr. Wade points out, in those days one could hardly entertain less than twenty guests at dinner without offending some near relative. Even when the list had been pared to the bone, you "broke down and invited Cousin Mattie. It simply would not do to leave out Cousin Mattie."

Or, he suggests, consider a typical after-church conversation on Sunday. "Won't you come home to dinner with us—your sister's family too, for they are visiting you and all of us do dearly love her. No, there will not be too many, for there are only two carriages-full of you, after all . . ."

Like other old Marshallville houses, the Wade home is partly furnished with heirloom mahogany and rosewood. In the hall and library are several fine family portraits painted by Kate Edwards, of Atlanta, who grew up in Marshallville.

Three miles west of town is the interesting white one-story Greek Revival house built by Dr. Wade's grandfather, the Reverend Daniel F. Wade. It stands far back from the road, surrounded by one-time cotton fields and one-time "quarters," now tenant houses. Born in this house was Dr. Wade's father, Dr. John Daniel Wade, who, like most physicians, took a broad view of life and religion.

"Doctor, can you explain the Immaculate Conception?" asked an acquaintance, apparently trying to fasten on him the odium of free thinking.

"I shall undertake it, sir," the doctor replied, "if you will first explain to me the more ordinary conception."

Samuel H. Rumph's Willow Lake Farm, with its rambling white Victorian house, is now owned by his daughter, Mrs. Warren Grice. Uncle Lewis A. Rumph came into the possession of a lovely old house on McCaskill Street in town—handmade bricks and a double gallery with tall Doric columns. This was formerly known as the Nixon-McCaskill house and is now the home of Samuel C. Rumph.

At the far end of Main Street stands the handsome George H. Slappey house—two-story, white frame with Doric columns—now the home of the Joe Clarks.

Directly across the street is a charming one-story version of the Grecian Doric, owned by Mrs. James Edgar Paullin, of Atlanta, who uses it as a part-time residence. Her husband, the late Dr. Paullin, was called to Warm Springs at the time of President Roosevelt's last illness and was with the President when he died. Dr. Paullin was at that time president of the American Medical Association. Equally important in Marshallville is the fact that Mrs. Paullin is the former Edna Frederick, descendant of original settlers.

In another of Marshallville's many lovely old houses, the Hamilton Felton place on McCaskill Street, lives a young bachelor, Richard E. Dodd, who forsook Atlanta for Marshallville, where he raises hunting dogs—and camellias.

You cannot stay long away from the subject of camellias in Marshallville. No matter what else you do, you also grow camellias. The temptation is to make a career of flowers as Dave Strother does at his Massee Lane Farm. For some residents, camellias have also become a money crop. Marshallville has two flourishing nurseries. Louise Turner has found art—and camellias—commercially profitable in water colors.

People have always "got along" together in Marshallville, both white and black. When a history of Macon County was published in 1933, Marshallville emerged as an extraordinarily complacent place:

"There seemed no elections ever—the same Sunday School superintendent, the same banker, the same teachers, the same librarian, the same commissioners, the same postmaster, the same Baptist preacher, the same night watchman, the same principal of the Negro school. Only the Methodist minister seemed to change." (And he was subject to appointments made by the Methodist Conference.) Even the garden club, organized in 1934, had the same president until a few years ago.

But Marshallville is not really a self-satisfied town. The Marshallville Foundation was organized not only to preserve what the town believes to be good but also to promote what might be better.

Marshallville's camellia shows were begun in 1938, and these are best summed up by Dr. Wade: "Their really unique quality is their setting," he says, "their being held in a small town, the yards and streets of which are filled with great oaks, with azaleas and early flowering peaches and magnolias, and with countless blossom-weighted camellias. And filled too with people, with 'native' people at every turn, bent for one day at least—and how long this is as the world goes!—on being irresistibly hospitable and charming, on giving to all of their guests a sweet sense of a new spring, like old springs before, a sweet sense of home, like the home that is with most people timeless."

CHAPTER 33

Playtime Plantations

GEORGIA'S rich playtime plantation belt reaches from Albany to Thomasville and spills over into Florida. Here are the great shooting preserves maintained by wealthy owners who live elsewhere most of the year—playtime plantations in the sense that upkeep is not dependent upon self-produced profits. Traditional hospitality and modern scientific experiments in agriculture happily reach a new high, unhampered by economic pressures. It's the Old South, streamlined.

Many of these estates were ante-bellum plantations. On some, the original white-columned houses live on in ageless beauty, notably at Greenwood, near Thomasville, one of the four or five homes owned by John Hay (Jock) Whitney, whose fortune is estimated at a conservative sixty millions. Among other interesting Greek Revival houses thus preserved is Pine Bloom, near Albany, the former home of Governor Alfred H. Colquitt, who was a leader in the effort to build a new South after the War Between the States.

Spread out in the neighborhood of Albany are fourteen of these luxury plantations. The Thomasville area includes thirty or more. Some of them serve as model farms and dairies and contribute widely to the general prosperity of the community. Some are communities within themselves, with a resident operating staff of several hundred persons. Melrose, near Thomasville, has its own motion-picture theater, the Show Boat, a replica of an excursion steamer, approached by a gangplank across a pool.

At Thomasville the plantation belt is no figure of speech. Two miles from the center of town, beautiful Pine Tree Boulevard circles the city. Beyond the boulevard are the great plantations, jointly comprising about 150,000 acres, one fourth of which is cultivated, with three fourths devoted to game and wild-life preserves. (The wild life includes bears.)

Photo by McLeod

FIGURE 97. Winnstead, near Thomasville, is the plantation house owned by Mr. and Mrs. Phillip Rust. The house was rebuilt about the turn of the century on the old foundation.

Many of these plantations are now in the hands of third-generation owners from the North, members of families who were originally attracted to Thomasville because of its seductively mild winter climate and other Southern charms, including an easygoing independence not dazzled by dollars.

William McKinley was a guest in the old Victorian Mark Hanna house on North Dawson Street when he was nominated for the presidency of the United States in the winter of 1895–1896. Thomasville had five winter hotels at that time. The name of the town's Paradise Park is a hang-over from the days when this recreation center was a part of the grounds of the old Piney Woods Hotel and the townspeople called it Yankee Paradise.

Annual shooting dog trials and horse shows are among South Georgia's pop-

FIGURE 98.   This ante-bellum cottage of the Misses Annie and Julia Wright in Thomasville is distinguished by hand carving within and without.

ular sports events, but the biggest event of all is Thomasville's annual rose show, which attracts anywhere from thirty to forty thousand visitors. This is a spectacular performance participated in by townspeople, plantation owners, nurserymen, in fact, everybody for miles around, and the competition is truly tough.

Thomasville's title, City of Roses, is no mere Chamber of Commerce slogan. Red radiance roses stage a dress parade alongside the streets of the town and Paul Scarlets gaily climb the telephone poles.

Many of the plantations open their doors for house-and-garden tours in connection with the rose show, which usually lasts two days.

Finest of the old houses and one of the finest in the South is Greenwood on the twenty-thousand-acre Whitney estate. A long magnolia-bordered avenue

301

leads from the high iron entrance gate to the gardens and the white-columned house.

The four tall Ionic columns are free-standing, with inverted laurel wreaths on the frieze of the entablature and a large magnolia rosette on the tympanum of the pointed pediment. Back of the columns is a two-story baulstraded gallery supported by smaller square columns. The first-floor balustrade is made up of spindles, but the one above is done in the more decorative wheat-sheaf design.

Greenwood was designed by an English architect, John Wind, for Thomas Jones, who settled here on a ten-thousand-acre tract in 1827. Construction of the house began in 1835 and was completed nine years later. It is said that Mr. Wind carved most of the interior woodwork himself and also the magnolia rosette.

Architect Stanford White—who was later shot and killed in a New York roof garden by Harry K. Thaw—figured in the history of Greenwood after it became the property of Colonel Oliver H. Payne, who willed it to Payne Whitney, father of Jock Whitney.

Stanford White pronounced the house a superb example of Greek Revival architecture. He added the wings at the sides which might well have been a part of the original plan. Mr. White also designed the sunken Italian garden at the right of the house, a great sweep of green centered by a fountain and a grouping of marble statuary.

Greenwood has many gardens and is one of the few places in the country where there is still an abundance of virgin long-leaf pine; one of the few places where timber of sufficient size for ships' masts could be obtained during World War II.

The lands devoted to agriculture at Greenwood are leased to Major Louis A. Beard, who has conducted here extensive experiments in the propagation of hybrid seed corn.

The main house at Greenwood remains closed except when the Whitney family are in residence. Mrs. Whitney was one of the three glamorous Cushing sisters of Boston. (The other two are Mrs. Vincent Astor and Mrs. William Paley.)

Mr. Whitney, born to millions, has tried his hand at many business ventures, most of which have paid off. He picked up a neat million and a half on the movie version of Margaret Mitchell's *Gone With the Wind*, which has a background similar to that of Greenwood. Associated with Selznick at the time the motion-picture rights of the manuscript were offered for sale, Mr. Whitney insisted on their purchase at a price which was then the highest ever paid for a first novel—$50,000.

Mr. Whitney, it is said, would like to give away as much money to worthy causes as the Rockefellers. Perhaps this is an inherited trait. An anecdote con-

FIGURE 99. The Columns, town house of Mr. and Mrs. Fondren Mitchell, on Park Front in Thomasville.

cerning the generosity of Colonel Oliver H. Payne, who formerly owned Greenwood, is told by E. R. Jerger, editor of the Thomasville *Times-Enterprise*.

"Colonel Payne received a bill for medical services from Dr. Tom McIntosh, who was a popular physician of the time in Thomasville, and a decided individualist," said Mr. Jerger. "Dr. McIntosh, a little man with a long beard and a high thin voice, always wore a top hat and, in winter, a cape. His bill to Colonel Payne was for $50.

"Colonel Payne sent him a check for $1,500.

" 'You don't owe me this,' the doctor told him in his familiar falsetto.

"Colonel Payne insisted that he did and without further argument Dr. McIntosh endorsed the check to a Georgia children's home, his pet charity. Colonel Payne then matched the check with another, made payable to the same orphanage, a total of $3,000, which the doctor accepted with thanks.

"Then turning to go, Dr. McIntosh asked humorously, 'Where's my $50?'

"It was immediately forthcoming."

Photo by McLeod

FIGURE 100. Residence of Mrs. Araminta Bailey in Thomasville.

FIGURE 101. Pine Bloom, plantation house of Hal Price Headley, near Albany, is the former home of Governor Alfred H. Colquitt. Note the unusual succession of porches.

Photo by Edward Vason Jones

At Greenwood, as on many plantations, the private cemetery remains the property of descendants of the original owner. Here, along with members of the Jones family, sleeps E. W. Clarke, of Paris, Maine, a Federal soldier who died in Thomasville in the final days of the War Between the States. Sleeping there too is Adjutant H. F. Jones, who gave up his life in that same war.

Miss Harriett Brandon, a great-granddaughter of Thomas Jones, says that the Federal soldier, ill with typhoid fever, was left behind when his unit marched north.

"He was left behind on the porch at the house of my grandmother in town, Mrs. David Brandon, who had been Harriett Jones. My grandfather was in the Confederate army, of course, and my grandmother, with the help of a young Negro boy, nursed the soldier through the long weeks of his illness, and somehow got letters through the lines to his family in Maine. She did everything humanly possible to pull him through and when he died, he was buried in the family cemetery out at Greenwood.

"Some years ago while traveling in Maine I detoured by Paris and called on the Clarke family. They gave me my grandmother's letters which had been handed down all these years."

The late H. Mellville Hanna, Cleveland, Ohio, industrialist, was one of the first of Thomasville's winter visitors to succumb to the lure of ante-bellum plantations. He bought three—Melrose, Pebble Hill and Winnstead. The first two are still owned by members of the Hanna family.

The original hand-hewn log dwelling covered with clapboard and first occupied by the Colson family back in pioneer times is now the central section of the large Dutch Colonial house at Melrose. All the plantation buildings are Dutch Colonial and all are painted to match the hard-surface, coral-colored clay and white sand of the plantation roads. Hedges of Cherokee roses border the highway along the property.

Melrose was largely developed by Mr. Hanna's son, Howard M. Hanna. Here is a fine Jersey herd and a green paddock for fine horses. On the day of our visit the third-floor servant's rooms were being torn out of the house for conversion to other use. Formerly the family brought a staff of white servants when they came South each winter. Now they depend on local labor.

In addition to its private motion-picture theater, the Show Boat, Melrose has a large glassed-in swimming pool. The handsome pool and bath houses at Thomasville's Glen Arven country club were a gift from Mr. Hanna. Melrose is now owned by two Hanna daughters, Mrs. F. H. Bolton and Mrs. Warren Bicknell.

The house at Pebble Hill Plantation, built by the late Mrs. Perry W. Harvey (she was Kate Hanna) is a glorified reproduction of the original white-columned house which was destroyed by fire.

Pebble Hill is now owned by Mrs. Harvey's daughter, Mrs. Parker Poe, who raises fine Jersey cattle and has done much to improve cattle breeding in Georgia. When not in Thomasville the Poes live in Lexington, Kentucky, where they raise fine horses. Mrs. Poe's mother inaugurated the system of visiting nurses for Thomasville plantations.

Also on the Pebble Hill property is Fair Oaks, the square-columned antebellum house built by Richard Mitchell.

Akin to Greenwood in design is Susina Plantation, known as Cedar Grove when it was the old Blackshear place. It is believed the same architect designed both Greenwood and Susina. Both houses have free-standing Doric columns and the familiar wheat-sheaf balustrade. Here, as at Greenwood, wings were added at a later date. Susina, now owned by Mr. and Mrs. James S. Mason, retains intact its Old South atmosphere.

Agricultural and livestock activities of playtime plantation owners are taken quite seriously. Thurman T. Scott, who raises Guernseys and Black Angus cattle at his River Creek place, came up one year with the international champion in Red Duroc hogs.

Thomasville has a number of charming old houses along its wide streets. One of these streets is shaded by a live oak which has been enrolled as the twenty-fourth ranking member of the National Live Oak society, of forty-seven tree members. The Thomasville tree has a limb spread of 146½ feet and its trunk, 49 feet high, is 21½ feet in diameter.

The one-story frame home of the Misses Annie and Julia Wright in Thomasville is distinguished by beautiful hand-carved woodwork in decorative design, both inside and out. Among many heirloom treasures that furnish the house is an old melodeon.

The Hardy Bryan house at 312 North Broad, owned by Mrs. Taylor Mitchell, is one of the oldest in town. It is a plantation type and a magnolia motif is introduced into the wood carving.

Miss Ola Mallette's handsome Georgian house at 342 North Dawson is one of the town's architectural gems. Others include the homes of Fondren Mitchell and Mrs. Araminta Bailey.

Albany, north of Thomasville, is linked to that city by what is perhaps Georgia's most scenic highway, U. S. 19. Beauty spots break out as you speed along, green hedges, magnolias, cedars, crape myrtles, fringes of brown-eyed susans and small wild purple flowers. At other points the highway cuts through spreading pecan groves or fields of crimson clover. Intermixed with the planta-

FIGURE 102. Iris Court, town house of Miss Cena Whitehead in Albany, was built for a bride of 1842–Miss Whitehead's grandmother.

tions are prosperous farms and dairies operated on a commercial basis which do their share of highway beautification.

This atmosphere of comfortable prosperity embraces the towns with their spic and span civic buildings and smoothly groomed grass plots.

A number of prominent Atlantians own plantations in the Albany vicinity. Robert W. Woodruff, chairman of the board of the Coca-Cola Company, is owner of Ichauway Plantation, where row crops and game preserve are competing attractions. Game and farming are joint interests at Hickory Grove, owned by Winship Nunnally. At John W. Grant's Wildfair it is game and row crops.

Pine Bloom, the old Colquitt plantation, with its lovely Greek Revival house,

FIGURE 103.   Hickory Grove, near Albany, is the game preserve and plantation of Winship Nunnally, of Atlanta.

is now owned by Hal Price Headley, of Lexington, Kentucky. Here is Mr. Headley's winter-training farm for his race horses. The horses go north in April for racing in Kentucky, New York and other points.

Governor Alfred H. Colquitt built the white Ionic-columned frame house in 1848. He served three terms as governor of the state and three as United States Senator. He was a Confederate major general, but when the War Between the States was over he worked equally hard for the rebuilding of the South and the reunion of the two sections. His former home takes its name, Pine Bloom, from the pine blooms of the surrounding trees.

Pine trees inspired the names of two other Albany plantations. One is Pineland, a fifteen-thousand-acre expanse of pine land, owned by General Richard K. Mellon of Pittsburgh. The other is Pine Knoll, owned by Thomas H. Daniel of Atlanta.

One of the first Greek Revival houses built in Albany is Iris Court, which in a way gave Albany its start as a town of many beautiful houses and many crape myrtle trees.

Iris Court is the home of Miss Cena Whitehead, and it was built in the eighteen fifties for her grandmother, Adelaide Eloise Stovall, who came to Albany in 1842 as the bride of John Jackson. They came in a carriage all the way from Milledgeville, 150 miles. Among other possessions in the carriage were the first of Albany's crape myrtle trees brought along by the bride. Iris Court was built to resemble her old home in Milledgeville, now known as the Conn house. The columns at Iris Court are square instead of rounded and originally encircled the house. In 1920 Miss Whitehead's mother, Mrs. J. R. Whitehead, had the back columns removed in order to add a spacious solarium.

Albany was just a cleared spot in the wilderness when young Mr. and Mrs. Jackson finally arrived in their carriage. They had a breakdown on the way but finally got going again. And just outside the new town they had to load the carriage onto a flat boat in order to cross the Flint River.

Colonel Nelson Tift, founder of the town, had not yet built the famous old bridge house. Now a business building, this interesting structure formerly was divided by a long hall which was the entrance to a toll bridge across the river. In early times the building was also used as a theater.

Iris Court was headquarters for Federal General Cooper, of Kentucky, who was in charge of military occupation troops stationed at Albany after the War Between the States. He brought his bride there, the former Miss Venable of Virginia. "We found them delightful people," Mrs. Jackson always said.

Architect Edward Vason Jones lives in his grandfather's ante-bellum town house, planned by a New Orleans architect who gave it the pleasing ironwork trimmings. "Grandfather built it because he was tired of living in town but the town long ago caught up with the house," Mr. Jones observed smilingly.

Albany's first brick house was built by Captain W. E. Smith in 1860. It has a square four-columned portico and is well preserved.

Albany's annual house-and-garden tours cover a lot of territory but everybody makes it back to near-by Radium Springs for the lavish buffet supper served there on Sunday nights.

CHAPTER 3 4

Ante-Bellum Beauties

*T*HERE is hardly a town in Georgia past the century mark that doesn't have one or more ante-bellum houses to link today with yesterday. Even when shabby, elbowed by business buildings and shorn of their once carefully tended lawns and gardens, the old houses still lend background to the town's social and architectural structure. They stand for something sturdy in human character that doesn't give up easily. Fortunately, many of Georgia's ante-bellum beauties are well preserved.

These old houses range all the way from the pioneer simplicity of the Dell house in Jacksonboro to the romantic elegance of St. Elmo in Columbus. And they reflect a variety of living equally broad.

Did Jacksonboro die of a curse, leaving the Dell house a lone survivor? Founded in 1794 as the seat of government of Screven County, this is now one of the dead towns of Georgia.

"The place had formerly a very bad character," says George White in *Statistics of the State of Georgia* (1849). "It was reported that in the mornings after drunken frolics and fights you could see the children picking up eyeballs in tea saucers."

A curse was placed on Jacksonboro in 1830 by Lorenzo Dow, traveling evangelist, when its citizens turned a deaf ear to his exhortations and also denied him shelter. The Goodall family, then living in the Dell house, were the one exception. They took him in for the night.

Next morning on leaving Jacksonboro, Lorenzo Dow removed his shoes, the better to shake from them the dust of the town. He pronounced a curse both upon the town and the townspeople—everything, everybody—except the Goodall family and their home.

In 1847 the county seat was removed from Jacksonboro to Sylvania. Whether or not the curse of Lorenzo Dow had anything to do with this, the town soon

FIGURE 104. The S. E. Butler house in Columbus was moved three hundred feet to the present site without disturbing its cupola, widow's walk or the Doric colonnade.

suffered a decline. Of the original settlement, nothing exists today but the old Dell house, built about 1815, a two-story frame structure, its hand-hewn beams put together with wooden pegs.

In Columbus the story is just the opposite. Progress and expansion have wrecked many fine old houses, but St. Elmo and other noteworthy examples of Greek Revival architecture remain.

At near-by Fort Benning, the world's largest infantry school, the commanding general lives in a spacious white-columned house which at one time or another has extended hospitality to most of the army's top brass. The fort, named for Old Rock, Confederate General Henry L. Benning, was once the plantation of Arthur Bussey.

General Benning's own plantation was situated near Columbus. He wasn't a general, of course, when he took for his bride the lovely Mary Howard Jones, who grew up at St. Elmo, built by her father, Seaborn Jones, about 1831.

Seaborn Jones was a prominent attorney and also served as a member of the United States House of Representatives. His wife, the former Mary Howard, was an aunt of Augusta J. Evans, author of the popular novel, *St. Elmo*, first

311

published in 1866. (One of its many reprintings appeared in 1949.) In her girl-hood, Augusta Evans was a frequent guest in the Jones home, then called El Dorado. Many people believe this house was used as the setting for her book. At any rate, when Jeremiah Slade bought the property about 1875, he changed the name to St. Elmo. The street and the surrounding residential section have also taken this name.

Though of Greek Revival architecture, this beautiful old house, now owned by Mr. and Mrs. Douglas Mobley, is distinctly individual. Delicately elaborate details build up a superb unity of effect, enhanced by the fine architectural balance of a massive façade and twelve Doric columns, forty feet high, which extend across the front and around two sides. These columns are crowned by a balustrade similar to the one that links them together at floor level on the wide portico. A hanging iron balcony in medallion design high-lights the entrance with its identical first- and second-floor doors, which have graceful fan- and side-lights. The house is built of handmade brick smoothed over with stucco, and shaded by great trees planted when a pioneer predecessor occupied the site.

Besides the visitor who inspired the name of the house, many other cele-brated guests have been entertained at St. Elmo. Two Presidents of the United States were guests, James K. Polk and Millard Fillmore. Other guests included Henry Clay and William Makepeace Thackeray.

The tower of the winds in ancient Athens inspired the Greek Revival Ralston-Cargill house in Columbus. Designed by Stephen Button of Philadelphia for Dr. Thomas Hoxey, it is known as the Lion House, because of the two massive Nubian lions that guard the entrance.

A few years after the War Between the States, a hoard of gold coins was discovered in a window casing of the house. It is said that the basement once had a subterranean passage to the old Racine Hotel in which a drove of mules was hidden while Federal troops occupied Columbus.

The stately ante-bellum house restored by Mr. and Mrs. S. E. Butler was moved three hundred feet to its present site without disturbing in the slightest the Doric columns, cupola or widow's walk. Among other Columbus charmers is The Elms, a Greek Revival cottage, built about 1832 by Hanson Scott Estes and enlarged by Lloyd G. Bowers, father of the present owner, Lloyd Bowers. Its old-fashioned box garden is a butterfly design.

Confederate General Joe Wheeler fell asleep over his maps at the old plan-tation desk in the study at Buena Vista, the lovely Doric-columned house of Mr. and Mrs. Thomas J. Glover in Newnan.

The reason for General Wheeler's exhaustion was reflected soon afterward in a letter written near Atlanta by General Sherman to Federal Major General W. H. Halleck in Washington:

FIGURE 105.   Confederate General Joe Wheeler made his headquarters at Buena Vista, the Thomas J. Glover house in Newnan. He fell asleep at the study desk after leading his Cavalry to victory in a fierce battle with the forces of Federal General McCook.

"August 1, 1864 . . . Colonel Brownlow reports from Marietta that he has just reached there, having escaped from a disaster that overtook General McCook's cavalry expedition at Newnan . . ."

The disaster was Joe Wheeler.

Buena Vista, in 1864, was the residence of Colonel Hugh Buchanan, then absent with the state militia. (Later he was Judge Buchanan and a member of the United States House of Representatives.) His young son, Edward, was at home, and until his death at the age of ninety-four, Edward never forgot the excitement of the household when Wheeler, the daring Confederate cavalry leader, rode up in his black plumed hat, gray uniform and crimson sash and asked if he and his staff could use the house as headquarters.

All over Georgia they remembered Wheeler like that, a man small of stature but a fine leader and fighter, fine enough for the United States Army to make him a major general in the Spanish American War.

Unopened letters addressed to Colonel Hugh Buchanan and bearing an 1864 Vermont postmark were found in the attic of Buena Vista when the Glovers bought and restored the old house. The letters were written by a sister from whom Colonel Buchanan became estranged because she so bitterly censured his allegiance to the Confederacy.

Colonel Buchanan enlarged the original house which was built in the late eighteen twenties by his brother-in-law, Edward S. Story, who soon afterward departed for Texas. The tall columns were a part of the later addition, as were the blinds, the first blinds to darken Newnan windows. The house has a cantilevered balcony and many other interesting architectural details. Like all of Newnan's old houses, and many of its new ones, Buena Vista is furnished with beautiful family pieces cherished through half a dozen or more generations.

Another charmingly restored Newnan house started out in 1854 at Oaklawn, nine miles from its present site. At that time the house with its one-story Doric columns had a raised basement. Carefully taken apart, it was rebuilt in town and is now surrounded by one of Newnan's finest camellia collections. This is the home of Mr. and Mrs. Edgar Hollis.

The handsome old Newnan home of Dr. Andrew Bonaparte Calhoun built in 1848 of handmade brick has tall columns at both front and back and beautifully carved interior woodwork. This is still occupied by members of the family, Mrs. Calhoun Hill and Miss Rebecca Hill. Family ownership continues in the name of Mrs. Arnold Broyles of Atlanta.

Not content with being beautiful, Mrs. Howell Newton, who lives in one of Forsyth's most charming old houses, took a course at the famous Cordon Bleu school of cooking. This training, passed along to her colored cook, results in an Old South menu with a French accent which surely transcends anything served in the spacious dining room of the Newton home a hundred years ago. Any fortunate guest of today can only wonder why more women do not cultivate this most potent of all charms.

Mrs. Newton not only had a family tradition to live up to but the tradition of her house as well. This two-story white dwelling which rests so serenely in its lovely garden was transplanted from Clinton many years ago, making the thirty-mile trip by ox team. Clinton, a frontier center of culture, was founded in 1807.

The Newton house has a small square portico with square columns and a sloping roof with wide overhanging eaves. It is exquisitely furnished in family heirlooms.

Is there magic in a rusty nail? An early owner of the ante-bellum Greek Revival house of Judge and Mrs. Frank Willingham in Forsyth was sure there is. He even thought he had proof.

This stately old house with tall Doric columns had several owners before

FIGURE 106. Residence of John Leon Hoffman, in Forsyth, where many refugees were given shelter during the War Between the States.

title was acquired by the present family. One of these early owners was the late B. R. Stephens, who was greatly troubled by the fact that a magnificent pecan tree on the property bore no fruit.

"Someone told Mr. Stephens if he would drive a number of rusty nails into the tree trunk that this would turn the trick," says Judge Willingham. A lack of iron was the trouble, according to the gentleman who prescribed the nails. Mr. Stephens followed this advice and sure enough, the very next year the tree produced a fine crop of pecans. It hasn't missed since.

"But," Judge Willingham adds, "I have always attributed this to the fact that another tree on adjoining property reached bearing age at that time and that what the older tree needed was the cross pollination this afforded. Mr. Stephens, however, was sure the rusty nails deserved at least a part of the credit."

The Willingham house is the only one this writer has seen in Georgia with an uneven number of columns. There are five across the front of its long porch. This interesting arrangement is due to the fact that the house—on an elevation

Photo by Drinnon

FIGURE 107. The old Blount house, near Haddock, is now owned by Dr. L. C. Lindsley. It was the former home of Mrs. Walter D. Lamar, of Macon.

overlooking the town and an unusually beautiful garden—has its steps at the end of the porch instead of center front. There was no necessity to space columns evenly on either side of an entrance.

Hill Ardin, a handsome white-columned house built by Cyrus Sharp in 1822, the year the town of Forsyth was founded, has a secret stair and unusually fine interior woodwork. A century-old cork tree stands on the grounds. The house was given its present name when it became the property of the Hugh Hardin family.

A fine old plantation-type house painted to harmonize with its garden is owned by Mr. and Mrs. J. L. Hoffman. The main portion of the house with its

FIGURE 108. Murder followed the writing of a name in the old Varner house at Indian Springs, where Creek Indian Chief William McIntosh signed a treaty ceding Creek lands to the federal government. His angry people shot him.

square columns and two-story porches is white, but the front walls of the porches are ashes of roses. Many refugees were given shelter here during the War Between the States.

Despite the fact that one of its choice old houses now graces Forsyth and that its most celebrated house burned down in recent years, architects still consider the town of Clinton a collector's item.

And this it is, in a double sense, for an avid lady shopper bought one of Clinton's houses some years ago simply because she coveted the antique scenic wallpaper which she transferred to her home in another town. This wallpaper depicted scenes from London's one-time Vauxhall Gardens and was still as fresh in color as it had been a century ago.

Clinton was a model town in the early eighteen hundreds—a cluster of gracious houses set in the midst of apparently endless acres of cotton. But things happened to Clinton. Its industries, including an iron foundry which turned out nine hundred cotton gins a year, were destroyed by the invading army during the War Between the States. Later the railroad bypassed Clinton. In 1905, nearly a hundred years after the town was founded, Jones County moved the seat of government from Clinton to Gray, close to the railroad depot.

But Clinton's old houses remain. Turn left, turn right on any of its unpaved clay roads and you find houses that have been there anywhere from six to seven generations. Mostly they are of Post-Colonial or Early Federal architecture. The ante-bellum Jade-Barron house, glistening white Greek Revival, is a comparative newcomer.

Original scenic wallpaper still adorns the living room of the home of Mr. and Mrs. W. R. Johnson at Clinton. Romantic in mood, it pictures ladies and gentlemen of the French court in classical outdoor settings. This was all painted by hand and there is no duplication of scene. The colors are still fresh though the paper has been on the walls since the house was built. Small front portico and square columns of this house show an architectural kinship to the Newton house in Forsyth.

Lowther Hall, the former Clinton home of Mrs. Frank Jones of Macon, burned to the ground some years ago. Its celebrated curving stair, framed by the arch of a wide central hall, was similar to that in Charleston's Manigault house.

Similar to both is the stair in the old Blount house, which still stands near Haddock between Clinton and Milledgeville. At the Blount house, the former home of Mrs. Walter D. Lamar of Macon, the hallway's arch is adorned with gold acanthus leaves. These are also used to produce a rich effect on center ceiling medallions, cornices and the niches flanking the fireplace in the drawing room.

This house, designed by Daniel Pratt for General John W. Gordon of the state militia, was begun in 1828 and completed five years later. It has a portico supported by two tall Doric columns and there is a hanging balcony. Some years ago the house was bought by Dr. L. C. Lindsley, who also owns Westover, described in the Milledgeville chapter of this book.

"A group of gentlemen's homes rather than a town," is the delightful description applied to Lexington in the *Garden History of Georgia*. Lexington, near Washington, was founded in 1808, and its old houses still give the town a leisurely and aristocratic air. The home of Mrs. R. F. Brooks, Sr., stands on a hill at the

FIGURE 109. The Little White House at Warm Springs where President Franklin D. Roosevelt died. This cottage, built according to traditional Southern architecture, was the Georgia home of the President.

end of a cross street, a gracious old house with tall Doric columns, surrounded by green lawn and venerable trees.

But most of the old houses are not visible from the highway. The one-time home of Governor George R. Gilmer, The Cedars, is almost hidden by its surrounding cedar grove. It is said that the main section of this house was built in 1800. Governor Gilmer bought the property in 1840, added a wing and a tall Doric portico which makes an unusual ell-shaped colonnade overlooking the old garden. The mounds of uncut stones collected by Governor Gilmer remain, one on each side of the walk. These are mentioned in his book, about early Georgians, but the location of the grotto from which the stones were gathered has been lost during the intervening years. Time has touched the old house too but has not impaired its dignity. The Cedars is now owned by James A. Reynolds.

President Monroe was entertained in 1819 at Woodlawn, the near-by plantation home of William H. Crawford. It is said they discussed here the policies resulting in the Monroe Doctrine. Crawford served as United States Senator, minister to France, Secretary of War under Madison, Secretary of the Treasury under Monroe and in 1824 was a candidate for President of the United States.

319

He fought two duels in support of his high political principles. Unfortunately Woodlawn was destroyed by fire in 1936.

The old home of Wilson and Joseph Henry Lumpkin still stands in Lexington, a frame house of strong, simple lines. Wilson Lumpkin served as governor of Georgia, and Atlanta was first named Marthasville for his daughter Martha. Joseph Henry Lumpkin, one of the founders of the Lumpkin Law School, was first chief justice of the Georgia Supreme Court.

One of the best preserved of Lexington's old houses was built by Stephen Upson in 1825. It is a spacious white clapboard house with a small, slender-columned portico suggestive of Mr. Upson's native New England. A low stone wall encloses the broad tree-bordered lawns and a beautiful box garden. This property was sold in 1903 to William King Howard and in 1951 was acquired by the present owners, Mr. and Mrs. W. E. Evans.

A girl member of the Confederate secret service, Fanny Fraser, once lived in the fine old Doric-columned house at 426 Atlanta Street in Marietta. This house is now owned by Mrs. C. O. Sanger, great-granddaughter of Fanny's parents, Captain and Mrs. John Fraser. Mrs. Fraser was a daughter of John Couper, whose plantation, Cannon's Point, on St. Simons Island, is described in another chapter.

Actually Miss Fraser started out serving as a volunteer army nurse, but proved herself a young woman of such discretion, poise and courage that she was soon called upon to gather information about the movement of Northern troops and to carry dispatches and other documents.

The opposing army got wind of these operations but was unable to secure proof. When General Sherman's forces reached Marietta, Fanny's sister, Rebecca, was brought before the commanding general for an official investigation.

But Rebecca also was equal to the situation. "She had a witty and trenchant tongue, the man did not live whose questions she could not parry, or when the necessity arose, answer with an air of innocence which made them feel that they were heartless brutes to have suspected her," declares Sadie Blackwell Gober Temple in her history of Cobb County, *The First Hundred Years*.

Built at the same time as the Sanger home was the house next door, owned by Mr. and Mrs. John Boston. Originally the two were occupied by brothers, Robert B. and Charles G. Bostwick. The tall white columns of the Boston house were removed at one time in its history but when later additions were made, architect Neel Reid also added—white columns.

A house with a past is Ivy Grove, the Marietta home of Mr. and Mrs. James Carmichael. When originally built in 1843 it was a well-proportioned Greek Revival structure with one-story columns on two sides. Like so many other houses, Ivy Grove later broke out in a rash of Victorian trimmings, topped by a tower.

Time passed, the house caught fire and the tower toppled. Mr. and Mrs. Morgan McNeel had the Victorian trimmings stripped away and Ivy Grove was restored to its original architectural self. While going through all these various phases it was owned by several generations of Mrs. McNeel's family.

In turn, the Carmichaels now cherish Ivy Grove, and you need an expert to tell you which of the furnishings is by Mr. Sheraton and which by Mr. Carmichael himself. A year of Mr. Carmichael's spare time went into the carving of finials for the posts of a handsome four-poster bed.

Tranquilla, one of the most impressive of Marietta's ante-bellum white-columned houses, is said to have been designed by the same architect who planned the group of beautiful old houses at Roswell, twelve miles distant. Tranquilla was built in 1849 by Andrew Jackson Hansell, who later became a Confederate general. Interestingly enough, General Hansell moved to Mimosa Hall in Roswell after the War Between the States when he was made president of the Roswell Mills.

The General's Marietta house was sold in 1869 to George Camp, whose daughter, "Miss Sallie," married George H. Keeler. One of his sons by a former marriage was O. B. Keeler, the late well-known golf writer; and his son, George Henry Keeler, now owns Tranquilla.

Two of Marietta's finest houses were built by John Heyward Glover, a leading Cobb County citizen of ante-bellum times. One of these is a former plantation house, with massive Doric columns, on the edge of town, discovered and restored some years ago by Mr. and Mrs. Fred Myers. The first step in its restoration was the replacement of 308 missing window panes.

Mr. Glover's town house at 504 Whitlock Avenue, now owned by Mrs. Leslie Blair, was built of handmade bricks and formerly had tall columns similar to those at Tranquilla. Mr. Glover's son, James Bolan Glover, gave it a new look in the Victorian era, which detracted nothing from its solid dignity.

Back of this house, and parallel with Wright Street, is one of Marietta's most charming small houses—also built of handmade bricks—a former slave cabin with a graceful sloping roof and wide chimneys. Now the home of Mr. and Mrs. Leon Gilbert, it was occupied by the Glover house servants in ante-bellum times. In later years, J. B. Glover converted the house into a six-room cottage for his daughter, Leize, when she married Marcus H. Field. Their two daughters, Mrs. Howard Harmon, of Atlanta, and Mrs. William Winburn, of Savannah, claim the distinction of having been born in a slave house.

Perhaps the largest Doric columns in Georgia adorn the home of Mr. and and Mrs. Frank Owenby on Kennesaw Avenue. This house was begun in 1841 by Archibald Howell and finished in 1849. The ceilings are fourteen feet high and most of the thirteen rooms are twenty-two by twenty-two feet. The Owenbys have five children, and Mrs. Owenby says their crowded life made her wish for a home as big as a courthouse. The old Howell house was the perfect answer.

Colonial Cottage Gardens, built about 1851, is the beautiful story-and-a-half house of Mr. and Mrs. Howell Trezevant. Six Doric columns march across its wide front porch. Inside the rooms are spacious and the ceilings high—just the right setting for Mrs. Trezevant's fine collections of old furniture, old family portraits, heavy silver, and china which includes a complete set of antique Meissen. This house was the former home of the headmaster of the one-time Georgia Military Institute at Marietta. It takes its name from the handsome boxwood garden at one side, planted by Mrs. Trezevant.

A superb job of restoration was done by Mrs. Robert Suhr at Sugar Hill, one of Marietta's loveliest houses, with columns front and back. Only the walls were standing, no windows, no doors. Now the big white house on its hill presents an enchanting picture which might have been preserved intact from a romantic past.

While many of Marietta's old houses have been cherished by succeeding generations of the same family, a number of others were restored when World War II brought a housing shortage to the town along with a bomber plant.

The cloistered seclusion of the beautiful North Georgia mountains is a setting for more than one century-old house. Some were built by early English and Scottish settlers after the removal of the Cherokee Indians in 1838. Others were the part-time homes of coastal planters and businessmen who brought their families to the up-country for the summer months.

A group of these early houses stands near Clarkesville. Two are especially interesting examples of American Gothic, designed by an architect named Van Buren.

Woodlands, which has its own private golf course, was built in 1848 by J. G. Kollock of Savannah, as a summer home. Even the library bookcases, made from walnut trees cut on the place, follow the design of the high cathedral-like doors. With its ten bedrooms, the house still serves admirably as a summer home for Kollock descendants, M. C., E. C. and G. J. Kollock of Atlanta and Miss Susan Kollock of Smyrna.

Blythewood is the year-round residence of Mr. and Mrs. Houstoun Johnston. It has many gables adorned with intricate carvings and topped by pinnacles. The terraced gardens are enclosed by iron fences which enhance the picturesque effect of the old house. These fences were collected by Mr. Johnston. One formerly surrounded the historic Independent Church in Savannah. The other guarded the gates at the old Carshed, as Atlanta's early railway station was called.

A fine Greek Revival house was built in this general neighborhood by General Duncan Clinch of South Carolina and is now owned by Barnwell Heyward.

The old Thomas Lumsden house was built in 1831, practically on top of a gold mine. There was wilderness all around and Indians. On one occasion Mrs. Lumsden was at home alone in the house with the children when seven or eight Indians appeared in the yard, all wearing war paint and carrying guns and tomahawks.

The young mother remembered stories of recent scalpings and was very much frightened but outwardly remained calm. One of the Indians she recognized. "John," she said, calling the Indian by his name, "I am here all alone with just the children. You will have to take care of us." John collected all the guns and tomahawks and brought them to her but she refused to take them. The Indians were given food and that night they slept on pallets in the house. Next morning they went peacefully on their way.

Mrs. Lumsden was the daughter of John L. Richardson, a pioneer settler in North Georgia, and her husband was a Scotsman. In a corner cupboard in the long sunny dining room of the Jesse Lumsden home are lovely pieces of china brought from Scotland when the first of the family came to this country. The George W. Williams house is now a home for orphan children.

A delightful Victorian Gothic house in the Nacoochee Valley was for many years the summer home of the C. W. Hunnicutt family of Atlanta and is now owned by Mrs. L. G. Hardman, widow of a former Georgia governor. Mrs. Hardman's wedding ring was fashioned of gold mined not far away.

They say Southerners get more Southern when they live away from home, and so the professional Southerner evolved. They say also that Northerners who come South to live become more Southern than the native-born. Something like this happened to Sanford Kingsbery of Derby Center, Vermont.

The Kingsberys came South to Carroll County, Georgia, in 1827. There is a legend that they planned to return to New England once Mr. Kingsbery had amassed a fortune. He made his fortune, all right, but he and his family went back to Vermont only on visits. Mrs. Kingsbery had planted a New England garden at their home, Oak Lawn, which still stands near Carrollton. Evidently she planted her heart there too and home is where the heart is, so they say.

Three Kingsbery sons fought for the Confederacy and while they were off with the Southern army the Northern army came by and burned the tobacco barn at Oak Lawn.

The house, which escaped the flames, is a two-story frame dwelling, originally built with twin-columned portico and a balcony railing in diamond design. The first piano in Carroll County stood in the parlor and people came from miles around to peep at it, much to the discomfiture of the family, who usually had guests already but had to ask the peepers in for a better look. This old square piano, shipped by water from Baltimore and brought from Charleston to Carrollton by ox team, now graces the home of a daughter, Mrs. W. C. Stripling in Fort Worth, Texas.

Mr. Kingsbery operated one of the state's finest stock farms. Two of his sons, Joseph and Charles, were among the founders of Atlanta's exclusive Piedmont Driving Club, which dates back to the days of fine horses and carriages. Here Joseph Kingsbery entertained President Grover Cleveland at a luncheon.

One of the noteworthy old houses in Elbert County is Rose Hill, near Elberton. The central part of the white frame house with its four-columned two-story portico was originally the home of Stephen Heard, acting governor of Georgia during the Revolution.

Here many years later the wife of Stephen Heard's grandson, Mrs. Eugene B. Heard, started the famous free Seaboard Airline traveling public library in memory of her young son who died at the age of twelve. The books she bought for him were the nucleus of the library now grown to about fifty thousand volumes. Everett St. John, president of the railroad at that time, agreed to give the books free transportation for the benefit of readers along the line traveled by the Seaboard.

When Mrs. Heard died, her daughter, Mrs. James Swift, carried on. When Mrs. Swift died, Mr. Swift married the assistant librarian and the work continues in the library at near-by Middleton. The Seaboard also continues to give free transportation to the books, although there was never any formal agreement beyond Mr. St. John's promise to Mrs. Heard. The books go to several Southern states. Rose Hill is now owned by J. Wade Johnson.

The William Allen house, built in 1784, is believed to be the oldest in Elbert County. It is now owned by E. C. Brown. Within the town of Elberton are other interesting architectural survivals, among them the beautiful square-columned Oliver home.

Both wine and brandy were served visitors to the old Fish home at Oglethorpe, in Macon County, according to the diary of James D. Frederick. Under date of March 21, 1856, he tells of going from his home in Lanier to attend court in Oglethorpe and have dinner with Colonel George W. Fish.

"Went and found Messrs. Miller, Blandford, lawyers, Simri Rose, editor, L. M. Felton, legislator, Ham Felton and myself, farmers. Directly after entering house we were invited to the dining room in the basement story to drink of wine and brandy. I took wine.

"Back in the parlor, we examined plates of Shakespeare, two volumes, costing $140. Then to dinner. There were three glasses to each plate, one for wine, one for champagne and the other for water. Soup constituted the first course, then wine. We were helped to meats, turkey, ham and so forth. This course through, champagne."

Colonel Fish was the victim of one of the state's most sensational murders in 1871. A certain Mr. Loyd, one of the two men later convicted and hanged, claimed the colonel had been paying too much attention to his (Loyd's) wife.

The old Fish home, built above a raised basement, the high front porch approached by a charming double staircase, is now owned by Edward P. Shealy of Atlanta. Similar in design is the old Stockton house at Oglethorpe, now the home of Mrs. T. C. Powers and her sister, Mrs. C. T. Harden. As in many old Georgia houses, the inside trim and hardware of the Stockton home were brought from England.

Violence is linked with the old Varner house at Indian Springs. Here in 1825 a treaty was signed that cost Creek Indian Chief William McIntosh his life. McIntosh, a man of mixed blood (he was a cousin of Georgia's Governor George M. Troup, then in office), had served the United States in the War of 1812 and in the Indian wars in Florida where he became a brigadier general. In February of 1825 he led his people in the signing of a treaty, by which the Creeks were offered $400,000 and an equal mount of western land in return for their remaining territory in Georgia.

McIntosh later retired to what is still called the McIntosh Reservation, a mile-square tract in Carroll County, granted him by the federal government, where he built himself a house. In the meantime the Creeks held a general council meeting and sentenced McIntosh to death. On April 30, 1825, more than a hundred angry Creeks surrounded McIntosh's new home and set it afire. Driven out by the flames which destroyed the house, McIntosh was instantly shot down.

The old Varner house at Indian Springs, long a private residence, was built in 1821 as a hotel and operated by McIntosh and Joel Bailey. The old registry desk at which the treaty was signed is still preserved. A long porch, with square posts, extends all the way across the front of the house and there are numerous front doors as was customary in stagecoach times.

There was always a room for tramps at Liberty Hall, the home of Alexander H. Stephens at Crawfordville. Now that the house and grounds are part of a state park, this room at the head of the dining room stairs is appropriately marked.

The sturdy white frame house, with a wide porch across the front, is otherwise much as it was when it was the home of the Great Commoner, a little man with a big brain. Stephens, who never weighed more than a hundred pounds and was a near-invalid, had a spectacular career as a statesman. He served as United States Senator, as Vice President of the Confederacy, as a member of the United States House of Representatives and died in Atlanta in 1882 while governor of Georgia.

Greensboro, Union Point and Greene County have an unusual number of

Greek Revival and other old houses. This was once a rich plantation section, and with a changed economy many of the county houses, now occupied by tenant farmers, show the heavy hand of time.

Among well-preserved survivals is the Park house, near the old Park mill on the Oconee River, still "in the family" as the home of Mr. and Mrs. Ed Askew.

The late Judge James B. Park was ten years old when he rescued his pet hen and kept her hidden in the house while Federal soldiers passed on the march to the sea. Everything else was taken, and he watched the three-story flour and corn-meal mill go up in smoke. "Our dwelling caught fire from the sparks and would have been destroyed except for a Negro servant, Cyrus Park, who remained on the roof with wet blankets," Judge Park later wrote.

The old Park home is the typical gabled, high-ceilinged white frame house of its era. The wide fireplace in the living room has a fine hand-carved mantel.

The oldest frame house in the county still stands near Union Point. Built by Redman Thornton of Virginia, it has a brick foundation, the space between the weatherboards and the laths filled in with brickwork. In the cellar you may see the heavy hand-hewn sills. There are three large rooms on the first floor and two on the second. The baseboards of the living room are made from a single plank two and a half feet wide. The big outside chimney on the northern side of the house has a built-in niche.

At Union Point also is Hawthorn Heights, the impressive Greek Revival house of Mr. and Mrs. Harold Lamb, named for the thick hawthorne hedge surrounding its eight acres of garden. In the garden stands one of the tea bushes sent to Washington from Japan by Commodore Perry when he opened the ports of that country in 1854. Nearly all the fine old furniture in the house has a family history. Several of the bedrooms upstairs are unchanged since they were furnished by brides of different generations.

Near Union Point, not far from the Georgia railroad crossing is Jefferson Hall, a beautifully proportioned house with tall Ionic columns. Jefferson Hall was built about 1830 by Lemuel Greene, who sold it to James Brooks Hart of Augusta. Mr. Hart used the house as a summer home. The railroad trains obligingly stopped in front of the door when the family traveled. About 1857 the place was sold to Ransom Harwell and remained in the Harwell family for many years. It is now owned by Mr. and Mrs. Clem Gunn.

Among Georgia's many interesting old estates is Casulon Plantation at High Shoals in Walton County, former home of the late Miss Sally Maud Jones. The original section of the house was built in 1825. Columns were added during the Classic Revival.

A house in cold storage is the 1774 log structure near Hoschton, once owned by Major James Cochran, Revolutionary soldier and later Jackson County's representative in the state legislature. General Andrew Jackson spent a night here on his way to the Seminole wars. Several years ago the house was dismantled but is still carefully preserved in accordance with a plan to re-erect it on a new site. Still owned by Cochran descendants, it is the property of Mrs. H. B. DeLaPerriere.

Louisville, capital of Georgia from 1795 to 1806, has its interesting old homes. So also have many other Georgia towns, Americus, Sparta, Talbotton, Cuthbert, Griffin, Barnesville, Thomaston and still others. An historic survival in Louisville is the old slave market, a large belfry-topped structure with open sides and ends.

All the old houses have their stories, stories which are a part of Georgia's past, the roots of its present. In touching the high spots here and there, it may seem to some readers that undue emphasis has been given to a certain war. Let it be remembered that this war was important in the history of the old houses, that it ended a way of life that brought many of them into being.

Perhaps it may be said that something of the Greek ideal was built into their white columns, an ideal that sought values in living which were beyond monetary standards. And this was well, for the old houses went through hard times. Some of them survived intact. Many others have been and are being restored. Gradually, all over Georgia, this seems to be happening. But it is only part of the larger picture. Farmhouses, tenant houses, rural areas in general, are taking on a new look. Georgia is building back. Much of the new building is modern but some of it is traditional too.

A white-columned cottage, traditional in design, was built at Warm Springs in 1932. It is the Little White House in which President Franklin D. Roosevelt died April 12, 1945.

Nothing has been disturbed since that sad day. The simple but charming six-room dwelling may still be seen as it was when the great wartime President spent his brief vacations here. In the comfortably furnished living room there are the old maps and the ship models he loved, the books he read—many mystery novels among them. There is the chair in which he was stricken with the fatal cerebral hemorrhage.

Now a national shrine, the Little White House attracts thousands of visitors every year. Near by is the great Warm Springs Foundation for the treatment of infantile paralysis, inspired by Mr. Roosevelt's own crippling attack of the disease and his first visit to Warm Springs in 1921, where he exercised in the warm waters of the swimming pool. Georgia Hall, the beautiful administration building of the Foundation, was erected by voluntary contributions of fifty thousand Georgia citizens. Its portico of white Doric columns is flanked by two long wings. Both the Little White House and Georgia Hall were designed by Georgia's own Henry Toombs.

CHAPTER 35

Portrait of a Lady: New South

SARAH Wadley Burt was serving champagne punch from the great silver punch bowl presented her grandfather when he was president of the Central of Georgia Railroad. It is a handsome bowl, measuring at least two feet across the top, with heavy raised decorations in an elaborate grape and leaf design.

As is usual among a large family connection, the bowl is often borrowed by Macon relatives or intimate friends when there is a wedding or a debut. This was one of the times it had been borrowed. As usual, there were admiring comments. But Mrs. Burt almost dropped the punch ladle when she heard one guest whisper to another, "They say it belongs to an old farm woman and that it's all she has left."

Mrs. Burt, the wife of Major William G. Burt, lives at Great Hill, near Bolingbroke, twelve miles from Macon, in the former home of her railroad-president grandparent, William Morrill Wadley. Mr. Wadley's pioneering practices in the South were simultaneous with those in the East of the great New York Central tycoon, Cornelius Vanderbilt. Both saw the far-flung possibilities of the combination of roads into what became the railway system. As early as 1869, Mr. Wadley leased the Southwestern Railroad and the Macon and Western, making them subsidiaries instead of competitors of the Central of Georgia. When stockholders were afraid to take a chance, Mr. Wadley leased roads in his own name and gave his personal check. The stockholders later said thank you with a beautiful mahogany dining-room chest containing, among other handsome pieces, the silver punch bowl.

Mrs. Burt smiled when reminded of the story—famous in Macon—about the punch bowl and the too-audible comments of a party guest.

"That guest was a little mixed up on some of the details," she said. "It was my grandfather Wadley, who had only one piece of silver left—a silver dollar—at

328

the close of the War Between the States. But she was right about one thing. I'm certainly an old farm woman."

Mrs. Burt smiled again, a gay warm smile. The farm is a two-thousand-acre plantation, on which she and Major Burt have successfully bridged a changed economic system by converting one-time cotton lands into a modern dairy farm.

You would never guess, driving south along U. S. Highway 41 in Monroe County, about halfway between Forsyth and Macon, that you were anywhere near this interesting old plantation. The road to the right looks like any other unpromising red clay road cut across an open field, with a wooded area in the distance.

On the night of Sarah Wadley's debut party this road was covered with wooden boards laid crosswise from main highway to house—a mile or more—just in case of rain. Flaming pine torches, held aloft by Negro servants stationed at intervals, lighted the guests along.

Today, after crossing the field, you come to a graded gravel-base driveway, which winds for half a mile through a grove of fine old trees. Suddenly, ahead of you, there is a clearing and there is the house, gray with age, surrounded by boxwood and old-fashioned shrubs and laurel and magnolias and great oaks, all enclosed by a waist-high lacy brick wall. The main gardens are outside the wall at the left, gently sloping downward to lose themselves in a velvet-smooth green pleasance which, in turn, is lost in shadowy woodland.

There are no white columns. The original house, one of the oldest in this section of the state, started out as the usual pioneer structure, with two rooms up and two down, a hall between and one-story shed rooms in the back. It now has twenty-two rooms. William Morrill Wadley bought the house in 1873, and enlarged and remodeled it according to the fashion of the day, which was Victorian. Mrs. Wadley, the former Rebecca Everingham of Cockspur Island, near Savannah, wanted a front porch. Mr. Wadley, who hailed from New Hampshire, wanted a stoop. The house has a front porch which has a stoop. It also has that incalculable quality called charm.

Having parked on the green forecourt outside the brick wall, you open the gate with pleasant anticipation. Immediately the surrounding stillness is shattered. All in full cry, dogs appear bouncing from everywhere, Doberman pinschers, cocker spaniels, and just dogs, six or seven at least. Thank heaven, all are wagging their tails. Anyway, Mrs. Burt, needing no doorbell, is now on the porch.

Whatever Sarah Wadley Burt's age, it is the age when her portrait should be added to other interesting family likenesses that adorn the paneled walls of the old home. It would be a portrait of a lady with black-fringed, vivid blue eyes, dark hair touched generously with gray, a lady with a charm and verve that have their roots in a rich, elemental vitality. It would be a portrait of a lady—New South.

She will tell you that all the feed and forage—except cottonseed meal and hulls—are raised on the place for a herd of two hundred purebred Guernseys. "And that's the truth," she will say, "but don't ask me how many gallons of milk we get a day. Nobody ever tells the truth about that. It's like the fish that got away."

She will tell you that Major Burt, now retired from the army, runs the farm—that she only does the bookkeeping. Some of the employees were born on the property, children or grandchildren of former slaves. But farm labor is still farm labor. This means that Major Burt may direct operations from the driver's seat of a tractor. It may mean that Mrs. Burt is at the wheel of the truck that delivers the big cans of milk to the distribution depot in Atlanta, eighty-odd miles distant.

It is whatever the day's work demands. She probably would not find the dairy farm so engrossing if its operation were less challenging. She probably would not enjoy her beautiful garden so much if all her outdoor activities were limited to gardening alone.

The plantation had its private race track when Mrs. Burt's father, George Dole Wadley, was a gay young blade, six feet tall, dark and handsome and given to wearing bright yellow or red silk waistcoats with his dress clothes. In the days before jet planes and hot rods, George Dole did pretty well with a two-wheeled sulky drawn by one of his fast horses. His favorite stunt was to meet the crack northbound express train at Bolingbroke and race it to the crossing. The object was to dash across in front of the locomotive.

George Dole Wadley never lost his "dash," even as a parent. "He was always going somewhere and taking us with him," says Mrs. Burt. "Somewhere" usually meant traveling in state in a private railway car and the destination might be Mexico, California or Canada. Or it could be New York and a trip to Europe. It was always something exciting.

Although there were eight Wadley children, it was George Dole who became manager of his father's plantation and, like his father, achieved prominence in railroad and financial circles. He married Georgia Tracy, daughter of one of the Confederacy's youngest brigadier generals, Edward Dorr Tracy, whose sword and sash hang beside the carved mantel in the book-lined library at Great Hill. Mrs. Burt's brother was named for the general. In an upstairs bedroom there are mementos of a later war—an army footlocker and an overseas helmet. This was the room of William Giroud Burt, Jr., who lost his life in World War II. The Burt's other son, George, named for his grandfather Wadley, is a member of the editorial staff of the Louisville *Courier-Journal*.

The railroad station, Bolingbroke, was so named soon after Mrs. Burt's grandfather, William M. Wadley, finished reading the life and works of Lord Bolingbroke. Great Hill was named for Mr. Wadley's boyhood home in Brentwood

Township, New Hampshire. It now represents three generations of additions and improvements. All the downstairs rooms have plaster ceilings and paneled walls. The mantels were carved on the place by a traveling German cabinet-maker. Each has a different design—sunburst, diamond, basket of flowers or fruit—which is something of an achievement when every room in a large house has its fireplace.

Some of the furnishings go back to New England ancestors, notably the handsome Queen Anne highboy in the back parlor. An exquisite Loewstoft bowl, also an heirloom, graces the top of the highboy, which is balanced on the other side of the room with a fine old desk. This is a delightful room, looking out toward the garden. Its paneled walls are gray-green and the comfortable chairs and sofas are covered with bright-flowered hand-blocked linen.

The Victorian overmantel mirror has its association with the colorful career of Mrs. Burt's grandfather. It is from the first of the coastwise steamers launched by the Ocean Steamship Company, of which Mr. Wadley was president and one of the founders. Hanging in the back hall is a picture of the *Rebecca Everingham*, named for his wife, which made its maiden voyage from Columbus, Georgia, to Apalachicola, Florida, in 1881 with Mr. and Mrs. Wadley aboard.

William M. Wadley rose from the ranks to be a railroad president and held that office from 1866 until his death in 1882. As Mrs. Burt has said, he was down to his bottom dollar when the War Between the States was over. But his ability as a financier was well known.

Sherman's army had made "hairpins" out of the rails of the Central and other Georgia railroads. (That's what the wrecking crews called them, after the rails had been heated red hot and twisted beyond straightening.) Mr. Wadley was offered the presidency of the Central at a time when that office was a challenge as well as an honor. But "he seemed to thrive on misfortune," his granddaughter says. Anyway, the railroad was soon on a paying basis.

Mr. Wadley's bold pioneering spirit, his brilliant ingenuity and resourcefulness, are no less effective when combined with the Old South charm of the distaff side of the family. Two of his daughters provide notable examples of this potent merging of inherited qualities—Mrs. William G. Raoul of Atlanta and the late Miss Sarah L. Wadley, both far ahead of their time in thinking and achievement. And now, his granddaughter, Sarah Wadley Burt.

CHAPTER 36

Wild Dogs in Atlanta

*T*HE sound seemed to start a long way off and first came to us from the northeast or the direction of Peachtree Creek. Mother said it sounded to her like the moaning of doves. But no doves or other birds were heard, even when the springtime came. The bluebirds were missed for three years. No, it was not the sound of doves, but the distant baying of dogs, dangerous dogs."

Miss Sarah Huff was telling about the wild dogs that overran Atlanta and threatened the safety of refugees who started coming home to a ruined city almost as soon as Sherman and his army began their march to the sea. The torch which left most of Atlanta in ashes was applied by the Federal army November 15, 1864. The Huff family, among the first to return, were back at home for Christmas.

Of Atlanta's 4,500 business and dwelling houses, they found only about four hundred still standing and most of these in damaged condition. It was an extremely cold winter. While the bodies of soldiers had been buried in shallow graves—later to be reinterred in cemeteries—the frozen carcasses of horses, mules and dogs killed in combat, littered the late battlefields around the city.

The city itself was a rubble heap. Wells and cisterns covered over with debris were among the many hazards encountered by those who sought to rebuild their homes. More than one citizen had to be rescued from these deathtraps when the earth apparently gave way beneath him.

But most vividly of all, Miss Huff remembered the wild dogs that slept all day amid the ruins and turned wolf pack at night.

"We had just got home from four months of refugeeing," she later wrote for *The Atlanta Journal Magazine*. "The baying of these animals in unison was the only sound to break the profound stillness.

"The dogs of refugeeing families had become outcasts," she explained. "The citizens, especially those living in the country, were apt to own several hounds and maybe three or four other dogs. In those trying times, even favorites could not be carried along because who—besides those especially invited, like my mother happened to be—could count on a welcome for themselves, much less for their cats and dogs?"

And so as desolation spread over the land, and the dogs grew lean and hungry, they became vicious. "The cat and the dog had changed places," Miss Huff continues. "Man's best friend had reverted to wolflike tendencies. But Tabby, who had been inconstant ever, welcomed us back home."

Tabby too, soon became a problem. "When a fire was made in the huge fireplace of the old log kitchen which was to shelter us until the big house could be repaired, in came the cats. Cats of all sizes, cats of all colors, white, gray, yellow, spotted and black. How could black mammy bake the corn dodger, boil the cowpeas or fry the tiny rashers of rancid bacon with ravenous felines glaring, ready to devour the scanty food before anybody could scare them away from the pot, the skillet or the half-canteen tin plates on the table."

The house in which Miss Sarah Huff was born in 1856 and lived in until her death in 1943 still stands at 70 Huff Road, N. W., on a hill overlooking the railroad tracks and Marietta Street. It was several miles from the 1860 city limits of Atlanta and was, in fact, a farmhouse.

A sturdy story-and-a-half frame structure with twin gables and a recessed front porch, it was built in 1855 by Jeremiah Huff on the foundations of a still older house. Because of its changing fortunes during the War Between the States, the Huff residence became known as the house of three flags. Between July 10 and 20 of 1864 it was used as headquarters by Confederate Major T. R. Hotchkiss. Later Federal Major General George H. Thomas established his headquarters there. After the family refugeed to Social Circle (Jeremiah Huff was in the Confederate army), a Scotch neighbor, George Edwards, raised a British flag over the house to protect it from vandals and the torch.

A letter, delivered eighty years after it was written by a spirited young woman who tells of would-be Yankee "beaux" and life between the picket lines of opposing armies, is a part of the interesting history of the old Perkerson house.

This substantial two-story frame house was built by Thomas Jefferson Perkerson in the late eighteen thirties—three miles from Five Points, Atlanta's present business center—before the city of Atlanta came into existence.

The letter, written by a daughter of the house, Elizabeth Perkerson—she signed it Lizzie—was penned on enormous sheets of an army hospital muster roll —sheets picked up in a Federal camp on the outskirts of Atlanta when the army left late in 1864 after burning the city.

Photo by Guy Hayes

FIGURE 110. Meadow Brook, in Atlanta, gives the street a sidewise glance. The old Colonel Robert Alston house was built in 1856; three dormer windows adorn front and back and the Doric colonnade extends around three sides.

Lizzie's letter, more than five thousand words long, never reached the brother for whom it was intended—Angus M. Perkerson, then a young Confederate artilleryman with Longstreet's Corps in Virginia.

In 1944—when soldiers of the South and the North were fighting together with European allies against fascism—the old letter was delivered to Angus Perkerson, Sunday Magazine Editor of the *Atlanta Journal*, a son of the Angus to whom it was originally addressed. This later Angus had also served as an artillery officer—in World War I.

The letter had passed through many adventures in its eighty years. In 1864 it had been rescued from a heap of mail dumped on the floor of the railway depot in Charleston and taken to Ohio by a Federal soldier—Samuel A. Wildman of the 25th Ohio Volunteer Regiment, later Judge Wildman of Norwalk, Ohio.

Many years later, after reading *Gone With the Wind*, Judge Wildman's daughter, Mrs. J. A. Fenner, of Cleveland, resolved to restore the letter to the family of the young Confederate soldier. With this purpose in view, she entrusted the letter, in 1944, to Mrs. Harvey Kurz, who was leaving Cleveland for a visit to Atlanta.

Mrs. Kurz said later, "I got quite a start when I consulted the Atlanta telephone directory and found the same name as that on the letter." She gave the Perkerson family quite a start too—for although a transcript of the letter had reposed in the collection of the Western Reserve Historical Association in Cleveland for many years—none of the writer's family knew of its existence.

Wrote Mrs. Fenner: "It has always been to me, and I know it was to my father, a matter of regret that these long pages, so vivacious and so gallant, were by the misfortune of war delivered into the hands of the enemy instead of those of the brother for whom they were written . . . I rejoice in the opportunity to restore them to the family."

Lizzie, a tall beautiful young woman with sparkling blue eyes and dark curls, describes the Yankee officers who came to call on the Perkerson sisters.

"A great many of them tried to be very friendly. The house was full of officers day and night, or that is, till bedtime. None of them boarded with us. They would walk down after supper with their shoulder straps shining like new money and their black boots and paper collars ever so fine. Think I like to have had a beau in the crowd. He was Captain Williams, of the Sixty-Eighth Ohio Regiment, and the hatefulest old scamp that ever made a track on soil. I want you to look out for him if you ever come in contact with Sherman's army, lay down your gun and take him by the back of the neck and shake him till he hollers, and then tell him it was done at my request.

"They didn't interrupt Pa or Dan in any way. Never asked Pa to take the oath at all. Nan (a sister) and I were in no way particular how we talked to them. I talked to them of *our army*, and my brothers, John and Dempse and Angus that were in *our* army all the time. It would aggravate some of them, others seemed to think it all right.

"They stayed here five weeks. And the maddest set when they found that Hood was in their rear and they had to leave you ever saw, I reckon. They thought that Hood had moved to Macon until he was clean across the river.

"Next morning early a woman that is living in Jim McCool's house sent for some of us to come over, that her child was dying. I went, and when I got there she wanted me to go up after Mrs. Sylvie, so I put out and directly heard cannonading in the direction of town, and when I got in sight of the Holland crossing I could see the guns. Our soldiers were firing from the hill at Sally Whit's place. So I began to feel sort of squeamish, but I ran up to the house, and while I was there they began to bring out our wounded to Sylvie's to dress their wounds. The fight continued for two hours . . .

"Well, it went on the same way until we began to see large fires in town, and then we were sure they were going to leave. That was on Saturday night. The fires continued until Monday night, and we discovered several large fires in the country. Till [Matilda] and I were on the porch looking at the fires when we heard the clanking of swords and spurs coming up the road. Well, Ang, if I had seen them building the fire to this house, I would never have felt more certain that we were gone up. But they came up to the poplar tree and turned out in this road and stood a few minutes and went back. In about two hours we heard them coming again. This time they rode up in front of the house and hollered. Till went to the door. They asked her what 'them dogs' were making such a fuss about. She told them she didn't know but supposed they were barking at soldiers that were riding around here, so they turned and went off and we soon discovered they were on picket on top of the hill, and next morning by sun-up the whole road was full of them and we found they were leaving sure enough, but going down the country instead of up.

"Well, they were passing all day and until 11 o'clock the next day, and since then I have felt free as a bird turned out of a cage. They didn't bother us much in passing. They sent in a guard without being asked for it. They told us they were going to play smash with the Confederacy, just going to sweep it out at one lick . . ."

While the picket lines of opposing armies were on opposite sides of the house, there was illness among the household. Lizzie's sister Matilda (called "Till"), whose husband, Jerry Gilbert, was in the Confederate army, came down with fever. Laid low by the same malady was Black Jim, a servant. "Well, our chance for a doctor was the Yankees," wrote Lizzie. "Dr. McCook, brother of the noted General McCook, treated both of them. He seemed to be a very good physician but they both like to have died."

When her mother became ill, Lizzie took the initiative. Driving "an old broken-down Yankee horse" and taking along her brother Dan, who was too young for military service, she started out early in the morning in search of a doctor who lived near Jonesboro.

"When I got to Rough and Ready I found a Confederate vidette who said I could go no further. I told him my business and also told him I was going on. Well, he told me I would find pickets on the road and to tell them to go with me to the lieutenant. . . . I told the pickets what he said. One of them said he thought from my looks that I could go to the lieutenant as well without him as with him. I told him I was of the same opinion, so on I went.

"Directly I came to a camp of some 10 or a dozen men. They halted me. I told them my business and after asking me a hundred questions about the Yankees, they ordered a man to mount and take me to the captain, who was still further down the road. . . . I answered all his questions and got for an answer 'You can go no farther.' I told him that I could and would. Well, he said he

Photo by Guy Hayes

FIGURE 111. Peachtree Golf Club, in Atlanta, was built as a residence for Samuel House in 1852. Free-standing Doric columns support a pointed pediment. The bricks were handmade by slave labor.

could do no better than send a guard with me to Fayetteville. I told him, all right, and drove on under guard."

At three o'clock in the afternoon they reached headquarters.

"The commander, after asking all the questions he could think of, gave me a pass and dismissed the guard. So there I was, my horse tired down and me 12 miles from the doctor's and 20 miles from home. But I put on a bold front and started again. At dark I was at Jonesboro and the horse so badly tired that I had to walk from there to Dr. Parker's, six miles. We got there at ten o'clock. Next day at 12 we got home.

"Dr. Parker thought he had to do something and didn't know what, so he gave Ma a dose of medicine that like to have killed her and went off and left

337

her worse than he found her. Well, she just remained in that condition until the next Tuesday, five days.

"When the Yankees commenced passing, Pa told some of the officers what a condition we were in and they sent three doctors in and they gave her medicine that relieved her almost immediately and she has been mending ever since . . ."

Lizzie tells of a neighbor's servant who made a classic remark when he left his master:

"He marched up to the door, made a polite bow and said, 'I now bid adieu to you and slavery,' and off he went.

"Our Negroes are all at home," she adds, "and they are the only ones in the neighborhood . . .

"We are cut off from the world as yet, but I hope we will be all right soon.

"Atlanta is a perfect mass of ruins. All the public buildings are gone except the City Hall. Whitehall street swept completely. Cousin Dan was up last week. He says he hasn't the shape of a house on the place, although he is coming back just as quick as he can get a place to go into. All the citizens are pushing back.

"We are making our calculations to live rather hard next year. But if we can live at all, I am not afraid that we will perish."

Although the old Perkerson house was preserved and still stands at 552 Perkerson Road, all the outbuildings, "gin house, stables, crib, smoke house, cook kitchen, the shop, garden and yard palings," were torn down and used by the invaders in building camps. "I do reckon there were five hundred here, knocking, cursing, ripping and staving all day, swearing they would tear the house down from over us if we didn't get out," Lizzie declared.

But the family didn't get out, and in 1934 at the age of ninety-seven, Lizzie died in the old house in which she had written her letter. For all the sentiments so vigorously expressed in that letter she had married a "Yankee," Sumner E. Butler, of New York. After his death, she came back home.

Lizzie was born in 1837 in a smaller house on the place while the main house was being built by her father, Thomas Jefferson Perkerson, one of the pioneer settlers of this section. The property (two land lots comprising 405 acres) remained in the family until 1943. A part of the land is now a city park.

The old white clapboard house has the strong simplicity of line typical of pioneer structures—gabled roof and end-chimneys, two rooms up and two down with a hall between. There are one-story shed rooms on each side of the recessed front porch with its slender square posts. Shed rooms and an ell at the back give added space. The downstairs rooms are plastered and the parlor and sitting room have decorative cornices. A simple and graceful stairway leads to the second floor.

The house still stands, but the one-time terrace and old-fashioned garden have been erased by a bulldozer and the house itself "modernized." Surrounding it are the houses and apartments of the Perkerson Park real-estate development.

The road in front of the house is said to be one of the few unchanged stretches of highway in the state over which Sherman's march to the sea proceeded. Dan, the young brother mentioned by Lizzie, often told in later years of how his eyes hurt after watching the soldiers march past all day with the sun glinting on their gun barrels. An old army map shows the Perkerson house marked as an identification point.

Atlanta's famous grand-slam master of golf, Bobby Jones, learned the game on links spread across the former meadows of the old Robert A. Alston property at East Lake, six miles from the center of town. Alexa Stirling, four times woman's national golf champion, also developed her championship skill on the East Lake Country Club course of the Atlanta Athletic club.

Mr. Alston, who was to die a violent death in 1878, built his white-columned house in 1856, to please his wife, the former Charlotte McGill of Charleston. It stands at 2420 Alston Drive, S. E., directly across the street from the golf course, and these former meadows inspired the name of the Alston property, Meadow Brook. The brook now helps to furnish water for the club's thirty-five-acre lake.

Interestingly enough, the old house, designed by an architect named Gunby, faces away from Alston Drive, which was laid out in later years, leaving the one-time front entrance at the side. Actually, this makes no difference, as the one-and-a-half-story Doric colonnade extends around three sides of the white frame house. It is said that these columns of solid cypress formerly surrounded the structure. Formerly also an arcaded passageway led from the back to the big dining room and kitchen. The house has dormer windows at both front and back, and though it now has fairly near neighbors on both sides, its great boxwood and tall magnolias preserve much of its individual atmosphere and privacy.

Mr. Alston and his family were hardly settled in the new house before war clouds began to gather and he found himself a captain of General Morgan's Confederate cavalry. Later he became a colonel and Morgan's adjutant general. For several months during the War Between the States these dashing raiders were camped in the Alston meadows, their restless horses nibbling grass where golfers now swing down the fairway.

In 1878, when Colonel Alston was a member of the Georgia House of Representatives, he led the fight which later abolished the leasing of convict labor to private industry. Several present-day Atlanta fortunes, so we are told, had their beginnings in the cheap labor available through this system of near peonage. At any rate, feeling ran high on both sides in 1878.

Photo by Guy Hayes

FIGURE 112. The old smokehouse of the former Samuel House Residence in Atlanta, now the golf shop at the Peachtree Golf Club.

It ran so high that Colonel Alston was shot by a former friend, who was said to be intoxicated at the time. Wounded, Colonel Alston was carried from the capitol—which then stood at the present site of the Western Union building on Marietta Street at Forsyth—to the present Ivan Allen-Marshall building across the street, where he breathed his last, a martyr to his convictions. His body was taken home to Meadow Brook for burial in the Decatur Cemetery.

Is Meadow Brook haunted? Author Minnie Hite Moody, who once lived in the old house, declares she often heard the clanking of sabers and the tread of military boots in the wide central hall and on the lovely winding stair.

340

This may have been a writer's vivid imagination but certainly there are bullet holes and other scars to prove that the house was near the battle lines in the eighteen sixties. Many noted guests were entertained here by Colonel Alston. Chief among them were the President of the Confederacy, Jefferson Davis, and Colonel Alston's good friends, Confederate Vice President Alexander H. Stephens and General John B. Gordon.

Many years later Bobby Jones grew up in a house not far away, a house actually within the grounds of the East Lake Country Club. As a child he began his golfing career here on the Atlanta Athletic Club's No. 1 East Lake course which covers the old Alston acres.

In all the tournaments in which he played in this country and abroad, Bobby Jones represented the Atlanta Athletic Club, and replicas of the four great cups that he won in a single year are on display in both the town and the country-club houses. Never before or since has any golfer won all four of these cups—the American National Amateur and Open, the British Amateur and Open.

Since that time Bobby Jones has played a leading part in the organization of two other golf clubs, at both of which ante-bellum plantation lands were converted into golf courses, and their former residences into clubhouses.

First of these is the Augusta National, over which the great Masters' tournament is played each spring in Augusta. (Described in the chapter, "Southern Charm and the Hell Bomb.")

The second is the exclusive Peachtree Golf Club, twelve miles north of Atlanta on Peachtree Road. In its early days this property, which came to be known as Southlook, changed hands many times. In 1852, according to records on file at the Atlanta Title Company, it was acquired by Samuel House. He it was who built the red brick, white-columned dwelling. The bricks were made from the red Georgia clay so conveniently at hand.

The carriage entrance is now the ladies' entrance, and the ladies have to be nimble enough to step pretty high, cars being lower slung than carriages were. The main stairway has been turned around to ascend from the back instead of the front of the wide central hall. On the second floor a partition between two rooms has been removed, giving the golfers a spacious grill with twin fireplaces. None of these changes has affected the mellow charm of the old house, which is appropriately surrounded by a great lawn, old boxwood and magnolia trees. The gardens and terrace include many unusual shrubs and tree plantings in addition to the traditional Southern favorites.

General Sherman and his staff spent a night here a few days before the Battle of Atlanta, and the neighborhood, Cross Keys, is mentioned in old wartime reports.

In 1903 the property was acquired by the late W. T. Ashford, whose daughter, Mrs. H. Cobb Caldwell, continued the development of its beautiful gardens. When the Caldwell family sold Southlook to the Peachtree Golf Club, Robert Trent Jones, the well-known golf architect, incorporated its many natural beauties into the general design of the golf course as originally visualized by Bobby Jones and his associates. Even the picturesque old brick smokehouse is utilized. It is the golf pro's shop.

Twelve miles west of Atlanta's city limits is an historic old house with six tall square columns which was once surrounded by the Indian village of Sandtown. Off the Cascade Road at the end of Sandtown Road, it stands on an elevation above a sweeping curve of the Chattahoochee River. It was a trading post in early days and a stagecoach stop on the route to Marthasville, the village which preceded the present Atlanta. The first post office of Sandtown occupied a room of this house now owned by J. H. Estes.

This was the first home of Andrew Campbell, whose father, William Campbell, emigrated here with his family in 1832, according to information collected by Mrs. Estes. Later it became the property of J. H. Wilson. Mr. Wilson refugeed to other parts when the South went to war in the 'sixties but filled the six big square porch columns with wheat in order to preserve his harvest from invaders. The wheat was conveyed aloft to the swinging balcony and poured into the columns, each of which held fifty bushels. When he returned, Mr. Wilson bored holes in the base of each column and out came the wheat. His family thought the house was haunted until an investigation proved that some joker among Northern troops had locked a billy goat in the attic—the only living creature on the place when the family returned.

The late Mrs. J. M. High, whose Atlanta house on Peachtree Street is now the High Museum, was a daughter of Mr. and Mrs. Wilson and was born in the Sandtown house.

In the rich bottom lands below the old dwelling is an Indian graveyard. About four hundred of the 825 acres of the Sandtown farm are now in cultivation, mostly sowed in cover crops, as Mr. Estes is gradually converting to a white-face Hereford stock farm.

Another handsome ante-bellum plantation house with tall columns still stands on the old Fairburn Road between Gordon Street and Cascade Avenue. It was built in 1856 by Judge William Asbury Wilson.

All these houses were a distance from the city. Nearer town is the old home of Colonel Lemuel P. Grant, minus its once-handsome columns but still standing near Grant Park. Land for the park was given the city by Colonel Grant, a native of Maine. He also erected the fortifications for Atlanta's defense against the Union army in the 'sixties.

One of Atlanta's most historic houses may be seen inside the Cyclorama at

Grant Park. This is the old Troup Hurt house, a substantial two-story structure reproduced on the mammoth circular canvas depicting the Battle of Atlanta. The house was directly in the line of fire and so realistic are the battle scenes that you expect to see the house burst into flame any moment.

Visitors from all over the world take time out to view this spectacular painting on a canvas measuring fifty feet in height, four hundred feet in circumference and weighing eighteen thousand pounds. The work was done by a group of German artists with a fidelity to detail which in no way interferes with the dramatic effect.

One of Atlanta's most famous houses is the Wren's Nest, 1050 Gordon Street, S. W.

The former home of Joel Chandler Harris, it is maintained by the Uncle Remus Memorial Association as a shrine to the memory of the author of the beloved Uncle Remus stories.

Here in this commodious gray Victorian house, Mr. Harris, then editor of *The Atlanta Constitution,* wrote many of the stories and books that brought him world fame. Here he and Mrs. Harris reared their family. Here he was visited by James Whitcomb Riley and other literary leaders of his day.

A shy man, Mr. Harris finally yielded to pressure and visited President Theodore Roosevelt in the White House. Later Mr. Roosevelt wrote, "All our family agreed that we had never received in the White House a pleasanter friend or a man whom we were more delighted to honor."

The Harris home got its name when a couple of wrens built a nest in the mailbox. Thereafter no one was allowed to disturb the box. And so, because they chose that particular box, the wrens also became famous.

Another Atlanta house with a writing background stands at 1401 Peachtree Street, N. E. It has tall white columns glimpsed through green magnolia leaves, and though built in fairly modern times is considered a fine example of Greek Revival architecture.

This was the girlhood home of the late Margaret Mitchell. Here she spent her vacations from Smith College, made her bow to Atlanta society, wrote short stories which national magazines were pleased to reject, decided to get the job on *The Atlanta Journal Magazine* which she held for four years.

This was her home until she married John R. Marsh and went to live in an apartment where she wrote—*Gone With the Wind.*

The Atlanta burned by Sherman began to build back almost before the embers cooled. It has grown far beyond the imagining of its early citizens and is still growing. In Augusta the old guard fears that city may become another Atlanta. Locally, the old guard fears Atlanta may become another New York.

343

Mrs. Blank and the Crazy House

*T*HEY were afraid Mrs. Blank might not like it at the hospital for mental patients. But when she got there, she found so many of her old friends, she felt right at home.

And there it was finally, bright as the first star of evening. Something I had learned about Mrs. Blank and modern living—learned from old houses.

Maybe it was the answer to a lot of things. Why husbands wander, why boys leave home, why daughters become unmarried mothers, why Mrs. Blank went quietly crazy, why few people feel secure any more. And it wasn't the atom bomb.

It was the foxholes.

Buffeted by crowds, deafened by din, our very lives menaced by motorized traffic, we retreat at day's end from the battlefields of so-called business and industry, to what?

To the foxholes for temporary shelter. They have little else to offer. No sanctuary. No renewal. These have been lost in an architectural and economic transition from the too-large houses of the past to the too-compact quarters of the present.

Of course, these foxholes are called apartments and houses. And they cost enough. But with bedrooms practically cut to bed size, ceilings closing in, "dining areas" in midget living rooms and closets too scarce and too small to hide even the family skeleton, is it any wonder so many people jump out of windows?

Not all of us live under these conditions, but that's where *you* may find yourself tomorrow, if present building trends continue.

344

Some years ago Atlanta's Mayor William B. Hartsfield warned that involuntary birth control is being forced upon newlyweds because too many of them cannot afford housing space for children.

"Small houses," according to the American Public Health Association, "are a menace to the health and happiness of American families."

We are "fast becoming a nation of middle-class slums," declares financial columnist Sylvia Porter. She draws this conclusion after a 1951 survey of new houses in the suburbs of New York, Washington, Denver and Omaha. Miss Porter found "shockingly small bedrooms, eight or nine feet long. Ridiculously inadequate closet space . . . definitely inferior and 'cheap' fixtures . . ." She also saw "intriguing lighting ideas, built-in television sets, some appealing gadgets. But," she asks, "are . . . gadgets more necessary than room to live and closet space? I doubt it."

Houses surveyed were selling for $12,000 to $20,000. "Even today that's a heap of cash," she points out. "In most instances the purchase of a home represents the major financial investment of the family's entire lifetime. It is the obligation of adult life, of family security."

(Family security. Isn't that the basis of national security?)

"High costs, scarce materials, expensive labor, credit restrictions . . . if this is the background—and it is—then it means our builders, architects, bankers and government officials must face up to the danger . . . and meet the challenge now," says Miss Porter. Otherwise, "before this decade is over, we will become . . . a nation of middle-class slums."

Let's go back to Mrs. Blank. When things got too hectic in the house she went out and sat in the family car parked in the driveway. She felt conspicuous but there wasn't anywhere else she could go and be alone. When she was sitting in the car like that, the family had learned to stay clear. Of course, sooner or later somebody wanted to go somewhere in the car and Mrs. Blank would have to be dislodged. But the brief respite helped. Then one day she just refused to go back into the house at all. And that was that.

It is pleasanter to contemplate my Aunt Maggie of an earlier generation. She lived in a big white house of no especial architectural beauty on a shady side street. Strange as it may seem now, there was only one bathroom in the entire house, but there were plenty of bedrooms. There was even a spare bedroom.

When Aunt Maggie wanted to get away from it all, she just retired upstairs, firmly closed the door and the green window blinds, dabbed eau de cologne on her temples and laid herself down on a big double bed in the cool, quiet dark. Life went on undisturbed downstairs. And short of the house catching fire, nobody disturbed Aunt Maggie when the door of her room was shut.

Aunt Maggie was a tower of strength, everybody said. She was always calm in emergencies. She was also dependable, warm-hearted and gay at other times. But she had to get away from things now and then. She called it inviting her soul—something she, no doubt, picked up secondhand from Walt Whitman, as a great many other people did. Uncle Bill had his privacy too when he retired to the study to chew on a cigar and read Shakespeare. That's what he said he read and there certainly were a lot of books, mostly in sets.

Of course, there was a general family sitting room. The parlor was usually running over with the friends of my older cousin, Abby May. Boy friends were "beaux" in those days. They all crowded around the piano and sang things like "In the evening by the moonlight . . ." The boys of the family and their friends held forth in the basement where a pool table had been set up.

Too young to be welcome by either group, I was frequently on the fringe, eavesdropping. On one of these occasions I heard my cousin Bill play-acting the part of district attorney. He was prosecuting a murder case and the other boys were supposed to be judge and jury. But they weren't very polite about it. They wanted to play pool. The fact that Bill grew up to be district attorney is beside the point.

The point is that here was a pleasantly uninhibited household, where people seldom got in each other's hair.

This was not the home of a rich man. This was what the Sylvia Porter of a generation ago would have called an average middle-class home, built in a day when it was recognized that people not only had to have privacy for taking baths but for recharging the human battery.

Or perhaps they only built houses that way because every married couple expected to raise a family and because there were plenty of servants. Perhaps women themselves are a little to blame for the way things have gone. They have said so often that they don't want a big house to keep without help. Reminded of modern electrical labor saving equipment, they have a pat reply, "Those things don't run themselves."

There's a joker in the resulting deal. Functional is the word for it. In the small, compact apartment or house, everything must serve not only one purpose but two or three.

Every simple routine act is a production for which the stage must be set.

You can't just drop into bed when you come home dead. You must let the bed out of the wall or unfold a sofa-bed or roll in the rollaway. Before any of this you must shift the furniture to make room for the bed. Even if it is a studio couch you wreck a crowded all-purpose closet getting out the bedding.

And that drop-leaf table. It looks so pretty with the books and the magazines and the flowers and all those other things on it. But you must clear them off before you make it look pretty another way—all set for dining. Sometimes you think if there were only yourself you might just eat out of the skillet but—well, you know how husbands are.

The tiny kitchen with all the wall cabinets is so convenient—until you try to use it. There never seems to be enough work space, especially when you clear the drop-leaf table after a meal. There's just nowhere to put the used dishes because the sink is already full of pots and pans. Sometimes you just stand there juggling them, but that's bad. Because the next step is throwing them. In the nick of time, you remember Mrs. Blank.

So you set the tray on the kitchen floor and go back to rearrange the drop-leaf table. In the meantime, for no reason, your husband makes a trip to the kitchen and you know what it is he crashes into.

This was the night you were going to straighten out that eight-in-one closet, but now you are too upset. That closet gives you a guilt-complex anyway. Didn't your mother tell you there should be a place for everything and everything in its place? Life certainly would be simpler that way. The trouble is the closet doesn't have walls of rubber. Everything in its place, indeed. Hah! The best you can hope for is somehow or other to get things out of sight. This means you frequently cannot find them again without a general upheaval which usually means a family upheaval too.

Talk about frustrations. Compact living is just one frustration after another. It's the frustrations that tire you, not the work.

So some people are beginning to discover. Take these young friends of ours, parents of three. They traded in their small house last year for a twenty-five-year-old nine-room house, plus breakfast room and sleeping porch. (Rooms were room size twenty-five years ago.

"Some of our friends thought we were crazy, of course," they admitted. "But ample room means less housework really, because the traffic is less concentrated. And there's less wear and tear both on the house and on the nervous system."

There was something else—something bigger than the sum of its parts—that they couldn't quite find a word for. "We think ampler room makes ampler living," said Mary, a little self-consciously. (Maybe you can't find ampler in the dictionary, but at least you know what it means.)

Even modern builders are beginning to realize that something is wrong with these smaller and smaller houses. So they leave out more and more partitions in order to give a "feeling" of space. The frontier cabins of our pioneer ancestors were without partitions. But even those hardy souls recognized the importance of privacy. Sheets or blankets were hung to make a dividing wall. Could it be that we are getting back to the cabin—a new kind of cabin, in a new kind of wilderness?

This writer has no quarrel with modern architecture and functional furnishings. Both are logical developments of our time and at their best express the great possibilities for beauty in a new and challenging art form. It is the cheating on space that turns an apartment or a house into a foxhole.

"How's it het?" asked the house-and-garden-tour pilgrim, as she gazed up at the high ceiling in the double parlor of a spacious old Georgia house.

"It ain't," her companion replied, straightening her funny hat before the tall gold-framed pier mirror.

This isn't typical Georgia grammar (and certainly anybody who can pay the nominal house-and-garden tour admission may take a look at how the other half lives) but it is typical national thinking.

Big rooms with high ceilings are expensive to heat. But they are not hot-boxes in summer. And, anyway, there's a happy medium. Incidentally, it might be well to remember that boys and girls are getting taller every generation—on orange juice, vitamins or something. The armed services found this out in World War II when the planes were not big enough for a lot of boys who wanted to be flyers.

My tour of Georgia convinced me that the old houses have something neither we nor Mrs. Blank have yet learned to do without. And it opened my eyes to something else. While traffic has been getting a strangle hold on the cities, modern transportation and communication have improved the smaller towns. They aren't what you thought if you got your ideas secondhand from Sinclair Lewis. It could be that the right combination is a smaller town and a bigger house. Anyway, a bigger house or a small house with big rooms.

"Perhaps spaciousness makes graciousness," said the owner of one beautifully restored ante-bellum house. "Of course, it sounds trite," she admitted.

It could be that she is right as well as trite. So often this is true. And the old houses do have something lacking in the shiny new small jobs.

They have something we, as well as Mrs. Blank, need badly. The old houses have an atmosphere of serenity—of sanctuary.

Bibliography

ANDERSON, MARY SAVAGE; Barrow, Elfrida DeRenne; Screven, Elizabeth Mackay; and Waring, Martha Gallaudet. *Georgia, a Pageant of Years.* Georgia Society of the Colonial Dames of America. Richmond: Garrett & Massie, 1933.

ARMSTRONG, MARGARET. *Fanny Kemble, a Passionate Victorian.* New York: The Macmillan Company, 1938.

AVARY, MYRTA LOCKETT. *Dixie after the War.* New York: Doubleday, Page & Co., 1906.

BARTRAM, JOHN. *Diary of a Journey Through the Carolinas, Georgia and Florida, 1765-66.* Philadelphia, 1943.

BARTRAM, WILLIAM. *Travels Through North and South Carolina, Georgia, East and West Florida, 1773-74.* Philadelphia, 1791.

BATTEY, GEORGE M., JR. *A History of Rome and Floyd County.* Atlanta, 1922.

BENET, STEPHEN VINCENT. *John Brown's Body.* New York: Farrar & Rinehart, 1927.

BOLTON, HERBERT E. and Ross, MARY. *The Debatable Land.* Berkeley, 1925.

BOWEN, ELIZA. *The Story of Wilkes County.* Edited by Louise Frederick Hays. Continental Book Co., 1950.

BREMER, FREDERIKA. *The Homes of the New World.* Translated by Mary Howitt. London: Arthur Hall, Virtue & Co., 1853.

BROWN, JOHN P. *Old Frontiers: The Story of the Cherokee Indians from the earliest times to the date of their removal to the West.* Kingsport, Tenn.: Southern Publishers, 1938.

BUSH-BROWN, HAROLD. *Outline of the Development of Early American Architecture; the Southern States. District——Georgia.*

CABELL, BRANCH, and HANNA, A. J. *The St. John's River.* New York: Farrar & Rinehart, 1943.

CANDLER, ALLEN D., comp. *The Colonial Records of the State of Georgia.* Atlanta, 1904-16.

CATE, MARGARET DAVIS. *Our Todays and Yesterdays.* Brunswick, Ga.: Glover Bros., 1930.
   "Fort Frederica and the Battle of Bloody Marsh." *Georgia Historical Quarterly.* Savannah, June, 1943.

CATE, MARGARET DAVIS; COLQUITT, DOLORES B.; and McCARTY, MARY WYLIE. *Flags of Five Nations.* Sea Island.

CONNALLY, MAJOR JAMES AUSTIN. "Connally's Letters to His Wife, 1862–65; Major Connally's Diary." *Transactions* of the Illinois State Historical Society for the Year 1928. Springfield: Phillips Bros., 1928.

CONYNGHAM, DAVID POWER. *Sherman's March Through the South*. New York: Sheldon & Co., 1865.

COONEY, LORAINE MEEKS, comp. *Garden History of Georgia*. Atlanta: Peachtree Garden Club, 1933.

CORRY, JOHN P. *Indian Affairs in Georgia, 1732–56*. Philadelphia, 1936.

CORSE, CARITA D. *The Key to the Golden Islands*. Chapel Hill: University of North Carolina Press, 1931.

COTTER, WILLIAM JASPER. *My Autobiography*. M. E. Church Press, 1917.

COULTER, E. MERTON. *Georgia, a Short History*. Chapel Hill: University of North Carolina Press, 1947.

   Georgia's Disputed Ruins. Chapel Hill: University of North Carolina Press, 1937.

   Thomas Spalding of Sapelo. Louisiana University State Press, 1940.

CRANE, VERNER W. *The Southern Frontier, 1670–1732*. Durham: Duke University Press, 1928.

CUMMING, INEZ PARKER. "Sweet with Bitter, Georgia Peach." *Georgia Review*. Winter, 1948.

CUNYUS, LUCY JOSEPHINE. *History of Bartow County*. Tribune Publishing Co., 1933.

DAUGHTERS OF THE AMERICAN REVOLUTION, THRONATEESKA CHAPTER. *History and Reminiscences of Doughterty County*. 1924.

DAVIS, WILLIAM COLUMBUS. *The Columns of Athens*. Atlanta, 1951.

DENMARK, ERNEST RAY. *Architecture of the Old South*. Foreword by Lewis E. Crook, Jr. Atlanta, 1926.

DICKINSON, JONATHAN. *Journal or God's Protecting Providence, Being a Narrative of a Journey from Port Royal in Jamaica to Philadelphia Between August 23, 1696, and April 1, 1697*. New Haven, Reprint 1945.

EDWARDS, HARRY STILLWELL. *Eneas Africanus*. Macon: Burke, 1920.

EGMONT, JOHN PERCEVAL, FIRST EARL. *Manuscripts of the Earl of Egmont, Diary*. London: His Majesty's Stationery Office, 1920–23.

FEATHERSTONHAUGH, G. W. *A Canoe Voyage Up the Minnay Sotor*. London: Bentley, 1847.

FEDERAL WRITERS' PROJECT, AMERICAN GUIDE SERIES:

   Georgia. Samuel Y. Tupper and Kathryn A. Hook, Supervisors. Athens: University of Georgia Press, 1940.

   Savannah. Chamber of Commerce, 1938.

   Savannah River Plantations. Mary Granger, Editor. Savannah: Georgia Historical Society, 1941.

   The Story of Washington Wilkes. Washington City Council, 1941.

FLANDERS, RALPH BETTS. *Plantation Slavery in Georgia*. Chapel Hill: University of North Carolina Press, 1933.

FOREMAN, GRANT. *Indian Removal, The Emigration of the Five Civilized Tribes of Indians*. Norman, Okla., 1932.

FREEMAN, DOUGLAS SOUTHALL. *The South to Posterity*. New York: Scribner's, 1939.

FRIES, ADELAIDE L., editor. *Records of the Moravians in Georgia*. Raleigh: 1905. *Records of the Moravians in North Carolina.*

GABRIEL, RALPH H. *Elias Boudinot, Cherokee, and His America*. Norman, Okla., 1941.

GAMBLE, THOMAS. *Savannah Duels and Duellists, 1733–1877*. Savannah, 1923.

GEORGIA HISTORICAL SOCIETY. *Collections*. Savannah, 1840——.

GILMER, GEORGE R. *Georgians, Sketches of Some of the First Settlers of Upper Georgia, of the Cherokees and the Author*. New York: D. Appleton Co., 1855.

GRAY, TOM S., JR. "The March to the Sea." *Georgia Historical Quarterly*, June, 1930.

HAMLIN, TALBOT. *Greek Revival Architecture in America*. Oxford University Press.

HANNA, A. J. *Flight into Oblivion*. Richmond: Johnston Pub. Co., 1938.

HARRIS, JULIA COLLIER. *The Life and Letters of Joel Chandler Harris*. Boston: Houghton-Mifflin, 1918.

HARTRIDGE, WALTER, and MURPHY, CHRISTOPHER. *Savannah, Etchings and Drawings*. Columbia, S. C.: Bostick, 1947.

HAYS, MRS. J. E. *History of Macon County*. Atlanta, 1933.

HENRY, ROBERT SELPH. *The Story of the Confederacy*. New York: Bobbs-Merrill, 1931.
 First with the Most Forrest. New York: Bobbs-Merrill, 1944.

HEYWARD, DUNCAN CLINCH. *Seed from Madagascar*. Chapel Hill: University of North Carolina Press, 1937.

HINES, NELLE WOMACK. *A Treasure Album of Milledgeville and Baldwin County*. Macon: Burke, 1936.

HITCHCOCK, MAJOR HENRY. *Marching with Sherman*. New Haven: Yale University Press, 1927.

HORN, STANLEY F. *Gallant Rebel*. New Brunswick: Rutgers University Press, 1947.

HOWARD, ANNIE HORNADY. *Georgia Homes and Landmarks*. Atlanta, 1929.

HOWARD, FRANCES THOMAS. *In and Out of the Lines*. New York: Neale, 1905.

HUFF, SARAH. "My Eighty Years in Atlanta." *The Atlanta Journal Magazine*, 1937.

JOHNSON, GUION GRIFFIS. *A Social History of the Sea Islands*. Chapel Hill: University of North Carolina Press, 1930.

JONES, C. C. *Dead Towns of Georgia*. Savannah, 1878.

JONES, MARY G., and REYNOLDS, LILY. *Coweta County, Chronicles for 100 Years*. Sarah Dickinson Chapter, Daughters of the American Revolution, 1928.

KEMBLE, FRANCES ANNE. *Journal of a Residence on a Georgian Plantation, 1838–39*. London; New York, 1863.

KIMBALL, SIDNEY FISKE. *Domestic Architecture of the American Colonies and of the Early Republic*. New York: Scribner's, 1922.

KNIGHT, LUCIAN LAMAR. *Georgia's Landmarks, Memorials and Legends*. Atlanta, 1913–14.

LEIGH, FRANCES BUTLER. *Ten Years on a Georgia Plantation Since the War*. London: Bentley, 1883.

LEVERT, OCTAVIA WALTON. *Souvenirs of Travel*. New York: Carleton, 1857.

LEWIS, LLOYD. *Sherman; Fighting Prophet*. New York: Harcourt, Brace, 1932.

LOCKWOOD, ALICE G. B. *Gardens of Colony and State*. Compiled and edited for the Garden Club of America. New York: Scribner's, 1934.

LONGSTREET, AUGUSTUS BALDWIN. *Georgia Scenes*. New York: Harper, 1897.

LOVELL, CAROLINE COUPER. *The Golden Isles of Georgia*. Boston: Little, Brown, 1932.

LUMPKIN, WILSON. *The Removal of the Cherokee Indians from Georgia*. New York: Dodd, Mead, 1907.

LUNT, DOLLY SUMNER. *A Woman's War-Time Journal*. Introduction by Julian Street. New York: The Century Co., 1918. Macon: J. W. Burke Co., 1927.

LYELL, SIR CHARLES. *Second Visit to the United States of North America*. London: John Murray, 1850.

MAJOR, HOWARD. *The Domestic Architecture of the Early American Republic: The Greek Revival*. Philadelphia and London: Lippincott, 1926.

MEAD, RUFUS, JR. "Letters and Diary of Commissary Sergeant, Fifth Regiment, Connecticut Volunteers." *Georgia Historical Quarterly*. Savannah, December 1948.

MITCHELL, ELLA. *History of Washington County*. Atlanta, 1924.

MITCHELL, MARGARET. *Gone With the Wind*. New York: The Macmillan Company, 1936.

MURRAY, THE HON. AMELIA M. *Letters from the United States, Cuba and Canada*. New York: G. P. Putnam's Sons, 1856.

NIGHTINGALE, B. N. "Dungeness." *Georgia Historical Quarterly*. Savannah, December 1939.

NIXON, RAYMOND B. *Henry W. Grady, Spokesman of the New South*. New York: Alfred A. Knopf, 1944.

ODUM, HOWARD. *Southern Regions of the United States*. Chapel Hill: University of North Carolina Press, 1936.

PARKER, CAPTAIN WILLIAM H. *Recollections of a Naval Officer*. New York: Scribner's, 1883.

PHILLIPS, ULRICH BONNELL. *The Life of Robert Toombs*. New York: The Macmillan Company, 1913.

Life and Labor in the Old South. Boston: Little, Brown, 1929.

POPE-HENNESSEY, UNA. *The Aristocratic Journey, Being the Outspoken Letters of Mrs. Basil Hall, written during a 14-months' sojourn in America, 1827-28*. New York: G. P. Putnam's Sons, 1931.

SHERMAN, WILLIAM TECUMSEH. *Memoirs of General William T. Sherman*. (Third edition, revised and corrected.) Webster, 1890.

SHERWOOD, ADIEL. *Gazetteer of Georgia*. Charleston: W. Riley, 1827.

SHRINER, CHARLES H. *History of Murray County*, 1911.

SMITH, CLIFFORD L. *History of Troup County*. Atlanta, 1935.

STOVALL, PLEASANT A. *Robert Toombs*. New York: Cassell, 1892.

TEMPLE, SADIE BLACKWELL GOBER. *The First Hundred Years, History of Cobb County*. Brown, 1935.

Bibliography

THACKERAY, WILLIAM MAKEPEACE. *Letters and Private Papers of William Makepeace Thackeray*. Collected and edited by Gordon N. Ray. New Haven: Cambridge, 1945–6.

WADE, JOHN DONALD. *Augustus Baldwin Longstreet, A Study of the Development of Culture in the South*. New York: The Macmillan Company, 1924.

WATSON, AMELIA M. *Among Untrodden Ways*. Original Manuscript, East Windsor Hill, Conn., 1915. St. Marys Library.

WALKER, ROBERT SPARKS. *Torchlights to the Cherokees*. New York: The Macmillan Company, 1931.

WHITE, GEORGE. *Historical Collections of Georgia*. New York: Pudney and Russell, 1854.

WHITE, GOODRICH C. "Old Oxford." *Bulletin* of Emory University. February 15, 1948.

YOUNG, IDA; GHOLSON, JULIUS; and HARGROVE, CLARA NELL. *The History of Macon, 1823–1949*. Macon Woman's Club, 1950.

INDEX